Make Money Online, Work From Home

From Newbie To Millionaire

Internet Marketing Success System Explained Step By Step.

by

Christine Clayfield

- Author of "Finding Niches Made Easy. 177 Free Ways to Find New Hot Profitable Niches".

Search for it on Amazon or buy it as an eBook on
www.FindingNichesMadeEasy.com

- Author of *"Drop Shipping and eCommerce. What You Need and Where To Get It"*.

Search for it on Amazon or buy it as an eBook on
www.DropshippingAndeCommerce.com

- Creator of www.worldwideselfpublishing.com *Video Tutorials*

You can buy matching companion video tutorials for this book here: www.VideosNewbieBook.com.

In the back of this book you will find a list of the video tutorials. You don't **NEED** the videos to make money online but in case you are the kind of person that learns a lot from video tutorials, you have the opportunity to buy them.

****

If you would like to receive my newsletter or interesting information about internet marketing, please opt-in on www.FromNewbieToMillionaire.com. You will receive an email when I have launched a new product or when I will be speaking at an event.

Do opt-in, I promise I will NOT send you a bundle of crappy affiliate links, just not my style! My money does not come from sending affiliate links to my subscribers but from multiple streams of income from my own products.

****

Published by IMB Publishing 2014. Published in 2011, updated in 2014.

Copyright and Trademarks

Disclaimer and Legal Notice

Table of Contents

Table of Contents

Part 12. Ways To Make Money - No Website Needed.............410

My Other Products

I have published books and built websites in over 90 different niches, but of course that's too many to list here. Below you can find a list of my other products that are Internet marketing/office related.

1) My book "Finding Niches Made Easy. 177 Free Ways to Find New Hot Profitable Niches".

Buy the **eBook** here: www.FindingNichesMadeEasy.com

Buy the **hard copy book**: search for it on Amazon

2) My Drop Shipping and eCommerce Book "DropShipping and eCommerce. What You Need and Where to Get It"

Buy the **eBook** here: www.dropshippingandecommerce.com.

Buy the **hard copy book**: search for it on Amazon

3) *My Self Publishing Success System Explained Step by Step in Video Tutorials*

I publish a new book, on average, every 2 weeks. These books are all in different niches, and I outsource all aspects of the book, including writing and cover design, except for the publishing, which I do myself. I explain EVERYTHING I do, from finding a niche to publishing the book worldwide in watch-over-my-shoulder style video tutorials: www.WorldwideSelfPublishing.com.

4) *My Break Reminder Software*

I have to try to reduce the time I spend on my computer due to a neck injury (you will read about it later). I used to use www.workpace.com, which is software that forces you to take breaks while on your computer. I had my own simplified version developed, which you can buy here: www.BreakReminderSoftware.com.

5) *My Repetitive Strain Injury Book*

The real-life stories in the book will make you think and will, hopefully, make you take regular breaks on your computer/mobile phones, etc.

The book is aimed at anyone who use our much-loved electronic gadgets too often, too long, without taking breaks. Nobody warns people about the permanent damage it can do to your body.

Buy the **hard copy book**: search for it on Amazon by author Lucy Rudford (pen name)

6) My Print Screen Software

When I was looking for a very simple print screen software application, without all the bells and whistles, I couldn't find it, therefore I had my own developed. I use it every single day and don't know how I could ever be without it.

You can buy it here: www.PrintingYourScreen.com.

Printing Your Screen, Screen Capture

★★★★★ The Software that Makes Printing Screen Shots And ★★★★★
Saving Screen shots *instant*.

7) Print a Kindle eBook

I don't like reading from a screen and searched A LOT for a reliable solution to print a Kindle book. You can grab your copy here free: www.HowToPrintAKindleBook.com.

How to print a kindle book from your PC. If you are like me and you prefer reading books from paper, this is for you. Before I knew how to print a Kindle book, I never bought any Kindle books, now I do because I print them and read them.

Please note there is a one-time charge of $29.99 / £19.00 to buy the Kindle Converter that I recommend in order to convert your Kindle to a pdf format that you can print. However, you have 5 days to test the product free. This converter is not my product and I don't earn any money from it if you buy it but it is a product that actually works. Works on PC, windows explorer. I have not tested it an an Apple computer.

More Information About Me:

www.ChristineClayfield.com

For more information about how you can make money as an affiliate selling my products, please refer to the end of this book.

IMPORTANT NOTE 1:

March 2013: A quick word about the Panda/Penguin updates.

1) This book was written before anybody was talking about Panda and Penquin. I can absolutely guarantee that my book is Panda/Penguin friendly.
A lot of my sites are doing even better for the main reason that I have always done my SEO really well and NEVER used anything automated. For some of my long tail keywords that have little competition, the SEO on my one-page-sales-wonders is not even THAT good on my sites but that is done intentionally because I can better that if need be to higher my rankings.

The Penguin update (second Panda update):
- penalises sites with keyword stuffing (which I have never done)
- penalises sites with automated link building (which I never use)
- penalises sites on which the backlinks are created too many too fast. I explain in my book to create backlinks ONLY to the extend that it is humanly possible to do.
- quality content is also very important (which I apply if appropriate, not for a sales page)
- penalises sites with black hat SEO (which I have never used)
- penalises sites with high bounce rates(when your visitors don't stay on the site for long)
- penalises sites with domain names not relevant to the content
- penalises sites with poor onsite optimisation (no internal links)
-more.... but the above are important.

It is exactly what I say in my book: NEVER buy anything automated and never do keyword stuffing and always use a domain name with the long tail keywords in it and put appropriate content on the site with internal links. My opinion is that good SEO is more important now than it ever was. The methods in my book can now be applied even with more success than before (if that is possible).

If you will apply exactly the same principles as explained in my ebook, you will most probably rank in Google, regardless of Panda or Penguin updates, and if you are targetting the "keywords with potential".
When Google "does one of their dances", I just adjust my dance moves so I can stay in the game. If you don't use anything automated, you can do the same.

IMPORTANT NOTE 2:

May 2014: A quick word about Google Keyword Tools.

I mention the termGoogle Keyword Tools in this book. Please note that Google Keyword Tools is no longer available and is replaced by Google Keyword Planner.

Search for it in Google and you will find this url:
https://adwords.google.com/ko/KeywordPlanner/Home .

You can still use this Keyword Tool free but you will need to set up an Adwords account with Google (search Youtube or follow the step by step instructions by Google when you sign up).

Setting up an Adwords account is totally free. Once you have set up your Adwords account, you can log in and use Keyword Planner. You do NOT have to spend any money with your Adwords account in order to use Keyword Planner. You do NOT need a website to use Keyword Planner. The general principle is exactly the same as Keyword Tools : you type in a keyword and Google will show you the monthly searches. The keywords will be shown in a different format than shown on this video but it is very simple to understand, you will see.

You can still download the keywords as described in this book.

The average search results are higher in Keyword Planner compared to what they were in Keyword Tools. Reason behind this is that Keyword Planner shows you the results on all devices (desktop computers and laptop computers, mobile phones and tablets). In Keyword Tools only searches for desktop and laptop computers were shown by default.

Conclusion: it is in principle all the same but you need to be logged into your Adwords account to be able to use Keyword Planner. The screenshots in this book are done with the old Keyword Tools except for the ones under "The importance of long tail keywords", which are from Keyword Planner. Once I publish a complete update of this book, I will remove all the Keyword Tools screenshot with Keyword Planner. As long as my methods still work, there is no need to update this book.

Best wishes,
Christine Clayfield.

Acknowledgments

For many years I have been sitting in front of my computer and even when I was occasionally sitting in my lounge I would work on my laptop. Was it worth it? Yes it was, but without the support and understanding of my husband and children it would not have been possible. I owe them a great deal and for their support I thank them from the bottom of my heart.

Thank you, thank you, thank you, to my dear husband. Your love is my life. Thank you for never complaining and always, without ever mentioning it, letting me work on my computer working away, often through the night, trying to make money on the internet. It has finally paid off. I could not have done it without your support. Thank you for letting me be me and never trying to change who I am, or who I want to be. I will always love you with all my heart.

Thank you, thank you, thank you, to my two beautiful intelligent twin daughters for being such respectful young adults. I do it all for you to try to give you a good future. Thank you for understanding why I spend a lot of time in my office. You know that the door is always open and always will be. I will always love you with all my heart.

Thank you, to my four step-children for accepting me and for loving your twin step-sisters. I hope you will always look after them.

Thank you Dad for all you did for me. I am so sorry I have never been an ideal daughter. Now that I am a Mum myself, I understand everything you did and said. Your hard lessons of trying to achieve something valuable in life have paid off. You would be proud of me now.

Thank you Mum for being there for me through difficult times when I was young. I love you.

Thank you to you, the reader, for the trust you put in me by reading this book. I hope you too will soon understand the power of the internet, and I hope that I can help you to make money online.

Foreword by Robert G. Allen

I have had the pleasure in meeting Christine Clayfield and she certainly is an inspiring lady! I am very impressed with her book. If you are serious about Internet Marketing, you need to read this book from A to Z. Her experiences in the online world of earning money combined with her ability to share her insights in written language which is easy to understand, makes this book a fantastic read.

In these pages you will find internet marketing strategies, wisdom and a bundle of practical tips to apply to your own business. It is hard to succeed on the internet without understanding all aspects of it. Christine's book breaks it all down into small chewable pieces that are easy to understand. Regardless of your level of internet marketing expertise, you will learn a lot from this book.

I do like the fact that she explains internet jargon at the beginning of her book unlike a lot of internet marketing books where the author assumes you understand all the terminology.

One of the many things I loved about this book is that Christine provides you with real-life income screenshots which makes it very authentic. Her in-depth-clearly- explained steps are easy to follow and understand. You can apply these steps and implement them in your own business, whatever niche you are in.

It is very clear that she has a lot of experience in internet marketing otherwise she would not be able to tell you the mistakes that she made so you can learn from them. She explains why some strategies work and why others are a waste of time. This book is packed with ideas that will help you to stay ahead of the competition. It is the perfect desk reference for any internet marketer! Anyone can earn money on the internet after reading this book and watching the video tutorials, *including you*. I know you'll learn things in this book you can't learn anywhere else. It contains dozens of powerful ideas and techniques which, when properly implemented, can take you on to success and fortune.

From Newbie To Millionaire will no doubt have a profound impact on a lot of people's lives and views on internet marketing.

Robert G. Allen *Author of these bestsellers: The One Minute Millionaire, Multiple Streams of Income, Multiple Streams of Internet Income, Creating Wealth, Cash in a Flash.*

Foreword by the author Christine Clayfield

Hello fellow internet marketer,

Thank you for buying my book on how to make a living online.

First of all, this book has first been published in 2011 and now, in May 2014, when I am writing this extra paragraph in this book, it continues to sell. Many people ask me if the methods explained in this book can still be applied today. Yes is the answer to that. I still build websites and monetise them , run ecommerce sites and publish books exactly the same way as I explain in this book. I have students who apply exactly what is written in this book and their site ranks in Google on the first pages. Other students have successfully published ebooks and books following my methods and their books are Number 1 on Amazon. Sure the internet changes and Google changes their "requirements" for sites to be shown on the first pages but as I do everything manually, I can easy adjust my sites in order to please Google. Some core principles of SEO have been the same for many years and will stay the same for many years to come. I will give you some examples of my sites later in this book. I always compare a website to a car: there are flash cars, small cars, big cars, small ones, nice and ugly ones, cars with lots of gadgets, etc.... but they all have one thing in common: they have a motor. Without a basic motor the car wouldn't drive. The same applies for a website: there are small websites, big ones, flash ones, ugly and nice ones, etc... but they all need basic SEO and some fundamental principles to be successful.

You might find that when you visit some of the websites in this book that the general look of some sites has changed but that can't be helped. If I would renew all the screenshots from the sites today, in one week they might have another look again.

Are you suffering from information overload? When I first started online, I know I was. I spent forever trying to learn a new trick or a new idea, and didn't actually put fingers to keyboard for a long time. There seemed to be so much to know that I never felt ready to begin.

There was a guide-for-this, a guide-for-that and all sorts of complicated guides to "technical software made easy" that were beyond my understanding.

I decided that once I got my head around this strange new world of internet marketing and started earning the amount of money I wanted, I would write the kind of book that I wish I had found when I began. This is that book.

However, 95% of internet marketers fail and at the beginning of my internet marketing venture, I was one of them. Luckily my persistence and hard work paid off and I am now earning money. I have found a way that makes me money and I have duplicated it in different niches. But it's not just me. Everyday more internet marketing millionaires are created. They know and understand the power of the internet. They understand how to make money on the internet, by creating a model or system that works for them, and duplicating it. That's what this book is all about. Now it is your turn to become an internet millionaire. You have made the right step. The fact that you have bought this book means that you are interested in earning money online. This is your opportunity.

Small opportunities are often the beginnings of great enterprises.

This could be your opportunity to start with one website and end up with a great enterprise.

From here you will discover how I am making money in my sleep. How? I now have lots of websites that I do not have to touch, I have many affiliates (people selling my stuff for a commission) selling all my different products, I have several successful advertising campaigns, and I have VAs (Virtual Assistants, these are people that you can hire to do any internet marketing jobs for you) working for me. The money keeps coming in without work from me. This can only be achieved after months and years of hard work. But don't let that put you off - you too can earn money in your sleep, it just depends how much work you are willing to put in.

> **What you will become rests with what you are willing to do.**
>
> **&**
>
> **One does what one is, one becomes what one does.**

Who the hell am I and why should you believe me?

I am a 54 year old business woman always looking for money making opportunities. If you Google me, you will probably not find out a lot about me as I have set up many websites without mentioning my name. This is because they are all in different niches. This is my first book/project in the internet marketing niche and you will only find my name on internet marketing related websites.

I mentioned briefly in the acknowledgements that I could not have achieved internet marketing success without the support of my dear husband. Let me just quickly mention his website www.thevintagecorporation.co.uk. He is the drummer and band manager of a nine-piece live band playing '60s and '70s music. If you Google "60s band Kent" and "70s band Kent" (the keywords that I have targeted), the band will show in Google on the first page. The domain name is **not** a good example of an ideal domain name (as you will find out later in the book) but hey, it's my husband's choice and I respect his choice. It is also not a monetised website like the ones I will be talking about in this book. Okay that's made him happy. I won't mention the band again.

Back to who I am. Let me tell you first what I am not:

- I am not a computer geek

- I am not a computer programmer

- I am not an IT consultant

- I am not a computer science diploma holder

- I am not a super duper clever person (I never did well at school)

I started with NO experience, NO support, NO training, NO special skills but figured it all out on my own and ultimately started to make money.

But this is what I am:

- I am a hard worker

- I can read, analyse and learn quickly

- I am eager to earn money

- I have a computer and I can copy and paste

- I have determination

- I believe in what I want to achieve

- I have a business mind and I can spot money-making possibilities

- I will not give up until I have reached my goal

If you are a person with the same thinking, you are on your way to earning money online.

The quality of most people's lives are a direct reflection of their expectations.

TOP TIP : Learn from the people who have proven that they know what they are talking about. Never take tips and tricks from somebody who is not experienced.

I strongly believe in this tip, whatever business you are in: always learn from people who have proven that they know what they are talking about. Ask yourself: "Did they prove that they know their stuff?" or "How much money has he/she earned?"

These pictures are proof that I know *the theory* behind internet marketing. On the left picture you can see 96 hard copy books that I have read. I have also bought or received over 400 PDFs or eBooks that I have studied (see left picture). I have over 50 binders with material that I bought and tried and I have purchased lots of training DVDs. Then there are the days I used to sit by my computer watching tutorials on how to make money on the web.

The screenshots below are proof that I know the *practical side* of internet marketing as well. Below are screenshots from some internet accounts.

Don't worry if you do not know exactly what these accounts are as that will become clear throughout the book.

One Adsense account shows earnings of $ 2709.81 or £ 1654.71 for December alone.

This Amazon account shows earnings of $2105.68 or £1292.26 for November.

This Clickbank account shows $2654.73 or £1629.47 in sales during October 2010.

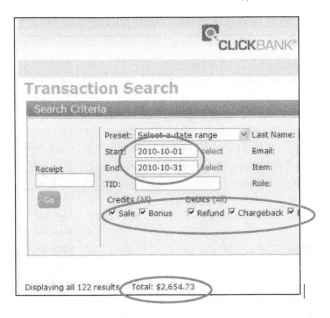

Another Clickbank account shows a total income of $3593.38 or £2205.62 from two weeks worth of sales: December 3 to December 17. This is $ 7186.56 or £ 4411.24 per month.

Daily Sales Snaps			
Fri	Dec	17	$290.64
Thu	Dec	16	$320.15
Wed	Dec	15	$210.20
Tue	Dec	14	$99.60
Mon	Dec	13	$358.60
Sun	Dec	12	$189.63
Sat	Dec	11	$320.50
Fri	Dec	10	**$125.88**
Thu	Dec	09	$420.99
Wed	Dec	08	$75.80
Tue	Dec	07	$89.66
Mon	Dec	06	$358.74
Sun	Dec	05	$89.60
Sat	Dec	04	$189.50
Fri	Dec	03	**$453.79**

This PayPal account shows $628.99 or £385.93 income during 12 days, which would be $1572.47 or £964.82 per month.

Date	Type	Name/Email	Payment status	Details	Order status/Actions	Gross	Fee	Net amount
22 Mar 2011	Payment From		Completed	Details	Print postage label ▼	£13.84	-£0.67	£13.17 GBP
22 Mar 2011	Payment From		Completed	Details	Print postage label ▼	£27.68	-£1.28	£26.40 GBP
19 Mar 2011	Payment From		Completed	Details	Print postage label ▼	£17.02	-£0.78	£16.24 GBP
17 Mar 2011	Payment From		Completed	Details	Print postage label ▼	£35.34	-£1.40	£33.94 GBP
17 Mar 2011	Payment From		Completed	Details	Print postage label ▼	£10.99	-£0.57	£10.42 GBP
17 Mar 2011	Payment From		Completed	Details	Print postage label ▼	£23.98	-£1.02	£22.96 GBP
16 Mar 2011	Payment From		Completed	Details	Print postage label ▼	£24.28	-£1.03	£23.25 GBP
16 Mar 2011	Payment From		Completed	Details	Print postage label ▼	£22.84	-£0.98	£21.86 GBP
16 Mar 2011	Payment From		Completed	Details	Print postage label ▼	£16.99	-£0.78	£16.21 GBP
16 Mar 2011	Payment From		Completed	Details	Print postage label ▼	£21.49	-£0.93	£20.56 GBP
14 Mar 2011	Payment From		Completed	Details	Print postage label ▼	£11.49	-£0.59	£10.90 GBP
12 Mar 2011	Payment From		Completed	Details	Print postage label ▼	£39.62	-£1.55	£38.07 GBP
11 Mar 2011	Payment From		Completed	Details	Print postage label ▼	£23.64	-£1.00	£22.64 GBP
10 Mar 2011	Payment From		Completed	Details	Print postage label ▼	£39.17	-£1.53	£37.64 GBP
10 Mar 2011	Payment From		Completed	Details	Print postage label ▼	£39.20	-£1.53	£37.67 GBP
9 Mar 2011	Payment From		Completed	Details	Print postage label ▼	£35.40	-£1.40	£34.00 GBP

And here's one of my book sales account showing $1080.00 or £665.28 from one month's sales.

United Kingdom Operating Unit - GBP Transations
Publisher POD Compensation Report for Internet Marketing Business
For Period of CUSTOM
Period: 02/10/2010 To 31/12/2010
Page: Summary

This report includes an open period, the amounts are not final.

(All transactions are liable to VAT at 0%)

Quantity	Net Sales	Print Charge	Setup Recovery	Other	Net Pub Comp	Rec Rem
112	922.88	-257.60	0.00	0.00	665.28	

One day of drop shipping/eCommerce sales (drop shipping will be explained later in the book):

24 Nov 2010	Pur	Accepted	707.66 GBP	58590969658262000384	VP
24 Nov 2010	Pur	Accepted	1,610.98 GBP	58590969658262000383	VP
24 Nov 2010	Pur	Accepted	358.02 GBP	58590969658262000376	VP
24 Nov 2010	Pur	Accepted	185.44 GBP	58590969658262000379	DE
24 Nov 2010	Pur	Accepted	50.09 GBP	58590969658262000387	DE
24 Nov 2010	Pur	Accepted	579.91 GBP	58590969658262000377	DE
24 Nov 2010	Pur	Accepted	778.25 GBP	58590969658262000382	DE
25 Nov 2010	Pur	Accepted	633.41 GBP	58590969658262000402	DE
25 Nov 2010	Pur	Accepted	126.93 GBP		
25 Nov 2010	Pur	Accepted	207.68 GBP		
25 Nov 2010	Pur	Accepted	88.30 GBP		
25 Nov 2010	Pur	Accepted	197.98 GBP		
25 Nov 2010	Pur	Accepted	88.39 GBP		
25 Nov 2010	Pur	Accepted	39.64 GBP		

On 24th November, daily total sales:

$10,615!

(£6,804)

I use ekmPowershop as my eCommerce software for some shops. Here is **one** account showing an average of two to three orders per day:

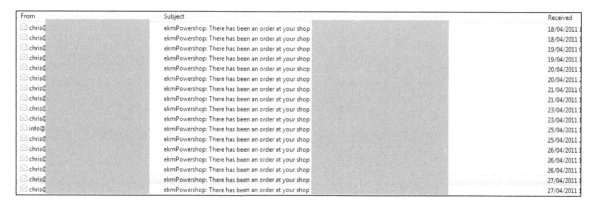

Total *including* eCommerce and drop shipping sales. Recap of the above screenshots:

$ 2709.81   or   £ 1654.71   Adsense income

$ 2105.68   or   £1292.26   Amazon affiliate commission

$ 4920.64   or   £ 3001.59   Clickbank average of both accounts shown

$ 1572.47   or   £964.82   PayPal sales

$1080.00   or   £665.28   Book sales account

$ 129,580.00 or £ 79.043.80   **Average** per month eCommerce and drop shipping sales
            (screenshot above is for one day only)

$ 141,968.60 Total $ per month or £86,622.46

X 12 months

$1,703,623.20 Total $ per year or £1,039,469.52

That is well over **$1,500.000 or £1.000.000 per year created from multiple streams of income.**

> **Important: Total income does not mean total profit. There is a big difference! VAT needs to be deducted where applicable and all expenses need to be deducted from the earnings in order to calculate the taxable profit. On top of that taxes need to be paid, after which your net profits can be calculated.**

The totals above are *excluding* any sales from paid traffic (people visiting your site) e.g. Pay Per Click (PPC) advertising, which is explained later in this book.

Here is an example: I spent $37.14 and turned it into $637.00 in one month – that is 1600% profit or $599.86 ! I run several PPC campaigns.

Displaying all 29 results.   Total: $637.00

Actions	Date	Time	Receipt	TID	Pmt	Currency	Txn Type	Item	Amount	Vendor
	2010-10-30			7S	MSTR	USD	Sale	1	$25.48	SAVMARRIAG
	2010-10-29			7S	VISA	USD	Sale	1	$25.48	SAVMARRIAG
	2010-10-29			7S	PYPL	USD	Sale	1	$25.48	SAVMARRIAG
	2010-10-28			7S	VISA	USD	Sale	1	$25.48	SAVMARRIAG
	2010-10-27			7S	VISA	USD	Sale	1	$25.48	SAVMARRIAG
	2010-10-26			7S	MSTR	USD	Sale	1	$25.48	SAVMARRIAG
	2010-10-25			7S	VISA	USD	Sale	1	$25.48	SAVMARRIAG
	2010-10-25			7S	PYPL	USD	Sale	1	$25.48	SAVMARRIAG
	2010-10-23			7S	PYPL	USD	Sale	1	$25.48	SAVMARRIAG
	2010-10-21			7S	MSTR	USD	Refund	1	($25.48)	SAVMARRIAG
	2010-10-20			7S	VISA	USD	Sale	1	$25.48	SAVMARRIAG
	2010-10-19			7S	VISA	USD	Sale	1	$25.48	SAVMARRIAG
	2010-10-18			7S	MSTR	USD	Sale	1	$25.48	SAVMARRIAG
	2010-10-18			7S	VISA	USD	Sale	1	$25.48	SAVMARRIAG
	2010-10-17			7S	MSTR	USD	Sale	1	$25.48	SAVMARRIAG
	2010-10-17			7S	VISA	USD	Sale	1	$25.48	SAVMARRIAG
	2010-10-15			7S	VISA	USD	Sale	1	$25.48	SAVMARRIAG
	2010-10-15			7S	VISA	USD	Sale	1	$25.48	SAVMARRIAG
	2010-10-13			7S	VISA	USD	Sale	1	$25.48	SAVMARRIAG
	2010-10-12			7S	VISA	USD	Sale	1	$25.48	SAVMARRIAG
	2010-10-07			7S	PYPL	USD	Sale	1	$25.48	SAVMARRIAG
	2010-10-07			7S	MSTR	USD	Sale	1	$25.48	SAVMARRIAG
	2010-10-04			7S	PYPL	USD	Sale	1	$25.48	SAVMARRIAG
	2010-10-03			7S	PYPL	USD	Refund	1	($25.48)	SAVMARRIAG
	2010-10-03			7S	VISA	USD	Sale	1	$25.48	SAVMARRIAG
	2010-10-03			7S	PYPL	USD	Sale	1	$25.48	SAVMARRIAG
	2010-10-02			7S	MSTR	USD	Sale	1	$25.48	SAVMARRIAG
	2010-10-02			7S	VISA	USD	Sale	1	$25.48	SAVMARRIAG
	2010-10-01			7S	PYPL	USD	Sale	1	$25.48	SAVMARRIAG

You are lucky, you can take advantage of the knowledge that I have gathered over the last five years. You can learn from me as I have done it all before, I have made the mistakes. You don't have to read 96 books or 400 eBooks. You don't have to buy over 100 different software programs or Clickbank products. You don't have to spend over $40,000 (mostly on advertising) to try to work out this internet thing. I've done all that for you and in this book you can read what I've learned. I have even signed up for internet gurus and now get their emails. Below is a picture of my inbox.

I used to read every single email, sign up for every internet marketing newsletter I could find and buy almost everything that any guru would rec ommend. And yes I did learn a lot. But now I do not even open the emails because I've discovered there is not much new to learn for me. All the guru emails that I receive now are just sitting in my "IM Sales Crap" folder. (IM = internet marketing) I saved all the emails especially so I can show you a screenshot in my book. I have saved up all the emails from 21 September 2010 until 27th May 2011, gathering 11546 emails during eight months. That is over 1440 emails per month or 48 emails per day. Knowing that it takes on average 15 minutes to investigate the email and study the offers emailed, brings us to the following calculations: 48 emails per day x 15 minutes = 720 minutes per day = 12 hours per day!

No wonder I never used to earn any money when I first started to investigate the internet marketing business! I have not even mentioned the 8047 deleted emails (Junk e-mails that I move to the Deleted Items folder).

I must add here that some gurus don't overdo it on their emails but most of them do. From some of them I receive two or three emails per day! Some of the internet marketing gurus give away good stuff and sell valuable information/DVDs. But be wary as there are a lot of cowboys doing business!

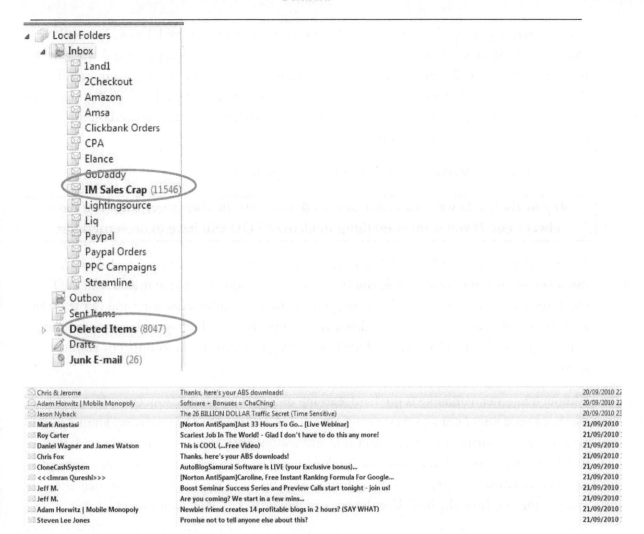

The emails highlighted in bold are unread emails started at 21 September 2010. The earlier emails are not bold. I started to investigate everything to do with earning money online about five years ago and now, I am finally living the dream.

To all those who dream of financial freedom, you can do it if I can !

Over the years I have read books and watched videos on (the following terms will be explained later) CPC, CPA, CPU, Adsense, mobile marketing, squeeze pages, article marketing, outsourcing, blogging, backlinking, landing pages, sales letters, list building, social networking, finding niches, affiliate marketing, driving traffic, video marketing and more and tried to make money in all these areas without success. Whatever I tried, I would either lose money, or break even or earn a little bit but never the amount I was hoping for. I was getting pretty fed up with it all. One morning I woke up and said to myself "I am not a quitter, I WILL make this work, I will build a website with a mixture of what I'd learned". So I did and I now have 96 websites (see screenshots later in this book), most of them based on the principle that I will teach you in this book.

It's your time, you can do it too. It's time for a change for you.

> **If you always do what you have always done, you will always get what you have always got. If you want something to change YOU will have to do something.**

Internet marketing is NOT hard. It is time consuming and there is a heck of a lot to take in but if you break it into manageable chunks, you can do it too. To start with you will NOT make any money sitting on your backside, you will have to put in some time and effort. After a while though, you WILL be sitting down and earning money. That is the beauty of internet marketing. EVERYTHING can be done from sitting in a chair in the comfort of your own home.

Although internet marketing is not hard, earning money through it is. Once you have read this book, you might not know everything about internet marketing but it is my aim to give you enough information to make you ready and confident to start your first website. If you watch the videos as well as reading the book, you will be even more ready! Perhaps none of us will ever know *everything* about doing business on the web; but hey, so what if there are crayons missing from the box? Use the crayons you've got to draw your picture.

> **You can make excuses or you can make money**

Do you need a lot of money to start with? No you don't. I will show you ways to earn money without a website but if you do want to start your own website, you can do so with just $19.99. You might not need money but you do need time. If you are not going to put in any effort, you will not make any money. Do bees get honey without work? No they don't.

> **No Bees No Honey - No Work No Money**

I will never say that making money on the internet is easy because it isn't. Well, it isn't at the beginning but once you will start to enjoy making money online, you will enjoy the internet.

If you want to get specialised in one specific field, you will need to dig deeper and learn more, but most aspects of internet marketing are covered in this book. Follow the steps in this book and spend time building traffic and you will probably start to earn money. You too can build websites and start earning money with your first one. When you can make $50 per month with one site, it becomes easier to make $100 per month with the same site. And once you can make $100 per month with one site, you can duplicate it and make $1000 per month with 10 sites. Always keep that in mind. But most of all...

Good luck! Just stay with it.

My warmest regards,

Christine Clayfield

Author, Entrepreneur, Infopreneur, Internet Marketer, Book Publisher, Public Speaker

Note: I am from the UK so this book is written in English spelling therefore you will see colour instead of color, optimise instead of optimize, socialise instead of socialize, etc..

September 2013. Important note added to this book:

If you are in the EU, you must investigate if your website is in regulation with The EU Cookie Law which comes into place on 26th May 2012. Just search for "EU Cookie Law". www.cookielaw.org says: "Most websites must offer users opt-in consent tools to allow cookies that pass information about your browsing activities to 3rd parties".

Remember: Nothing is going to happen unless YOU make it happen.

Introduction

> **If you already know a lot about internet marketing, I suggest that you go straight to 'Part 3: Niche research' as that is where my method actually starts.**

1. What is internet marketing (IM)?

Wikipedia definition: Internet marketing, also referred to as e-marketing, web-marketing, online-marketing. It is the marketing of products or services over the internet.

In other words, it is promoting your business or website online with the methods that are available through today's internet marketing technology.

It is very popular across the world because the set-up costs are minimal, you can choose your work hours and you can reach customers worldwide.

Internet Marketing is also known in the internet world simply as IM. Throughout this book I will use the acronym IM.

2. Important to mention before you start reading this book

- Whenever I say "Google your keyword", what I really mean is search for your keyword in whichever search engine you want. According to statistics Google owns the largest share of the search engine market, followed by Yahoo!, Search, Bing, Ask and lots of other smaller search engines.

- This book is also based on trying to please Google with our website but a lot of the search engines apply the same methods to decide which pages display for a certain keyword, although all search engines have their own algorithms (the formula that each search engine uses to evaluate web pages and to determine if their relevance and value are good enough to be shown in the searches). Consequently, whatever techniques that I use for ranking will work for most search engines.

- At times in the book I mention the same thing twice or more. There are two reasons for doing this: firstly because I firmly believe that repetition makes you remember things better and secondly because some readers might only read a few chapters in this book and not understand that particular chapter when reading it should I have left certain information out.

- At the time of printing this book, all websites were fully functional. If you come across a website, a plugin, etc…that is no longer available (the internet changes all the time), I suggest that you search online for an alternative.

- The methods outlined in this book are designed to try to get on the pages of Google with our keyword (the words people type in to search for something) in the organic ranking (on the left underneath the ads) not the sponsored links. Research has shown that these are the websites clicked on most often when people have typed in a keyword.

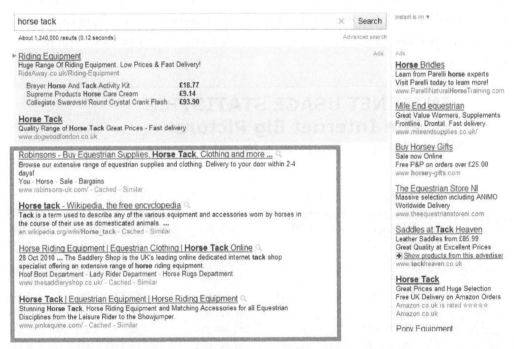

Organic ranking in frame, rest is sponsored ranking (top and right).

-   Once you start earning money, you will have to pay taxes on your income. Just because you've earned it on the internet does not mean it is not taxable. If only it were like that, life would be marvellous. Make sure you check the legalities of the country you live in.

- You will see some "one-liners" dotted throughout this book. These are statements that I believe in or that I apply in my private life and in my business life. I have chosen to share these with you as I think they can be valuable when applied.

- Where amounts are shown in different currencies e.g. $ and £: the currency conversion used was correct in November 2010 but is subject to change.

3. How big is this internet marketing business ?

This is how big: 1,966,514,816 Internet Users (see the picture below), a lot of which either speak English or use English-speaking websites. That is 1.9 billion internet users! More than five billion people have mobile phones and over 78 million can go online with their phone. This means that no matter what you are selling, somebody is likely to want your product right now. Absolutely everything and everybody is coming online. Online sales are rising each year. Millions of people are proving that they are willing and able to be sold to, whether you're selling a product or a service.

INTERNET USAGE STATISTICS
The Internet Big Picture
World Internet Users and Population Stats

WORLD INTERNET USAGE AND POPULATION STATISTICS

World Regions	Population (2010 Est.)	Internet Users Dec. 31, 2000	Internet Users Latest Data	Penetration (% Population)	Growth 2000-2010	Users % of Table
Africa	1,013,779,050	4,514,400	110,931,700	10.9 %	2,357.3 %	5.6 %
Asia	3,834,792,852	114,304,000	825,094,396	21.5 %	621.8 %	42.0 %
Europe	813,319,511	105,096,093	475,069,448	58.4 %	352.0 %	24.2 %
Middle East	212,336,924	3,284,800	63,240,946	29.8 %	1,825.3 %	3.2 %
North America	344,124,450	108,096,800	266,224,500	77.4 %	146.3 %	13.5 %
Latin America/Caribbean	592,556,972	18,068,919	204,689,836	34.5 %	1,032.8 %	10.4 %
Oceania / Australia	34,700,201	7,620,480	21,263,990	61.3 %	179.0 %	1.1 %
WORLD TOTAL	6,845,609,960	360,985,492	1,966,514,816	28.7 %	444.8 %	100.0 %

NOTES: (1) Internet Usage and World Population Statistics are for June 30, 2010. (2) CLICK on each world region name for detailed regional usage information. (3) Demographic (Population) numbers are based on data from the US Census Bureau . (4) Internet usage information comes from data published by Nielsen Online, by the International Telecommunications Union, by GfK, local Regulators and other reliable sources. (5) For definitions, disclaimer, and navigation help, please refer to the Site Surfing Guide. (6) Information in this site may be cited, giving the due credit to www.internetworldstats.com. Copyright © 2000 - 2010, Miniwatts Marketing Group. All rights reserved worldwide.

Source : http://www.internetworldstats.com/stats.htm

These days a company without a website is not considered a professional company.

You have to get in there while you still can. There are still some good untapped money-making niches. Building an IM business from zero is much cheaper than building a normal business outside the internet. You can also build an IM empire much quicker than you can build a normal business, because you can reach millions of people with the internet all over the world.

4. Who is this book **NOT** suitable for?

If you want to find a get-rich-quick scheme without putting any effort in, this book is certainly not for you. Everything that I do to earn money online involves working very hard to start with.

If you want to earn $20,000 online in one month from now, you can forget it because that is not possible with my system (nor with any system).

This initial picture on how to make money might even look a bit depressing, as I stress throughout this book that you must work hard to see results. But hey, taking over $1,500,000 per year can hardly be categorised as depressing now, can it? Stick with it and you will find happiness and smiles.

Whatever the mind of man can conceive and believe, it can achieve.   *Napoleon Hill*

5. Who is this book for?

This book can be helpful and very useful to:

- Anybody who wants to earn money working from home eg. Stay-at-home Mums or Dads

- Anybody who has a website

- Anybody who wants to create their first website

- Anybody who wants to earn money on the web without a website

- Anybody who wants to learn about free traffic

- Anybody who wants to learn about paid traffic

- Anybody who wants to earn money as an affiliate

- Anybody who wants to earn a lot of money working from home

- Anybody who is already earning money, but wants to pick up some tips and tricks or find traffic techniques

- Anybody aged between the ages 10 and 100 who wants to put some effort into earning money online

- I think you get the idea, it is suitable for anybody who is involved with internet marketing

Try and you might - Don't and you certainly won't.

6. What is actually in this book?

The idea of this book is to summarize what I have learned over the past years. I am outlining a strategy that works for me. You can copy my strategy and hopefully you too will be making good money soon. I have 96 websites.

Want proof? Here it is:

The majority of my websites – 83 in total – are hosted with www.1and1.co.uk simply because I prefer to work with their platform. The other 13 are hosted with www.godaddy.com . On the screenshot below you can see that I am logged into my account (it says logout on the right-hand top corner of the screenshot) and it shows that I have 83 websites in total.

This is a screenshot of my 1and1 account, showing 83 sites in "My Domain Overview":

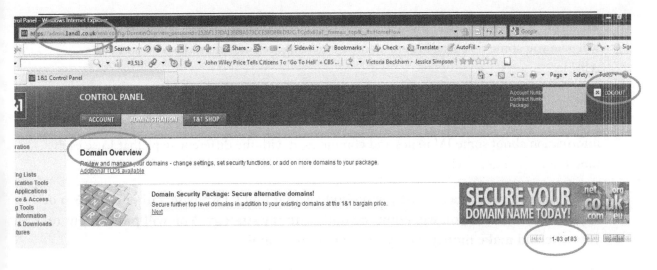

This is a screenshot of my Godaddy account, showing 13 sites in "My Account":

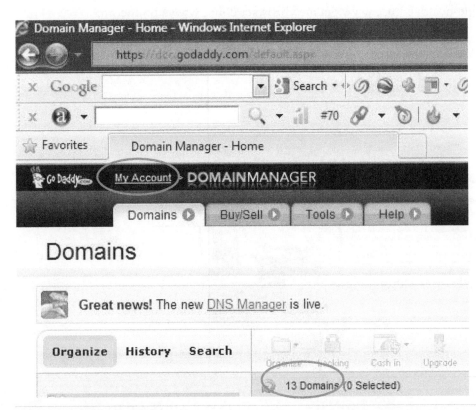

Throughout this book I will share with you the knowledge that I have gained over the years. I will give you some tips, insights and some interesting websites that I have found to be reliable.

This book will, for the most part, explain the exact steps I go through when I set up a new website. I'm not hiding anything or missing anything out. This book is about giving information about some IM issues and combining it with the different steps that I use each time I develop a new website.

There are two main reasons why somebody would build a website: either to inform or to generate income. You will combine both with my strategy. You will put content on your site and make money with your money-making link.

Here are a few examples of how your site could look. These sites all have content on and have all sorts of money–making links on the site. These are the types of sites that I have in all different niches and I will be explaining step by step how to find new niches and how to put the money making links on your site. The vast majority of my sites are with multiple streams of income. Here are a few examples (not my sites): www.active.com , www.herniated-disc-pain.org, www.spine-health.com, , www.getanewbrowser.com , www.about.com,

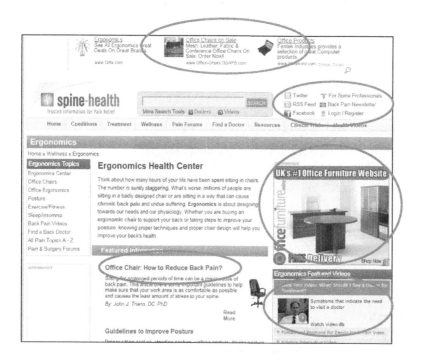

On the screenshot above you can see money-making links and good content : CPA offers, Adsense, videos, share icon, Affiliate Products, and more. All these terms will be clear to you at the end of this book.

Building a website does not need to be complicated and earning money online is not complicated either. Your website can look simple but sophisticated.

> **Simplicity is the ultimate sophistication.**
>
> Leonardo Da Vinci

If you follow my steps, ideas, tips, tricks and insights in this book then you'll have a site that you can start testing and tweaking for yourself, and you can really maximise the amount of money you make.

I am explaining a lot of different ways that you can earn money, without going into too much detail on each subject in IM. If, after reading this book, you think Facebook is the way to go for you, you need to buy another book that focuses on Facebook. If you think you will really enjoy YouTube marketing, buy an extra book specialised in that subject. This book gives you an overview of the internet's money-making possibilities. Find the one that you like most and focus on that.

Study, analyse, try things, learn what works for you and learn what you like doing most. Once you have found that, stick with it and concentrate on it until you master it.

7. You need to look after your health. Believe me. I know.

Consider this as a very important message from one internet marketer to another. Believe me, I have learned the hard way. For years I sat working on my computer for hours and days in the wrong position, in the wrong chair, without any breaks. On some days, I would switch my computer on at 8am and work on it until 1am the next morning. My punishment for this: I have been diagnosed with cervical spondolysis (a non-curable condition) in my neck, with disc space between C5, C6 and C7 most affected. Want proof? Here it is. As I always like to prove what I say, here is a picture of my neck's x-ray and MRI scan. You can see on the first picture that the space between disc C5 and C6 is thinner than all the other spaces. The second picture shows a bulging disc pushing pressure on the spinal cord and its nerves fibers. Permanent nerve damage can be caused when a bulging disc in the neck is compressing a nerve for a long period of time.

 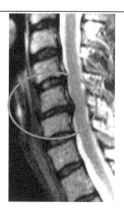

Now I cannot work on the computer as much as I would like to because when I do, my neck starts to hurt. I now have two choices: work a long time and give myself pain or work less and have no pain. As health is more important than money I obviously choose to work fewer hours. I can still work about ten hours per day on the computer but certainly not longer in order not to make my condition worse. I am not telling you this out of self-pity as I am very happy with what I have achieved. ***I am telling you this so you don't make the same mistake.***

I always ask myself, and I assume you do too, when somebody is selling something that he is making money with, why would he sell it, why would he not just do it himself without telling the world about it ? You could ask the same about this book. Why am I giving away my system for others to apply if I am making money with it? Well now you know the reason. In my case, it is for health. My health is the reason I have decided to write this book. It was my plan to build another 100 sites over the next few years but that will not be possible after my diagnosis as I always like to oversee everything (I am a control-freak) that my staff and outsourcers are doing, which all takes up a lot of time. I am now very happy with the number of sites that I have and therefore other people can build sites with my system.

I am a professional internet marketer and always will be as I **love** it. The fact that I cannot work as much as I would like to is not a major disaster for me because a lot of my work is now done by my staff, or by outsourcing, and a lot of my sites will provide me with income on autopilot for many years to come. ***Please please pay attention to the following. What I am about to say truly is very important for your health.*** I feel that it is my duty to tell everybody in an office environment about the dangers of working constantly on a computer. I would not want you to make the same mistakes as me. If somebody had told me five years ago what I am going to tell you, I would not have a problem with my neck now. As an internet marketer you will be sitting in front of the computer for hours and hours and maybe even days. **Most people think that an office environment is a place with very low risk of injury. I thought the same until I had excruciating shoulder pain when I woke up one day. The truth is a lot of musculoskeletal disorders are caused in office environments. These disorders develop because of repetitive strain to the body's muscles, tendons, ligaments, joints and nerves. Back, shoulders, neck, arms and hands are most commonly affected resulting from computer injuries (work-related musculoskeletal disorders).**

The two most important things that you need to know:

1. Make sure that you are sitting in the correct position on your computer. Search for "correct posture at a computer" and you will find a lot of information. Search for "ergonomic office chair" and change your office chair if you have to.

2. Make sure you take regular breaks. Staring at a computer screen with your head and neck always in the same position is very straining for your neck.

I use my own developed software: www.breakremindersoftware.com and in my opinion this should be installed on each computer that is sold anywhere in the world. It is not available for Apple computers. www.workpace.com is similar, more sophisticated software and I believe available for Apple computer. The software monitors the time you work on the computer and it alerts you when you need to take a break. It shows you general exercises that you can do while sitting on your chair. You can set it to block your keyboard during breaks so you cannot work. My settings are as follows:

- I have a break for 20 seconds every 10 minutes and I've set the software so that my keyboard is blocked. Therefore every 10 minutes I do some gentle neck exercises.

- I have a 10-minute break every hour and my software is set so my keyboard is blocked, which forces me to get up and do something else for 10 minutes.

If you can afford it, invest in www.breakremindersoftware.com. It is the best piece of software available for an office environment. You have been warned: install it as a matter of urgency if you can afford it. If you cannot afford it: force yourself to take regular breaks. There are similar programmes on the market : simply search for "office timers" or "office break timers".

Sorry to have to be the one to tell you but i-Pads, laptops and mobile phones are a lot worse for your neck than a normal computer screen. This is because your face is always pointing downwards, so your neck has a lot more strain on it.

Also, finger arthritis is predicted to be a major worldwide problem in years to come, as people use their phones for too long. The finger movement involved in texting and moving a mouse causes Repetitive Strain Injury, resulting in arthritis for a lot of people.

You can read about Repetitive Strain Injury in my daughter's book: www.PainInTheThumb.com It is also available on Amazon.

Correct posture at the computer: **Bad posture at the computer:**

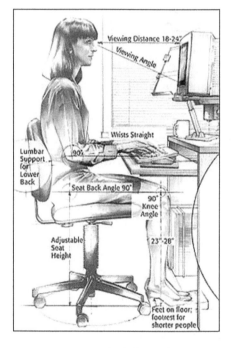

(Source: www.ergonomics-info.com)

Please do not ignore this message, it really is very important, I cannot stress it enough.

8. Total Cost to build a website

It is possible to earn money on the internet without having a website. I will give plenty of examples later in the book. However, with my method you do need your own website for each niche you are targeting.

How much will building a website cost you? I'm not going to lie to you. Setting up a website *does* cost money - so don't believe the hype that this is all money for nothing. Don't be afraid though, the bare essentials will cost you about $20, but there are extras that you should invest in if you really want to hit the ground running.

a) The crucial "can't do this without them" elements

- A domain and hosting account (plus free email address) with www.godaddy.com - this is the one thing that you cannot avoid buying. You want to have a website that makes you money, so you're going to need to buy a website, which means having a domain name and a hosting account (explained more later) - $19 per year.

- Web design software. I will talk about Wordpress mostly in this book, which is completely free. WordPress is a free, Web-based software program that anyone can use to build and maintain a website or blog.

- Autoresponder Software – As internet marketer, you must, must, must have a way of capturing your visitors email addresses so that you can keep them coming back, and sell to them. This can be done with an auto responder like www.aweber.com. Prices for autoresponders range from $0 (for up to 500 Subscribers in MailChimp) to $19.95 p/month (with www.aweber.com, which is the best autoresponder, in my opinion). You do not need Aweber for each website that you are designing. Therefore if you have 20 sites, each site only costs you $1.00 per month. Once you have over 2500 opt-ins (people who filled in their e-mail address) the monthly payment goes up slightly. If you are not sure yet how committed you are, start with MailChimp because it is free at the beginning. However, if you decide afterwards to change to Aweber it will not be possible to transfer the email addresses (unless your opt-ins decide to opt-in *again* when you ask send them an email saying you have changed your autoresponder) and you will have to start building your list again. Don't worry if you do not know want an opt-in and autoresponder is, it will be explained later.

b) The recommended extras that will earn you more money

- Market Samurai – www.marketsamurai.com. This software is one of my favourite tools for online research. It offers brilliant keyword research and search engine optimisation tools. It gives a deep insight into keywords and competitors for that keyword. Every internet marketer should get to grips with it. It is the best possible investment you could ever make when it comes to making money online. You'll easily make the money back because you'll be able to find the keywords that you can easily dominate - $97 (*one off payment, free upgrades and support for life*). The advertised one-off payment is $147 but if you subscribe for a seven-day trial you automatically get $48 discount.
- Scanner - For our Royalty Free Book Method (will be explained later what this is). If you want to really speed up your money-making then this is crucial and cheap - $40
- Books on your niche - The best way to find out information and ideas for content on your niche site is reading books - $0 (*go to your local library*) to $10 (*for a stack of second-hand books from Amazon or eBay*)

Conclusion:

- The crucial things you need: domain name and hosting - $19 per year

- Recommended extras – Market Samurai at $97

Total - $116

If you think that sounds like a lot then you're wrong. How much do you think a bricks and mortar business costs to get off the ground?

$20,000? $40,000?

How long do you think it takes them to re-pay that initial investment? Somewhere around five to ten years is a fair estimate.

In contrast, your new business will cost you a maximum of $116 to start up and could earn it all back in one month.

It's a no-brainer: spend a tiny amount of money and you could earn a LOT of money.

What to buy	Cost
GoDaddy domain name and hosting	$1.66 per month ($19 per year)
Market Samurai	$97 (if bought after trial download)
Aweber	$19.95 p/month for multiple accounts
Wordpress	*Free*

Top Tip : When you buy anything online, always Google "keyword" + "discount coupon" or "keyword" + "discount voucher" or "keyword" + "voucher code". You will be amazed how many discount vouchers are available online. You can also visit www.voucherhub.com to see what's available. All you need to do when you order a product is get the discount code and paste it when you check-out. You can save yourself anything from 5% to 50% discount if you're lucky.

9. Where have all the customers gone?

The vast majority of searchers never look past page two of a Google search. Owning a website is like owning a high street shop in a busy shopping street. If your site is on page one you are located at the entrance of the busiest shop in the high street, so you are likely to earn money as long as people are going to the high street. If your site is on page two you are located near the entrance of the busiest shop in town so you are very likely to stay in business. If you are outside the first two pages of a Google search, you have a tiny little shop on a tiny little corner at the end of the busy street- where nobody ever walks. These little shops constantly change owner because nobody can make any money out there.

Fact is that in most towns, the high street shops are less busy than then they were ten years ago. Why? Because people shop differently these days. People shop from the comfort of their homes and use the internet to find places to buy stuff. In the high street people enter shops, have a look around in each shop, and eventually buy something in a shop that they like. On the web people visit site after site and buy something on a site they like. So there are two things that are obviously important: to develop a site that people like and to make sure people can see your shop to "walk in" on the web. Conclusion: a shop needs to be in the middle of the high street to survive and make money. Likewise your website needs to be on the first pages of Google to make money (unless you will use paid traffic to your site).

So, "Where have all the customers gone"? Simple – they've gone online.

How do people decide where online to buy?

- **Google**: Well first of all, they Google what they want and see what comes up. In order to display in Google, content and links to your website are important.

- **Blogs**: People find shops on Google, but if they have not heard of the shop, they are likely to type in "shop+review" or something similar. The results of such a search are often blogs, where people review, shop and rate their experience.

- **Social media**: people will ask their friends if they have heard about a shop or join forums to see if anybody has bought from it before.

All these three aspects are covered in this book, from making sure people find you in Google to blogging and social media.

To conclude, you must move your shop to where the customers have gone. Whatever business you start on the web, selling physical products or selling eBooks or sending affiliate links or launching a new shopping site, you NEED traffic. No way around it. Just as you need customers for a high street shop to survive, you need traffic on your site to survive and make money. That is why a big chunk of this book is focused on traffic. The traffic methods that I describe in this book can be used for any websites, not just the kind of sites that I suggest you build.

10. Password nightmare solved

You need a system for your passwords. It's a certainty. You will create hundreds of accounts and it will be impossible to remember all user names and passwords. I used to keep them all on a spreadsheet, with nothing on my computer for security purposes. I have been spoofed before, so I am extremely careful with passwords and web security and so should you. Anyway six months later I would have manually added another 30 passwords to the sheet but because I had no digital version I had to type in the first 100 passwords AGAIN to add the other 30! Print it and bin it again and the same scenario when I had an extra 30 passwords to add.

Then I came across www.Roboform.com and all my problems were solved. Roboform remembers all your passwords, is a doddle to use and is safe. I use www.roboform2go.com

for all my laptops. This is exactly the same principle but all the passwords are stored on a USB stick so you need the USB stick to open it. This is because somebody could steal your laptop but at least without the USB stick, there is no way they have easy access all your passwords. You will create a password in order to get to your other passwords, so even if somebody steals your stick, they won't get your other passwords.

Roboform can also store other information like your name and address, and email address. You can also set up different identities, which can be great submitting articles under a different pen name. Note: Roboform does not work on Opera or Apple, but Apple has its own version: www.1password.com.

Caution: it is essential to have anti-virus software (e.g. Norton) *and* Anti-Spyware-checking software(e.g. Super Anti Spyware Professional) installed on your computer. I have found that an all-in-security like Norton is not sufficient, you also need separate anti-spyware. And please, if you are serious about IM, don't just install the free versions that are available on the internet.

Part 1. Can Anybody be an Internet Marketer ?

1. How can internet marketing be compared to running a "normal" business?

All you need is a computer and an internet connection to make money online, right? Well, I am afraid it's not that simple. In my opinion anybody with a tiny little bit of business acumen and common sense can make money on the internet. A person with a lot of business attitude and business knowledge has a slightly better chance of making it. The buying attitudes, reasons and motives of customers buying on the web are very similar to the ones buying on the high street. A lot of business principles can be applied to marketing online and off-line so people who are aware of these business principles are just one step ahead of others. Having said that, you certainly do not need business knowledge to make it. It is just an advantage and not a necessity.

> **Don't try to fit in if you are born to stand out. Don't join the rat race.**

The traditional elements of marketing are the "four Ps". These also apply to the IM business. The point I want to get across here is that IM is comparable to doing business outside the internet. An internet business is like running a normal business; it will need your full-time attention to succeed.

Here are some business terms that are very well known in the marketing/business world outside the internet and can also be applied to the IM environment.

a) The 4 Ps are:

- **Product**. Your product is whatever you are selling, online or offline.

- **Price**. Your price needs to be realistic compared to comparable products on the market, in our case on the web.

- **Placement** is about your distribution channels. Where and when are your products going to be available? There is one big difference here with normal marketing because products are available online 24/7.

- **Promotion** is your channels of communication with your customers and prospects.

If there is a problem somewhere with your sales, on the web or outside the web, you need to investigate each P to see which is causing the problem.

b) AIDA

A = Attention. Get your visitor's attention, in our case by building a website with various sources of potential interest.

I = Interest. Get your visitors interested in what is on your site.

D = Desire. Give your visitors the desire to click on something on your website. In our case we are trying to make the visitor click on something that makes you money.

A = Action. Your visitor takes action and clicks on one of the links on your website. All links are links that make you money, so the principle you need to follow when designing your website is to include as many money-making links as possible.

c) 80/20 rule

80% of your sales come from 20% of your customers applies very often in any business environment. This also applies in keyword research, as 80% of your sales will come from 20% of your keywords that are used in, for instance, an adword campaign. It is therefore important to look after that 20% of your customers and to focus on the 20% of your good keywords.

d) Rule of 10

A sales representative can get 100 prospects gathered at an exhibition. Out of these 100 prospects he might get ten more interesting leads, and out of those ten leads one person will buy his product. If he is lucky, the sales rep could get between 2% and 5% of sales out of his 100 prospects. That is a principle that I have always applied in all my businesses.

How does this work in IM? If 100 people click on your ad and one person buys your product, you have a conversion rate of 1%, which is acceptable in IM. A realistic IM conversion rate (discussed later in more detail) is between 1% and 5%.

e) Know your competitors

Knowing your competition is vital whatever business you are in. Further in the book I will give you some tools to "spy" on your competition.

f) Supply and demand – pricing policy

If a manufacturer makes a product and there is a large demand and no competition, they will probably sell the product with a high profit margin as there is no competition. If other manufacturers start to produce similar products and bring them to market, the first manufacturer will probably have to reduce his price, as it is likely that the other manufacturers will have a lower selling price.

The same applies for the pricing of eBooks: if you find a niche and there is no competition you can sell your eBook for a high price. If five other people publish an eBook in the same niche, chances are you will sell less, and have to lower your price to stay competitive in the market.

g) Benefits, benefits, benefits

When selling any products, you HAVE to concentrate on what the benefits are for the customer when purchasing the product. If you are selling a product online, exactly the same applies: benefits, benefits, benefits. Don't say "We make good quality chairs" but instead say "Your back pain could disappear forever with our chairs".

h) Only two sales

There are only two reasons for sales in any sales environment, on the web or outside the web:

- A solution to a problem

- A fulfilment of a need or dream

i) Put on other shoes

If you want to be in business you need to put yourself in your customer's shoes. What would you like to see if you were a potential customer? Look at the world, your product, your sales letter, your eBook, etc… as a potential customer. If you visit a website, what would you like to see ? Develop the website in that way.

j) KPI indicators

KPI stands for Key Performance Indicators – also called Key Success Indicators and are used a lot in businesses outside the web environment. As an internet marketer you also need to analyse as many aspects of your website as possible and try to improve it all the time. Just like the giant supermarkets know more about your spending habits than you do, you need to try to find out what the searching habits of your customers are. The purpose of a KPI is to measure a certain activity, analyse the data and learn or improve.

k) Last but not least: **Your USP =Unique Selling Point.** What is unique about your product? How do you stand out from your competition?

2. What skills does an internet marketer need?

My success in the IM world did not come overnight. I have read, I have analysed, I have tried, I have learned and what I've learned, I've put into action. I have made lots of (expensive) mistakes.

You can forget about working only one hour a day to earn millions. That is living in a dream world. If you are prepared to spend a lot of time on the computer and if you are prepared to work hard and learn from your mistakes, you have a good chance of making it. However, you will have to learn a lot of skills in a short time in a very competitive business.

In order to succeed on the internet you need to have some knowledge in a large variety of fields. There is no need to be an expert from the start in all the different fields as you will learn as you go along. Any business owner will tell you that it is hard work running a company. The same applies for an IM business. If you are planning to do all the work yourself, without outsourcing any of it, you will need some skills from all the professions listed below. To succeed, you will need a mixture of these 25 skills:

- **Website builder.** You will need these skills as that is the aim of the game: build websites with money-making links. In order to build good websites, you will also need lots of the skills listed below.

- **Graphic artist.** You will have to be creative in how you arrange the layout of your website. You must think about where to put images and text. You have to know what colours match and what colours clash when seen together. You have to know what typeface to use and what size the typeface should be.

- **Computer expert.** You don't really need to be an expert but you certainly need to have some computer knowledge. You will have to be able to work with different software programmes (such as graphic layout programmes and graphic design programmes) as you will need to resize pictures or reduce their resolution. Knowledge of some basic HTML, a web coding language, is an advantage but not a necessity.

- **Marketing expert.** You need to have some marketing knowledge. It will be a huge advantage if you know what 4P's, AIDA, Maslow triangle and market segmentations are. When your website is designed, you need to know what your target market is, who your target customers are, who your competition is. Not only do you need to know about it, but you also have to be able to analyse the information to your advantage.

- **Sales person.** You need to know how to sell, what price to sell for and who to sell to. One big advantage: you do not need to wear a smart suit, shiny shoes, red socks or a polka-dot tie ☺.

- **Accountant**. You need to work out your profits as an affiliate, and you need to know how to calculate 65% profit on a product. You need to know how much profit is left for you if you give away 70% commission to your affiliate.

- **Mathematician**. You need to work out conversion rates and use spread sheets to work out a total of your profits.

- **Writer.** You need to write articles and write content for your site.

- **Photographer.** You need to work with photographs, so you will need some basic photo editing skills to know what resolution means, what pixels are, how to save a photograph as a JPEG and so on.

- **Logo designer.** You will need to design a header for your site. You can also outsource this.

- **Psychologist.** You need to know about your customers' behaviour. Analyse in what style to write and to sell for your target customers. You need to realise that selling to teenagers and silver surfers is different and you must adjust your style of writing accordingly.

- **Behaviour analyst.** You need to know where on your screen to put a "buy it now" button. You need to know which part of your screen your visitors look at first, according to studies.

- **Video Expert.** You are likely to work with videos, so you need to know the best format to save a video for the quickest download. You need to know what MPEG and WAV mean.

- **Typist.** You need to be able to type more than five words per minute. If you are a very slow typer, you are losing valuable time. You can always get a copy of Dragon Naturally Speaking, available on Amazon, which is speech recognition software: you speak and the computer types it in MsWord. It is amazing software.

- **Logical thinker**. You need to think about the logic of the page order on your site. Also, think about if your text flows logically.

- **Business person.** You need the business instinct to spot money-making opportunities and exploit markets. You will need to make business decisions and foresee any changes needed, and be able to adapt to those changes.

- **Analyst.** You need to analyse information from several sources, put it all together and make decisions based on your analysis. Ask yourself: what market are you selling to? Who are you are selling to? What are they buying? Are they spending money? You need the skills to conclude that if somebody has been advertising something on the web for the last two years, he must be making money, so you could try the same thing. You need to know what to pay attention to, and what to ignore.

- **Organiser.** You will, without a doubt, need some organisational skills. You need to organise the files on your computer in folders. You will need a system to instantly find a password when it's required.

- **Risk taker.** You need to be able to make calculated risks decisions in case you are going to spend money on paid traffic methods.

- **Copywriter.** You need to be able to write in a style that makes people order from you. The ability to write interesting sales copy is very important.

- **Researcher.** You will need to research your niche and be able to conclude what is important information for your potential customers.

- **Planner.** You need to be able to plan when you will design your site, when you will drive traffic to it, when you will try paid traffic.

- **SEO expert**. The most important for your website is to rank in Google, therefore SEO (Search Engine Optimisation) knowledge is essential.

- **Webmaster.** You will need to be able to publish your site to the search engines. You need to know what an IP address is and what hosting means.

- **Judge.** You need sound judgment and the ability to recognise a lie. There are lots of scam artists on the web who are often very convincing.

So there you have it! That is 25 skills that you will need to become a successful internet marketer. And I am not joking. To become successful, you need a blend of these skills, abilities and talents. Most of all you need entrepreneurial flair and business instinct. Maybe now you understand why most online businesses fail and why a lot of people give up. Even if you will be using ready-to-use templates and software or an online shop, you will still need the majority of the skills above. Even if you decide to outsource everything you still need to know all the basics about IM, as you will have to check and correct the work delivered to you by outsourcers.

But there is hope: you do not need all these skills from the start. But you will need them all in order to become a successful internet marketer. Fortunately you can learn a lot of these skills by reading about them. No-one was born wise; it comes from making more good choices than bad ones and learning from the bad ones. In the beginning you will probably, just like me, feel like you're not getting anywhere, but be positive and stay focused and keep your spirits high.

> ## A good idea without business skills is not a good idea.

If you only remember one thing after reading this book it should be this: take action. Copy what I do when I build a website. The system works for me so it can work for you. Take action: start now, set yourself a goal. Stop buying all sorts of sales guides, stop going to courses and stop never DOING anything. You need to take action NOW.

> Do not wait; the time will never be "just right." Start where you stand, and work with whatever tools you may have at your command, and better tools will be found as you go along. *Napoleon Hill*

Skills + action = success

> TOP TIP : write down what you are going to do and tell your friends what your plan is. Did you know that you are 49 times more likely to get something done if you write it down? On top of that you are 49 times more likely to do it if you tell all your friends that you are planning to do it. That is 2401 (49 x 49) more likely to get things done if you write it down AND tell your friends. You know what to do.

On top of the blend of skills that you need to become a super affiliate, you also need to: Be prepared to work hard - Be determined and persistent - Have a strong money earning desire - Have the willpower to keep going when things go wrong - Be willing to outsource - Invest your profits in your next project - Focus on one thing.

> **Be like a stamp: stick to one thing until you get there**.

3. YOU need to stay in control.

I must admit, I did try and earn money on the web 'the lazy way' and bought some software that would set up all the sites for me, and host them for me for a monthly fee. That's all I did when I started my internet venture: buy stuff that would promise to make me rich by doing nothing. Boy did I learn the expensive way that this stuff does not work. Once I bought the software the provider would tell me that I needed to host my domains with them or that I was forced to buy my domain names with them. In other words, I wasn't in control. That used to annoy me and put me off ever buying from them again.

YOU need to be in control of your domain names and your hosting.

YOU must decide when you want don't want a domain name any longer.

YOU must be able to change content on your site without having to ask permission.

YOU must be able to change some keywords if need be.

YOU want to decide when and if you are selling your site.

You do NOT want to open a support ticket to BEG for your domain name to be cancelled, only to be told that you had entered a two-year contract, and nothing can be done. I have done all that and it becomes annoying and frustrating. Don't make the mistakes that I made. I will tell you now: 'the lazy way' does not work and 99% of the time you are not in control. The programmers or software providers are in control.

I will show you in this book how to build a website, how to rank in Google and how to make money with your sites, and most importantly how YOU will be IN CONTROL of every aspect of your site. Sounds simple? That's because it is. With a bit of effort and a bit of commercial thinking, you can do it too.

Do you know a very rich person who makes all his money by advertising on Facebook? Or do you know a very rich person who earns all his money from writing articles? I don't. That's because these people are workers in a large factory, in this case the factory is the web. Yes they earn money. But who earns the most and will always earn the most? Yeah that's right: The boss. The one who owns the website, in this case Facebook and the article site.

Sure you can earn good money on the web by not owning a website but you will earn most when you own the website (with affiliates selling for you) and when YOU are in control of everything. That's also why automated systems are no good because you are not in control. The only person making a lot of money from those systems is the seller, the one who owns the software.

Important: Although I strongly emphasise that being in control is important, it is equally important to outsource some of your work. Now this may sound like a contradiction but it isn't. In my opinion you need to know first what you are talking about and only then can you give work to outsourcers. That's why it is important for you to do all the work yourself for your first few websites. You still need to check the work that your outsourcers are doing, therefore you will still be in control as you need to control your outsourcers.

TOP TIP: BE THE BOSS, BE IN CONTROL.

Part 2. Some Internet Marketing Terminology Explained

I always assume that everybody knows what an eBook is or what affiliate marketing is, but every time I start talking to somebody who is not involved with IM, I realise that most people do not understand commonly used internet terms. For this reason I will explain some terminology that I will use a lot in this book. I will explain it in such a way that a total newbie can understand it. It's frustrating when authors assume that you understand internet terminology, so I'll explain.

- What is a niche?

I will talk a lot about niches in this book but what is a niche? A niche is a small part of a topic or subject. A car market is a niche: that is a niche where all people are interested in cars. Mercedes is a sub niche from the main niche (a niche within a niche), as it is a manufacturer of cars. You can keep digging deeper into a niche: a yellow Mercedes would be another sub niche of the Mercedes niche. A yellow Mercedes with yellow leather chairs (digging deeper again) would be a micro niche in that sub niche. In this book I will sometimes talk about sub niches and micro niches that have the potential to make money. I will simply call it "niche" throughout this book.

Recap:

Market or niche: Car

Sub niche: Mercedes

Micro Niche: Yellow Mercedes

Here's another example:

Market or niche: Tennis

Sub niche: Serving

Micro Niche: Serving left-handed

The internet is ideal for finding niche markets. You can join groups, forums, communities, chat sites and social websites and talk about your niche, sub niche or micro niche. In "the olden days" you would have to go to exhibitions, join clubs, phone people or write thousands of letters in order to find people who love yellow Mercedes'. All you need to do these days is Google Yellow Mercedes and it's likely that you will find potential customers. And the extra bonus? You can sell to people all over the world.

Why are micro niches of significant importance? Research has proven that when people do not *immediately* find what they want on a site, they will leave it. Take our example of Mercedes: a searcher types in "yellow Mercedes" and comes across the site that has not focused on the keywords yellow Mercedes. He sees all red, black and blue cars and leaves the site. The next site he comes across shows four pictures all with a Yellow Mercedes. He will no doubt have a look on the site because he knows that it contains relevant information.

The longer he stays on your site, the more chance there is that he clicks one of your money-making links. That's exactly what you will be doing when you have read this book: building a site on yellow Mercedes (using our example) and filling it with content that can earn you money. For instance, you'll sell books on yellow Mercedes, sell DVDs about yellow Mercedes, sell a miniature yellow Mercedes, sell yellow paint for a yellow Mercedes and so on. And no, you do not have to stock or ship any of these products, that's the beauty of affiliate marketing (see a bit further).

Here are some more examples of niches, just so you get the picture: piano players, twin mums, translators, model train builders, yoga trainers.

Sub-niches would be: standing-up piano players, twin mums over 40, Spanish translators, and so on.

- What is an eBook?

'eBook' stands for electronic book (also known as digital book). It is called a digital product because it can be downloaded immediately after purchase and there are no shipping costs. It is basically a normal book but published in electronic format. Rather than reading words from a hard copy book, you read them from your computer, laptop or from devices called eBook readers such as Amazon's Kindle. Apple calls its eBooks, iBooks.

There are free eBooks available and the eBook market is expanding all the time. There are now millions of eBooks for sale on the web on thousands of different topics. An ebook is usually delivered to the buyer in PDF format (Portable Document Format). If you want an eBook at 3 o'clock in the morning, you can go on a website, buy one with your credit card or PayPal account and you can be reading it five minutes later. No queuing in the shops - great stuff. You just buy it online like you would buy a DVD of your favourite film. I love eBooks, but personally I print mine and read them from paper as I always need to make notes in the books I read.

eBook availability is crucial. Imagine you can't sleep at night because you have excruciating pain in your left leg. You want a remedy NOW. You are browsing the web and see a picture that looks like a book and its title is "Proven remedies to stop pain in your left leg. Your pain can be gone in 5 minutes". Click on the book and in all likelihood it will be an eBook that you can buy for between $15.00 and $47.00. Once bought, you can download it and your pain can be gone in five minutes.

Want to know another interesting thing about eBooks? Most of them have a 60-day guarantee, because a lot of them are registered with www.Clickbank.com (see a bit further) and Clickbank gives an automatic 60-day refund period – no questions asked. If you do not like the eBook about the leg remedy, you can ask for your money back – even if you have already read the book. That's why it's important to sell informative eBooks otherwise people will ask for a refund. People usually ask for a refund if they are not happy with what they bought. If they think that they received value for money, they are unlikely to ask for a refund.

- What is affiliate marketing?

Remember the days when the guy from the insurance company would come and sit in your kitchen and try to sell you insurance? The "older" generation reading this will remember. When he sold you some, his boss – the insurance company – would pay the sales guy say, 10% commission. That is affiliate marketing the old fashioned way. I guess you could also call it commission marketing because that's what it is: somebody gets paid commission for selling somebody else's product. The insurance company is the affiliate merchant, or vendor, and the sales guy is the affiliate as he gets commission from a sale.

Now imagine this scenario on the internet: the insurance company has a website that sells insurance. The sales guy has a website that tells you the pros and cons of insurance and here and there on his website he puts a link that, when you click on it, you have the chance to buy something. If you buy via that link, the insurance company will pay the sales guy commission.

So in this case you are the sales guy that will be selling for other companies, and every time you sell something, the company will pay you commission. You are the affiliate (the one who receives the commission) and the insurance company that will pay you is called the merchant or the vendor. All you need to do is put the same affiliate links on your website that refer to the insurance companies' website, and you get paid when somebody buys via that link. Where and how to get your money making affiliate link will be covered later in the book. Everything else is automated. Commissions range from 1% to 75%. Physical products usually pay between 2% and 25% commission but www.Clickbank.com, which sells mostly digital products, can pay up to 80% commission or even more.

A merchant is an online retailer with a website where you can buy products or services.

An affiliate or online publisher is the person who drives visitors to the merchant's website and gets paid commission when customers buy something by clicking on the link that is on the affiliate's website. An affiliate drives buyers to the merchant's sites and gets paid for it. The merchants pays the affiliate commission only when a sale is made. The affiliate will sell your product or services for a commission. Affiliates are other internet marketers or other website owners.

www.amazon.com is a good example of a successful affiliate merchant business, which it started in 1996. They now have over 400,000 affiliates (Amazon calls them associates). A vendor is the person who is selling his goods on Amazon and Amazon gets paid commission (or a vendor's fee) every time the vendor sells something. The vendor of course gets the money for the purchase of the goods (minus Amazon's commission). All administration and collecting of the money is done by Amazon.

www.amazon.com and www.comparethemarket.com are probably two companies that you have heard of before but never realised that they made money in affiliate marketing.

Amazon is a merchant as you can sell their products as an affiliate but in a way Amazon is also an affiliate network as all administration is done by them.

Affiliate marketing is literally everywhere on the web. Websites without any money-making links are hard to find these days.

Affiliate networks are automated websites on which merchants can put their name to say they are looking for affiliates to drive traffic to their websites. You, as an affiliate, go to the affiliate network to grab an affiliate link to put on your website. The affiliate network pays you your commission. All you need to do is stick a link on your site and drive traffic, all the rest is done automatically for you. I will give some examples of trustworthy networks later in this book.

Affiliate marketing is the whole automated set up to do with affiliates, merchants and affiliate networks.

Here's a good example of an affiliate link. I searched for Cat Training and www.thecattraining.com was shown in Google. Here is a screenshot from their site.

I have circled 'Amazon Store' to draw your attention. When you click on 'Amazon Store', you will be directed to this screen:

Amazon Store

When you click on any of the products, you will be taken to Amazon.

When you buy a product via Amazon, the owner of www.TheCatTraining.com will receive commission from Amazon because people are buying via their affiliate link.

Once you are into affiliate marketing you will never look at a website the same way again. You will constantly look for links on the top of your browser. You will constantly look for new ideas. A lot of people search for "top 10 digital cameras" or " best flat TV" or " review video software". Years ago I used to believe the reviews on websites. Unfortunately reality has taught me that some websites don't publish honest, impartial reviews. They will award top prize to the company with the affiliate link that pays them the most money.

All the "Buy" buttons will be an affiliate link. The first 'buy' button might take you to the Amazon store; the second 'buy' button might take you to a computer store. So if the website owner earns a lot more from the Amazon link, he might put that first even if it doesn't merit the win.

Some review websites do give honest opinions. But be cautious with what you buy and what you believe on the web.

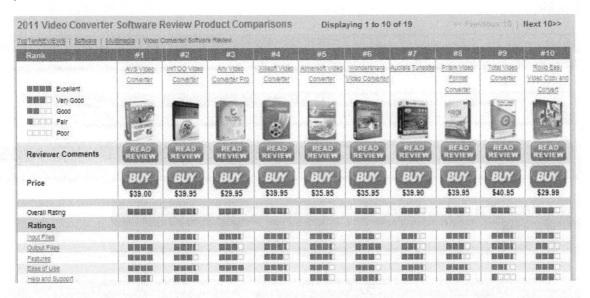

Here's an example of an affiliate link that you might see in the browser when you click one of the Buy Buttons:

If you come across any website – once you are an internet marketer – you will probably pay a lot of attention to what is in the browser bar on the top of your screen. Anything that says something like ID6487541 or Affiliate = 789p or IDlink 1290 tells you that somebody is earning money from affiliate marketing.

So the website owner (in this case the one with the website showing all the buy buttons) is the insurance guy, or affiliate, sitting on your table who earns commission. The website that you navigate to (in this example regnow.com) when you click the 'buy' button is the merchant who pays the commission to the affiliate.

As an internet marketer you can become an affiliate and sell other people's products BUT it is even better to have your own product and let other people sell it for you. All you need to do is become a merchant (by asking people to sell your products).

Here are a few screenshots from the browser bar where it is very obvious that it is an affiliate link. The give away can be: ID, Partner, TID, Link 1234, Affilatecode…., AFFIL1234, Cookie,…..

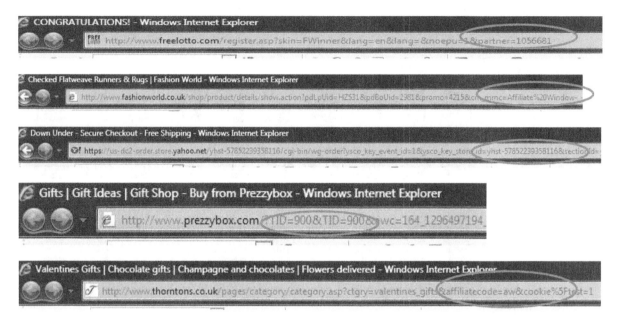

There is one big problem with affiliate marketing and the clue is in the name: **marketing**. The affiliate network does not help you with that. Getting a site stacked with affiliate links is easy but getting visitors to your site is a lot more difficult. It's the marketing of your site that is going to be the hardest. But no worries, after you've read this book I am sure that you are ready to tackle that problem.

Origin of Affiliate Marketing (source :Wikipedia)

The concept of revenue sharing—paying commission for referred business—predates affiliate marketing and the Internet. The translation of the revenue share principles to mainstream e-commerce happened in November 1994, almost four years after the origination of the World Wide Web.

The concepts of affiliate marketing on the Internet was conceived of, put into practice and patented by William J. Tobin, the founder of PC Flowers & Gifts. Launched on the Prodigy Network in 1989, PC Flowers & Gifts remained on the service until 1996. By 1993, PC

Flowers & Gifts generated sales in excess of $6 million dollars per year on the Prodigy service. In 1989, PC Flowers and Gifts developed the business model of paying a commission on sales to The Prodigy network. Tobin applied for a patent on tracking and affiliate marketing on January 22, 1996 and was issued U.S. Patent number 6,141,666 on Oct 31, 2000. Tobin also received the Japanese Patent number 4,021,941 on Oct 5, 2007 and U.S. Patent number 7,505,913 on Mar 17, 2009 for affiliate marketing and tracking.

Cybererotica was among the early innovators in affiliate marketing with a cost per click program.

During November 1994, CDNOW launched its BuyWeb program. CDNOW had the idea that music-oriented websites could review or list albums on their pages that their visitors may be interested in purchasing. These websites could also offer a link that would take the visitor directly to CDNOW to purchase the albums. The idea for remote purchasing originally arose because of conversations with music label Geffen Records in the fall of 1994. The management at Geffen wanted to sell its artists' CDs directly from its website, but did not want to implement this capability itself. Geffen asked CDNOW if it could design a program where CDNOW would handle the order fulfillment. Geffen realized that CDNOW could link directly from the artist on its website to Geffen's website, bypassing the CDNOW home page and going directly to an artist's music page.

Amazon.com (Amazon) launched its associate program in July 1996: Amazon associates could place banner or text links on their site for individual books, or link directly to the Amazon home page.

When visitors clicked from the associate's website through to Amazon and purchased a book, the associate received a commission. Amazon was not the first merchant to offer an affiliate program, but its program was the first to become widely known and serve as a model for subsequent programs.

- What are cookies?

Affiliate Marketing gets even more interesting because some merchants work with Cookies: 2-days Cookies, 7-days Cookies, 14-days Cookies, sometimes even lifetime Cookies. A Cookie is a text file that contains a form of ID (Identification) and is placed on a computer by a website. I will explain it from an affiliate marketing view. You, as the affiliate, are driving traffic to the merchant's website with your affiliate link. A visitor clicks on your link and so visits the merchant's website. He might not buy anything and leave the site but the merchant has left a cookie on the visitor's computer. If that visitor returns to the site within 7 days of his first visit, you will still receive commission because the merchant has left a 7-day cookie. If the same visitor returns to the site on the eighth day after his very first visit, you will not receive commission.

If the visitor decides to go directly to the merchant to purchase the product, without clicking the link on your website, you will still earn commission because the visitor has your cookie on his or her computer and your affiliate ID is remembered. Once a cookie expires, the memory of your affiliate ID information also expires.

Each cookie has an expiry period, starting when the visitor clicks on your link for the very first time, and ending after a certain time. When signing up with affiliate networks, try to find merchants with lifetime cookies. There are not many but try to focus on finding them, it is worth it. Quite a lot of affiliate merchants do not offer any Cookies at all.

If you ever want to clear your cookies, there are two easy ways to do it:

1) Go to Internet Properties on your computer, click Delete under browsing history and make sure to tick Cookies on the next screen

2) Run a Spyware program (I use Spybot.com) and it will find cookies. You can then instruct Spyboyt to remove them

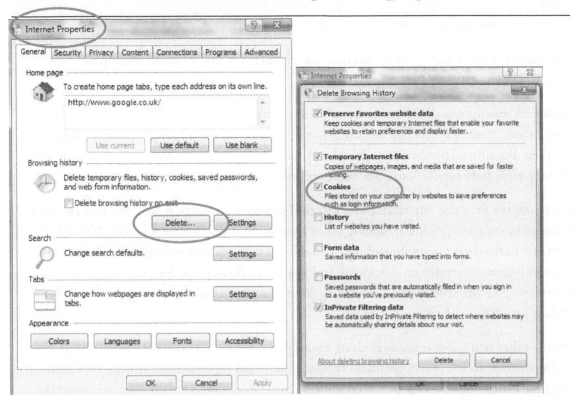

- What is Clickbank?

Well, in their words:

Clickbank Is The Web's Most Trusted Digital Marketplace. Founded in 1998, ClickBank is a secure online retail outlet for more than 70,000 digital product vendors and 110,000 active affiliate marketers. **ClickBank makes a sale somewhere in the world every three seconds,** safely processing more than 27,000 digital transactions a day. They serve more than 200 countries, and are consistently ranked as one of the most high-traffic sites on the web. Source: www.Clickbank.com.

Clickbank is the largest affiliate marketplace on the internet. Without Clickbank the internet would not be the same for many affiliates. In my opinion, you can't really be an internet marketer without having an account with Clickbank. There are internet millionaires who have never sold anything themselves but earn all their money as an affiliate, selling other people's products.

Clickbank is also known simply as "CB" in the IM world.

Clickbank is sort of like Amazon but only for digital products. You can sign up at www.Clickbank.com.

Clickbank mostly sells digital products: eBooks, software, videos. The products range from 'how to stop your dog barking' to 'how to make money on the internet' and everything else in between. Because all products are digital and the delivery cost is zero, the commission rates are very high: between 50% to 75% and even more.

Clickbank is a database where affiliates can find products to sell or where vendors can find affiliates to sell their products. Signing up as an affiliate with Clickbank is free. If you have written an eBook on "piano repair" but you are not very good at selling or building websites, you can become a vendor on Clickbank and put your eBook there for anybody to sell. In return you give the seller part of the selling price. As an example, you keep 40% and the affiliate gets 60% when a book is sold.

On the other hand, if you know nothing about piano repair but you think that there is a gap on the internet to sell books on piano repairs, you would sign up as an affiliate on Clickbank and find a piano repair book to sell on your website. You would get 60% (or whatever the commission rate is) of the selling price because you have put in most of the effort in the sale of the eBook.

To sign up as a vendor you need to pay a one-off fee of $49.95. You sign up as a vendor when you have your own product and you want to put in on the marketplace. You want people (affiliates) to sell it for you and you pay them commission for every sale.

Once you have signed up with www.Clickbank.com and you are a Clickbank affiliate, you will be given a unique hyperlink (or 'hoplink') to the product you want to promote. Then anyone who clicks your link and buys the product will earn you a percentage commission. How to get that link onto your website will be covered later in this book.

Clickbank is the internet marketer's dream come true. The big advantage of Clickbank is that it has its own payment processor, so you can sell products and charge people to their credit card – Clickbank does all this for you automatically. Before Clickbank was online, you would have to get your own merchant account from your bank, and as a new business that would be almost impossible. **With Clickbank, you can sell stuff online without ever having sold anything before - Clickbank will charge your customer.**

Clickbank collects the money from the buyer, pays the affiliate the commission and pays the vendor the rest.

Here's the example as a website developer: You are developing a website about pianos and piano repair but you do not have the knowledge to write an eBook on the subject. Here are the steps you need to take:

- Sign up **as an affiliate** on www.Clickbank.com. Visit the market place, search for piano repair and find the product you want to sell.

- Look at the different products and for the product that you like, choose 'Promote'. Later in this book I will discuss other things to look for but at the moment I just want to point out how easy it all is to get a money-making code.

- When you click "promote" your affiliate link will automatically be created and you will be shown a code. Copy that code onto your website for a picture or anchor text like this: Buy a piano repair book here : with the hyperlink function of your web design software, you need to paste that link to the underlined text. When somebody clicks that link, they will go to the sales page of the piano repair book and Clickbank will pay you commission on the sale.

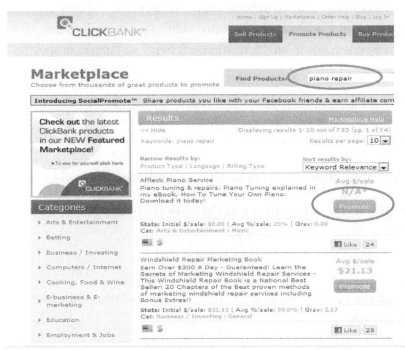

Shown above: Find the product you want to sell, search for 'piano repair' and click 'promote'. You will be given an affiliate link to put on your site.

Here's the example if you are the eBook writer who would like to find affiliates to sell your book: You have the knowledge of repairing a piano and you have enough material to write an eBook (approx. 60 to 150 pages) about the subject. Here are the steps that you need to follow:

- Write your eBook

- Design a very simple cover

> **There is never any justification for things being complex if they can be simple.**

- Convert it to a PDF ('save as' in Microsoft Word and choose 'PDF-format').

- Make one page of text explaining why your eBook is wonderful and what it can do for the buyer

- Design a website with a sales page **and** an affiliate page. For examples of how an affiliate page can look like, visit Clickbank, open some websites and scroll to the bottom of each website where you will see "affiliates click here" or " make money with this", etc…

- Sign up **as a vendor** on www.Clickbank.com

- Put your eBook on the marketplace for affiliates to sell it

- Check your Clickbank account regularly to see how many books you have sold

There is no need to write the eBook yourself or do any of the work yourself; you can outsource it as you will read later.

Who gets paid what?

Suppose the eBook cost $29 and the vendor says that the affiliate receives 70% of the sale and the vendor keeps 30% of the sale.

$29 x 70% = $20.30 This is what the affiliate gets (the person selling your book)

$29 x 30% = $8.70 This is what the vendor keeps (you as the writer of the book)

BUT Clickbank is a commercial institution. So Clickbank needs to get paid for its work. Clickbank charges 7.5% of the sales price + $1.00 per sale.

$29 x 7.5% = $2.17 + $1.00 = $3.17 Therefore $3.17 is Clickbank's profit.

$29 - $ 3.17 = $ 25.83 So this amount is what the vendor and affiliate get paid.

$25.83x 70% = $18.08 This is the amount that the affiliate gets paid in his Clickbank account.

$25.83x 30% = $7.74 This is the amount that the vendor gets paid in his Clickbank account.

When you sign up with Clickbank you can choose how you get paid: by bank transfer, cheque or international cheque. You can set a minimum when you want to get paid e.g. $100, $200, etc… This means that as soon as you have $100 in your account, Clickbank will pay you. If you have not been paid enough by the end of each month, your balance will be moved to the next month.

TOP TIP : To start with, sell eBooks as an affiliate. As soon as possible, write an eBook yourself about your niche because then you can list your eBook on Clickbank and an army of affiliates can sell it for you.

Being an affiliate has the following advantages:

- No licence fees needed

- There is no contract to sign with anybody

- You can log onto your work anywhere in the world

- You can make money while you sleep (after you have put in some hard work)

- You can sell in any country, worldwide

- You can sell in any niche

- You never have to process orders

- You never ever have to ship orders

- You never ever need to worry about stock take, over stock or left over stock

- You never need a customers' service email or telephone number

- You never need large start-up capital to begin trading

- You never need a Payment Processing Gateway (a bank that charges your customer's card)

- You don't need employees

- You don't need sales experience

- You don't need to know anything about the niche to sell in it

- You have no production costs to worry about

- You never have to leave your house

- You never have to speak to anybody if you don't want to

- You can choose the hours you work

- You can be your own boss

- You can start up a business that can grow 200% or more each year, which is almost impossible to achieve in a business outside the web

- You never have to go to the bank to pay in cheques, as all is done electronically

- You never have to chase late payments as all is paid in advance

- There are no cash flow problems (if you manage your money correctly) as you receive your money immediately

- No refund worries as CB does this for you – everything is automated

So Clickbank is all about vendors and affiliates, but how does a vendor earn money from an affiliate? Do I have to email the vendor each time I have made a sale?

A lot of people ask me this. It all sounds a bit complicated to start with but once you have used it once or twice you won't believe how simple it all is.

You must have come across websites that have underlined text, and if you click the underlined text, it re-directs you to another website. In a way, that is what Clickbank does. But it just has a fancier word for it: hoplink. If somebody clicks on a hoplink, it means that they are re-directed to the page with your hoplink on so you make money.

A hoplink is the linking format that Clickbank uses. It puts the affiliate cookie into the user's computer and then takes the user to the sales page of the product. A general Clickbank hoplink looks like this:

http://AFFILIATE.VENDOR.hop.clickbank.net

AFFILIATE in this case is your Clickbank username or nickname.

VENDOR in this case is the vendor's Clickbank username or nickname or the owner of the product that you are selling via your affiliate link.

Suppose the affiliate is called SUE876 and the vendor is called JOHN123, the hoplink would look like this:

http://SUE876.JOHN123.hop.clickbank.net

Therefore each person who sells a product from the vendor would have a unique hoplink. If the affiliate would be called HORSEMAN998, the hoplink would look like this:

http://HORSEMAN998.JOHN123.hop.clickbank.net

The vendor and affiliate nicknames can be ANYTHING you want, as long as the name does not already exist in Clickbank.

You must use your hoplinks all the time when you want to promote or sell a product. This is the only way that you will receive your commissions. Suppose you send an email to your friend with a Clickbank hoplink that looks like the above. When your friend clicks on the hoplink and buys your product, Clickbank will know to pay you your commission because of your **unique** hoplink.

When somebody clicks on your hoplink, Clickbank will know that you made a sale and will pay commission into your account. Clickbank does everything automatically. It is like a miniature accountancy system, because it keeps a record of all the sales made and it keeps a record of who gets how much commission.

To create a hoplink, you have to visit www.Clickbank.com and search for the product that you want to promote and your hoplink will automatically be created when you click "promote" next to the product description.

If you have only one traffic source the above hoplink will be okay but when you use several methods to generate sales, you will want to know from which traffic method the sale is created. So, add a TID (or tracking hoplink or tracking identification) to the above hoplink. Your affiliate link will then look like this:

http://SUE876.JOHN123.hop.clickbank.net/?TID =ABC where ABC could be: friend's email or facebookID or website or blog (see hoplink below), or whatever you want it to be.

http://SUE876.JOHN123.hop.clickbank.net/TID=BLOG

Your Clickbank account will show you which TID each sale was made with, so you can see which one of your traffic sources is doing well. You should try to use tracking hoplinks as much as possible, as this will help you to learn which of your methods is working best and which are not working at all. There will be more about TID later in this book.

Important: Clickbank changes their rules sometimes so make sure you know the rules before you start working with them as a vendor or as an affiliate.

- What is article marketing or bum marketing?

Most people think that article marketing is the same as bum marketing. The main difference is that with bum marketing you find an untapped niche and an affiliate product in that niche. You write an article with keywords, which makes it easier for your article to rank in the search engines. In article marketing you would focus on the keyword "dog" but in bum marketing you would focus on the keyword "how to stop your dog barking". In article marketing you would send your visitor to your website with a lot of information about dogs. In bum marketing you would send your visitor straight to your affiliate landing page selling an eBook about how to stop your dog from barking.

Here's Wikipedia's definition of article marketing: *It is a type of advertising in which businesses write short articles related to their respective industry. These articles are made available for distribution and publication in the marketplace. Each article contains a bio box and byline (collectively known as the resource box) that include references and contact information for the author's business. Well-written content articles released for free distribution have the potential of increasing the authoring business' credibility within its market as well as attracting new clients. These articles are often syndicated by other websites, and published on multiple websites.*

And here's the simple explanation: you write a short article about your subject, then publish it to article websites or article directories with a resource box or your link. People who find your article will click on your resource box which contains your link, and that will make you money. The resource box is a small box underneath your article that contains your website link. For example: you write an article on 'how to brush your teeth' and in your resource box you put an affiliate link (the link you are given when clicking "promote" for the product you want to sell) to a Clickbank product or an affiliate link for toothbrushes on Amazon. Google loves certain article websites so assuming that you have written a unique article on 'how to brush your teeth', Google might list the article website. Your article will be read by people looking for information on 'how to brush your teeth' and when they click on the affiliate link in your resource box and buy via that link, you will make money.

Here is an example of articles ranking on page one in the search results: ezinearticles.com and articlesbase.com, which are both article marketing directories.

How to **Properly** Clean **Your Teeth** | eHow.com
How to **Properly** Clean **Your Teeth**. The proper way to **brush** and clean **your teeth**.
www.ehow.com › Health › Dental Health › Teeth Cleaning - Cached - Similar

How To Brush Your Teeth Properly - Brushing Your Teeth Properly
Brushing your teeth properly goes a long way in maintaining proper oral hygiene. Go through this article and explore step-by-step instructions on how to ...
lifestyle.iloveindia.com/.../how-to-brush-your-teeth-properly-4997.html - Cached - Similar

How to Brush Your Teeth Correctly
10 Jun 2009 ... **Brushing** of **teeth** is something that we do everyday and many of us do it with our eyes closed without bothering to see whether we are doing ...
ezinearticles.com › Health and Fitness › Dental Care - Cached - Similar

How to Brush Your Teeth Correctly—personal Dental Care
2 May 2008 ... **Brushing your teeth** twice a day will extend the life of your teeth and improve your health. Learn brushing techniques that will enhance your ...
www.articlesbase.com › Health › Dental Care - Cached - Similar

With article marketing, you do not need to own a website or have any experience at all. Find a good niche with a shortage of articles, find an affiliate product that can earn you money and that's it, you can make money. It is as simple as that.

Any internet marketer will tell you that article marketing is a good way of increasing sales. It is also an effective way of adding one-way links pointing to your site. More about links later in the book. Exchanging links with another site is still a good way of getting links both ways, but the search engines place more emphasis on one-way links (like article marketing) than two-way or reciprocal links.

What are article directories?

Article directories are websites where anyone can submit an article for inclusion in the directory. The article directories are free for anyone to visit or take content from. Some article directories require you to create an account while others don't. Once you have submitted your article you need to wait for it to be approved by the article directory.

According to the rules of article marketing, people can copy the content of your article to use as content on their website. But in order to do that, they also have to copy your resource box. So one article can get you several links and can get you on several websites. You will need to read the terms and conditions of every article website to which you submit, but most of them have the same rules.

Good article marketing works. I will give you some good article marketing rules under the 'free-traffic' section of the book.

- What is an opt-in box?

An opt-in box is another way of saying "somewhere for your visitors to enter their email address to receive updates and emails from you". Once a visitor has given you their email address, they have "opted-in". An opt-in box normally resembles the layout of the examples below:

Wikipedia definitions:

Opt in email is a term used when someone is given the option to receive "bulk" email, that is, email that is sent to many people at the same time. Typically, this is some sort of mailing list, newsletter, or advertising. Obtaining permission before sending e-mail is critical because without it, the email is Unsolicited Bulk Email, better known as spam.

There are several common forms of opt-in email:

Unconfirmed opt-in

A new subscriber first gives his or her email address to the list software (for instance, on a web page), but no steps are taken to make sure that this address actually belongs to the person. This can cause email from the mailing list to be considered spam because simple typos of the email address can cause the email to be sent to someone else. Malicious subscriptions are also possible, as are subscriptions that are due to spammers forging email addresses that are sent to the email address used to subscribe to the mailing list.

Confirmed opt-in (COI) or double opt-in

A new subscriber asks to be subscribed to the mailing list, but unlike unconfirmed opt-in, a confirmation email is sent to verify it was really them. Many believe the person must not be added to the mailing list unless an explicit step is taken, such as clicking a special web link or sending back a reply email. This ensures that no person can subscribe someone else out of malice or error. Mail system administrators and non-spam mailing list operators refer to this as confirmed subscription or closed-loop opt-in.

Some marketers call closed loop opt-in "double opt-in."

The term double opt-in was coined by marketers in the late '90s to differentiate it from single opt-in, where a new subscriber to an email list gets a confirmation email telling them they will begin to receive emails if they take no action. This is compared to double opt-in, where the new subscriber must respond to the confirmation email to be added to the list.

Some marketers contend that double opt-in is like asking for permission twice and that it constitutes unnecessary interference with someone who has already said they want to hear from the marketer.

The term double opt-in has also been co-opted by spammers, diluting its value.

Opt-out

Instead of giving people the option to be put on the list, they are automatically added and have the option to be taken out.

End of Wikipedia definitions

Here is an example of how a confirmation request email can look like after somebody opted-in to receive a newsletter :

IMPORTANT: **Just one more step before you can get my newsletter.**

Click on the Link in the Confirmation Email!

- Check your inbox for your confirmation email. Click on the link in the email to verify your subscription.
- If your confirmation email isn't in your inbox in 15 minutes, check your spam or junk mail folder (sometimes they get put there by mistake).

As an internet marketer you should always try to get double opt-ins by sending your opt-ins a confirmation email – see the above screenshot. Your opt-ins are then telling you twice that they want the information: first when they opted-in and a second time when they receive the confirmation email and click the confirmation link.

The double opt-ins are better as the chances of the emails ending up in your visitor's spam box are smaller. However in my experience a heck of a lot of emails (that I signed up for with double opt-in) end up in my spam box anyway.

This is called building a list. You have a list of 1000 people if 1000 people have opted-in.

- What is email marketing?

Email marketing is one of the best ways - if done correctly - to keep existing visitors coming back and to market your offers directly to their inboxes. All you need to do is send the people who opt-in an email on a regular basis with links that will earn you money. The people that will receive your emails have given their permission, so it is permission-based email marketing and for this reason is not categorized as spam. Predictions are that in 2012 some 400 billion emails will enter inboxes every day. As much as 75% to 80% are spam or unwanted emails.

To sell a product, you sell yourself first. People have to like the sales person that is sitting on the other side of the customers' desk, otherwise the customer will not order. This is the same in IM: with email marketing you have a change to build a relationship with your customers. Give them good content, or interesting freebies and they will start to like you, giving you a better chance of selling to them. Lead generation is huge on the internet.

- What is an auto responder?

An auto responder is a software program that automatically sends out emails on a pre-scheduled basis to all opted-in people on your list.

Once you have built a list, the idea is that you send them some freebies or send them a newsletter or an affiliate link etc… You can't possibly do all this manually each time you receive a new opt-in. An autoresponder does this automatically for you. Let's say you want to create a 5 part email course. You set the intervals for the emails, say once a day. All you need to do is type in the emails once in your auto responder software and your list will get an email once a day. Anyone joining your list will automatically be sent those emails for the next 5 days.

So the owner of the list uses autoresponder software to set up a sequence of emails that go out at regular intervals.

You must have an auto responder when you have an opt-in box on your website.

You will have seen these messages at the bottom of your emails :

To unsubscribe or change subscriber options visit:
http://www.aweber.com/z/r/?jAx…..

When you click on that click you will be unsubscribed. By law you need to put an unsubscribe button at the bottom of each email you send. If people no longer want to receive your emails and click unsubscribe, your auto responder will remove that person automatically from your list and your next pre-scheduled email will no longer be received by the person who has unsubscribed.

Which auto responder is best?

The best email auto-responder on the market, is in my opinion www.aweber.com, but a good, free alternative is MailChimp (if using a limited list).

Here's a list of automated email auto responders:

www.aweber.com RECOMMENDED
www.getresponse.com
www.autocontactor.com
www.mailchimp.com

You have to make sure that you use a professional auto responder service because that way you are protected from spam complaints. If you can provide proof of subscriber opt-in you are in a strong position.

A video about www.aweber.com is included with my video tutorials. Please visit www.VideosNewbieBook.com to get access.

- What is 'hosting'?

Once you have decided on your domain name, which is the name of your site, such as www.yourdomainnamehere.com you need to make sure that somebody will host your website. This means somebody has got to store your website somewhere so people can access it. When you have built a website on your computer and it has been published to the web, people need to be able to see it. If 1000 people want to look at your site, they won't come to your home or office to do it, so you need to have a place where your site is "hosted" so that all 1000 people can look at it at the same time. This is what a hosting company does; they will give your site a space on their massive computer servers so people can view it. You pay the hosting company a fee to host, or store, your site.

When choosing a hosting company, you need to look at two factors: web disk space and bandwidth, both explained in the next few paragraphs.

Another reason why you need a hosting company is because of the bandwidth (see explanation below) on your computer. If you host your website yourself and have an internet connection speed of 1MB on your home computer, it will take several hours for a customer to download a movie. A hosting company might have a 250MB internet connection speed, meaning your customers can download the movie much quicker.

Choose your hosting company carefully. You can spend a heck of a lot of time designing your site but if it is slow to load due to a poor hosting plan, visitors will move on to another site. I recommend strongly not using the free or very cheap web hosting companies.

- What is bandwidth and what is the difference with web disk space?

This often confuses IM newbies.

What is 'disk space'?

Disk space is also called data storage or hosting space. It is the amount of data that the hosting provider allows you to store. Images, audio files, visual files, multi-media files and graphics all take up a lot more space than simple text. If your site has 20 pages of mostly text, your total disk space needs will probably be under 1MB. If you have a site with lots of graphics and multimedia, you need a lot more disk space.

> **Top Tip: To find out how much disk space you need for your website, simply put all your website files into one folder on your PC. Right click the folder and choose 'properties', which will show you the total space needed to store your website.**

What is 'bandwidth'?

Bandwidth is the amount of traffic that your hosting company allows between your website on their server, and the visitors to your website. It is a measure of total data transferred in one month to and from your site. Each time a visitor looks at your site, it is downloaded from your hosting company to be viewed on the internet. If you go over the amount of bandwidth with your hosting company they could charge you an extra fee, visitors might not be able to see your site or it will be downloaded very slowly.

Think about bandwidth as cars on motorways (highways in the US). If you are the only car on the motorway, you can drive quickly but the more cars the slower you're forced to go. You are also not able to overtake another car when you are stuck in a queue. With low bandwith your visitors cannot download things quickly and will be stuck in a queue when wanting to download a file if two people want to download it at the same time.

How much bandwidth do you need?

For most small businesses or personal sites 2GB of bandwidth per month is usually enough. Most hosting companies will include this in their cheapest package. Traffic to your site is the number of 'bits' that are transferred on the internet. One gigabyte (GB) is 1,024 megabytes. To store one character, one byte of storage is needed.

- Imagine that you have 100 filing cabinets in your office.

- Each of these filing cabinets has 1000 folders in it

- In each folder there are 100 papers

- On each paper are 100 characters

- The total of all these is 1 GB (100x1000x100x100)

How much bandwidth you need depends on what type of website you are building. If people can download MP3 songs or movies from your website, and you are expecting a lot of visitors, you will need a very high bandwidth because each MP3 song is, on average, about 4MB. A movie can be up to 1000MB or 1GB. In this case, if you only have a bandwidth of 1GB, when two customers want to download a 1GB movie, they cannot do it at the same time. Remember, in my comparison with motorways and cars you cannot overtake a car when in a traffic jam. The second one in the queue will probably receive an error message. This will result in your customer having a negative impression of your site, which of course you must avoid. If you are expecting ten thousand visitors to your site per day, you need to choose the correct bandwidth plan with your hosting company. Most hosting companies offer the facility to start with low bandwidth and upgrade it at an extra cost.

Companies offer a variety of bandwidth options in terms of your monthly gigabyte allocation.

Work out how much bandwidth you need is not as simple as calculating how much disk space you need. But the following formula will give you some idea: Size (or disk space) of all your web pages including all graphics X numbers of visitors you expect each day X number of pages your visitors will view X 30 days per month = total monthly data transfer, or bandwidth.

The amount of emails that you send also counts in the bandwidth. If you often send hundreds of emails with very large files attached, it will count towards your bandwidth usage.

If your website gets lots of visits per month, through Google or from affiliates sending traffic to it, you need more bandwidth, not necessarily more space.

Quite a few hosting companies now offer unlimited bandwidth, as you can see from the screenshot below taken from www.godaddy.com. More and more hosting companies start to offer unlimited space and unlimited bandwidth.

Economy 4GH
£1.23 /month

- **10 GB** Space
- **Unlimited** Bandwidth
- **100** Email Accounts²
- **10** MySQL Databases (1 GB ea.)
- **FREE** Google® Ad Credits†

Deluxe 4GH BEST VALUE!
£4.97 /month

- **150 GB** Space
- **Unlimited** Websites∞ & Bandwidth
- **500** Email Accounts²
- **25** MySQL Databases (1 GB ea.)
- **FREE** Google® Ad Credits†

Conclusion: disk space is the amount of storage space your website needs on the server of your hosting company. Bandwidth is the traffic that passes through your hosting company to your website.

- What is traffic?

Getting traffic to your site simply means getting people to see your site. It is no good having a site if nobody can find it. To put it very simply: *traffic = visitors = people looking at your site.* Always use different traffic techniques because not everybody uses the same method of finding products on the web. If you are selling a product outside IM you would use different methods to try to find customers. You can go to exhibitions, you can sell at markets, you can call people and make appointments and you can place advertisements in magazine and newspapers. If you're selling products on a market, the more you visit the more you sell because different people in different areas go to different markets. Exactly the same happens online: different types of people will search for your products; from different religions, different traditions, different intellectual levels and different backgrounds. Everybody has different knowledge and people use their own knowledge to search for products. If you only focus on getting traffic with Facebook, you are missing out on all the people that do not use Facebook. I will discuss free traffic and paid traffic later in the book.

- What is PLR- Private Label Rights and what are Resell Rights Products?

Resell Rights Product are products that somebody else made but you can sell. This is a very easy way for a newbie internet marketer to start, as there are products available with ready-made websites, ready written eBooks and articles, readymade sales letters and so on. The downside of these types of products is that they are PLR (Public Label Rights) and Google does not like PLR therefore Google will not show your pages in the search results because it will be duplicate content for Google. If you want to rank in Google: don't use PLR by just copying and pasting. PLR is brilliant **IF** you re-write it.

Some internet marketers believe that if you make your home page with unique content and all other pages with PLR content, Google will still show your site. Personally, I have not seen many examples of that.

Using PLR products is easy and can make you a lot of money; if you become an expert at driving traffic to your sites. I suggest that you try our free-traffic methods first before you get involved in paid traffic.

Another downside is that other people will be selling exactly the same product. But hey, the internet is such a vast place, with so many ready-to-buy people surfing in thousands of different niches, that it is a not a big problem.

The people who will buy your product most often are not internet marketers. Therefore they will not know that your product is a PLR product, as they won't even know what a PLR product is. PLR, in the form of just copy and paste the text of an article for instance, is only a big problem if you want to rank in Google.

There are basically three different resale rights. I have listed the most important points about the three different types below. You have to make sure that you understand what you are allowed to do when you sell a product. Don't worry though, all good websites that sell Resell Rights Products will explain very clearly what you can and cannot do with their products.

- Simple Resale Rights

- You can sell all the products and keep all the profit yourself without having to pay any royalties to the product publisher
- The person that buys your product is not allowed to sell it on
- There might be a restriction to the minimum price you need to sell it for
- Sometimes you are not allowed to give it away

- Master Resale Rights
- The same rules apply as for the Simple Resale Rights but with these rights you can sell the resale rights for the products. This means that the customer who buys from you, can sell on to his customers.

- Private Label Rights (or white label rights)
- These are the best and therefore generally the most expensive
- You can modify the product as much as you want before selling it
- You can put your own name on the product and claim you made it yourself. Isn't that cool? Something to show off to your friends!

There are lots of good websites where you can buy PLR products, which are listed later in the book. Simply search for "your keyword" + " PLR".

Conclusion: PLR is brilliant to give away to your subscribers and it is also brilliant to use as content **but only** if you re-write it otherwise it becomes duplicate content.

How can I see if text is duplicate content? How can I see if my article is duplicate content? How can I see if the PLR products that I want to use is already used a lot? These are questions that people frequently ask me during my courses.

All you need to do is type into Google the text that you want to check in between inverted commas. I typed in: "Men and women can be affected by hair loss and it happens to be a very serious matter". By putting the text between inverted commas, Google will show you the text that *is exactly the same* in the results in **bold**.

The result on the screenshot below shows about 16,400 results for exactly the same text! You can therefore conclude that there are a lot of people who have used exactly the same text on their website, and probably never even noticed the spelling mistake in the sentence (effected should be affected). The exact same text is listed in bold in Google.

I hope that you can see the problem with PLR products: thousands of people can use it and because Google does not like PLR, it will not show your site. So your chances of ranking high in Google are much smaller than if you write your own text. From the screenshot below you can see how much Google likes article directories as – even with PLR articles on – Google still shows the sites on page one. But in this case it is only because I have typed in a long sentence to search for and therefore I have asked Google to match the sentence **exactly**. If you search for "hair loss", which is what people would normally search for, none of the websites with PLR on them would show.

"Men and women can be effected by hair loss and it happens to be a very serious matt ×

About 16,400 results (0.14 seconds)   Ad

► Did you mean: "Men and women can be *affected* by hair loss and it happens to be a very seriou matter"

Combat Hair Loss
14 Jun 2009 ... Men and women can be effected by hair loss and it happens to be a very serious matter. Anybody that is having hair loss do not have too many ...
www.articlesbase.com › Health › Hair Loss - Cached

Stop Balding with Natural Home Remedies
Men and women can be effected by hair loss and it happens to be a very serious matter. Anybody that is having hair loss do not have too many options for ...
www.homemademedicine.com/stop-balding.html - Cached

http://www.webinxs.com
Men and women can be effected by hair loss and it happens to be a very serious matter. Anybody that is having hair loss do not have too many options for ...
www.webinxs.com/articlesdirectory/ezineready.php?id... - United States - Cached

All The Things You Need To Know About Hair Loss
29 Dec 2010 ... Men and women can be effected by hair loss and it happens to be a very serious matter. Somebody that is experiencing hair loss really does ...
healtharticles.cz.cc/all-the-things-you-need-to-know-about-hair-loss/ - Cached

Things to Know About Hair Loss | Round About Midnight
4 Feb 2011 ... Men and women can be effected by hair loss and it happens to be a very serious matter. Anybody that is having hair loss do not have too many ...
www.roundaboutmidnight.com/things-to-know-about-hair-loss/ - Cached

Information About Hair Loss
29 May 2009 ... Men and women can be effected by hair loss and it happens to be a very serious matter. Anybody that is having hair loss do not have too many ...
www.articleintelligence.com/Art/.../Information-About-Hair-Loss.html - Cached

- What is Click Through Rate (CTR) and Conversion Rate (CR)?

What is CTR ?

An advertisement's CTR is how many people will actually click on your ad if Google shows it 100 times. Usually a realistic CTR is between 1% and 10%. Any more is considered very good in the IM business.

CTR is a really simple fraction that looks like this:

$$\frac{\text{Number of people who } \textbf{clicked your link } (\textit{clicks})}{\text{Number of people who } \textbf{saw your link } (\textit{impressions})} \times 100 = \text{CTR (in \%)}$$

In Google Analytics and Google Webmaster (explained later) the "Number of people who saw your link" are called "Impressions" and "Number of people who clicked your link" are simply called "Clicks".

Very often the term CTR is used when the term CR is mentioned.

What is CR?

CR stands for conversion rate: if 100 people visit your site, how many will actually buy or perform the action required? A realistic conversion rate is between 1% and 5% in case. Higher conversion rates are possible but it depends on what you decide counts as a conversion - filling in email address could be considered a conversion.

CR is a straight-forward equation and describes the percentage of people who performed a certain action on a page or bought a product.

$$\frac{\text{Number of people who } \textbf{performed an action}}{\text{Number of people who saw } \textbf{your page}} \times 100 = \text{CTR (in \%)}$$

The simplest example would be a one-page sales letter. On this kind of page, the conversion rate would be the number of people who bought the product, divided by the number of people who looked at the product, converted into a percentage.

Knowing your conversion rates means you can test different elements of your site and check the impact it has on your number of sales.

Think about how powerful increasing your conversion rate can be, and how all these little changes can seriously add up. If you double your conversion rate, you double your income. To really hammer this home: testing and increasing your conversion rate means you earn more money without worrying about getting more traffic!

A simplified explanation to make it easy to remember:

People who saw your website and clicked on it = Click Through Rate (CTR)

People who saw your website and bought something = Conversion Rate (CR)

- What is URL and IP-address?

URL stands for Unique (or universal) Resource Locator. It is also known as an internet address, or web address. For instance, www.yoursitehere.com is your URL.

IP stands for Internet Protocol. Every computer, router, modem or other device (such as a printer or scanner) that is connected to the internet is automatically assigned a unique number known as an IP address. These IP addresses consist of four numbers separated by periods (also called a 'dotted-quad') and look something like 172.16.254.1.

In comparison to the postal infrastructure, if you do not have a postal code or a zip code, you would not be able to receive any mail by post. Without an IP address for each device connected to your PC, it would be impossible to receive or send any data over the internet. The IP address can often be used to identify the region or country from which a computer is connecting to the internet. That's why it is important to choose a hosting company in your own country if your targeted visitors are based in your country.

- What is SEO?

SEO stands for Search Engine Optimisation. It is the process of developing your website with a view to rank in Google in the organic or natural listings (not paid listings) following certain rules, which are mostly keyword related. SEO is a technique which, when applied correctly, can result in the search engines finding your site and ranking it higher than millions of other sites.

- What is HTML?

HTML is a computer language and stands for Hyper Text Markup Language. It scares a lot of people because it consists of a lot of codes and looks like this:

```
href="http://www.nitrotek.co.uk/skin/m/1298243920/skin/frontend/default/electronicsstore3/cs
e3/css/boxes.css,/skin/frontend/default/electronicsstore3/css/menu.css,/skin/frontend/defaul
default/default/css/magentweet.css,/skin/frontend/default/default/css/menubuilder.css" media
<script type="text/javascript"
src="http://www.nitrotek.co.uk/skin/m/1266627222/js/prototype/prototype.js,/js/prototype/val
aculous/effects.js,/js/scriptaculous/dragdrop.js,/js/scriptaculous/controls.js,/js/scriptacu
,/js/varien/menu.js,/js/mage/translate.js,/js/mage/cookies.js" ></script>
<link type="text/css" rel="stylesheet"
href="http://www.nitrotek.co.uk/skin/m/1274378045/skin/frontend/default/electronicsstore3/cs
<link type="text/css" rel="stylesheet" href="http://www.nitrotek.co.uk/js/auit/editor/css/ed
<!--[if lt IE 8]>
<link type="text/css" rel="stylesheet"
```

If you visit any website and right-click on any page and choose "View Source" you can see the HTML code. HTML is the small building blocks that make up a webpage.

Everything explained in this book ***does not*** require any knowledge of HTML. Most website design packages do not require the website builder to know HTML, but it is handy to be able to work with HTML as you can then make changes to the site you would otherwise not be able to make.

- What is outsourcing and can outsourcing sites be trusted?

Outsourcing is simply giving a task to somebody, and paying them to do it. Outsourcing on the internet is done on outsourcing websites. Almost anything can be outsourced on the internet. The general principle on these sites is the opposite of eBay. As eBay is an auction site, the product goes to whoever pays the highest price. On outsourcing websites the freelancer bids low on a job in order to win the work. For example, freelancer A might quote $200 to design a five-page website but freelancer B might undercut A with a quote of $180. www.elance.com is my favourite outsourcing site.

The screenshot below gives you an idea of how much work is outsourced.

Today on Elance

47,782

Jobs Posted (last 30 days)

378,548

Contractors

$381,562,612

Work done (to-date)

You can get an outsourcer to write a 150-page book on any subjects for $500 or £307. As writing a book with unique content (not just PLR products copied and pasted) will take several weeks, you might wonder why somebody would do this for $500. The reason is that a lot of people who are registered on Elance are based in sub continental countries. The cost of living in such countries is much lower than in western countries, like the USA or the UK.

So it is a win-win situation: the outsource freelancer gets a lot of money and the person giving him the job gets a good price. Make sure to check the feedback from the person you are thinking of hiring because you will need to select somebody who can write perfect English, without spelling mistakes. There are a lot of native English speakers on the outsourcing sites but in my experience they quote higher for the jobs.

There are very professional people and companies getting work on Elance as you can see from the next screenshot. Earning over $1 million with 35 jobs and five-star ratings, you can conclude that this is a trustworthy company to deal with.

Xicom Technologies Ltd.

16 | ⭐⭐⭐⭐⭐ 5.0 | $1,142,886 Earnings | 35 Jobs | Web & Programming | 🏭 India

Xicom is a CMMI Level-3 certified software development company with a strong team of 100+ highly skilled IT experts, catering result-oriented and cost-competitive solutions to SME's across the world. Why...

▶ Portfolio | Skills: PHP4, ASP.NET 2003, Advanced PHP, LAMP, Dot Net Fundamentals

---

How does outsourcing work on Elance?

Stage 1:

- You post a detailed job describing what you need your outsourcer to do. Make sure that you provide as many details as possible. If you ever have to dispute the work supplied, you can refer back to the original job description.
- Freelancers will send you proposals.
- You can analyse the proposals. Outsourcing sites are based on feedback and trust ratings. If somebody offers you a price for a job, but has only done two jobs and both received negative feedback, you should not choose that person to do your job. However, if somebody offers you a price and has done 25 jobs with 25 positive ratings, they are a much better candidate. Most people will show you samples of previous work to help you decide.
- **Word of caution:** Be cautious when a person only has one job and one positive feedback. The feedback could come from friends or family. Everybody has to start somewhere...

Stage 2:

- You decide which person you want to hire and he or she will accept the previously set terms of payment eg. 10% deposit, 50% when most work done and 40% on completion and delivery of the job. All people I 've worked with did not ask for a deposit at all.
- In order for the freelancer to make sure that you have the money to pay him once the job is done, you put the money in Elance Escrow. You only release the money to the freelancer when you are happy with the job.
- Elance describes this as follows: *Elance Escrow is a safe and efficient way to pay for work delivered online. Once a job is awarded, the client and provider define and agree upon milestones, and funds are then placed into Escrow. Providers can quickly and safely begin working knowing that*

payment is secure and will be released once work is completed, and clients are protected knowing their funds are securely held in Escrow and will only be released to the provider when work is delivered and accepted.

- You can constantly track progress of your job in your workroom.

Stage 3:

- The work is done and sent to you for approval.
- If you are happy with the work, you release the funds in Escrow (see screenshot below) and everybody is happy!

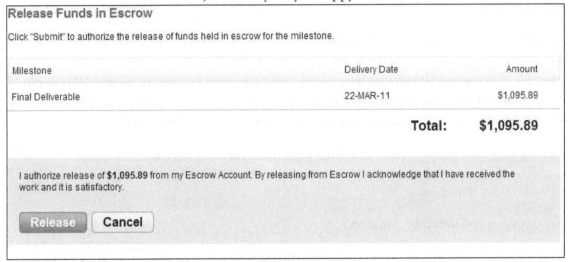

Release Funds in Escrow

Click "Submit" to authorize the release of funds held in escrow for the milestone.

Milestone	Delivery Date	Amount
Final Deliverable	22-MAR-11	$1,095.89
	Total:	**$1,095.89**

I authorize release of **$1,095.89** from my Escrow Account. By releasing from Escrow I acknowledge that I have received the work and it is satisfactory.

[Release]   **Cancel**

Outsourcing is a bit like hiring employees. Sometimes it works out and sometimes it doesn't.

Can these outsourcing sites be trusted?

Thousands of businesses use outsourcing sites everyday to hire and manage online, so yes they can be trusted. If you trust eBay and Amazon, you can trust the well-known outsourcing sites as the principle is more or less the same: 99% of people who do business on those sites can be trusted but unfortunately there are dishonest people everywhere on the web. The outsourcing sites listed below are very well known in the internet business.

Here are some reliable outsourcing websites where thousands of freelancers bid for all sorts of jobs: writing, translating, web design, slideshows, marketing, admin, multimedia, design, engineering, finance, legal, manufacturing... the list goes on.

www.elance.com RECOMMENDED, my favourite

www.fiverr.com There are a huge amount of services here for $5: backlinks, more Twitter followers, installing your website for you, consulting... you can even pay a woman to dress up in a cat-suit and jump around shouting whatever you like (although that will probably not help you earn money from your site).

www.freelancer.com

www.guru.com

www.microworkers.com RECOMMENDED This site is brilliant for getting lots of small jobs done at once and can cost a tiny amount per job ($0.20 per 250 word article, for example). If I wanted 100 articles with 250 words each, then I'd post an ad and 100 people would each write me one article. The turnaround is extremely quick, it's cheap and if you don't like the quality of a submission then you simply reject it and you don't pay for it!

www.odeskresources.com : you can follow per hour what your outsourcer is doing

www.peopleperhour.com

www.mturk.com Owned by Amazon

> **Top Tip : Use the first money you make through internet marketing to get yourself a VA (Virtual Assistant). A VA can do almost any internet marketing relating jobs for you. You can hire a full time VA for approx. $426 or £275 per month. Most workers accept Paypal so you can pay them online.**

Good sites to find VA's:

www.onlinejobs.ph

www.bestjobs.ph

- What is a blog?

Blog is short for "weblog" and it is a type of website, or part of a website, that is regularly updated by the author.

Updating a blog is called 'blogging' and the person who keeps the blog is called a blogger. The owner of the blogging website will put new articles on the sites regularly; these are called posts, blog post or entries. The posts on a blog are listed in chronological order with the latest addition at the top. Blogs are usually written on a particular niche and nowadays there are blogs on any niche you can think of, resulting in blog communities where people can comment on blog entries. People can share ideas, learn from other comments and also do business with others in the same niche.

To learn about blogs, read a few, leave some comments or ask questions.

If you see "write a comment" or "tell us what you think" or "share your ideas" or "speak your mind" or "leave a reply" with a comment box underneath it, you are looking at a blog.

Example of how a blog comment entry can look:

Example of how your comment is displayed on a blog (in case your name is Keith):

- What is a landing page or 'squeeze page'?

A landing page is also called a 'lead capture page' or 'squeeze page'. The purpose of a landing page is to build a list, convert visitors into customers or to make visitors perform an action, such as filling in their personal details. Some landing pages are cleverly done by internet marketers. In the example below it appears all a visitor has to do is fill in some information in order to get an idea on how much a loan would cost. What they do not tell you on the landing page is that you need to fill in your email address once you click "start your request". Job done for the internet marketer, who owns the website, as the company now has your email address and can bombard you with emails about loans with their email marketing.

A landing page is very often used for online advertising. It is the web page that appears once you click on an advertisement. The landing page is often a page where you have to fill in your email address (opt-in box) in order to reach the actual advertised website. The landing page relates to the subject that is advertised, so if you click on an ad for losing weight, the landing page will be about losing weight.

A lot of pay-per-click campaigns (PPC) will send you to a landing page.

Sometimes a landing page is integrated into what looks like a normal website page, as in example three of the landing pages below.

A website that looks like a normal website with a small opt-in box is usually called a squeeze page rather than a landing page.

Here are some examples of landing pages:

Example 1:   Source: http://www.landingpagewebdesign.com

Example 2:

Example 3:

- What is a sales page or pitch page?

Okay, now you know what a landing page is, but what is a sales page or pitch page?

A sales page, sales letter, pitch page, one-page sales wonder, sales wonder page are all the same : it is the page with the sales text on that leads to people hitting the 'Buy It Now' button.

These pages, definitely the ones in the "how to make money on the internet" niche, are mostly designed by people who are specialised in writing sales copy or converting sales pages. Guru sales pages, like the ones with gravity 400 (best selling product) and more on Clickbank, can cost up to $10,000 per page. A lot of these sales pages stretch to between 20 and 35 A4 pages.

These sales pages are written in a way to make the visitor believe that they really need to buy a product. They are written in a sophisticated way, based on many psychological studies on how to influence a visitor's mind and how to make customers buy a product.

Unfortunately for the visitor, very often the products under-deliver once they have hit the 'Buy It Now' button.

A badly written sales page is pointless as it will not lead to people buying the product, and is called a poorly converting sales page.

Writing a well converting sales page is an art and is best left to professional copy writers.

You could try it yourself if you feel confident and learn from the professionals. I suggest that you print 20 well-written sales pages, the ones with high gravity on Clickbank. You will see that most of them follow the same pattern, picture positioning and style of writing. A lot of pictures and text are repeated on the same sales page because most people will not read every letter on the sales page but scroll through it. The professional sales writers know what parts of the sales letter you will read and what parts you will ignore.

It is a bit confusing as sometimes an advertisement will send you to the sales page. In which case, the guru's call their sales page their landing page as it is the page that you land on when clicking their ad.

Here's the definition:

The main difference between a landing page and a sales letter is that a landing page aims to collect data to build a list and a sales page is designed to make a customer buy something. A landing page will not have a 'Buy It Now' button but a sales page always will. A landing page can, once the data is collected, lead to a sales page.

Word of caution about make money sales pages.

There are some very good sales pages on the internet that will give you exactly what is described on the sales letter. But a lot of the sales letters in the "Make money on the internet niche" promise a lot and deliver nothing.

1. Often when you click "Add to Cart" there is a recurring payment that you automatically agree to, which either was not mentioned at all on the sales letter, or was hidden. I have done it myself: I got very excited about a sales letter, saw 'Buy It Now' for $47 and when I saw £47 in bold, quickly went onto the next screen and clicked OK resulting in being rebilled the next month. The extra problem with this is that if you request a refund from Clickbank, you are asking for a refund for the initial $47 which is the actual sale. As Clickbank considers this as "refund done" it is much harder to get a refund for future billing amounts and you cannot do it unless you start opening support tickets. For this reason I always buy recurring-payments-software with PayPal as they have a simple "stop recurring transactions or subscriptions" button.

2. The amount on the sales letter is always **excluding** VAT. So if you buy something for $47, it will cost you $56.40.

3. Clickbank has a 60-day "no reason asked" refund policy, so I recommend always buying products that are listed on Clickbank . If you buy products not listed on Clickbank , you might end up in a refund merry-go-round, going round and round in circles to get a refund.

4. One-time offers on sales pages: "This price is for today only" or "You have 20 minutes to decide as after that the offer will be gone". Just ignore them. In 99% of cases the special offer will still be there a week later.

- What is PPC (Pay Per Click Advertising)?

Pay Per Click is one of the best ways to get traffic to your site. The idea first started with affiliate marketing and it is now a billion dollar industry.

It is also known under the following names : Pay Per Placement, Pay Per Performance, Pay Per Ranking, Pay Per Position, Cost Per Click.

PPC is an advertising system used on search engines, content websites, blogs, advertising networks. The advertiser – you – only pays when a user clicks on your ad. Within one hour of launching your ad campaign your site can be seen by thousands of people.

When a user types in the keyword matching your keywords, the advertising network will show your ad. This is the best thing about PPC as the traffic you receive from it is targeted. You can sometimes dominate the market with PPC. All administration is done by the PPC-networks and all you need to do is set up the ad campaign and decide which keywords you want to pay for when people click on your ad. You will also need to decide how much you want to pay per click : the more you bid per click, the more often your ad will show.

PPC advertising is usually done with the following steps:

- Set up an account with the PPC network.

- Write an advertisement (you can easy copy this from Clickbank sales pages). Vendors on Clickbank won't mind you copying their stuff as you use it to create sales for them.

- Make a landing Page for your ads. This can be an affiliate link or your own site.

- Create a keyword list or create an ad campaign.

- Set how much you want to bid for the keyword

- Place the ad.

You can track how many people have visited your site through your ads and track how much your ads are costing you. You can set a daily budget and you can immediately stop your ads from being shown if you are not making any money. More about PPC networks later in the book. You have certainly seen Google Adwords, which is a PPC network.

- What are Adwords and Adsense?

Google Adwords is the largest PPC (Pay per Click) network. Google has two different types of network: the search networks (Adwords) and the content networks (Adsense). As a default, Google places your ad on both networks. The search network is the one that you have probably seen often when searching with a keyword. The websites shown in the boxes below have paid for an Adwords campaign. In this case the keywords "dog training" show these sponsored links when somebody searches for those keywords. When somebody clicks on the sponsored ad, the advertiser or the person who is running the *adword campaign has to pay Google money.* That is why this type of advertising is called Pay Per Click as the advertiser only pays when the visitor actually clicks on the website.

Adwords look like this:

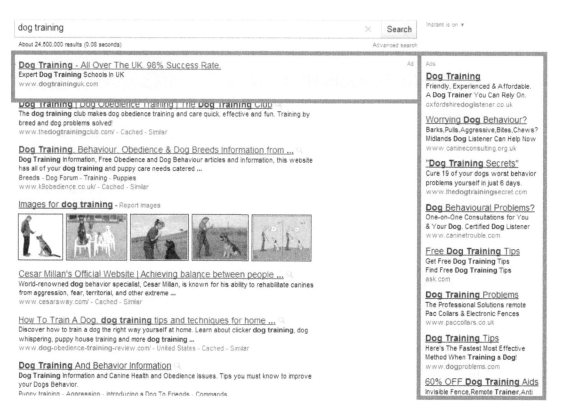

The content network places your ads on relevant websites. In other words, Google places ads and images automatically on the websites that have chosen for ads to be placed on their sites. When somebody clicks on those ads, *the website owner gets paid by Google.*

PPC will be explained in a lot more detail later in the book.

Important note: At the time of writing this book, Google announced that instead of calling their ads "Adsense", they will call them "AdChoices". They will still be called Adsense in your Google Account but at the bottom of the ads that you can see on websites, it will say "AdChoices". So instead of "Ads by Google" as you can see on these screenshots, it will say "AdChoices". I will refer to them as Adsense in the rest of the book. Google constantly changes their Adsense rules so make sure you are aware of their latest rules and regulations.

Adsense looks like this :

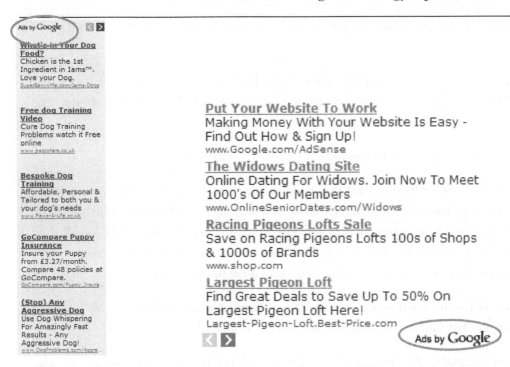

Adwords = a website owner paying for his website to be shown in the searches. Each time somebody clicks, **the website owner pays Google** per click.

Adsense = a website owner decides that he wants Google to place relevant ads on his site. Each time somebody clicks the ads, **Google pays the website owner** per click.

If a website owner pays $1.00 per click for Adwords and opts for search network **and** content network, he can decide an amount he wants to pay for Adwords ($1.00) and a separate amount he wants for Adsense ($0.60).

- What is an automated system?

An automated system is where you pay for things to be done automatically for you. There are automated systems available on just about everything in online marketing: link building, content pulling, blog commenting, article submission, social marketing, getting traffic, website creation, ad creation and so on.

For instance, you could buy software that automatically builds websites for you, based on certain keywords that you enter in. What the sales letter selling the automated system does not tell you is that thousands other people will have exactly the same website as you if you do this.

Do the automated systems work? In my opinion, no. They all have more disadvantages than advantages. I have bought several because, to start with, I thought I could make money the lazy way and have everything done automatically.

There might be the odd good one around, but the vast majority of them do not work.

Ask yourself, if the seller is buying stuff that really works, why doesn't he conquer every market in every niche himself? He could earn buckets and buckets of money. Why on earth would he sell his secret to conquer the market? He can easily take on some staff (on all the sales pages it clearly states you can earn hundreds and thousands of dollars in a matter of weeks or months) and make them apply his automation on his own websites.

In my opinion ALL automated systems (well 99% of them) are a complete SCAM. NO successful website that ranks in Google is completely automated.

Your website is integral to the success of your business. **YOUR** website, not somebody else's. If you want to change something to the automated sites, you very often can't without technical support and they might never answer your question when you contact them.

Usually the following rule applies: If it is too good to be true, it probably is.

- Automated traffic or automated linking: Yes or No?

Only one word to remember: NO.

There are lots of products available that promise to get you 20,000 visitors in two days or to make you $5000 by tomorrow morning. I have tried several on some of my new websites. In case Google would ban my site because of the automated traffic system, I never used one of my established sites to test for the automated systems. The result on each and every one of the automated products that I have bought? Nada, ziltz, rien du tout, nothing, niks, zero.

The "one-page sales wonder" sales pages for these products are written by extremely good copy writers. Gurus pay up to $10,000 or more to have a sales page done for them. So do they work from a sales point of view? Yes they do. They are written so well that anybody who reads them wants to hit the "buy it now" button, including myself. Five years ago I bought many such products but none of them ever earned me a cent.

From Newbie to Millionaire   114

Some very big problems with these big-promise-automated-systems:

- Google is more clever than you think and works out scams and automated systems very quickly. Search engine robots are "programmed" to ignore and reject stupid tricks and schemes. Sure an automated system might work for the first few users who bought it for two or three days but by the time hundreds of people have bought them, people will drive traffic the same way (as sold in the system). Google soon works this out and won't show the websites on the first page.

- Very often these big-promise-traffic-systems are based on sending 1000's of emails or thousands of visitors to *very* untargeted prospects, which won't ever convert into sales. The automated emails will no doubt end up in the user's spam or junk emails, clearly marked with the first word SPAM in the title of the email. So most people don't even open them.

- Some of the systems and software products sold as "automated systems" operate outside of Google's user guidelines, so Google can immediately ban your site.

- Webmasters who care about their website and topic will never link to any garbage links anyway, because they know that Google is very good at scrubbing link quality.

- When you buy an automated system for building websites very often you need to buy the domain names and the hosting from the seller. This is in total contradiction with what I strongly believe in : that YOU need to be in control of all your domain names and hosting. You probably already have a hosting company, why on earth would you pay an extra monthly fee to host domain names with the seller's hosting company.

- The biggest problem of all is that you are NOT in control. What if the company who sold you the system goes out of business, or stops the traffic system all of a sudden? You've lost your money and you get nothing, because you don't even know what it is they provide because they do it for you.

- If Google does another dance (when Google changes it algorithms now and again, it is called a Google Dance), then you are not in control. With the system that I follow, things can easily be adjusted even if Google dances! I say: Dance Away Google! Some people say that a Google Dance is a slight fluctuation in the search results due to server updates. When one server is updated, another is used, which might have older data on it and so might not have all the backlinks registered. The fact is Google has its own secrets and always will have but Google Dance is a well know term in the IM world and it just means things change and you need to be in control to change them at your end accordingly. With automated traffic, you are not in control at all as you have to follow the system that you bought.

Remember you can't control the wind but you can adjust your sails. If Google controls the way it ranks websites, you can adjust your websites and keywords accordingly but only if you are in control.

The websites that promises you to be number one in Google are NO DOUBT SCAMS as it is impossible to guarantee it. The seller of these types of sites is not Google and Google constantly changes it's algorithm. Nobody knows the Google rules.

If a company phones you or sends you an e-mail saying that they can get you on Page 1 with SEO, the first thing you should do is Google something like " SEO, how to be on the 1st page in Google". If that company is not on the first pages, you know that they cannot even do it for their own website!

- Automated website creation: Yes or No?

Only one word to remember: NO.

Automated website creation is where a one-page wonder sales page that promises to make you bundles of money (by next week!) by creating websites automatically for you just by typing in a keyword or a domain name.

I bought all this sort of nonsense myself when I first started so I bought an automated website creation deal from an IM guru and I was very happy because the product would do all the work for me and build automatic websites that would look smart and professional. I was very disappointed that I was forced to host with the guru for the sites that were created automatically, because the guru did not tell me that on the sales page! A nice looking website was created for me BUT ten minutes later when I did a search, I was no longer impressed!

Why? The screenshot below explains: one of the sentences of the automatically created content on this automatically created website is: "with the vast amount of online money making opportunities that invade the market, choosing can prove to be quite difficult". I copied that sentence and placed it in Google search between inverted commas. The result: 40 other sites came up with exactly the same text. I could not believe it! Surely with that duplicated content my chances of ever being shown in Google were zero. I will never buy anything automated again and I now realise that when it sounds too good to be true, it probably is. Hard work will rank you in Google, automated sites won't.

"With the vast amount of online money making opportunities that invade the market, cl

Page 4 of 40 results (0.29 seconds)

▸ Blogsbot Blog » Available Online Money Making Opportunities
25 Dec 2010 ... **With the vast amount of online money making opportunities that invade the market , choosing can prove to be quite difficult.** ...
blog.blogsbot.net/tag/available-online-money-making-opportunities/ - Cached

Blogsbot Blog » Finding Legitimate Online Money Making Opportunities
25 Dec 2010 ... **With the vast amount of online money making opportunities** ...
blog.blogsbot.net/.../finding-legitimate-online-money-making-opportunities/ - Cached
➕ Show more results from blogsbot.net

Affiliate Marketer's: Turn Traffic Into Bucks - Online Money ...
5 Feb 2010 ... **With the vast amount of online money making opportunities that invade the market , choosing can prove to be quite difficult.** ...
affiliate-marketers-ashraf.blogspot.com/.../turn-traffic-into-bucks-online- money.html - Cached

ezines | autorespondemarketingtips.com | Page 14
6 Feb 2010 ... **With the vast amount of online money making opportunities that invade the market , choosing can prove to be quite difficult.** ...
autorespondemarketingtips.com/category/ezines/page/14/ - Cached

Kelly S. Brown - ezinearticles.com Expert Author
With the vast amount of online money making opportunities that invade the market , choosing can prove to be quite difficult. This is more true now than ever, ...
ezinearticles.com/?expert=Kelly_S._Brown - Cached

Turn Traffic Into Bucks: Online Money Making Opportunities-Make ...
17 Feb 2011 ... **With the vast amount of online money making opportunities that invade the market , choosing can prove to be quite difficult.** ...
www.makemoneyonlinefromhome24.com/turn-traffic-into-bucks-online- money-making-opportunities/ - Cached

Blog - www.onlineschool4makingmoney.com
16 Feb 2011 ... **With the vast amount of online money making opportunities that invade the market , choosing can prove to be quite difficult.** ...
www.onlineschool4makingmoney.com/blog/ - Cached

Blog - www.makemadmoneyonline.com
16 Feb 2011 ... **With the vast amount of online money making opportunities that invade the market, choosing can prove to be quite difficult.**

- Automated blog posting: Yes or No?

Only one word to remember: NO. Here is a good example why not :

A new comment on the post "Demersal Fish" is waiting for your approval
http://icefishingtactics.com/demersal-fish/

Author : Madelbawd (IP: 109.230.220.96 , 109.230.220.96)
E-mail : ubifeke@yahoo.co.uk
URL   : http://danielctavares.com/dominios-dreamorama.cc/memberlist.php?mode=viewprofile&u=821
Whois : http://ws.arin.net/cgi-bin/whois.pl?queryinput=109.230.220.96
Comment:
how to unlock iphone 3gs
click
unlock iphone 3gs 4.2.1
unlock iphone 3gs 4.3.2
unlock iphone 3gs 4.3
unlock iphone 3gs

http://heroes-wow.dyndns.org/forum/member.php?u=592
http://indianmtforum.com/memberlist.php?mode=viewprofile&u=996
http://club.sinofrance.org/index.php?showuser=149038
http://mywarez.jetforum.net/memberlist.php?mode=viewprofile&u=2954
http://club.sinofrance.org/index.php?showuser=149038

http://www.sainegestion.org/archives/1753?succes=true#comment-3224
http://oliviachile.com/?p=664&cpage=1#comment-24450
http://www.pocketpcaddict.com/forums/site-announcements/12950-want-free-games-want-pocket-pc-addict-editor-257.html#po
http://phoenixmt2.cba.pl/forum/viewtopic.php?p=255#255
http://www.flyprivate.net/join.htm

Hey, i have been having alot of problems wit my CPU and its been very slow and i keep getting those Online Spam pop ups where using certin programs. It ether doesnt open or cant find certin programs. I officially got sick of it when i bought a 200$ iPod Touch problem with windows installer in mid installation. Please Tell me a way to fix my computer! the first person whos answer solves m

Often with automated blogging the comments are totally irrelevant to the websites. The above screenshot is a comment about unlocking iPhones posted on a website about Ice Fishing Tactics. The webmaster will never approve your comments, so it is a waste of time. Google will also know that the comment is irrelevant to the site if the webmaster has his setting as "automatically approve all comments".

Important: If you are planning to drive traffic to your site with paid traffic methods or social websites, etc… it does not matter at all if you use automated methods. Just don't use it if you want to rank in Google.

Part 3. Niche Research

After my rather large introduction and IM terminology explanation, I can now get to business. I believe I needed to explain these to make you understand some basics otherwise you would not understand the terminology used in this book.

In this first part called Niche Research you will learn how to find a new niche with potential and you will check if your niche has the potential to make money.

The fundamentals of IM the way it works for me are:

-   Find a target market or niche

-   Offer a solution on a website

-   Drive traffic to your website with the offer on

-   Put an opt-in box on your website to create more sales

-   Put money making links dotted around the pages, in an organised manner

-   Sell an existing ebook as an affiliate and if it sells well, create and ebook and a hard copy version of the ebook

-   Duplicate it for another niche

Okay, before we start thinking about building a website, you need to find a niche with potential, a niche that can make you money.

People tend to make a really big deal out of finding a niche (or topic or market) for their website when, in reality, it can be surprisingly straight forward.

You HAVE to spend a lot of time and effort in investigating your niche. This is THE most important step in your initial research of finding a niche with potential. When I say with potential, I mean with potential to be shown in the search engines, with potential to earn you money. Pick the wrong niche and you are immediately fighting a losing battle and the changes of earning money are basically zero.

It is not essential to pick a niche that you are personally interested in.

From Newbie to Millionaire

You need to have a commercial attitude when picking what niche to target - find something where there's interest and money to be made. Try not to go into this thinking "I really want to make a great-looking website", but instead should think "I want to create a site that's got the potential to make me lots of money".

You need to find a niche that could work with my suggested method, even if the niche is about a subject that you were not interested in before. If you will be building 20 sites in the future, these 20 sites are unlikely to be about your hobbies, as I assume that you do not have 20 hobbies. Who has? However, you need to be prepared to research and analyse your niche: if you absolutely hate spiders, do not design a website on spiders. Even if it does look like a very good potential money-making niche, I would suggest you don't start it.

I've got sites on a wide range of niches that I am not interested in personally. The motivation to write and update them comes from the money aspect - this is how you should be thinking. Think money, don't think interest. Of course, if you can find a niche that you are interested in (e.g. your hobby) and it can make you money, pick that niche first. But I believe you should never bet on one horse or put all your eggs in one basket. In other words, build websites in lots of different niches. If you build ten websites, three might never make you any money (we all make mistakes), four might make you a little bit and three might make you a lot.

> **Experience is the name we give to our mistakes.**

Wherever you are, whatever you are doing, look around, analyse and constantly look for a niche that you can investigate with my method. I was sitting in a traffic jam a few years ago, looked outside and saw pigeons on the pavement. When I came home, I did my keyword research on racing pigeons and my next niche was born. I now have a very high earning website on pigeons. Finding an idea for your website can be that easy! Did I know anything about pigeons? No but I know how to rank in Google with pigeon-keywords and I know how to monetise a website. I do know a little bit about pigeons now as I have read books and written articles. It will all be clear to you throughout this book. I've outsourced an eBook on Racing Pigeons, which is on Clickbank, and the hard copy also sells on Amazon.

A few months later I saw an article in the paper about Micro Pigs, or Teacup Pigs, becoming more popular as pets. I started my research and I now have an eBook about Micro pigs on Clickbank and a hard copy book on Amazon.

These are just two examples of how I came up with new ideas. It is not difficult to find ideas if you constantly think about it. Ask all your friends and family what they are interested in and if they have ever searched the web and could not find the answers to their questions. Investigate the potentials in that niche and maybe that could be your next site.

I also have good earning websites on phobias: go to www.phobialist.com where you can see a list of all the phobias.

A recommended book in this niche-subject is "The Zulu Principle : Making Extraordinary Profits from Ordinary Shares" by Jim Slater. Available on www.amazon.com .

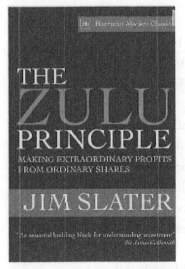

Although this book is about trading shares, the message in this book is very clear: you can become a leading expert in any niche or micro niche in a very short time just by studying and analysing that niche. Slater applies his method by specialising in a certain type of share and situation surrounding that share. The book is all about finding a niche and then attempt to dominate it. Slater suggests that you need to become an expert in your niche and your expertise will enable you to outperform the markets in niches neglected by others. The same principle applies on the web, if you, as an internet marketer can find a lucrative niche and specialise in it, you can make money. The ability to find a niche and dig deeper into that niche is an extremely good skill to have as an internet marketer.

1. Things to think about when choosing your niche

You should always keep in mind the reasons why people spend money. Purchases are made for the following reasons (in all walks of life, not just online):

- To solve a problem they are having
- To fill a basic need
- For convenience
- To give them peace of mind
- Increasing their image or ego/peer pressure/showing off
- For their entertainment

- To make them wealthier (this could mean either saving money or making money)
- For knowledge
- To replace something they've lost or broken
- For value - people can't resist bargains

2. Niches NOT to pick

There are a lot of gurus who tell you to pick a popular niche: health, wealth, books, electronics, insurance and so on. I disagree. I never pick these niches because it is an enormous task to rank highly for them.

My decision whether to build a website around a niche is mostly based on my keyword research and whether the niche can be monetized or not. The subjects listed below however are subjects that I do not recommend for a newbie. Reason? With these subjects/niches it is almost impossible to beat "the big boys". Let the "big boys" play the "big game". If you want to open a food store in the USA, you do not want to compete with WalMart and the likes. It is impossible and a losing battle. It is better to accept that you cannot compete with them and to start a very specialized food store instead. The same applies for websites: the enormous companies spend enormous amounts of money to rank in Google on the first page, or they spend an even bigger amount of money on advertising. Insurance companies employ extremely clever webmasters. I wouldn't like to compete with them and I recommend you don't waste your time either. 15 years ago it was relatively easy to build a website on insurance and rank on the first pages but in 2011 that is an almost impossible task, unless you are very experienced.

Here are my Top 10 niches to avoid. It is the list of the niches that I do not recommend for newbies:

- Insurance

- Debt consolidation

- Mortgages

- Loans

- Real estate

- Computers

- Automobile

- Forex (Foreign Exchange online trading)

- Booking holidays online

- Making money online

Here are the top four that most gurus say to try:

- Dating and relationships

- Health and fitness

- Lifestyle

- Self-help

If you can find a *micro* niche with potential in one of those four niches, that might be do-able.

Personally I think that all these niches are over-populated so I do not even try to rank for them.

Don't worry; there are a lot of micro niches left untouched with potential.

Niches NOT to pick because of homonyms or "double keywords".

Suppose that you think "How to get rid of a mole in your garden" could be good keywords to build a website for. When you type "mole" into Google, you will see that some websites are about moles as skin growths, and some websites are about moles in the garden. This is what I call a "double" keyword: a word with a double meaning, also called a homonym.

Homonyms generally include two categories of word types: homophones and homographs.

Homographs are words that are spelled the same but have different meanings. Here are a few examples:

Mole: animal/skin growth

Parrot: a bird/a wireless device

Suit: piece of clothing/to fit in with

Canary: a bird/canary islands

Homophones are words that sound the same when you pronounce them, but have different meanings e.g. allowed and aloud, buy and bye. You see it gets complicated, that's why I call them "double keywords".

I never build websites or set up PPC campaigns with double keywords because there will be "double" competition on Google and other search engines. Websites not even related to yours will rank. Why make it more difficult than it already is to rank in Google?

Talking about niches: in my book: "Finding Niches Made Easy", I explain the exact steps I take before deciding on a new niches.

3. Check points for your niche

- Always check if your niche is in a market where people are spending money.

- Make sure whatever you sell is a long term product in the market, unless you are happy selling products that are only popular in the short term, or are seasonal.

- Do the customers that you are targeting have money to spend? There is not a lot of point selling luxury yachts to homeless people.

- Is there already too much competition? If you are planning to write a guide or an eBook on your subject, search for " keyword" + "guide " and " keyword" + "eBook".

4. How to find a new niche or test if your niche has potential

There are several ways to judge the potential of a niche. You need to do a bit (a lot actually) of market research in your niche before deciding if it is good.

It is a good start if there are commercial sites (such as shops or eBay) in the search results and Google Sponsored Listings (also known as *Adwords*) on the right-hand side of the search results. If you can find low competition keywords around this niche, as explained in the next section, then you're in business!

If there are no commercial sites listed and no Adwords listings at all then this may be a dead market and not worth pursuing. However, if you have found in your niche research that there is a lot of demand/searches for your keyword and no competition, you might have found yourself a winner.

Here are a few ways to get ideas on your new site or to find out if your idea has potential.

- Google search: if you search for your niche keyword and all the sites on the first three to five pages are sites with hardly any content or no keyword in the domain name, that is a very good start. This might mean that it will be easy for you to rank but needs more investigation before you can decide.

- Google Alerts. Sign up to www.Google.com/alerts and get emailed at regular intervals whenever anyone blogs or talks about your niche. If there's a lot of movement then it may be a good niche. Even if you have decided on your new niche, I suggest that you keep Google Alerts on because it flags blogs, forums and more that are relevant to your niche each time you receive an alert. Each time you see a new blog in your niche, write the blog domain name on your to do list as you can get links from the blog once your own website is developed. If you don't have a "to do" list, you need to make one.

- Google Trends. Have a look on Google Trends www.Google.com/trends for hot searches and hot niches. Google Trend is very interesting. You do not want to start a new niche which has gone down in search consistently for the last two years. Google Trends has clear graphs so in a matter of seconds you can see if your niche is potentially a good one. For instance, you might see on the graph that your keyword is seasonal or that it gets peak searches only in two months of the year. The graph below shows "stand up comedy" as a consistent niche for over six years.

- Google Zeitgeist. Fastest rising and fastest growing niches: www.Google.com/zeitgeist Find out what people have searched for.

- Yahoo News. Find out what people are talking about: www.news.yahoo.com

- Lycos. Find out what the latest trends and hot topics are: www.lycos.com

- Toluna. http://uk.toluna.com/test is a website where brand new products are tested. You can get great ideas here. Some products might never be released but other products will have huge potential for a website. A website with a new product as a keyword in the domain name is good, but check the legalities and trademarks.

- Alexa hot urls. -www.alexa.com/hoturls

- Pricegrabber. Visit www.pricegrabber.com to search for keywords and a top 200 will be shown, which is updated daily. Find a product and do your research in Keyword Planner or www.marketsamurai.com. , which will be explained later.

- Amazon Top 100. Go to www.amazon.com. This is an excellent way to identify hot new markets. This is updated hourly.

- Choose a category from the drop down menu e.g. electronics

- Type in your keyword e.g. flip video, and click 'Bestsellers'

- This will show you the Top 100 best-selling products in that category.

Each time you dig deeper into a specific category, it will show you the best sellers.

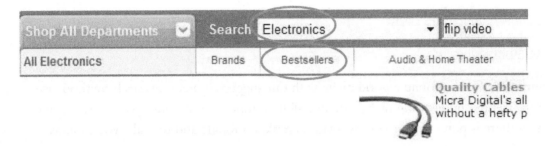

- Magazines. www.magazine.com will give you a list of almost every magazine there is. People who publish magazines have done a lot of research and concluded that there is a market out there for that subject. Find a magazine in a niche and do your research with Keyword Tools and www.marketsamurai.com. . I will explain later what this is.

- Dummies. Go to www.dummies.com and click on latest books or new releases. If Dummies has decided to make a new book, you know that there is a market for it. Learn from the big guys, they have the money to do the research.

- Will your eBook be in a popular niche? Find out:
http://www.barnesandnoble.com/bestsellers/top10everything.asp

- A good way to look for sub-niches. Select your category and look for sub-niches:
http://pulse.ebay.com

- Visit www.ebooks.com and go to 'Most Popular Subjects' to see what sells well. Do a search in your niche. If no eBook is listed and there are a lot of searches per month, you might have found a winner.

- Visit http://product-index.ebay.com/best_selling_1.html to see the best-selling products on eBay to give you some ideas.

- Visit www.technorati.com and search for a blog in your niche.

- http://fr.toluna.com for new products in France.

- www.nichebotclassic.com

- www.nicheday.com receive a new niche, every day

- www.surveymonkey.com

- www.twittertrendingtopics.com

- www.trendwatching.com

Important: If you have found a good niche with our suggested niche-research-method (see further) the trends and growing niches are not all that important, because your research has shown that there is potential for your website to rank in Google and to make you money.

> **TOP TIP : The fact that you are not an expert in a field should not put you off. You will learn about your niche as you go.**

5. See what your competitors are doing

- Visit www.spyfu.com. Here you can download competitors' keywords and adwords. This is not free.

- If there are too many websites with PR5 and upwards as your competitors, you might have to re-think. Don't worry I will clarify later what this means. For now just put it on your "to-do-when-you-start-a-new-niche" list. Firefox (web browser) gives you PR rankings underneath each website.

In my book "Finding Niches Made Easy", I explain in detail what steps I take before entering a new niche.

Part 4. Keyword Research

A *keyword* is whatever you type into the search box in a search engine. *Keyword research* is using a set of tools to discover what keywords people are searching for. If we know this, then we can build a site that targets people's searches.

1. Importance of long tail keywords.

In this chapter we will look at finding *long tail keywords* - keywords with multiple words in them, sometimes called golden keyword. These type of keywords are less searched for, less popular and less competitive but when you target these keywords collectively they can drive a lot of traffic to your site. These keywords are very specific to what you are selling. Long tail keywords are also cheaper per click if you use paid traffic.

If you were looking for information on how to cook a fish pie, what would you search for? Would you search for "fish pie"? No, you'd more likely search for exactly what you want: "how to cook a fish pie".

This is an example of a long tail keyword. These kinds of keywords will have fewer searches than short (single word keywords), but the person searching will be looking for something more specific, which is good for us: it means we can build a site that perfectly suits what they're looking for! Google shows the keywords that the searcher typed in **bold.** Subconsciously people will first click on the websites that show their keyword in bold. **Long tail keywords have a much better conversion rate than short keywords because you will get quality targeted traffic. People type in exactly what they are going to buy and land on your site.**

If you could buy the domain name www.howtocookafishpie.com, that would be your first step towards success. But you must follow all the other rules for success as with a good domain name only, and nothing else, you won't make it in the internet world.

It is much better to rank for lots of low competition long tail keywords than not to rank for high competitive short keywords. You can find these long tail keywords with a keywords research tools.

Long tail keywords enable you to narrow your search down to only the sites that have the information you're looking for. They are used on a website to bring visitors to a certain web page or when the visitor is searching for something specific. Likewise, they are used by a web publisher in search engines to bring surfers to a web page within their site, rather than their home page. If you are building a website about cheese, you would NOT target to rank for the word cheese. Instead, it is much better and easier to target for words like "Spanish artisanal cheeses" or "Dutch Gouda cheese" or "English extra mature cheese", etc.

An Example of Finding Long Tail Keywords with *Keyword Planner.*

Once signed in to your Adwords account, go to "Tools" on the top and select Keyword Planner from the drop down menu.

Click on "Search for new keyword and ad group ideas".

Type in your keyword and make sure to check the settings, e.g. Language, Locations, etc. I always set this to:

- All locations
- English
- Google: Here, you can also choose Google and search partners.

- You can fill in **negative keywords** if you wish, e.g. free. This will NOT display searches for someone who types in "free book", as clearly you don't want to target those people. You can also customise your search, but I always leave that as default. You could say, for instance, only give me keywords that have over 1000 searches per month.

I have typed in "weight loss supplements" as keyword and clicked "Get ideas".

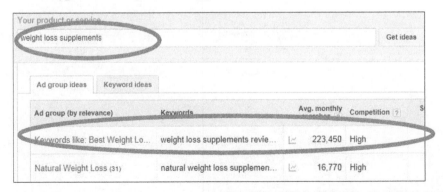

Next, you'll want to look at the average monthly searches that the keyword has. In our case, as shown on the above screenshot, there have been 223,450 **combined** searches for all the keywords (combined searches means the total of searches for different keywords added together)

Important to mention: the result of the monthly searches is based on exact searches.

When you type in [weight loss supplements] in the *Google* search box, you can see it shows 3,530.000 results. That is A LOT of results, so the competition for this keyword will be hard. We need to find another long tail keyword with less competition!

When you click on "Best Weight Loss", as shown below, you will get different keywords.

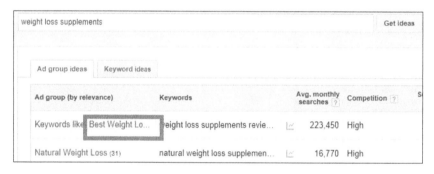

When you click on "Best Weight Loss", this screen will appear:

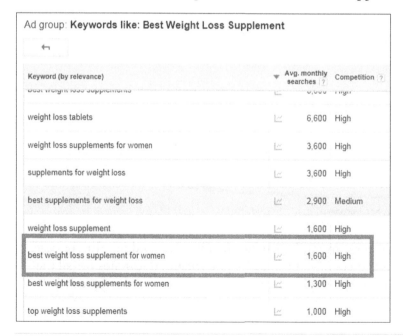

Note that you can see the search results for long tail keywords. Have a look at the keyword "best weight loss supplements for women" and paste that into the search box in Google.

You can see that the number of results is immediately a lot lower, at 1,020.000, so it will be an easier job to rank for that long tail keyword. While the competition is still higher than you would like, it is better than the first keyword you tried. If I were building a website around weight loss for women, I would have at least three different pages on my website, each focusing on the three long tail keywords shown on the next screenshot:

- weight loss tablets: 6,600 searches per month
- weight loss supplements for women: 3,600 searches per month
- best supplements for weight loss: 2,900 searches per month

Note that some of the searches are basically the same, e.g. single vs. plural or "for women" added. I would combine these small differences in searches and focus on all of them on one page of my website. With the above, I just want to show you how easy it is to find long tail keywords to rank for.

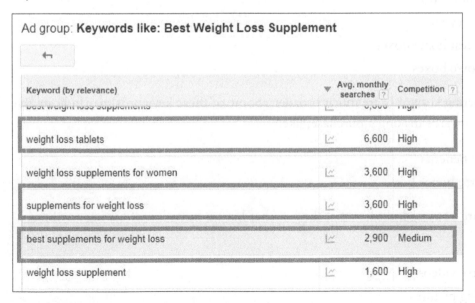

2. What makes a good keyword to target?

A basic explanation is:

- One with low competition
  AND
- High searches

There are two types of keywords:

- Information gathering keywords - people looking for information, not to actually buy something.
- Buying keywords - the visitor has made up their mind that they want a product and you just need to guide them to your page to make the sale.

Both of these can earn money: *buying keywords* can get you sales, while *information gathering keywords* can earn you advertising revenue.

Buying keywords and key phrases are things like:

- buy horse box
- purchase horse box
- horse box reviews
- compare best horse boxes
- Top 10 horse boxes

Information gathering keywords are much broader. Some of these keywords may indicate the person is leaning towards making a purchase, like:

- horse box benefits
- which horse box is best

Some keywords are a strong indicator that the searcher has no intention of buying anything, such as:

- funny horse videos
- horse riding pictures

Basically, we need to look at three things when we're choosing our niche:

1. Demand
2. Profitability
3. Competition

We will be covering these points throughout this book.

We'll be working with www.marketsamurai.com. and the Google Keyword Tool in this guide. Market Samurai is explained first (payable option) and Google Keyword Tool is free to use.

TOP TIP: Pick a niche with potential and pick a very specific keyword in that niche. There might be fewer searches but there will also be less competition.

When looking for keywords to target, it may be useful to use something called 'Google Related searches' to get ideas.

To use this, perform your search as usual on Google and then click "Related searches" on the bottom left of your screen.

All results
Sites with images
Related searches
Timeline
Dictionary
Reading level
Translated foreign pages

Reset tools

This will bring up other keywords that people typed in that are relating to your keyword, in this case "benefits of relaxation", that you've first typed in Google.

benefits of relaxation

About 18,600,000 results (0.20 seconds)   Go to

Related searches

Related searches for **benefits of relaxation**:

benefits of exercise	disadvantages of relaxation	drawbacks of relaxation
benefits of meditation	risks of relaxation	limitations of relaxation
benefits of sleep	problems of relaxation	side effects of relaxation
benefits of massage	advantages of using relaxation	negatives of relaxation
benefits of rest	costs of relaxation	income support of relaxation

You can then type in "benefits of exercise" (the first related keyword in the list) in Google and do Related searches again for that specific keyword, which will give you even more related keywords.

3. Finding the keywords to target with Market Samurai

Market Samurai is a truly awesome piece of software. It's the one thing I couldn't live without when I'm doing my research. Market Samurai may seem expensive at $99 but I've never found anything that's even half as good for keyword research.

Another thing to remember is that this is a *one-off payment* of $99, whereas a lot of other keyword tools have monthly subscription fees. The advertised one-off payment is $147 but if you subscribe for a 7-day trial you automatically get $48 discount (August 2011). You can purchase Market Samurai here: www.marketsamurai.com.

A video on keyword research for "Micro Pig" with Market Samurai is included with my video tutorials. Please visit www.VideosNewbieBook.com to get access.

Market Samurai can look a bit complicated to start with but once you have watched the video, it doesn't take long to get used to the software.

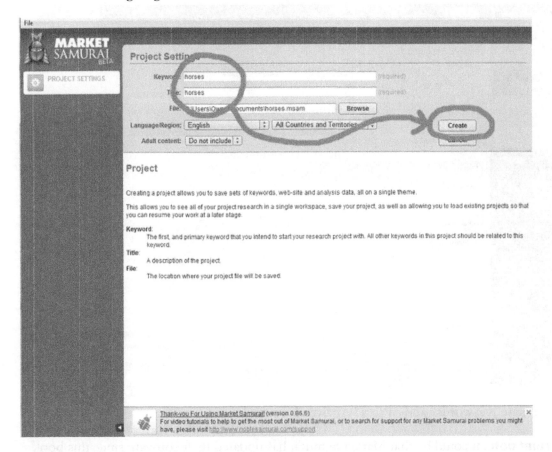

Step 1

Open Market Samurai and enter your niche into the "keyword" section and press enter. In this example we'll type *horses* into the box... hopefully we'll find a great sub-niche we can target! The rest of the information will fill automatically. Hit the "Create" button.

Step 2

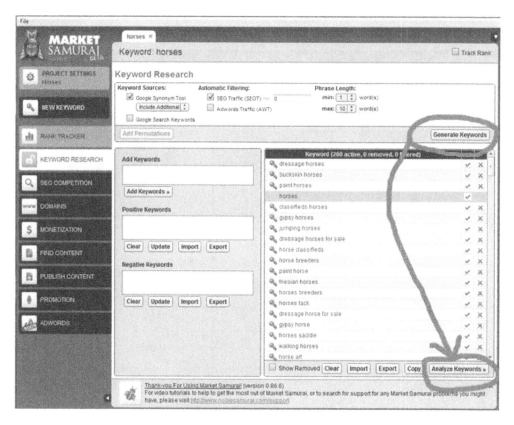

Hit "Generate Keywords" and Press "Analyze Keywords"

Important note: it could be that Market Samurai has updated their software since this book was published. In that case, these screenshots might be different to what you will see on your screen. If that is the case, I suggest you watch the Market Samurai Video Tutorials on their website, once you have bought the product.

Step 3

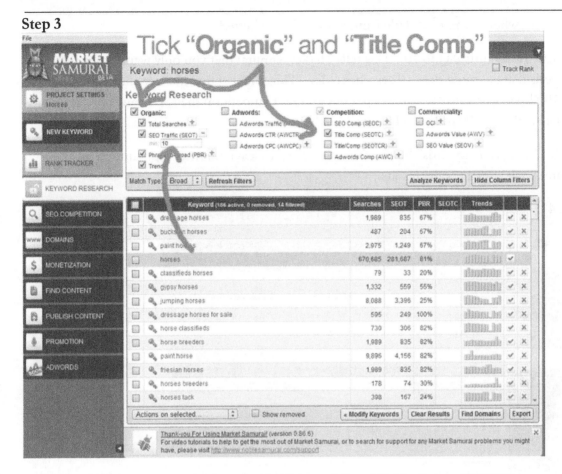

Deselect everything except the box marked "Organic" and "Title Comp SEOTC".

SEOTC stands for SEO Title Competition. "Title Comp" is short for "Title Competition" and tells you the number of sites in Google with that keyword or phrase in its page title, like this:

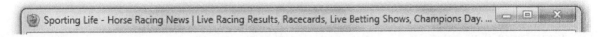

It's a good bet that this site is targeting the keywords "Horse Racing", "Horse Racing News", "Live Racing Results", "Racecards" and so on.

If we wanted to rank for any of these keywords then this site would be one we'd have to beat in the search. This Title Competition is a good way of judging how many other sites are optimised and actively trying to get in the search results for the same keywords as you.

Obviously, when it comes to Title Competition, less is better!

Set SEO Traffic (SEOT) to 10 - This tells Market Samurai that you only want to see the keywords that get more than 10 searches a day. This might sound like very little but if you find 100 keywords with 10 searches per day and no competition then you can easily dominate them all and get 1000 potential hits every 24 hours.

Hit the "Analyze Keywords" button. You may have to leave Market Samurai for a few minutes while it gathers the results.

Step 4

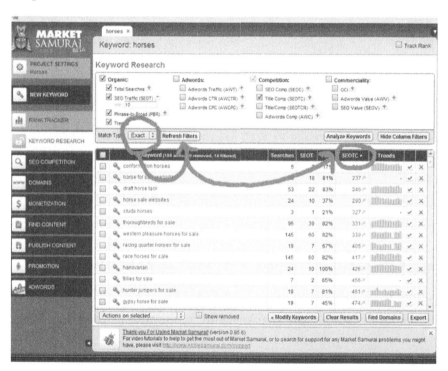

When Market Samurai's finished doing its thing, change 'Match Type' to 'Exact' and click the tab 'SEOTC' to list all the keywords in order of Title Competition.

This gives you a list, starting with the easiest keywords to rank highly in Google, going up to the keywords that will be close to impossible at this stage.

I will get back to Market Samurai but first I need to explain what the different search methods mean as it is important to understand them.

The "Match Type" is basically how people are searching, and is a very important thing to understand.

What is Match Type?

In the screen shot above, take the search phrase "race horses for sale".

If "Match Type" is set to **broad** then the number of searches displayed will include those words in any order; it shows the amount of people searching for:

- race horses for sale
- horses race sale for
- sale for race horses
- for horses sale race

or any longer phrase with the keywords "race horses for sale" - like a user searching for "winning race horses for sale in the UK"

That's what the "82%" in PBR (phrase-to-broad match) means. It's telling you that 82% of people searching for this keyword will type in exactly "race horses for sale", while the other 18% are typing in a different combination of these words.

By setting your "Match Type" to **'Exact'** it gives you the number of searches that the key phrase ("key phrase" is a term used for keywords including more than one word) gets *written exactly as you see it*. This is useful because if you find a keyword or key phrase that gets a huge amount of broad match searches per day, but has a phrase-to-broad match of 1%, then it's only being searched a small amount.

Below is a recap, which is important to remember for your keyword research in any search engine. Suppose we search for: *race horses for sale*.

- **Broad match:** only type in the words in the search engine, without putting the words between " " or [ ] : the searched for words will show up in any order. Not always relevant searches will show. So your search would include the following:

- race horses for sale
- horses race sale for
- sale for race horses

- for horses sale race

- **"Phrase match"**: the order of the words has to be correct to show. Other words can be included either side of the phrase but no other words are allowed in between any words of the search words. You type your search like this with quotation marks or inverted commas at beginning and end: "your search word or phrase here". Your search would include:

- *race horses for sale* in England
- help me with finding *race horses for sale*

It will not show: race horses and dogs for sale (because and dogs are in the middle)

- **[Exact matches]** : your exact phrase will show and nothing else. You type your search like this with square brackets at beginning and end: [your search word or phrase here]. Your search would include:

- *Race horses for sale* and nothing else. Nothing else will be shown, not even this: race-horses for sale, or racehorses for sale.

Broad match = keywords without " " or [ ] = any words or any order of words will show.

"Phrase match" = "your keywords" = order of words has to be correct and no words in between.

[Exact] = [your keywords] = only exact wording searched for will show

---

> **TOP TIP : As an internet marketer, it is very important to always search for keywords in "phrase match" or [exact match].**
>
> **Even if you are not going to be an Internet Marketer, never search for more than one keyword with broad match as you will get more accurate search results.**

The following two screenshots show you what a difference the two different searches can make: 1,170,000 searches against 28,800 searches shown.

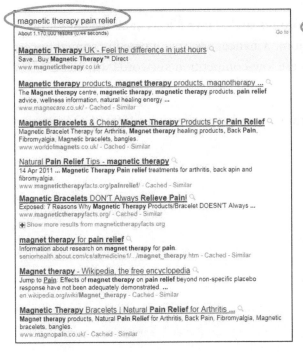 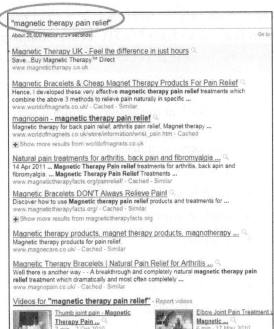

In April 2012, I've added this note to this book: At the moment, it is not possible to fetch lots of data for lots of keywords together with Market Samurai. You need to "check" each keyword.

Market Samurai explains on their site why they have that restriction: *Instead of being able to fetch the SEOTC / SEOUC data for every single keyword you have, we've added a "check" option next to each keyword, which will retrieve the data for that keyword only. This means that you can retrieve this valuable data on a keyword-by-keyword basis, after you've applied your other filters.*
This restriction on being able to fetch large blocks of SEOTC / SEOUC data is a result

of a restriction within Google on the number of SEOTC / SEOUC data that can be retrieved in quick succession.

It might be possible that Google will allow this again in the future as Google constantly changes their rules. Even with this restriction, I find Market Samurai still the best keyword research tool.

Picking the keywords

Okay, back to www.marketsamurai.com. keyword research. Have a look at all the keywords with fewer than 1000 SEOTC (Title Competition). Chances are, if you typed in something as broad as "horses" as your initial keyword, all these low-competition keywords will be on completely different things.

Let's take a look at our results. Among other things, our keywords under 1000 SEOTC are:

- conformation horses
- horse for sale websites
- draft horse tack
- studs horses
- hanovarian
- hunter jumpers for sale
- tack classifieds
- horses breeder
- buy horses

These are all a bit too wide ranging for our niche site. Remember, we want a site that's almost entirely based around one small niche because, in Google's eyes, the site will be more relevant to targeted keywords.

For example: you've got more chance ranking for keywords containing "studs horses", and all related keywords, if your entire site is laser targeted and optimised for this sub-niche.

Now we try to dig deeper into the "horse" niche.

Refining Your Niche

Hit the "Searches" tab and sort all your keywords by number of searches per day, starting with the highest searched first.

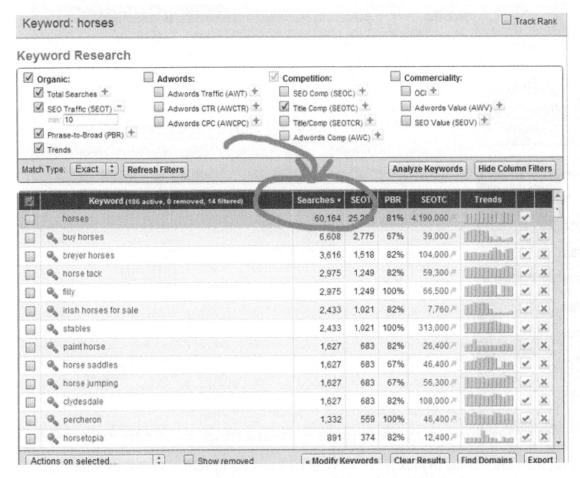

These are the most-searched-for keywords that are based around the keyword "horses".

Take a look at these top-keywords and make a note of which ones you want to research further.

From the list in the screen shot above, I decided to look into "horse tack" because, having a quick look, horse tacks are available on Amazon and sell for hundreds of pounds (meaning we could earn a lot from affiliate sales). I think we've found our niche!

Hit "New Keyword" and enter *horse tack*.

Re-do Steps 1 to 4, except this time set the SEO Traffic (SEOT) to 'min: 1 search per day'.

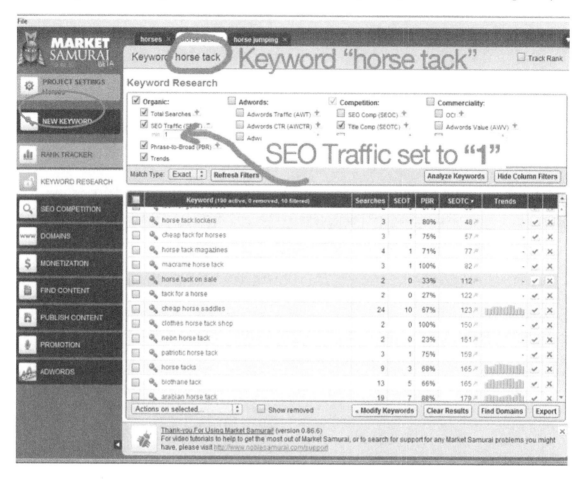

Now, these are starting to look good: we've got a lot of highly related keywords, with a lot under 1000 SEOTC (Title Competition). These are the keywords that we are going to target to rank in Google. We also have a lot of highly searched for keywords with slightly higher competition (which we can target after pursuing the low-competition ones).

4. Finding the keywords to target without Market Samurai

It is possible to do your keyword research for free without using Market Samurai. It will be more time consuming but will give you very similar results.

The Method

Enter "keyword tool" into Google:

keyword tool

Google Search   I'm Feeling Lucky

Advertising Programs   Business Solutions   About Google   **Go to Google UK**

© 2010 - Privacy

and click on the first result, the "Google Keyword Tool"

keyword tool

KW Research | AW Sandbox | Traffic Estimator | Trends | Insights | Sktool | 100 | CSV

About 84,300,000 results (0.14 seconds)

Keyword Tool - Google AdWords - Online Advertising by Google ☆ - 14 visits - Nov 4
Enter one **keyword** or phrase per line to see what related word searches your ad will show on.
https://adwords.google.com/select/**KeywordTool**External - Similar
#1 | PR: 6 | Y! Links: 813,000,000 | Alexa: 1 | Business

Next, enter "horses" into the search box, with the rest of the options set as shown below:

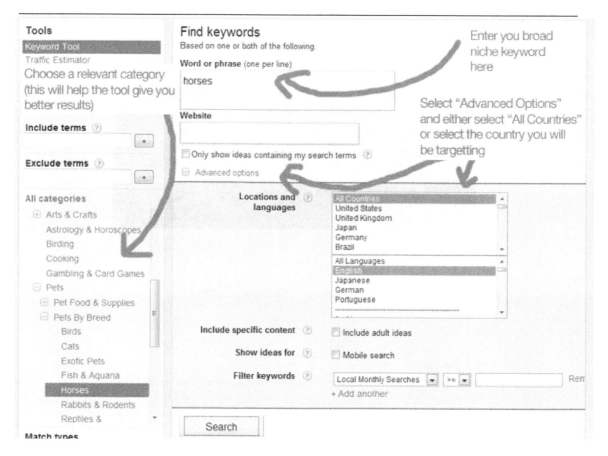

This will output a host of keywords based around the word "horses".

Note: the Google Keyword Tool (GKT) traffic estimates are given in MONTHLY amounts, whereas Market Samurai (MS) gives the figures in DAILY searches. To compare the two either divide the GKT results by 31 or multiple the MS results by 31.

Sort the results by "Global Monthly Searches" and leave the "Match Type" set to broad for this stage. We're going to dig deeper into the keywords shown here, so we want to know how many times different variations of these keywords are searched for, which is what "Broad" gives us.

Now, we're looking for keywords broadly relating to actual types of products, or things, at this stage so scroll through the results and make a note of all of these.

Having a look through, I would delve deeper into:

- horse tack, horse saddle, horse boots, horse trailer, horse stables, horse artwork

These are all sub-niches of the broader horse niche, each with possible money-making opportunities from affiliate sales/CPC advertising/information products.

Delving deeper into the sub-niche tick "Only show ideas containing my search terms" *(1)* and set your match type to [Exact] *(2)* then enter each of your selected sub-niches into the "Word or phrase" box, one by one *(3)*:

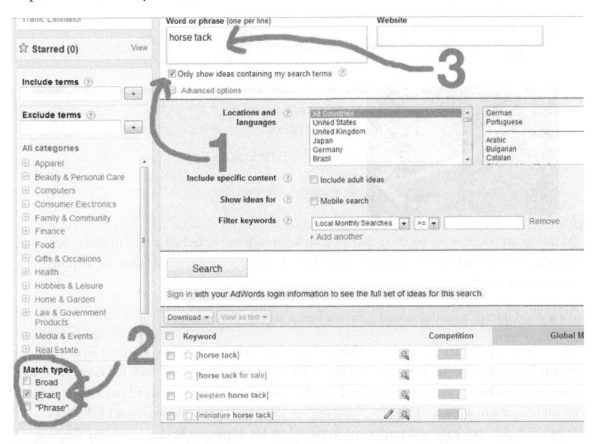

Sort these results by "Global Monthly Searches" and download the results as a "CSV for Excel":

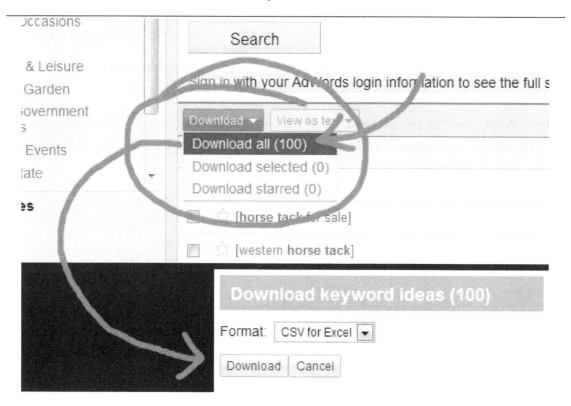

At this point you may be worried that all your keywords are searched a tiny amount each month, and be thinking "what's the point? Why don't I go for keywords that are searched more frequently?".

It's a good question, and one that I have a better answer for:

The reason is that these keywords will be easy to rank for, because low searches frequently means low competition. If you have a list of 100 keywords that you'll rank for easily then the amount of visitors your site receives will quickly add up with each keyword you target. Start by building a site with say 15 pages, focusing on 15 of the best keywords (out of the 100 keywords). So each page will target one keyword. A lot of people have a hard time figuring out what content to write for their sites but, with this list, you'll never have that problem, while making only half the effort to appear on the first page of Google. You can still build pages with different keywords (ones that are more difficult to rank for) as once people are on your site they will hopefully have a look around. Then they will find the pages with keywords that are more difficult to rank for.

You'll also notice that you'll start ranking for more commonly searched keywords, because of the amount of good, well-targeted content on your site, so it's a double win.

Anyway, back to our research!

Open up your newly-saved .csv file in Excel and delete everything except for the columns:

- Keyword
- Competition
- Global Monthly Searches

Then add the title "SEOTC" to the first empty column, as shown below:

	Keyword	Competition	Global Monthly Searches	SEOTC	
1	Keyword	Competition	Global Monthly Searches	SEOTC	
2	[horse tack]	0.66	8100		
3	[horse tack for sale]	0.88	1600		
4	[miniature horse tack]	0.77	590		
5	[western horse tack]	0.8	880		
6	[cheap horse tack]	0.87	480		
7	[used horse tack]	0.84	480		
8	[dis...]				
9	[hor...se tack stores]	0.81			
10	[en...]		590		
11	[hor...se tack shops]	0.81	480		
12	[hor...wholesale]	0.83			
13	[draft horse tack]	0.69	480		
14	[horse tack supplies]	0.87	590		

Keep everything in these three columns and delete everything else. *Add SEOTC as the header of this column*

Now that we know the average monthly searches for each keyword, we can go ahead and start checking the title competition for each one, or "SEOTC".

Take each keyword, starting with the most-searched-for and enter it into Google in the form shown below:

allintitle: "YOUR KEYWORD OR PHRASE HERE"

Google will then display all the pages that you will be competing against. Make a note of the number of results and put them under the SEOTC column next to each keyword:

---

allintitle: "horse tack for sale"

KW Research | AW Sandbox | Traffic Estimator | Trends | Insights | Sktool | 100 | CSV

About 3,320 results (0.23 seconds)   Number of competing

Horse Tack for sale United King sites is 3,320. Enter this
We have a range of horse tack for sale Ur   or sale
including rugs, saddles, boots, bridles, reins in the SEOTC column
www.friday-ad.co.uk/uk/horses-and-eques
#1 | PR: 0 | Y! Links: 182,000 | Alexa: 23,373 | Business for the keyword

Horse Tack For Sale   [horse tack for sale]
Horse Tack For Sale/Wanted.Saddles, Bri   Bins,
Miniature Tack,Stolen Items etc.
members.iinet.net.au/~allholden/oz/horsetack/index.html - Cached - Similar
#2 | PR: - | Y! Links: 229,000 | Alexa: 8,707 | Business

Gainesville Equine Services & Horse Tack for Sale

Do this for all the keywords and then save the changes to your spreadsheet.

The keywords to target first are those with under 1000 title competition.

Our next step is to see if this is going to be worth our time.

5. Are there enough searches and is there low enough competition?

The next thing to do is check if there are enough searches and if there is low enough competition to be able to rank on the first page of Google quickly.

Getting on the first pages of Google is *extremely difficult*. Try to buy a (short) domain name with a keyword like "internet marketing" or "hypnosis" or "arthritis" and you will find it impossible. Most domain names with the most-searched keywords are all taken. There must be hundreds of websites with the word 'arthritis' in but when you Google 'arthritis' the majority of the websites shown on the first three pages do not even have the keyword in the domain name. Where are all the other websites? They have moved to the back of the high street where nobody ever goes! All the people who bought a domain name with the keyword

---

'arthritis' in, didn't make it to the top of Google. But there is hope. With my keyword research system, it is possible to rank highly in Google.

Go back to Market Samurai. On the last screen you were on, click "Export" in the bottom-right of the screen to save these results as a .csv file, to open in Microsoft Excel.

Opening this file will give you the following:

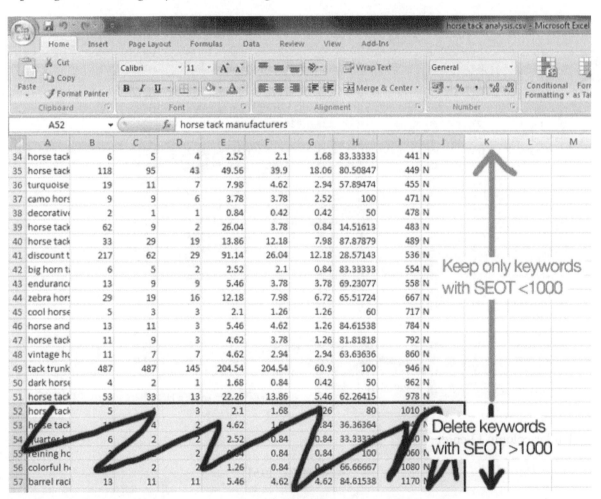

The spreadsheet above should say: " Keep only keywords with SEOT**C**<1000" and " Delete keywords with SEOT**C**>1000"

Because we're only interested in the keywords with fewer than 1000 competing titles (at least for now), delete everything with a competition of greater than 1000.

Now, column D contains the exact number of searches per day for each of the keywords.

We want to know the total amount of traffic we're going to get once we dominate these.

	A	B	C	D	E	F	G	H	I	J	K	L	M
28	horse tack	5	4	2	2.1	1.68	0.84	80	360 N				
29	barrel raci	398	118	79	167.16	49.56	33.18	29.64824	363 N				
30	horse sad	217	145	95	91.14	60.9	39.9	66.82028	371 N				
31	spanish h	9	6	5	3.78	2.52	2.1	66.66667	426 N				
32	draft hors	19	16	13	7.98	6.72	5.46	84.21053	431 N				
33	horse tack	29	24	19	12.18	10.08	7.98	82.75862	432 N				
34	horse tack	6	5	4	2.52	2.1	1.68	83.33333	441 N				
35	horse tack	118	95	43	49.56	39.9	18.06	80.50847	449 N				
36	turquoise	19	11	7	7.98	4.62	2.94	57.89474	455 N				
37	camo hors	9	9	6	3.78	3.78	2.52	100	471 N				
38	decorative	2	1	1	0.84	0.42	0.42	50	478 N				
39	horse tack	62	9	2	26.04	3.78	0.84	14.51613	483 N				
40	horse tack	33	29	19	13.86	12.18	7.98	87.87879	489 N				
41	discount t	217	62	29	91.14	26.04	12.18	28.57143	536 N				
42	big horn t	6	5	2	2.52	2.1	0.84	83.33333	554 N				
43	endurance	13	9	9	5.46	3.78	3.78	69.23077	558 N				
44	zebra hors	29	19	16	12.18	7.98	6.72	65.51724	667 N				
45	cool horse	5	3	3	2.1	1.26	1.26	60	717 N				
46	horse and	13	11	3	5.46	4.62	1.26	84.61538	784 N				
47	horse tack	11	9	3	4.62	3.78	1.26	81.81818	792 N				
48	vintage h	11	7	7	4.62	2.94	2.94	63.63636	860 N				
49	tack trunk	487	487	145	204.54	204.54	60.9	100	946 N				
50	dark horse	4	2	1	1.68	0.84	0.42	50	962 N				
51	horse tack	53	33	13	22.26	13.86	5						
52				=SUM(D2:D51)									

Add the total number of searches for all remaining keywords

Under column D enter

$$=SUM(D2-D51)$$

(Where we have entered 51, you would enter the row of your last keyword in the list)

This adds up all the searches and tells you exactly how many daily searches are being made for these keywords. In our case, this adds up to 705 exact searches per day, which is a number I'd be happy with.

Really, any number above 500 exact searches per day suggests a good candidate.

(Remember, these are the keywords we are likely to rank *easily* for to start getting traffic quickly - we will move onto the bigger keywords once we have taken over these).

Targeting the best, easiest keywords to begin with

Highlight the remaining keywords you have in Excel and press CTRL and C to copy.

Go back to Market Samurai and hit "Modify Keywords" at the bottom of your results.

At the next screen press "Clear" to erase everything and then paste your keywords from Excel into the "Add Keywords" box:

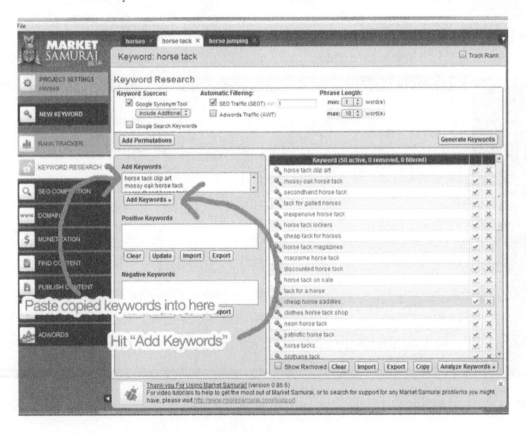

Press "Analyze Keywords" and, on the next screen, organise them by number of searches, keeping the same settings as used previously, but with SEO Traffic (SEOT) set to a minimum of one this time:

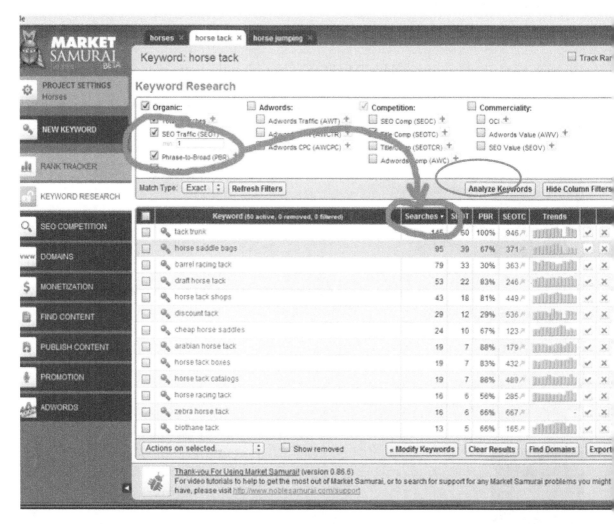

Right, now we have something to build a website around!

Judging competition for keyword

To start, you need to install SEO for Firefox. This is another search engine, like Google, which some people use. Visit www.firefox.com to download it. It is free. Also visit www.seobook.com and sign up for a free account. The guys running that website are seriously knowledgeable and you should read some of their material when you have a chance: it's brilliant.

Right, so download *SEO for Firefox* from SEOBook.com. When installed, right-click the icon in the bottom right of the Firefox window and select 'Options'.

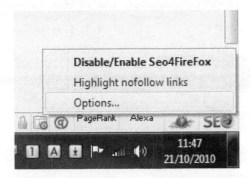

On the next screen press "Hide All", and then set PR, Alexa and Y! Links to "Automatic" - these are the three main things we need to know about our competition.

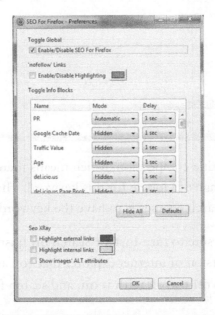

Now to check your competition.

Let's start with the highest searched-for keyword, with under 1000 title competition. Looking at our screenshot from Market Samurai, this is "tack trunk":

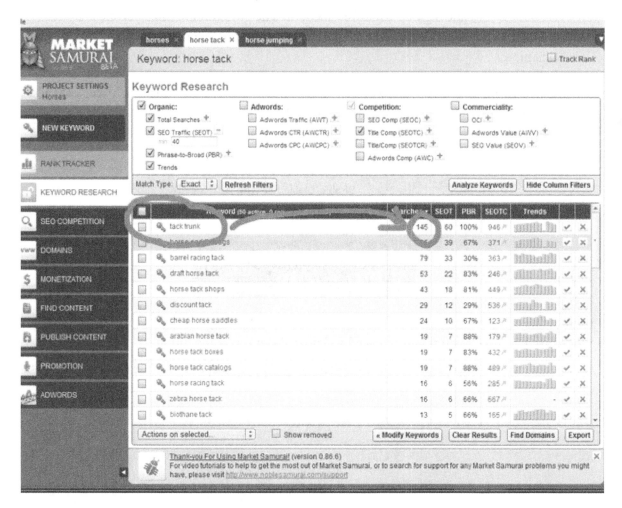

Now we know it has got low title competition, which means there aren't many sites actively trying to appear on the first page of Google for this keyword. The first thing you do when optimising your site for the search engines is to have the keyword in the title.

So we go to Google - making sure to turn Instant Search off (just google how to do this as it can vary depending on the version of internet explorer that you are using). **This is important: *SEO for Firefox* won't work with it on,** and search for *tack trunk*.

This gives us the following screen in Firefox:

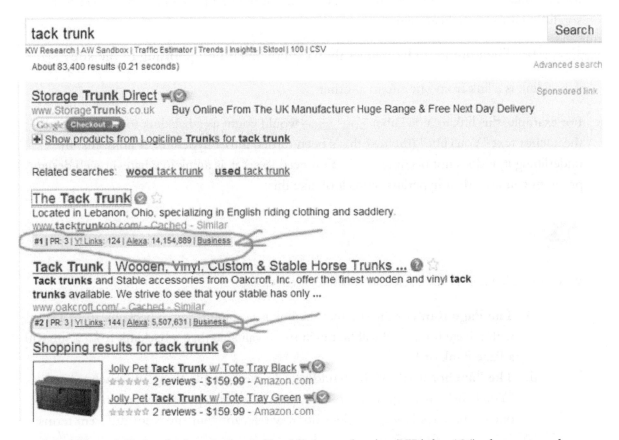

Underneath each listing is the number of backlinks to the site (Y!Links: 124), the page rank (PR:3) and the Alexa rank (Alexa : 14,154,889). The Alexa rank is a rank given to every website on the internet. It gives every website a rank based on the amount of visitors it receives. An Alexa rank of 1 would make your site the most-visited place on the whole internet. You can find the top 500 Alexa sites at www.alexa.com/topsites

Now, on this search result screen we need to pay special attention to a few things:

a) The average page rank of all the sites in the results

Page Rank (PR) is how much Google likes a website. It goes from 0 to 10 (10 being a handful of the biggest sites on the internet, such as Adobe, Google and Apple).

Your site will start with a PR 0 and will find it harder to appear in the first page of Google than a similar site with a higher PR. If all the sites on the first page have PR of over four you'll find it tough to beat them.

b) The number of backlinks that Yahoo! has found pointing to the site

A backlink is a link from one site to another.

For example, this link to YouTube: YouTube - would count as a backlink to that site, with the anchor text "YouTube" (the text that's been turned into a hyperlink or link). Just by underlining it, it does not become a link. You need to set it as a link in whatever web design program you use. Most hyperlink icons look like this:

When Google looks at the backlinks to a site, it checks:

c) **The Page Rank** of the site that the link is coming from - a backlink from a site with a Page Rank of 9 will be much more valuable than a backlink from a site with a Page Rank of 1.

d) **The "anchor text" of the backlink.** In the example above, the anchor text was "YouTube". It's important to understand the concept of anchor text because it's one of the ways Google decides on how relevant your site is for different terms.

A good analogy of how this works is to think of all the sites competing for a keyword as politicians trying to get elected into Parliament or Congress. Each backlink is a vote for that candidate. Google would look at my link to YouTube above and say "okay, this counts as one vote for YouTube.com to be top of the search results for the keyword *YouTube*".

The winning candidate will be the one with the overall highest number of votes (there are other factors that also decide on the search result listings, but this is a good start).

e) The kind of pages that show up.

It's a good sign if you can see Yahoo! Answers pages, or sites with just that keyword in the domain (like "http://www.horse-tacks.com") because it shows it's possible to rank highly with a bit of SEO work.

If you see any Web 2.0 sites (like Squidoo, Wordpress, Blogger) listed on the first page then that's also a good sign.

It's also good if the first page is full of sites that have a PR of between 0 and 3, and some of them don't have the keyword in the title and they've got a low number of backlinks. More about backlinks later in the book.

There are a number of other keyword tools available, so it is a case of finding one that you like. Examples of other tools:

> www.goodkeywords.com
> www.soovle.com = to get ideas for long tail keywords
> www.wordpot.com
> www.wordtracker.com RECOMMENDED
> www.wordstream.com
> www.keyworddiscovery.com
> www.hittail.com
> www.keywordspy.com
> www.micronichefinder.com
> www.ppcwebspy.com
> www.senuke.com is another keyword tool but is expensive, as it has lots of other
> features built in. Their keyword research is based on www.wordtracker.com
> www.seohat.com
> www.webnaster-toolkit.com

6. Will your new niche actually make you any money?

Now that you have decided that it is possible to rank in Google with your niche, you need to check if there are products available for you to make money. We need to, at this stage, quickly check five things and later in this book these five will be explained in more detail as I show you how to put them on your site. The reason I need to mention this now is to find out if there is money to be made. If there are no affiliate products available at all, it might be a good idea to start investigating a new niche.

The five most important money making points to look at are:

a. How much can you earn with Adsense?

b. Are there relevant CPA (Click Per Action) Offers available in your niche?

c. Are there relevant Clickbank products available?

d. Are there Amazon products available in your niche?

e. Are there other good affiliate schemes available in your niche?

a. How much can you earn with Adsense?

You've probably seen Google AdSense all over the internet. It really is a very simple concept:

- You sign up here: www.Google.com/adsense/
- Google will give you a code that you place on every page on which you want ads displayed
- This code examines the page it's on and then Google shows ads that are relevant to the content
- When someone clicks on one of those links, you get paid... simple!

To find out how much you could potentially earn per click, you need to go to the Google AdWords tool here:

https://adwords.Google.com/select/KeywordPlanner

Enter your niche into the box and select "all countries" (or whatever country it is that you're targeting), and also "Only show ideas containing my search terms".

Hit "Search".

When it's loaded click the button marked "Columns" and select "Estimated Avg. CPC" and then sort your results by this.

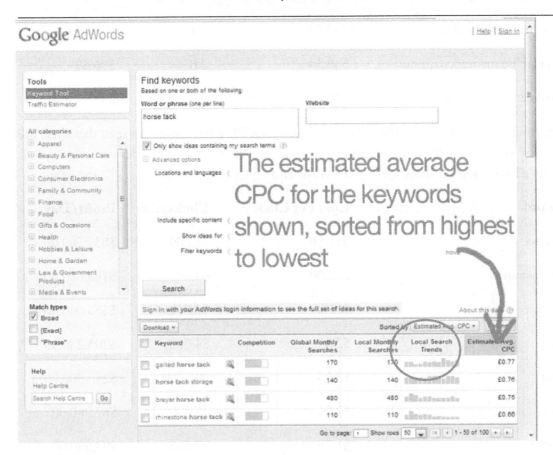

This will give you a list of the keywords that offer you the highest payout on AdSense. The "Estimated Avg. CPC" is the estimated amount that you would earn per click on your AdSense ads, so is the amount Google will pay into your account each time somebody clicks on one of your ads. AdSense needs to be placed on pages that are well optimised for one keyword. **If AdSense can't decide exactly what your content is then the ads will be irrelevant to your site, meaning no-one will click them and you won't earn anything.**

Here are a few examples of VERY profitable Adsense keywords. The amounts next to the keywords are the payout for Adsense per click, and the number next to this is the number of clicks expected per day.

Keyword	Cost Per Click	Clicks/day	Profit/Day
Auto insurance quotes Florida	$57.00	0.1	$ 0.00

Audio conference calling	$55.32	0.1	$ 0.00
Universal life insurance quote	$48.34	2.0	$96.68
Consolidate college loans	$45.09	0.5	$ 0.00

Okay, you can see that the payout is very high per click BUT have you also seen that there are hardly any visitors per day. So you can only earn a very small amount per day or nothing at all. Now let's have a look at these lists of keywords and CPC:

Keyword	Cost Per Click	Clicks/day	Profit/Day
Insurance	$17.50	49,000	$857,500.00
Auto insurance	$29.00	6400	$185,600.00
Mortgage	$13.00	12,000	$156,000.00
Hotel	$2.40	84,700	$203,280.00
Acting	$2.25	106,000	$238,500.00
Computers	$2.06	33,000	$67,980.00
Furniture	$1.70	57,400	$97,580.00

See the difference in the last column Profit Per Day? Of course you do. The lesson to remember here is that it is a combination of expected clicks per day AND Cost Per Click that is going to make you a lot of money. Finding a keyword that is expensive and pays you a lot of money per click is worth zero, nothing, if nobody clicks on it. You need to find the keyword that pays a lot per click AND has a reasonable number of visitors per day.

Figures are rounded up and were correct at the time of printing, but are likely to change.

See the $29.00 per click for Auto insurance? This means that if the insurance company advertising with Adwords only receives 3% clicks, it will cost them $ 5568 or £3461(6400 searches per day x 3% = 192 x $29.00) per day to be on the top of Google Adwords !

The next thing you need to do is find products that will make you money either to send to your list for email marketing or to put on your website. This is very important because once you have built a website and you start building your lists, you need to have available products to send to your list. Don't worry if you do not understand this at the moment, it will become clear later in the book. All you need to remember for now is that you HAVE to find products that you can make money with otherwise it is better to find a new niche and start your initial niche-research again. Without money-making affiliate products, you will not make any money.

b. Are there relevant CPA offers available in your niche?

If you've not promoted CPA offers before, don't worry, they're very straight-forward. CPA stands for "cost per action" and basically means you get paid for every visitor that performs a certain task.

For example:

You could promote a link to a page that asks people to enter their email address into a box. Every time someone clicks on your link and fills in their email address, you get paid.

You will have seen graphics like these, which are CPA offers. The website owner earns money when somebody does the required action via the link.

When the visitor takes a free trial or fills in their email address, you will get paid. In the "Get a quote" example, when the visitor requests a quote, you get paid.

Why are companies prepared to pay you just to give them a potential customer? Targeted customers or targeted traffic refers to people who are looking for specific information on the internet. If somebody types in "how to lose weight" they are a targeted customer in the 'losing weight' niche. Targeted potential customers are very important to any company, whether the companies are online or not. This is why companies spend fortunes on exhibitions, flash brochures, sales people and so on. Most medium to large companies employ sales guys with flash cars and flash mobile phones to go and visit people who are interested in what they are selling. The majority of potential customers visited by these sales people will not buy immediately. Salesmen will follow up with a sale call as a second attempt to try to convince them to buy the product. You probably had those annoying sales calls yourself. Professional sales people who go on the road are very expensive for a company. Companies have to pay their wages, sales commission and expenses. But in order to find targeted customers or customers that are interested in what they are selling, it is very often money well spent. Without those expensive sales people, there would be no targeted customers to turn into buyers.

The same happens online. But it has now become a lot cheaper for companies to find targeted customers. That's why companies are prepared to pay you money if you give them an interested potential customer. You put their CPA-offers on your site, they receive targeted customers and it costs them nothing to put it on your site. Instead of having a few expensive sales people, who can visit a maximum of say five potential customers per day, they can have thousands of websites with their CPA offers on. Instead of the sales people calling to try to sell products, targeted customers are sent emails with the products for sale. It is a lot less expensive. This is one of the reasons why exhibitions and expensive sales people are becoming less popular for companies, because the internet is a much cheaper place to get targeted customers.

I hope now you understand what CPA-offers are and how they work.

To find what CPA offers are available on all the different networks, visit www.offervault.com and search for your niche. The first place you should check when searching for CPA offers in your niche is www.offervault.com. Think of it as a huge offer-directory, listing all the offers available on the majority of all the CPA networks. Once you find something you like, sign up with the host network and start marketing the offer!

 You may have to be a little broader to find something here - searching for "horse tacks" found nothing, but searching for "horse" gave the following results:

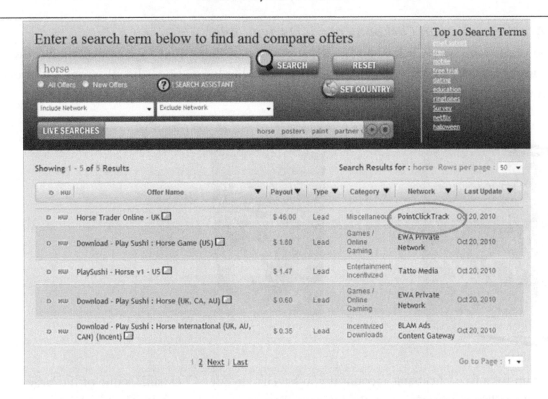

The name under the 'Network' column is the affiliate network you have to sign up to, in order to be able to promote the offer. The affiliate network will give you your code to put on your site.

The Horse Trader Online CPA offer has a $46 payout, which is a great one to promote because you know anyone looking for horse tacks is going to have a horse (forgive me for stating the obvious!).

Don't worry about understanding everything at this stage. We will go into exactly how to put these elements on your site later in this book.

All you need to do at the moment is to check www.offervault.com to see if there are CPA offers available in your niche. If there are no offers, it does not necessarily mean that you cannot build your website. It only means you will not earn any money from CPA-offers.

c. Are there relevant Clickbank products available?

You've probably seen Clickbank eBooks before on websites. They look something like the picture below. When you click on the picture of the book, you go to the sales page and order form at the bottom of the sales page.

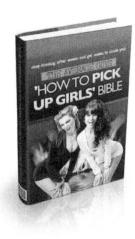

Sign up for a free Clickbank account if you haven't already. Clickbank is one of the largest digital product marketplaces on the internet. Sign up at www.Clickbank.com. You might as well sign up now because if you are serious about making money on the web, you cannot ignore Clickbank and, as a beginner, you will find it fantastic.

For now, all you need to do is to find out if there are Clickbank products available to put on your site to sell. Later in the book I will show you which other websites are good to use and how to get your affiliate code from Clickbank to put on your site. Even if there are no products available on Clickbank, that does not mean that the niche you are planning to build is not a good one. We can put other affiliate links on, or you can write your own eBook and put it on your site. I strongly recommend to put an affiliate ebook on **each** site as you can earn a lot of money with them.

To find out if there are Clickbank products available, follow these steps:

- Log into your account. You can also visit the 'Market Place' without having an account but you won't be able to grab your affiliate link.

- Go to 'Market Place'

- Choose your niche category and browse to see if there are products available.

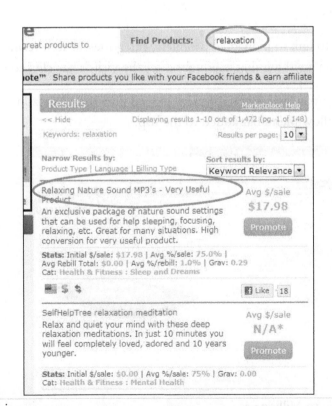

- That's all you need to do for now.- remember the only thing that we are doing now is checking availability. You have seen that there are products available at a reasonable payout each time you sell a product.

The following websites are free resources that give a goldmine of information for Clickbank products:

www.cb-analytics.com

www.CBEngine.com

www.CBTrends.com

But don't worry about this now, I will discuss these later.

d. Are there Amazon products available in my niche?

Amazon has a great affiliate scheme, offering a commission of around from 3% to 8.5 % on all its products.

It allows you to link to individual products, categories, search results and more, and get commission on anything that is bought after the visitor has clicked on your link!

On every page you visit (once you have logged into your Amazon Associates Account) you will see the follow menu bar added to the top:

Clicking "Link to this page" will give you your affiliate link for whatever you're viewing. This means that if anyone clicks your affiliate link and then happens to buy something from Amazon, you'll get commission (even if it wasn't the original item you linked them to).

e. Are there other good affiliate schemes for your website?

Search for *"your niche" + affiliates* on Google and find sites in your niche that offer affiliate schemes. This way you can find products that may not be available anywhere else, and that are highly targeted to your audience. These affiliate networks all work on the same basis: you choose the product that could sell in your niche, get an affiliate link and put that link on your website.

Some examples of other places to find affiliate products to promote:

> www.affiliatefirst.com
> www.affiliateguide.com/residual.html - list of recurring commissions
> www.affiliateprograms.com
> www.affiliatescout.com
> www.affiliatewindow.com RECOMMENDED
> www.associateprograms.com is a directory of affiliate programmes
> www.cj.com (commission junction) RECOMMENDED
> www.ebaypartnernetwork.com
> www.lifetimecommissions.com - list of recurring commissions
> www.linkshare.com RECOMMENDED
> www.paydotcom.com
> www.shareasale.com RECOMMENDED

- If you have decided to buy www.marketsamurai.com. you can look under commercialization to find products to promote
- Or simply search for "your keyword" + "affiliate"
- Or search for your keyword and see who is ranked on the first page. Open each site and scroll down to the bottom of the pages. Companies that are looking for affiliates will have (usually at the bottom of the pages) words like: "Make money with us" or "affiliates click here" or "referrals commissions"

You don't have to put all the monetisation elements discussed in this book on your site. For some sites, you can just use Adsense, CPA offers and affiliate links. www.costhelper.com is a good example of this and the webmaster had done a great job putting affiliate links on this site combined with lots of content.

Top Tip: Always make sure – wherever possible – that you make your affiliate pages open in a new browser page in order to keep your website open. Once visitors click on one of your links they are unlikely to go back to your site. This really is very important as the longer your website stays open the more chance there is that people will click on one of your links.

Part 5. Creating Your Site

Now that you have investigated your niche, found a good niche with good money-making potential and done your keyword research, it is time to build your website.

You will **NOT** earn a lot of money if your sites look like this: www.soulwax.com/2007/

> **First of all, have a look at how NOT to design a website: www.webpagesthatsuck.com and make sure that you are never listed on this site** ☺

1. How to design your site

When you have found your niche and you have concluded that it is a good niche where people will spend money and where there are products available to use as commercial links, it is important to know that there are three ways to deliver products or services that we will sell.

a) **Digital**. The goods are delivered online, with immediate access. Examples are: eBooks, MP3s, audio files, streaming videos. We will focus on selling eBooks.

b) **Physical**. The goods are posted or shipped to the buyer. The buyer does not have immediate access but prefers physical products. Examples are hard copy books, DVDs, audio CD. We will focus on selling books and DVDs from Amazon.

c) **Experimental.** The visitor can attend seminars, webinars, conference calls, receive email mini courses and more.

Instead of using one delivery method we will have all three on our website. We will sell eBooks (a) on our website. The buyer can also buy the physical book or CDs (b). The buyer can also opt-in for an email mini course (c) or we will find Affiliate Products with webinars(c).

Three birds with one stone!

If we get 10,000 visitors to our website, there is no way of knowing which type of product they like to buy: a), b) or c). So we will make sure that every type of buyer can buy from our website and we will give the buyer some extra information on the way.

We will build our site with the free Wordpress software - don't worry, it's easy to install, and I'll show you how.

If you'd rather use a different program to create your websites then here are some good ones. Some of these are templates, some are software programs and others are 'drag and drop' websites.

- **Serif Webplus** - www.serif.com/webplus RECOMMENDED. If you can use word or any design program, you can use Webplus. It is WYSIWYG (What You See Is What You Get) based software. If you can work with Coreldraw or Quark Xpress (design software), you can also use Webplus with ease. You can buy it from www.amazon.com

- **Microsoft Expression Web 3** - www.microsoft.com/expression RECOMMENDED, ideal for designing one-page-sales wonders. You can also buy it from www.amazon.com

- **Weebly** - www.weebly.com. Recommended for Newbies. This is a very easy platform for designing your website. Hosting is free if you are happy with a URL like this : www.yourkeywordhere.weebly.com or you can pay for hosting and choose your domain name. With Weebly you can create free websites and blogs. It is a very easy click and drag interface and I highly recommend it.

- **Homewebsitecenter** - www.homewebsitecenter.com A great website. Here you can have your own website with an eBook to sell in three easy steps. Simply fill in your PayPal address and your website is ready. There are several upgrades possible but even with the completely free version, your website is created in under five minutes. Simply drive traffic to your site and start earning money. Highly recommended for newbies who want to test driving traffic to a site and not worry about ranking in Google. The paid version gives you a bunch of website statistics as well.

- **Moonfruit** - www.moonfruit.com Drag and drop website building.

- **Webs** : www.webs.com

- **Artisteer** - www.artisteer.com

- **Free Website Templates** - www.freewebsitetemplates.com

- **Kompozer** - www.kompozer.net

- **Instant Site Launcher** - www.instantsitelauncher.com

- **90 Second Website Builder** - www.90-second-website-builder.com Drag and drop website building
- **Mrsite** – www.mrsite.com
- **4 templates** - www.4templates.com

If you're not good at creating your own images and logos, then here are some places where you can get someone else to do them for you:

- www.20dollarbanner.com Get any website banner done for just $20
- www.designgururyan.com A great graphics designer
- www.domydesignstuff.com Another great graphics designer

I am not going to go too deep into discussing web design, as that could take up an entire book all by itself. There are, however, a few important things that you should remember when designing your site. Here are my top design rules:

1. **Use graphics sparingly** - In 2009, only 63.5% of online United States households had a broadband connection. The other 36.5% were accessing the web through dial-up modems. Graphics (such as pictures and charts) take a long time to load. If you use heavy graphics, that take a long time to load, you can lose one third of your potential customers because they will lose patience and move to another site. The graph below shows that there are still a lot of households with low speed connections. You can check the speed of your broadband, if you are in the UK, at www.broadbandspeedchecker.co.uk **or** www.speedtest.net **or** www.ozspeedtest.com

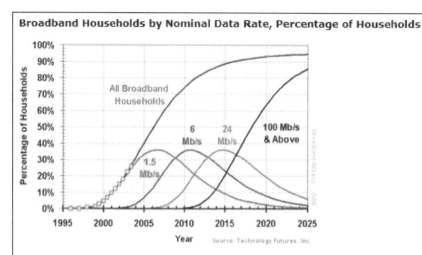

Broadband Households by Nominal Data Rate, Percentage of Households

This figure shows TFI's basic forecast of broadband penetration (from all providers) and the migration from one generation to another. By 2010, about 75% of U.S. households will have broadband service, and about 12% of households will subscribe to very high-speed broadband (at least 24 Mb/s).

2. **Avoid using moving images and streaming video** - These can also seriously limit the speed at which your website loads. These slow loading times can cause visitors to leave your site before they've even read any of your content.

   You can check the speed of your website with YSLOW from Yahoo! Yslow analyzes web pages and suggests ways to improve their performance. For more information go to http://developer.yahoo.com/yslow/

3. **Nobody likes side-scrolling** - Keep your website suitable for 1024 x 768 screen dimensions and you'll ensure that over 96% of people can see all of your content without annoying side-scroll bars. If you go any larger than that, there will be visitors who have to scroll left and right. The 800 x 600 resolution, which was the standard a few years ago, is almost non existent now. You will be able to set your screen size in your web design software.

   The table below shows the best screen resolution size to design a website:

Date	Higher	1024×768	800×600	640×480	Unknown
January 2009	57%	36%	4%	0%	3%
January 2008	38%	48%	8%	0%	6%

January 2007	26%	54%	14%	0%	6%
January 2006	17%	57%	20%	0%	6%
January 2005	12%	53%	30%	0%	5%
January 2004	10%	47%	37%	1%	5%
January 2003	6%	40%	47%	2%	5%
January 2002	6%	34%	52%	3%	5%
January 2001	5%	29%	55%	6%	5%
January 2000	4%	25%	56%	11%	4%

Source : www.stayonsearch.com

4. **Don't use Flash elements**. Flash (Adobe Flash) is a multimedia platform and to create animation video and activity on web pages. It is very often used for advertisements and games. Google can't understand Flash and so won't know what your website is about. This will be a real problem when you start trying to get on page one of the search results. A person who does not have Adobe Flash Player installed will not be able to see your site. Although sometimes Flash can look great, flashing elements can put people off.

Flash ain't cash!
---

5. **Don't have music that plays automatically** - Your music taste will not be the same as everyone else's. If you really *must* have music on your site then make sure it's easy for your visitors to turn 'off' or 'on' as they require. Make sure that you use royalty free music, or you'll have to pay for the rights.

6. **Include lots of internal links** - Have links to your other pages at the top, left and bottom of the page because Google likes this.

7. **KISS** Remember to KISS, which stands for: Keep It Simple, Stupid. Ugly and earning money is better than beautiful and earning nothing. The key to web design is simplicity, not sophistication and overload. Don't try to look like an internet giant, instead focus on what makes you money.

8. **Low resolution pictures** – if you do use pictures on your website, make sure that you use low resolution images as otherwise they will take too long to load and people will get bored and leave. Most software programs now have an option "save for web" to save a picture.

9. **Low resolution videos** – if you do use videos on your website, make sure that you use low resolution ones as otherwise they will take too long to load.

10. **Your font size should be minimum 12pt.** Remember that your visitors can be of all ages and older people often even find size 12 a bit too small to read. Some analysts say that font size 14pt is better. Try it and test it.

11. **Use a standard font:** the best fonts for the web are Arial, Verdana, Calibri and Tahoma. If you use unusual fonts and your visitor does not have that font on their computer, they will not be able to read the text very well.

12. **Add to Cart** Check-out buttons convert better than 'Buy Now' or 'Order Now' buttons.

13. Be clear. Your visitors must see in **the first few seconds** what the site is all about.

14. **Put the opt-in box above the fold**. 'Above the fold' is the first thing people see when the webpage opens. When a visitor scrolls down, they are then looking at "below the fold". Important headlines should always be above the fold. I also recommend putting an opt-in box above the fold.

15. **The 'above the fold' screen.** The first screen visitors see is your website's prime selling space and what you put on it can determine your success. Don't make it "overcrowded".

16. **Make sure a link is a link.** Only underline text if it is a link. Don't underline to emphasise text otherwise people might not click your money-making links. Make sure that a visitor can clearly see what is clickable and what isn't. The standard is to underline clickable links. You could change the colour of the links, too.

17. **Leave enough white space on each page.** Pages that look too busy are abandoned very quickly and your chance of making money is gone.

18. **Don't put thousands of words of text without any sub headers**. Use sub headers and bullet points wherever possible. Visitors will not read every word on your site but they will scan through it and read what interests them.

19. **Text must be easy to read.** No green text on a green and red floral background please.

20. **No white text on black background.** Research has shown that a lot of people do not like white text on a dark coloured background. Older people especially and people with impaired vision find it hard to read. Stick to black text on a white background, as people are used to reading it.

21. **No welcome/intro pages or Flash pages.** I have never understood why somebody would want intro pages on their site. They say "enter". Euhh! Yes of course I want to see your site, that's why I clicked on it. Duh!

22. Check your text for **spelling mistakes.** Get friends to proof read it as you are unlikely to see your own mistakes.

23. **Don't use lots of colours** on your site or non-matching colours. Below is a chart that interior designers use. The same rules for interior design apply for websites: it all has to be pleasing to the eye and have a cosy and comfortable feel. The rule from the wheel below is: opposite colours are complementary colours. Colours that are next to each other should never be seen together. Google "colour chart" to see the colours.

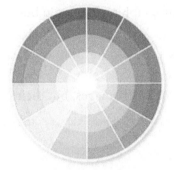

TOP TIP: Don't build a website full of pop-ups, flashing images and moving graphics. Research has shown that people immediately leave sites like these and, on top of that, Google cannot see the fancy stuff on your site so it is better to use the space for content.

Do not try to please yourself by building marvellous-looking sites. Instead please yourself with the money you will earn by putting decent content and lots of money-making links on your site.

Make sure that ALL the pictures, music and videos that you use are royalty free. There are institutions out there who only try to find websites that use non-royalty free products. You might get a letter in the post one day with a heavy fine if you do not abide by the royalty free rules. The consequences could be huge and result in a lawsuit.

For that reason you should always either buy stock photos or stock images, or make sure you use images that are under the Commercial Commons licence (i.e. royalty free). Stock images are pictures on stock photo websites to be used or bought by other people. Usually you are required to provide a link to the source where you got the picture from, but read the terms and conditions of the site.

Use these sites for royalty free photographs and videos:

- www.sxc.hu The images under "results for" are free to use and royalty free. The images under "Premium result for" are payable.

- www.INeedAGreatStory.com Royalty free stories, videos and infographics. Here you buy credits to allow you to buy content.
- www.gettyimages.com They have a HUGE range of stock photos you can buy, but can be expensive.
- www.dreamstime.com This site also contains a massive amount of stock images, but their prices are slightly cheaper.
- www.bigstockphoto.com
- www.dreamstime.com
- www.fotalia.com
- www.istockphoto.com
- www.publicdomainpictures.net
- www.shutterstock.com

- www.flickr.com Search for images with the Creative Commons licence. These images can be used legally, and freely on your site (although may sometimes require a credit).

To search for images go to the Flickr Advanced Search and check the box next to "Only search within Creative Commons-licensed content" and then search as normal:

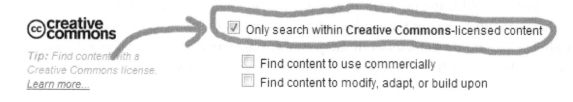

For royalty free music clips :
- www.royaltyfreemusic.com
- www.shockwave-sound.com
- www.slicktracks.com

TOP TIP : A photograph of yourself on your site lets people know that you are a real person. If you don't like your own photograph you can always create an avatar: www.sitepal.com (not free), www.cartoonyourworld.com, www.mywebface.com

---

A website must look and feel good for the visitor, and they must immediately have a good impression when landing on your site.

You never have a second chance to make a good first impression.

---

2. Choosing the domain name

At this point you should have chosen your niche and have a list of the keywords you're going to target (both the small easy ones and the slightly harder ones). Before you can start developing your site, you need to get a domain name and hosting.

A domain name is very important. The domain name www.insurance.com was sold for 35.6 million dollars. This was only for the domain name not for the content of the site. *Source : www.enbeeone3.com*

Here are some tips regarding the choice of your domain name.

1. ALWAYS ALWAYS get a domain name with the keyword in that you want to target. This is VERY important for ranking purposes. Everybody likes their own name (almost everybody) or the name of their company but calling a website www.JohnSmith.com or www.SmithAssociates.com if your site is about furniture does not give Google any clues that your site is about furniture. Your domain name is one of the first things Google looks at to rank your site.

I always go for domains that contain the name of the niche and, unless it doesn't make any sense, use plurals. In our horse tacks example I would probably buy a domain like:

- horsetacksreview.com
- horse-tacks.com
- thehorsetackshop.com

The reason I use plurals is because Google places emphasis on the keywords in the domain name. If the domain name has the phrase "horse tacks" in it, Google will assume it's about horse tacks.

By putting a plural in there you will rank for both "horse tack" (you'll see it in the search results highlighted like this: horsetacks) and "horse tacks". Adding "shop" to the end of a domain name is a sneaky way of still getting the plural keyword in there (highlighted in Google search results as horsetackshop).

2. I recommend that you buy your own domain name (not use a free one like yourkeyword@weebly.com). It is more professional and you have ownership and control if say you want to sell it.

3. Put your keyword or key phrase at the beginning of the domain name, not at the end. If you keyword is "dog food in bulk" www.bulkfoodfordogs.com is an okay domain name. But this one is a much better one: www.dogfoodinbulk.com

4. Domain names with model numbers in them are a good idea if there are enough searches for a certain model number e.g. www.Hobie16Catamaran.com , www.RemoteControlHelicopters107g.com, etc…

S107G is a model number for a remote control helicopter. By using the plural helicopters in the domain name Google will see it as helicopters **and** as the model number S107G. If the domain name would have been www.S107GRemoteControlHelicopter.com, the domain name would not rank so well for helicopters (plural) as a keyword. The important message to remember here is: always try and put as many keywords as possible in your domain name.

5. Whatever domain name you choose, always check out the legalities. Some, such as Twitter, Facebook, Apple, iPad, iPod, Olympic are trademarks and cannot be used in your domain name. You don't want to spend a lot of time building a website only to have to take it down

later due to trademark infringement. You can search for "keyword+brandprotection" or "keyword+registered trademarks" to find out more information.

6. You could even use common misspelled words as domain names.

7. It is always best to buy the .com or .uk or .org domain names (or the extension of whatever country you are in) ahead of .net domain names. I suggest that you don't buy extensions like .biz or .us or .info as these are used a lot by spam websites so search engines and visitors often ignore them.

If you have a shop that only supplies goods in your country or you have a site that only supplies services in your country, it is best to have a domain suffix from your country such as .co.uk or .fr or .nl.

8. Avoid hyphens. However, if your keyword is not available without hyphens, it is better to buy a domain name with hyphens than to have no keyword in the domain. One reason I try to avoid hyphens is when somebody types in your domain and forgets to type the hyphens, they will go to your competitor's sites. Another reason is that Google will probably think that the domain name without hyphens is older, as domains with hyphens only started to appear when the domains without hyphens were already taken.

9. Make it easy to remember.

10. Make it easy to understand –never have to think about how to spell your domain name.

11. Make it easy to say in your head, and anybody else's head.

12. If possible, make it easy to understand and read for the non-English or non-American people who visit your site.

13. Make sure you don't make your domain name too long, such as www. howtolooseweightreallyfastandeasy.com.

14. Make it easy to read in the browser bar. Letters l and i next to each other are difficult to read : ilillili. So are the letters m, n and r: mrnmrn. A vowel at the end of a word and at the beginning of the next word is often difficult to read.

15. Definitely avoid double "e" e.g. www.largeenamellockets.com

16. Avoid two letters the same next to each other. As if someone forgets to type in one letter, they might end up on your competitor's site and never get to yours. Sometimes two letters the same next to each other also makes it difficult to read. I usually type my domain names in MsWord and underline them. That way, you can see how people see it when it appears underlined as a link and decide if it is easy to read.

17. Make sure that you choose "auto renew" when buying a domain name otherwise, if you don't pay attention at renewal time and forget to renew it, it could be gone. You should get an e-mail as a reminder for renewal but just in case you miss the email, your domain name will still be renewed.

18.If the main keywords are already taken as a domain name and you want to use "guide" or "training" after your keyword and that is also taken, use a similar word. I suggest you type in "guide" and "training" in the online thesaurus to see which other words you could use.

If you are not very creative and need some help, visit www.squadhelp.com to receive 200+ suggestions for your domain – at a small fee.

The following websites all have different tools to help you create a domain name :

www.123finder.com

www.bustaname.com

www.domaintyper.com

www.nameboy.com

www.namestation.com

www.savespell.com

www.shoutdomains.com

www.stuckdomains.com

You can check if your domain name is available here. You can also buy domain names here:

www.123-reg.co.uk

www.1and1.com RECOMMENDED

www.checkdomain.com

www.godaddy.com RECOMMENDED

www.namecheap.com

www.register.com

www.ukreg.com RECOMMENDED

For a video on how to buy a domain name and set up hosting with GoDaddy, visit www.VideosNewbieBook.com.

3. Hosting

You can buy a domain name from one company and have the hosting done by another company. Personally I prefer to use the company I bought my domain from to do the hosting as well.

If you have an Australian website and you are targeting a market in Australia, it is always best to choose a hosting company with an Australian server. If you are based in USA, choose a hosting company with a USA based server and so on. This can be important for search engine ranking purposes.

I've always used GoDaddy (www.godaddy.com) and 1and1 (www.1and1.com) for my hosting. If you're still looking for a hosting provider then I recommend www.godaddy.com, especially if you make mostly Wordpress-based websites.

Generally I prefer www.1and1.com because I like their platform better than GoDaddy's and in my experience they have better customer services, which you can contact late during weekdays and also on weekends. Each time I have phoned 1and1 with a problem, I had an immediate answer, but I cannot say the same for GoDaddy.

Another advantage of www.1and1.com is that you can have almost unlimited free emails for each domain name, if you choose the business option. With GoDaddy you only get *one* email account but you can purchase more.

However, for Wordpress sites, I have come across some problems with www.1and1.com and therefore www.godaddy.com is recommended if you are planning to use Wordpress.

Here some other reliable hosting companies:

www.hostgator.com

www.hostmonster.com

www.justhost.com

4. Buying an old domain

Google loves old websites. It views them as more reliable and will put them on the first page on the search results much more rapidly than it would a new domain.

If you have money to invest ($15 upwards) then you can purchase a domain that has expired from the GoDaddy auctions - doing this has worked very well for me in the past.

Where to buy domains:

- GoDaddy - www.godaddy.com search for auctions.
- NameBoy - You can enter words you're looking for in a domain and it will give you a list of both old and new domains available - www.nameboy.com
- 123-Reg - www.123-reg.co.uk
- 1and1 - www.1and1.com
- Namecheap – www.namecheap.com

5. Buying a complete, ready made site

It's possible to buy complete, ready made websites with all the graphics, domain name and content already completed. Check the website content is 100% original because Google doesn't like copied material.

Complete sites can be purchased from as little as $90 from www.Flippa.com , which is an auction site, similar to eBay, where you can buy domains and websites instead of physical goods.

Places to purchase full websites:

- www.flippa.com Domain and website auction site
- www.sedo.com : for domains that are already receiving traffic

There are a few important things to mention if you are thinking of buying an old domain or a readymade website.

- Try to buy a domain name with your keyword in.
- Never buy a domain name that was related to adult content or gambling. You can check this with www.archive.org and type the domain next to 'waybackmachine'. This will give you a list of dates where you can see what the domain looked like on that date.
- Make sure the domain name does not contain any words that are a trademark.
- If the domain name is already listed in DMOZ (a huge database of human-added websites) and Yahoo directory, that is good because Google likes websites listed in these.
- Search the site for popularity. Go to www.alexa.com and type in the domain name. This will give you the number of visitors and some traffic figures.
- In Google type: "info:www.domainnamehere.com". Google will give you some information about the site. Try to find how many pages are indexed by Google. The more pages that are indexed, the better.
- In Google type: "link:www.domainnamehere.com". Google will show you the links the domain has.
- You can type in the domain at http://siteexplorer.search.yahoo.com and Yahoo will show you the domain's links.

> **TOP TIP: Try to design your own website so you are always in control. You do not need an expensive web design company that charges you $35.00 per month to maintain your site and hosting. They charge you silly web design prices and each time you want a tiny change made to your site, it will cost you money again.**

6. Installing Wordpress and setting up the site

Please visit www.VideosNewbieBook.com to get access to a video on how to install Wordpress on a site.

I use Wordpress for a lot of my sites because everything is straight forward and it is completely FREE. You can update the content at the click of a button, add a number of plugins to make it do anything you want and it's instantly SEO friendly (optimised with keywords for the search engines) straight out of the box.

I use the following Wordpress Themes (a theme is a certain look for a website with built in design and site options): Church, Thesis, TwentyTen, Neoclassical, Convergence, Lifestyle, Concept X, LifestyleChild, ProSense….. nothing extremely fancy or special. There are free themes and payable themes.

Installing Wordpress on www.godaddy.com couldn't be easier, as you are about to see.

Once you've set up your hosting account with GoDaddy, go to

http://hostingmanager.secureserver.net

and log in using your account details.

You'll find yourself on this screen in www.godaddy.com :

Clicking on the highlighted "Your Applications" will take you to the GoDaddy applications installer:

Search for, or click on "Wordpress", and then hit the "Install" button on the next page:

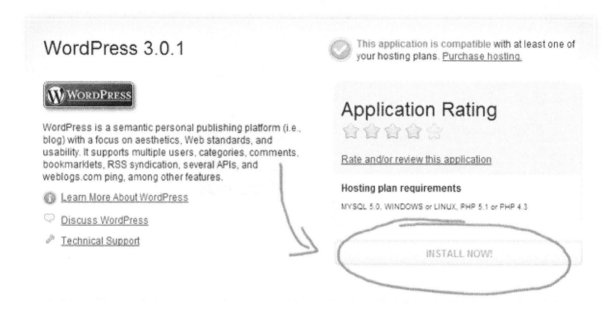

Follow the on-screen instructions to set up Wordpress on your recently purchased domain.

For database description use "[whatever the domain name is] Wordpress"

For the database password use something you'll remember easily.

When asked what folder to install it into, leave the box blank to install into the root directory

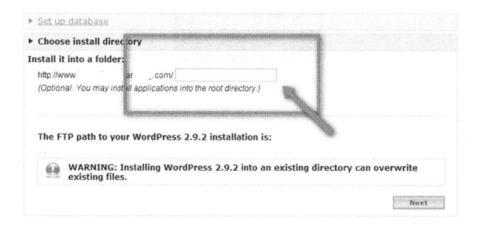

Set the email as your main email address, and the titles for them as the domain name (i.e. if your site is called horsetacks.com, enter "Horse Tacks").

Username: admin

Password: [set a password]

Then click "Finish"!

Once it's installed go to *http://www.yourdomain.com/wp-admin* and log in with the account details you set when you installed.

Setting it up

Adding Plugins

A plugin is a small piece of software that adds extra functions to your Wordpress site. They are easy to install and there is a huge library of them to choose from.

Below is a list of the most important plugins you need to install, and what they do.

To begin, click "Add New" under the plugins tab, on the left of your screen.

On the next screen, search for, and install:

a) All in One SEO Pack

This is a free plugin from Wordpress. Search the plugin database for it and it will allow you to:

- Add your own custom titles to each page and post, and
- Add the right meta-keywords for each page and post,

as well as offering a few other exciting pieces. Trust me, download it!

b) StatPress

This is a really simple site analytics program. It's no-where near as advanced as Google Analytics, but it'll tell you where your most recent visitors came from, what they searched for, how many visitors you should expect in a month and so on. It is really useful for checking your stats on-the-fly.

c) Easy Privacy Policy

If you're planning on putting AdSense on your site then a good privacy policy is one of the Google requirements.

d) SEO Smart Links

Automatically sets chosen phrases as links. This is great for SEO purposes and to help users navigate around your site. From my experience, around 15%-40% of all clicks away from a blog post are through these smart links, which makes it an easy way to guide visitors to where you want them.

From an SEO point of view, setting the phrase "horse tacks in Canada" to always turn into a link pointing to your page which is optimised for the phrase "horse tacks in Canada", is another way to make a vote for that page relevant to that key phrase.

e) AdSense Now!

Automatically places your Google AdSense code wherever you want it, which saves a lot of time messing around with code.

f) Google Analytics for Wordpress

This allows you to link your Google Analytics account with your Wordpress page, without adding the Google tracking code to every page.

g) Google Analytics

This is a free tool from Google that shows you a huge amount of statistics about your site. Link it with your *Google Analytics for Wordpress* plugin and it will tell you an amazing amount of information about your site.

h) Google Webmaster Tools

Link this with your Google Analytics account and in a week or so (as it gathers data) it will tell you:

- What keywords you're ranking for in Google
- Your average position in Google for each keyword
- The number of times your listing has been viewed in Google and the number of people who clicked on the link when they saw it
- The number of backlinks to your site and the most-used anchor texts
- And a lot more

Basically it's a great way to see what keywords you're ranking for and what position you're in. It means you can keep track on how your backlinking and SEO efforts are affecting your Google rank. Webmaster Tools gives you information on how your site appears on the internet: what keywords you're ranking for, any HTML errors, keyword densities on your site and more.

Your site layout

Your site layout has a big impact on the amount of money you make.

Think about this extreme example: if all of your affiliate links are at the bottom of the page, in an unreadable font colour, what is the likelihood that someone will see them and click on them? Very small.

Studies looking at eye movement of internet users show that users often read web pages in an F-shaped pattern: two horizontal stripes followed by a vertical stripe, as you can see in the image below. Not only that, but they'll view your page fast. If they don't see what they want immediately then they'll press the back button and never return.

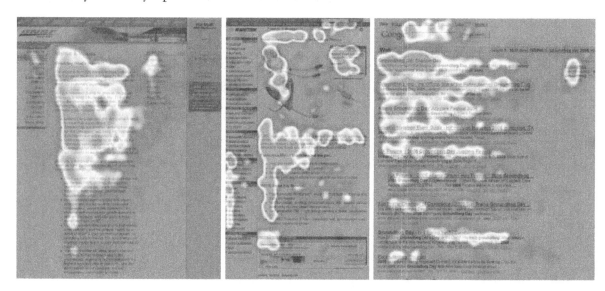

(Example illustration from useit.com)

Obviously this isn't a set-in-stone rule, but start thinking about what you can do to draw the eye to exactly what you want visitors to see.

Organising our keywords

Now you have a list of the most searched for keywords that you will easily be able to rank for, each of which will need a page on your site.

Creating the content

Each of these low competition keywords that you want to rank for need PAGES on your Wordpress site that are Search Engine Optimised.

Don't worry, this is seriously easy as long as you use the great plugins listed below. These truly are things that I use every day. They basically make the whole SEO thing so easy that it doesn't even matter if you've never heard about it, or previously found it impossible.

- *SEOPressor Wordpress Plugin* www.seopressor.com

This little thing has revolutionised how I look at SEO. I swore I'd never fully understand SEO and then I found this plugin.

Now, at the bottom of every post or page I can type into the box under the Wordpress text editor the keyword or phrase for which I want to rank in Google.

I just write my content and press "save draft". Then, I get an on screen message telling me exactly what I need to do to make it perfectly optimised, with a rating out of 100. Just follow the steps and you can sit back, knowing that you've done everything right for Google!

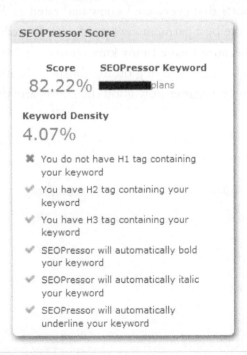

SEOPressor gives you a score and tells you what you need to change for your site to go from an 84% score to a 100% score. The above screenshot shows your site does not have a Header 1 (H1) tag containing your keyword.

I love SEOPressor. It'll cost $47 (for one website) to purchase it but it's the best money you could possibly spend (in terms of importance, it is equal to Market Samurai!).

You can get this here: www.seopressor.com

-   *SEO Doctor Firefox Extension*

Once you've written your post using www.seopressor.com then this Firefox extension will come in handy. Open up the page you've just created and in the bottom left of the Firefox window you'll see a grade out of 100, similar to SEOPressor.

You may notice a slight difference between the grade you get from SEODoctor and the grade you get from the SEOPressor plug-in. SEOPressor analyses your actual content and SEODoctor examines how that content's actually displayed online, and takes things like Load Time and internal links into account.

Imagine buying a pair of shorts that everyone I knew had rated as 90% amazing. 100% amazing would make them the best garment ever produced. But when I tried them on, they only looked 80% amazing because I have funny knees (not really). SEOPressor is the overall rating, SEODoctor is the equivalent of trying on the shorts. Always take SEODoctor's verdict as final because it doesn't matter how good the shorts are, they have to suit you.

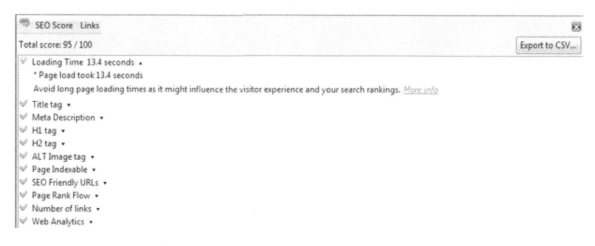

Part 6. SEO – Search Engine Optimisation

What is SEO and why is it so important?

SEO = Search Engine Optimisation, or how to rank in Google following certain rules.

Your website constantly needs visitors to make money, just like your shop in the high street constantly needs customers. SEO is very important to make sure that the customers keep finding your shop and that you do not end up hidden on the fifth page of Google.

SEO is talked about a lot among webmasters because it is very important. For a newbie it can be a bit confusing but I hope that all will be clear to you when you've read this book. SEO is not an exact science and it will take you a considerable amount of time to create a site that is worthy of a good search engine ranking.

SEO is something that any new online business must familiarize themselves with. After all, when it's done correctly, it is your ticket to true online success. There are a few SEO tools online that you can gain access to for free or at a nominal fee—some of which are described in this book in brief.

While you don't have to be a complete expert at SEO to start building your website business, it will be extremely helpful if you are somewhat familiar with SEO and what it can do for you. Therefore, I strongly recommend at least reading the Beginner's Guide to SEO on www.moz.com before delving too deep into launching your business. You'll be amazed at how much it can help you build your site, research competition and market your site later on.

None of the SEO rules apply if you are planning to send traffic to your site with PPC ads or with social media. SEO is only important if you want Google to show your website when someone types in your keyword.

What is the difference between On Page SEO (OPSEO) and Off Page SEO (OFFSEO) ?

The sort of SEO we will cover here first is OPSEO – this is On Page Search Engine Optimisation. This is very important for Google ranking. On Page SEO means designing your website in a search engine-friendly way, by using keywords throughout the site, title tags, meta tags, header tags and more. This is also called internal and external web optimisation. You can't do one and not the other to rank highly in Google. The OPSEO (internal) are changes you make ON your website and OFFSEO (external) is the stuff that you do outside of the design of your site.

By doing OPSEO correctly you have a good chance in the SERPs = Search Engine Result Pages, or the listings pages returned when you search for a keyword.

Have you ever wondered how search engines decide how to rank your website in their results pages? Or how they know exactly what's on your page and what it's about?

They send out robots (or "bots") that crawl your site, paying particular attention to the elements we are about to discuss. If you get these things right then you stand a much better chance of appearing in the search results for the keywords you want. **Use your keywords mostly on the top and the bottom of each page.**

> **Top Tip: use commonly misspelled words or model numbers as keywords in either your domain name, title tags or meta description. The person who typed in the misspelled word probably does not know how to spell it correctly anyway. It is amazing how many visits I get on pages with a misspelled word. Google Analytics gives me this information.**

Off Page SEO refers to work done outside the design of your website or when the website is finished to help you rank in the search engines. Off Page SEO is a continuous process: it means getting backlinks to your site and promoting your site on other websites, building your credibility online. It can also be done through article marketing, joining forums and so on.

To summarize ,On Page SEO is important when you build your site and Off Page SEO is about getting traffic to your site, which will be covered later in this book.

In order to develop a successful site you need to keep two things in mind - you are aiming to please Google but you must also aim to please the searcher, and you must know what searchers are looking for and what keyword they use.

According to recent studies OFF Page SEO is now more important to Google than On Page SEO: 30%-40 % for On Page SEO and 60%-70% for Off Page SEO. A few years ago On Page SEO was clearly the most important (about 90%).

SEO is very detailed and you can get books just on this subject. I am only going to cover the most important basics. If you apply these rules, you should be able to rank highly in Google.

I have to tell you that I believe ranking in Google is overcomplicated by many people. I will give you some examples of my sites, where very basic SEO has been applied and these sites have been ranking on page one since I've published them, years ago. I have NEVER touched any of these sites as I believe in the following: "if something works, leave it alone". Panda or Penguin have never bothered me for most of my sites.

In the foreword in this book I mentioned that some core principles of SEO have been the same for many years and will stay the same for many years to come. Let me show you some of my examples/

The liquorice and the nougat sites listed below are also good examples that an ecommerce does NOT need to be very big to rank. Of course, I am not making £22,000/$35,000 per month from these sites, but they do give me a nice monthly income with little work.

So here three of my sites:

1) www.micropigshed.com This site creates income from book sales and from Adsense and ranks on the first page for the following targeted keywords:

- keeping micro pigs
- micro pig diet
- how to keep micro pigs
- micro pig food
- looking after a micro pig
- micro pigs care

- micro pigs book

Well, I hope they are still ranking well when you are reading this book. They were when I finished writing the book (In 2011).

2) www.liquorice-licorice.co.uk I have intentionally built this site NOT to rank for the word liquorice on its own, as the competition was too large, but for the keywords listed below. The site is shown on page one in google.co.uk for all these keywords:

- double salt liquorice

- doube salt liquorice UK

- triple salt liquorice

- Italian liquorice

- liquorice for diabetics

- Dutch liquorice

- Belgian liquorice

- buy liquorice online

- buy liquorice

- gelatine free liquorice

- sugar free liquorice

Note: searches vary, therefore every day different websites are shown by Google. Knowing that Amazon , as a high authority site, sells a lot of liquorice, you might have noticed that often my site is listed **before** Amazon.

Why did I choose that domain name? It is one of those words that is difficult to spell for some people. Some people will type in 'liquorice' and others will type in 'licorice'. Liquorice is the way it is spelled in the UK and licorice is the American way. I have used both in my domain name to rank for both markets, although the keywords that I have targeted are mostly intended for the UK market, as most of my customers are in the UK, but some UK customers will also search for "licorice".

3) www.nougat-nougat.co.uk This site ranks for the following targeted keywords:

- Italian nougat cakes

- Belgian nougat

- wedding nougat cakes

- gelatine free nougat

You see, ranking a site is not THAT difficult as there is nothing special about the three sites that I have shown you but they are all built with the important factors in mind, listed below. They don't tick all the must have elements that should ideally be on your site (discussed later) but the sites rank well therefore I leave them alone.

THE most important factors for building a website that will rank in Google for years, in order of importance, are:

- Practice the basic SEO rules (see next page)

- Focus on long tail keywords

- Don't build a site in an over saturated market.

- NEVER EVER use anything automated on your site or any of your other sites: no automated websites, no automated back links, no automated articles feed, no automated video feed, etc...

- You need a low bounce rate. When visitors leave your website immediately after they've opened it, Google can see this and that means you have a high bounce rate. If you have a high bounce rate and Google has seen it, Google will decide that there isn't much interesting to see on your site therefore your site will be ranked down.

- You need regular visitors (with a low bounce rate).

- Put the must have elements on your site e.c. privacy policy, etc... discussed later.

Perhaps you have noticed - if you had a look at the above websites - that there are no social media buttons or "likes" on the site. Some people say that these days it is impossible to rank in Google without having some social media on your site. I hope these websites prove that you don't NEED social media to rank.

OK here are the basic SEO rules.

1. Keywords in the URL

Along with keywords in your site's page titles, keywords in the domain name and URL are hugely important if you want to rank quickly.

One of the quickest ways to rank for a keyword is to have that keyword in your domain name.

i.e. http://www.YourKeyword.com

I recommend naming your domain after your broad niche so that you can have a wide range of items and information available, while still benefiting from the keyword-rich domain name.

This means, in the example we've been using, we would have the domain:

http://www.horsetacks.com rather than *http://www.yellow-metal-horse-tacks.com*

- In my research I have concluded that shorter URLs usually perform better in the search results.

- Shorter URLs are also more likely to be used by other internet marketers for links and so on.

- Bad URLs make it unclear for Google what your site is all about. With good URLs you tell the search engines what you want your page to be ranked for.

An example of a bad URL : www.hypnosis.com/index.&?89=76=ahtr?52

An example of a good URL : www.hypnosis/list/coverthypnosis (coverthypnosis is the page name)

Want proof that keywords in the domain name are very important? Have a look at the screenshot below, which tells you enough. When my site www.FromNewbieToMillionaire.com had no content on at all, only the words "web site under development" Google displayed my site on the 1st page, out of 3.810.000 results. Note that I did not type the keywords in "exact search".

Important note: Once Google 's robots will see that my website is a one-page-sales wonder, it **might** not show it again on the first page (Google does not like one-page-sales-wonders) but it will show other pages that have targeted the keywords "from newbie to millionaire". If it **is** shown on the first page, it means that the website gets a lot of traffic or Google cannot find any other sites that are more relevant to show first, showing the importance again of having your keywords in your domain name. Sometimes, if there is not a lot of competition, the website with the keyword in will be shown, even it is a one-page-sales-wonder.

from newbie to millionaire

About 3,810,000 results (0.17 seconds)

▶ Just another WordPress site :: From betting **newbie to millionaire**
25 May 2011 ... From betting **newbie to millionaire** .... Tags: best, betting, bookmaker, casino, millionaire, newbie, odds, software, win, winners ...
frombettingnewbietomillionaire.com/ - Cached

from newbie to millionaire to billionaire. | Marketing With You ...
18 Oct 2010 ... "**from newbie to millionaire** to billionaire". talk about going full circle in the past 90 days. you see 90 days ago I took a leaf out of the ...
marketingwithyou.com/newbie-millionaire-billionaire/ - Cached

Home
From Newbie To Millionaire. Home. Web site under development.
fromnewbietomillionaire.com/ - Cached

2. Page title tag

The title tag is one of the most important parts of SEO to get right. Make certain that your keyword is there as it's what Google places a lot of weight on. It's what your users will see in Google and it's what will appear on the top of the browser window.

Do not go over 70 characters in length for your page title.

Give each page a title (or tag) containing a keyword. You can give your page two titles by putting a " | " between the two keywords or phrases eg. How to design a logo | logo design. This will count twice as a keyword for Google. To get the " | " key, use shift key plus the key on the left of the letter Z on your keyboard (on a QWERTY keyboard).

> **TOP TIP : Do not include stop words in your keywords and search phrases. Google ignores these and considers them irrelevant. Do not use stop words in your meta title, meta keywords, links or header tags. Here is a list of some commonly used stop words.**
>
> And   Be   I   In   Me   Of   On   The

> **TOP TIP :** The keyword that you want to rank for in the page title needs to be early in the title. This is important for Google. So do NOT use this: "Secret Tips Revealed about how To Stop Your Dog From Barking". Instead use: "Stop Your Dog From Barking Secret Tips Revealed" because the "Stop Your Dog From Barking" is more important than "Secret Tips" in the search.

3. Meta description or meta tags

In Google's search results your meta description will appear in bold under your title. The 'meta tags' or 'page description' are the two lines that appear in Google underneath the 'title tag'.

You need to write a good description because it is the one thing that users have to decide whether or not to visit your page.

Do not go over 350 characters in length.

> **Horses** and **horse** training, care, **tack**, and supply info.
> Horses, horse information, horses for sale, horse classifieds. We answer some of the most common questions about horse breeds, horse care, **horse tack**, ...
> www.horses-and-**horse**-information.com/ - Cached - Similar

Title tag = the underlined text = Horses and horse training, care, tack, and supply info.

Meta tag or page description = Horses, horse information, horses for sale, etc.......

4. <H> tags or header tags

<H> tags tell the search engines what is a heading on your website. H1 is the page heading, H2 is a sub heading and H3 is a sub, sub heading.

> Every page should contain ONE H1 tag (no more, no less) which must contain your target keyword.
> Next you need ONE OR MORE H2 tags also containing the keyword.
> And, lastly, ONE OR MORE H3 tags containing your keyword.

Some web design programs call them Title, Header, Subtitle. In your Wordpress post/page editor these different H tags are called Heading 1, 2 and 3 and can be accessed by clicking the drop-down box that says "paragraph":

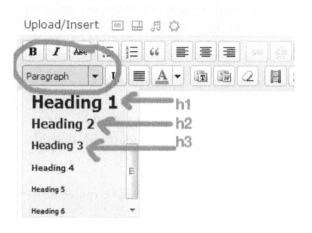

Microsoft Word headers:

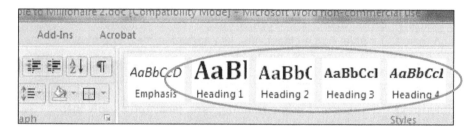

All web design software that I have come across have these headers built in. So if you call a page name "coverthypnosis" as your page title tag, you would also put a header on that page as "coverthypnosis".

5. Images should have the keyword in their filename and as their alt tag

Google, or any other search engines, cannot recognise pictures on your website (not yet anyway) but if you give each picture a keyword, Google will recognise the keyword. Each page should have at least one image on it, and that image's filename should be in the format: your keyword.jpg /.png/.gif (suffix depends on file format).

When you insert the image onto your site you also need to set the "alt tag" as your keyword. This is easy to do in Wordpress, as shown below :

If you are not using Wordpress then you should put the alt tag in manually. The code for it is:

```
<img src="http://www.yourdomain.com/images/your-keyword.png" alt="your keyword" />
```

If you're using a website design program then try right-clicking the image and clicking "properties". There will be a section marked "alternate text" or "alt text". This is where you you enter your alt tag keyword.

You must give every picture on your website a name because Google counts it as a keyword.

Do the test on your website, or on other websites. When you see a picture on the page and you move your mouse over the picture, you will see the picture name either on the screen or at the bottom left corner of your browser window. That is the Image Alt Tag. If no name appears when you hover over the picture, it means that no Image Alt Tag was used or, in other words, the picture was not named with a keyword in the title.

Google's picture search won't find your picture of a Ferrari 658 if you put it on the web with a reference " DCMB999002". It might show it if you give your picture a name like " My Ferrari 658".

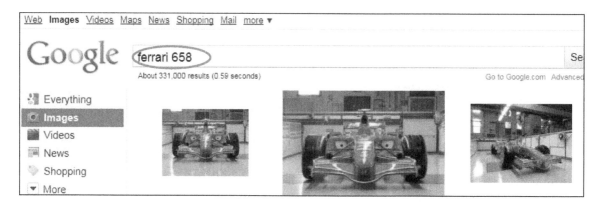

6. The pages must be named according to the content that is on them

If the page name is "safe dog collars" make sure you are talking about or selling dog collars on that page and not dog medallions. Your keyword that is in the page name must also appear a few times in the page content.

I repeat this again to stress the importance: Every page on your website should have a unique title tag. It should describe the content of that page so when it shows up in Google, the visitor will find what they expected to see. This is important for Google ranking because if every visitor leaves the page in a matter of seconds, Google will notice this and might rank you lower.

TOP TIP : Forget the one-word-keywords and try and rank with long tail keywords. It makes your SEO job a lot easier and you will rank more quickly. Always design a separate page for each long tail keyword on your site and use that same keyword on each page in your content. Example: You are building a site on muscle training. Instead of trying to rank for "muscle training", you try and rank for "muscle training for legs". The title tag of one page should then be "muscle training for legs". On that page, use the keyword "muscle training for legs" spread out over that page. Do the same for "muscle training for arms", etc...

7. Keyword density.

Aim to have the keyword make up somewhere between 2% and 4% of the text on each page of your site.

Any more than this and Google may consider it "keyword stuffing" (the practice of repeating a word over and over again to try to influence your Google position) and ignore your page.

Any less than this and Google may not realise that your page is about this keyword.

Always put your keyword in the first AND last sentence of each page.

Always make some of your keywords **bold** or *italic* on each page, to emphasis them to Google as Google does recognise bold text.

8. Learn from your competition

In any business, online or off line, you need to keep an eye on your competitors and try to better them. You can find out what keywords they rank for on the first pages.

Search with your keyword and look at the first three pages to see which domain names show. Click on each domain name and once on the website, put your cursor anywhere on the page, right-click and choose "view source". This will give the web page's source code, which will look something like this :

```
ww.pettag.co.uk/acatalog/Tags_for_Horses.html - Original Source
Format
<HTML><HEAD><TITLE> Pet Tag Engraving Horse Tags Horse Tags</TITLE><Actinic:BASEHREF
VALUE="http://www.pettag.co.uk/acatalog/"/><META NAME="ACTINICTITLE" CONTENT="Horse Tags"><META HTTP-
Type" content="text/html; charset=iso-8859-1"> <META NAME="Keywords" CONTENT="Horse Tags, Horse Ident:
Horse ID Tag, Pet Tag">
<META NAME="Description" CONTENT="Pet Tag Engraving Services - Horse Tags">
<META NAME="ActinicKey" CONTENT="fe4b34e8eae9d5de86a1d6d5818f89ef0">
<META NAME="Generator" CONTENT="accxecom5">
  <SCRIPT LANGUAGE="JavaScript" SRC="actiniccore.js" TYPE="text/javascript"></SCRIPT><script language=
<!--
function MM_swapImgRestore() { //v3.0
var i,x,a=document.MM_sr; for(i=0;a&&i<a.length&&(x=a[i])&&x.oSrc;i++) x.src=x.oSrc;
```

Now you can see the page how Google sees it. You need to view the source code of a minimum of ten first domain names and it's better to do all 30 of the domains from the first three pages of your search. Either copy and paste all the information next to TITLE TAG, META KEYWORDS, META DESCRIPTION or do a print screen of all the websites. Analyse and learn. See what keywords and what sort of websites your competitors use to get on the first few pages of Google.

You can also do the opposite. Go to pages 20 to 30, right-click "View Source" and see why those sites are *not* ranking on the first pages of Google.

You can find out how well optimised your competitors' sites are by using www.webceo.com or www.spyfu.com (not free).

Check out how many links the websites have or what PR the site is. If you use www.firefox.com you can see this information instantly underneath the website.

To better your competition you need to develop your website so that Google sees it as more relevant. You might have to do better SEO or optimise your site better. You might just beat them with that extra link. There is no golden rule that applies here: you just have to research and learn.

Yahoo Site Explorer gives information about your competitors' sites.

www.marketsamurai.com. has a great tool to learn about your competition. You can evaluate the top 10 sites in your niche and Market Samurai also gives your competitor's anchor text.

9. Activity

This is a tricky thing to quantify. Since one of the latest Google algorithm updates, Google now looks at "activity" as one of the factors it takes into account when ranking a website. This could mean a number of things: comments your blog posts receive, frequency of updates, forum activity (if you have a forum on your site), or the time people stay and browse on your site. The general rule of thumb is to update your site, or have some form of user interaction, at least once a week.

10. Number of links per page

Google will only scan a maximum of the first 100 links on a page, maybe even fewer than that. Keep the amount of links to around 50 (with over 25 of them as internal links).

TOP TIP : Make some of your keywords on your pages Bold, Italic or Underlined in order for Google to see them easier.

TOP TIP : Use your targeted keyword in the first sentence and in the last sentence of each page.

Summary SEO :

Remember: where do your keywords go?

1. In URL, best at the beginning

2. In Page Title, best at the beginning

3. In Meta Description or Meta Tags, best at the beginning

4. In Header tags H1, H2, H3, etc....

5. In Alt Text (pictures), best at the beginning

6. Name the pages according to the content on them

Important: **Make one separate page on your site per keyword you want to target. Focus on one long tail keyword on each page.**

7. In Content : keyword density is important

8. Learn from your competition

9. Activity is important

10. Links are important; Authority Site Links are brilliant

11. Put several internal page links on your site

TOP TIP : Apply good SEO to your site first and providing that you are in a low competition niche, you will probably rank in Google. If this does not work, check out how your competition made it to the 1st pages (by doing "view source" on their site) and work on your SEO. If that fails, you can use traffic methods from this book to drive traffic to your site to increase your chances of Google ranking.

- Example layout of a website, showing best practice on-page SEO. The following is for a page optimised for the key phrase "micro pig feed".

`<title>` tag *(less than 69 characters)*	Micro Pigs | Micro Pig Feed
Meta Description tag *(less than 156 characters)*	Find the best micro pig feed at the Micro Pig Shed.
Meta Keyword tags *(your webpage keywords)*	Micro pig feed, micro pig feed, micro pigs feed, micro pigs feed, feed for micro pigs, what to feed micro pig, what do micro pigs eat, what do micro pigs eat
`<h1>` tag *(most important title should only be one per page)*	Basics of Micro Pig Feed
`<p>` tag *(body text paragraph)*	Basic micro pig feed should contain several basic elements... Whenever possible, provide your pig with unlimited grazing on chemical-free grass. If this is not possible, add high-quality hay such as alfalfa or oat to the micro pig feed. This roughage is very important, but feed within reason!
`<img>` tag	IMAGE - given the alt. tag "micro pig feed"
`<h2>` tag	What Should Be In Micro Pig Feed?
`<p>` tag	Fifty percent of the balance of the micro pig feed should be a good-quality commercial pig food. There are pelleted foods on the market specifically for miniature pigs. Feed pig starter to pigs under two months, and adult food to all others. Since you are not planning to send your pig to market, do not use pig grower or finisher.
`<h3>` tag	Know what micro fig feed you're looking for?
`<p>` tag *(links to other pages on your site)*	<ul><li>Micro Pig Feed Product A</li><li>Micro Pig Feed Product B</li><li>Micro Pig Feed Product C</li><li>Micro Pig Feed Product D</li></ul>
Footer	Site Map | Disclaimer | Privacy Policy | Help All Contents Copyright 2011

If you want to design a page on "micro pig training", you would replace "micro pig feed" with "micro pig training" and of course change the content accordingly.

- Another example layout of a website, showing best practice for on-page SEO. The following is for a page optimised for the key phrase "horse tack trunk" (paragraph content taken from Wikipedia):

<title> tag *(less than 69 characters)*	Horse Tacks | Horse Tack Trunk
Meta Description tag *(less than 156 characters)*	Find the best horse tack trunk for you at our horse tack site.
Meta Keyword tags *(your webpage keywords)*	Horse tacks, horse tack trunk, horse tack trunks, best horse tack trunks, cheap horse tack trucks
<h1> tag *(most important title - should only be one per page)*	Horse Tack Trunk Basics
<p> tag *(body text paragraph)*	Horse tack trunks are a place to store away all the horse tacks you have probably accumulated over your years' horse riding. Tack is a term used to describe any of the various equipment and accessories worn by horses in the course of their use as domesticated animals. Saddles, stirrups, bridles, halters, reins, bits, harnesses, martingales, and breastplates are all forms of horse tacks.
<img> tag	IMAGE - given the alt. tag "horse tack trunk"
<h2> tag	More About The Contents Of Horse Tack Trunks
<p> tag	Saddles are seats for the rider, fastened to the horse's back by means of a *girth* (English-style riding), known as a *cinch* in the Western US, a wide strap that goes around the horse at a point about four inches behind the forelegs. Some western saddles will also have a second strap known as a *flank* or *back cinch* that fastens at the rear of the saddle and goes around the widest part of the horse's belly.[
<h3> tag	Know what type of horse tack trunk you're looking for?
<p> tag *(links to other pages on your site)*	• Horse Tack Trunk A • Horse Tack Trunk B • Horse Tack Trunk C • Horse Tack Trunk D
Footer	Site Map | Disclaimer | Privacy Policy | Help All Contents Copyright 2011

Depending on the amount of content you have in between your <p> tags, you may want to put your key phrase in once or twice. You want to aim for an overall keyword density of about 4% (meaning that around 4% of the content on the page is your keyword).

- The "perfectly optimized page" for the example keyword phrase "chocolate donuts".

Page Title : Chocolate Donuts | Mary's Bakery

Meta Description : Mary's Bakery's chocolate donuts are possibly the most delicious, perfectly formed, flawlessly chocolately donuts ever made.

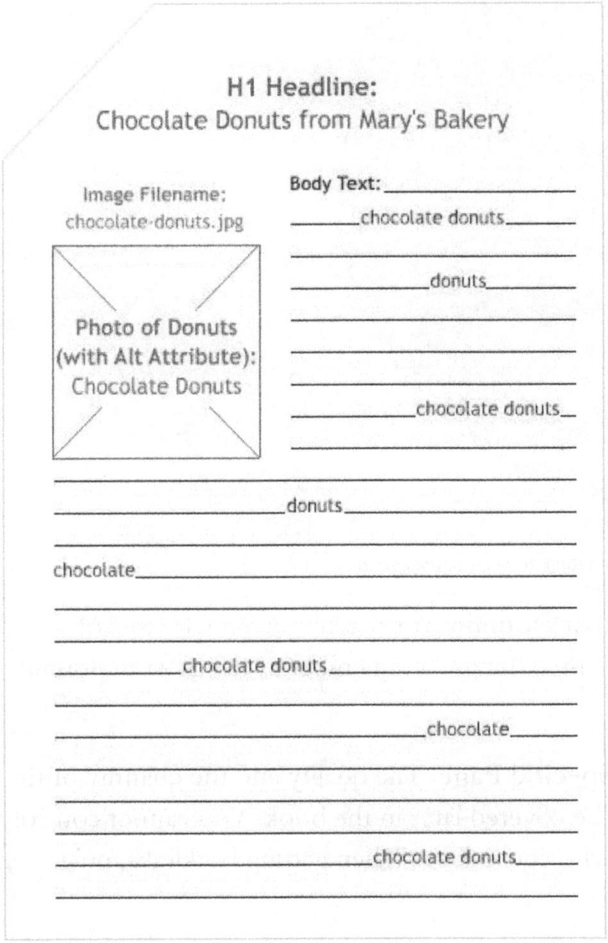

H1 Headline:
Chocolate Donuts from Mary's Bakery

Image Filename:
chocolate-donuts.jpg

Photo of Donuts
(with Alt Attribute):
Chocolate Donuts

Body Text:_____
_____chocolate donuts_____

_____donuts_____

_____chocolate donuts_

_____donuts_____

chocolate_____

_____chocolate donuts_____

_____chocolate_____

_____chocolate donuts_____

Page URL: http://marysbakery.com/chocolate-donuts

On the Pie Chart Below you can see the importance of the keyword on page optimization.

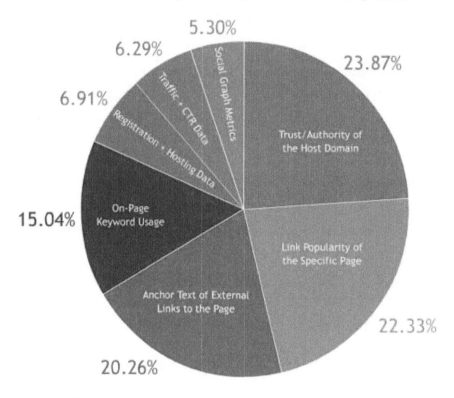

Components of Google's Ranking Algorithm
(According to 72 SEOs Surveyed for SEOmoz's Biennial Search Ranking Factors)

Source : http://www.seomoz.org/blog/perfecting-keyword-targeting-on-page-optimization

First: 23.87% Trust/Authority of The Host Domain. A trusted domain with lots of visitors, lots of content and inbound links. Three things to remember as the most important : domain age, good content, quality links.

Second: 22.33% Link Popularity of the Specific Page. The quality and the quantity of the inbound links are very important. This will be covered later in the book. You cannot control who links to your site but you can control who you link to. When getting backlinks, only ever link to relevant sites.

Third: 20.26% Anchor Text of External Links to the Page. It is important to have anchored links coming into your page. You need the correct anchors from quality sources. If you point to a relevant page on a website, you should use keyword rich anchor text e.g. instead of "click here". Here are some stop-dog-barking tips is much better than Click Here for Tips. It is better for two reasons: firstly because the visitor immediately knows what to expect when clicking the link and secondly because for search engines the anchor text is another link with relevant keywords. So instead of using Anchor Text, use Descriptive Anchor Text, like this one: Here are some stop-dog-barking tips.

Fourth: 15.04% On-Page Keyword Usage. Keyword density should be about 2% to 4% maximum. Not enough and your site might not rank, too much and it is considered keyword stuffing. Trial and error is the only way to find out.

Fifth: 6.91% Registration-Hosting Data. Google likes old domain names. They know that spammers will never register a domain for longer than one year. Google also does not really like .info websites because very often these are used by spammers as .info domain names are cheaper to buy. If your target market is Australia, you must make sure that you have a .com or .au website and also with an Australian server.

Sixth: 6.29% Traffic – Click Through Data. You have done a lot of work and your website ranks in Google BUT most visitors who visit your website immediately hit the back button. To Google this means that the information on your site was not interesting enough for the visitor to stay, Google will rank it lower. Unless you work really hard on the content, the website will not rank on the first pages again. Google will also keep a record of the amount of times your website is shown and clicked on.

Seventh: 5.30% Social Graph Metrics. Google never used to take this into account. If Google finds out that your website is liked by a lot of people, it will show higher in the rankings. This is where social networking and the backlink strategies discussed later in this book are important. You need to open an account with Facebook, Twitter, Digg, Propeller and so on and get people talking about you or pointing to your site.

SEO Conclusion : On page SEO takes a long time if you want to do it right BUT it will pay off. It is the most important thing for getting free traffic. Your hard work will be worth it once you type in your keyword and your website is listed first! You will probably never forget that moment. I still remember the first time I ranked on the first page with my keyword.

That's when I realised that if I can achieve it for one site, I can duplicate my method for other sites or outsource the building of more sites.

Some of the most important things that determine your ranking success with Google:

- SEO: keywords in domain name and on your site

- Content: you must have good unique content

- Links: you must have other sites that link to yours

- Reputation of your site, mostly coming from social media e.g. YouTube, Facebook

- Activity on your site: if nobody ever visits your site or if visitors stay only briefly, Google will not be impressed.

It is not enough to have an extremely well optimised website with ON Page SEO as there is more work to be done, all of which will be discussed in this book.

> **TOP TIP : You need to investigate your keywords BEFORE you start the design of your site. Design your site around your keywords.**

11. Number of results myth resolved

The following information is especially useful to newbies. When I first started online, I was confused. Suppose I searched for horse and got 185,000,000 results, does this mean that I have to compete with over 185 million pages about horses? Surely that is not possible!

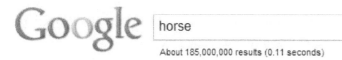

No it is indeed not possible but that's not how it works. Let me explain.

The number of results means nothing in terms of competition. If there is a large number for the results then there is a lot of interest in the subject. The search results will include ALL the websites with the word 'horse' on any page , this means websites selling DVDs with 'horse' in the title, or horse riding holidays, etc… all *irrelevant* to the horse tack niche. The only websites that you have to compete with are the first eight pages of results, so that's a maximum of 80 websites. The reason for this is that Google will list lots of websites that have the word horse in it but that are poorly SEO optimised. Google will also show pages with a lot of unrelated stuff on. The bottom line is the only ones you have to worry about are the ones that are listed on the first eight pages. To show you how important long tail keywords are, here's an example.

Google shows 339,000,000 for the exact search for "Mercedes" :

Google shows 55,100 for the exact search for "yellow Mercedes"

Conclusion: your competition is immediately less if you refine your keywords and want to rank for "yellow Mercedes" compared to "Mercedes".

To close the SEO-section here are a few ways of how to **never** rank highly:

-   Black Hat SEO (keyword stuffing)

-   No title tags or very bad title tags

-   Irrelevant domain names

- Using link farms (see further in this book)

- Using lots of Flash all over your website

- Irrelevant content or not enough content

- Using wrong keywords on different pages e.g. giving a page a title tag "stop dog barking" and then not using any of these three words on that page.

12. Do you need one website per niche ?

Another question that a lot of internet marketing beginners ask me is: "If I want to build ten different websites in ten different niches, do I have to buy ten different domain names?" Now that you have read about the importance of SEO and keyword use on your site, I think you might guess the answer: yes it is indeed better to have one website per niche. If the niches are totally different you have to buy different domain names because the searcher for your keyword will want to see a site with ONLY the information that they're interested in. If somebody types in "fly fishing" in Google and opens a site that has "fly fishing" and "how to make candles" on it, they will soon leave your site.

If you have different subjects in one niche e.g. arthritis in your neck and arthritis in your foot you could create several pages within one website and have arthritis as your main domain name. Each page would then have to be optimised for the correct keyword. So one page would focus on arthritis in your neck and another page would focus on arthritis in your foot. The majority of websites on such subjects are built this way.

However, in my opinion it is better to create two different websites, the first one called www.arthritisinyourneck.com and the second called www.arthritisinyourfoot.com. I have mentioned the importance of targeted customers before and this is another good example. A person who has neck-arthritis might not have foot-arthritis so is more likely to stay on your site for a while (assuming that you have decent content) if your site is relevant to them. The longer they stay on your site, the more chance your money-making links will be clicked.

It is also important to have two different sites for ranking purposes, as having the keywords in your domain name is important.

In case you choose to build two sites I suggest that you place links on each website to your other website(s). For instance, on the website about your neck you could put: <u>here you can find information about foot arthritis</u> (link to your other site).

Part 7. Creating Content For Your Site

When creating your content, you should always keep in mind exactly who you're writing for. You need to know your audience, know what they expect and know what they want.

You shouldn't just know your audience though. In any business, you must know your competition as well. See how the biggest websites in your niche have arranged their sites and note the kind of language they use.

In my book "Finding Niches Made Easy" are lots of websites listed that you can visit for content ideas. My book also includes Advanced Search Techniques, to find the things you are looking for much quicker.

Important: Your visitor cares only about himself and not so much about you. For this reason, use the word "YOU" a lot more than the word "we" and "me", at a ratio of 75% (you) to 25% (me or we).

Some good places to find articles and content to either buy, or learn, from are:

- www.screensteps.com This tool is brilliant if you want to produce an informative "How To" guide that includes screenshots.
- www.howstuffworks.com Huge range of high quality content that you can re-write
- www.ehow.com Step-by-step guides to do just about anything
- www.theanswerbank.com
- www.allexperts.com
- www.answerbag.com

If you decide to purchase Market Samurai, you can click on "Find Content" for your keyword and Market Samurai will give you a list of options. To get your copy, visit www.marketsamurai.com.

CONTENT IS KING. FACT. Content is definitely what can make or break your chances to rank highly more than anything else and it is what makes you different from your competitors. It also makes other websites in your niche want to link to your site. The links that other websites give you is a sign for Google that your site is worthy

of ranking for your market. More links means more traffic from other sites and traffic from other sites means Google will rank you higher.

Google is always hungry for content. Make sure that you feed the crawling robots. The more good content, the better. Good content is a MUST HAVE on your site.

Before I get into my method of getting content, I want to talk about the two types of Wordpress updates:

- Pages
- Posts

"Pages" should be where you write and create your keyword researched articles. "Posts" should be where you upload content that isn't necessarily keyword researched.

This is because "posts" are more like a news-stream, whereas "pages" are static areas on your site that are laid out much like a classic website would be.

Here are some methods to get content for your site.

Chapter 1. Content Methods

The best method for writing content is simply to write it yourself, but this can be time consuming. Here are a few ways of getting content.

1. The book method: The Copyright-free book or public domain method

I will not give a definition here about copyright free and public domain because the rules and regulations are different in each country. Check your country for all legalities. Just Google "public domain" or " when is and a product copyright free", etc… In general, royalty free and public domain means that you can use content and change it without permission from the author. Anything which legally has no owner is public domain, so it belongs to the public and they may use it any way they choose. If something is under Copyright Protection, you cannot use it without the author's permission.

Public domain used with a business attitude, or an "I-want-to-make-money" attitude, can earn you money.

You can even remove the author's name, edit the book and sell it as your own. Once you have modified a public domain product, it becomes your property.

In the USA there are some general rules for a work to be considered public domain:

- If the work was published in the United States before 1923. No exceptions.

- All work created after 1 March 1989 is Copyright Protected for 70 years from the date the author dies.

- All work made for hire after 1 March 1989 is Copyright Protected for 95 years from publication or 120 years from the date it was created.

There are more factors that determine whether something is Public Domain or not in the USA. Investigate if the book or article you want to use is indeed Public Domain.

Did you know that there is work available as Public Domain from William Shakespeare, Mark Twain, Jane Austin, Hans Christian Andersen, Charles Dickens, Agatha Christie, Albert Einstein, Charles Darwin and more?

Is there money to be made with public domain content? Sure there is!

- Walt Disney started his billion dollar empire with a public domain source: the fairy tales of the Grimm Brothers.

- Did you know that almost all the movies played on TCM (Turner Classic Movies), the cable network company were public domain when they started? The creator had a business idea, using public domain work to get rich. As it has become a very popular TV channel, he now earns lots of money from advertising.

How can you find public domain work ?

- Visit www.books.Google.com where you can find books on many different subjects. In the advanced search you can select books that are published before 1923. For books that are out of copyright, you can read and download the entire book.

Click Advanced Search :

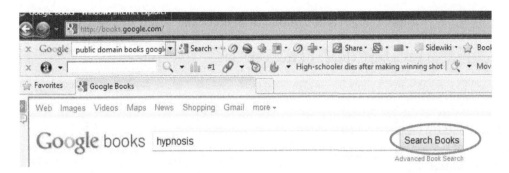

In the publication date, set the last date as January 1923 and hit the 'Search' button. This will show you all the books that are published before 1923, which are public domain books.

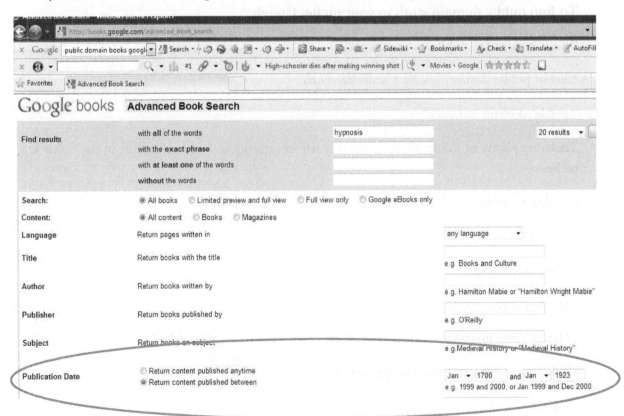

- Visit www.glutenberg.com for royalty free books.

- Visit www.archive.org for material that is available to the public.

- www.authorama.com has a large list of public domain books

- www.bartleby.com has a large choice of free content

- www.bibliomania.com

- www.internetarchive.com

- www.literature.org

- www.publicdomainreport.com

To find public domain work in your niche, Google :

" your keyword + public domain work"

" list of public domain books + your keyword"

" public domain websites"

There are plenty of Public Domain books, articles, music, and films available in the following niches:

- Children books

- Mind reading

- Natural remedies

- Home cures

- Handwriting analysis

- Television series and radio programmes

- Business books

- Books on hobbies

- Books on collecting

- Masterpieces of literature e.g. Shakespeare, Dickens, Poe

- Thousands of non-fiction books

- Family books about education, children, relationships

- Historical books

You will be amazed what is available as public domain material.

My scanning method to create content explained.

Ingredients you need.

This method may require some initial investment, but will save you an unbelievable amount of time and money. I have to be honest, I'm slightly nervous about giving this tip away: it's been a personal secret for some time!

If you:

- Struggle with writing content on a niche you know nothing about
- Hate spending hours writing articles or posts for your site
- Aren't a native English speaker
- Are just plain lazy and want to make creating quality content easy

Then this is for you. ***Please visit*** www.VideosNewbieBook.com ***to watch a video on this subject.***

Initial requirements:

a) An A4 scanner

You don't need a fancy scanner, just one that is large enough to scan a book, and that's reliable and quick. I personally use a Canon LiDE100 Colour Image Scanner ($98 or £61.00)

b) A copy of <u>ABBYY Reader Express</u> ($90 or £56). Search for "finereader Abby" if you want to order one. This OCR (Optical Character Recognition) software links up with your scanner, will take the words off the page, and put them into Microsoft Word.

Every time you rewrite an article from the internet for your site, chances are it's been rewritten thousands of times by hundreds of other people. If your version is even slightly similar to someone else's version then Google will simply ignore all your content and you'll never get that much-needed Google first page ranking.

A lot of eBook writers will buy 10 to 20 physical books, read them and put it all together into one eBook in their own words. With this method you don't need to worry about absorbing and organising this huge amount of information, you just rewrite one small section as, and when, needed.

Also, if you've ever used or thought about using outsourced workers to write articles for you, you may be paying $1 per article. By using my out of copyright book method you can get up to a hundred articles for the price of one second-hand book.

Tip: check with your library. Maybe they have an out of copyright book section. If they do, you can get your content completely free (this is true in the UK but I am not sure other parts of the world).

The recipe for my method

Find some out of copyright books or public domain work related to your niche. If it is in PDF-format, print a copy and put that under the scanner.

Find a short section of about 250-500 words that you think would make a good article, post or page. If you have your list of keywords to target, you can find passages based around that keyword. If you want to rank in Google for "horse tacks" then find a passage about horse tacks.

Lay the book, or printed version of the book, open on the relevant page on your new scanner like this (this is the scanner I use):

Hit the "Scan To Microsoft Word" button and give it a minute.

Next you will have a Word document with an exact digital copy of the book. It'll even match the font and formatting and in all the time I've used it, it's never made a single mistake.

This scanned section can then be edited and pasted into Wordpress to be optimised with www.seopressor.com for whatever keyword you're targeting.

Honestly, if this hasn't just given you a "WOW!" moment then you're not impressed quickly. The video on this subject is called "Scan with Abbey Fine reader". Please visit www.VideosNewbieBook.com to get access to the video.

You can use these edited versions as articles, posts, pages, anything!

As an added tip, here's one of the ways I use this method:

- Use Abbyy Reader Express to scan in as many short chunks of text as I can find in all the books I have. These sections are text that I think work well on their own, and make sense out of context.
- Re-word each scanned section.
- Go into Wordpress and create a post on each of these scanned chunks and *backdate them so that a post is made every X days* (I personally have a post every five days, but it's up to you how often you post).

Now I've got quick, high-quality content that will be updated on my site regularly, without lifting another finger!

2. Rewriting PLR articles

PLR stands for *Private Label Rights.* These kinds of articles allow you to edit and change as much as you want and can be a great way of finding new content. Make sure that you rewrite the content to a good level though, otherwise Google will ignore it - if it finds content on your site that someone else has, your site may be completely ignored and will not appear in the search results.

You can give away PLR articles on your opt-in page. You can use PLR articles to re-write your own book. PLR articles are brilliant but only if you use them to give away. If you are driving traffic to your site with Paid Traffic methods, it does not really matter all that much if you have PLR articles on your site. But PLR is a definite no-go if you want to rank in the search engines, unless you re-write them.

Good PLR sites or sites to get content:

www.cloneforsuccess.com = PLR with squeeze page
www.contentgoldmine.com
www.glutenberg.org
www.INeedAGreatStory.com Royalty-free stories, videos and infographics. You buy credits to allow you buy material.
www.plrpro.com
www.resellrightspack.com
www.sitecontentideas.com
www.super-resell.com
www.theplrstore.com RECOMMENDED

3. Google Translate to re-write articles

If you want a quick way to rewrite articles you've scanned or articles you've found, then the following method might help. You can transfer PLR articles into unique articles with this method.

- Go to the Google Translator –translate.Google.com
- Paste your article into the box.

- Set English as the language you're translating from, and German as the language you're translating, then hit 'translate':

- Now copy the translation back into the box and translate from German to English:

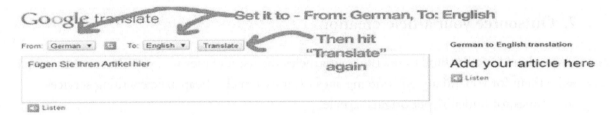

For longer articles translating back to English or any other language will give you a differently worded version. For greater rewording try translating it again, this time into Dutch or French until you're happy. You will need to read and edit the final version to ensure it is grammatically correct.

4. Interview method

Whatever your niche, there will be people that you can contact and interview over the phone, by email or, if they are local, by simply going to see them. You can get brilliant unique content this way. I found that a lot of people are willing to be interviewed without asking for money, simply because they love their business (which in this case is your niche) and are proud to be chosen to be interviewed. Sometimes they ask a very small amount or sometimes they are very happy if you give them a credit in your article or eBook or website.

5. Gutenberg.com

All articles on www.gutenberg.com are free and you can use them for anything you like.

6. Dragon Naturally Speaking

Dragon Naturally Speaking is a speech recognition software package developed and sold by Nuance Communications for Windows. Many years ago I bought several versions that simply would not work but I am very impressed with version 11.

You train the software to recognise your voice. Once that is done you simply talk to the computer through a microphone. The computer writes whatever you say into Microsoft Word. I use this method more and more as you can "speak your thoughts" which are typed in automatically for you. I love it. It's a pleasant way to create quick and easy content.

7. Outsource your article creation

If you don't have the time to rewrite your articles then sometimes it pays to have other people write them for you. Many outsourcing sites offer extremely cheap article writing services, sometimes for under $1 per original article!

Best places for article writing outsourcing:

www.99centarticles.com
www.agentsofvalue.com
www.elance.com RECOMMENDED
www.fiverr.com RECOMMENDED A huge amount of services, including some funny ones!
www.freelancer.com
www.guru.com
www.ifreelance.com
www.microworkers.com RECOMMENDED
www.mturk.com
www.need-an-article.net
www.odeskresources.com
www.peopleperhour.com

Chapter 2. Add Compelling Headlines for your Posts/Pages

A headline on your website needs to draw people in. It needs to be compelling. It needs to arouse such curiosity in the reader that they have to read your content.

The nature of the internet and the way we read content, especially on the web, means that if we're not immediately gripped by what we see, we'll move on. This is why a good headline is so powerful.

All headlines fall into nine broad categories. Some fall into more than one.

If you understand these basic types then you're on your way to crafting copy that sells.

Spend time writing your headline. Write down a few and narrow them down to the best one.

Good words to use in your headline and sales letter:

- benefits
- more benefits
- free
- profit
- new

- now
- secret
- easy
- saves
- guarantee

- today
- first
- how to
- amazing
- special offer

1. The no-nonsense, direct headline

No messing about, no complicated cleverness, just straight to the point.

Examples:

- 25% Off All Women's Underwear
- Free Pencil Sharpener For Every Subscriber

2. The subtle, in-direct or pun headline

These kind of headlines are slightly more clever and are commonly employed by tabloid newspapers. There are two main types of these: the pun and the indirect sell.

Examples:

- The Pun: Much Ado About Muffin
  At BA - A British Airways flight attendant was suspended for stealing a muffin that a passenger left uneaten on his tray.
- Indirect Sell: Where Will You Wear Your New Hat? - Above an article selling new hats. This kind of headline makes the reader curious - "What hat?" "Where *would* I wear this hat? At the beach?" and helps to subtly get them more interested in what's on offer. If they imagine themselves with a new hat then there's a chance they'll be warmed up to the idea of purchasing one.

3. The news or press release headline

Examples:

- Tesco Opens 500th Store In UK
- Boy Band "Take That" To Reform

4. The "how to fix your problem" headline

Imagine you're writing an article to help people with a specific problem. It's a good bet that these people will be looking for an answer to their problem. What better way to let them know that your content is the answer to their prayers than by saying "How To Fix Your Problem"?

Examples: How To Tune a Guitar / How To Cure Your Acne

5. The straight-up question headline

You only have to look at an issue of any women's magazine to see how powerful these kind of headlines can be. They ask a question that resonates with the reader, by asking a question readers have asked themselves in the past, or questions that makes them think "oh, that's true, why *is* that?".

Example:

- Do You Lock The Door When You Have A Bath Even If No-one's Home?
- Why Do Your Parents Irritate You So Much?

A more clever and subtle way of using this is to present a question readers have never thought to ask, then imply that they *should* be worried about the answer.

- Why Are You Still Paying Full Price For Your Rent?
- Do You Know The Damage Your Keyboard Is Doing To Your Hands?

6. The "Demand and Command" headline

Uses strong verbs and calls to action to get straight to the point, telling readers exactly what they have to do.

Examples:

- Take Your Medicine NOW
- Subscribe To My RSS Feed

7. The "X Reasons Why Y" headline

You'll see these all over the internet because they work. You haven't got to always use "reasons why", just the number format. The best format is to start with a number, then a sensationalist adjective (terrifying, unbelievable, disgusting, amazing) and then write the subject of the list in your content.

Examples:

- 7 Delicious Tricks That Will Turn You Into A Super-Chef Overnight
- 6 Scary Things The Bible Didn't Teach You
- Top 10 Mistakes Dog Keepers Make
- 5 Amazing Tips to Improve Your Health
-

8. The social proof headline

People like products that other people like, regardless of the benefits one product has over another. Just look at the huge number of tissue brands, all selling almost identical products, repackaged.

People think: I've heard of Kleenex. I've seen my friends use Kleenex. I think I'll buy some Kleenex. The headline helps to bypass the reader's critical functions because: X amount of other people can't be wrong and it shows seemingly impartial evidence that what you're offering really is great.

These headlines can be crafted in a number of ways. They can be a straight-up testimonial, or they can inform the reader exactly how many other people are already doing what you want them to do.

Example: 18,956 People Are Making A Full-Time Living By Following From Newbie to Millionaire.

9. The "added authenticity" headline

Try looking at the benefits of your product from a different point of view and adding authenticity with some small, powerful qualifiers.

Let's say you've discovered a type of food that can make racing pigeons fly faster. Your first attempt might be something like:

"Superfood That Turns Racing Pigeons Into Nuclear Powered Homing Missiles"

It's good, it's punchy, it's intriguing. But, if you add just a few extra elements it can be transformed into a killer headline:

 "26 Year Old Motorcyclist Stumbles On Superfood That Turns Racing Pigeons Into Nuclear Powered Homing Missiles Easily and 100% Naturally"

Adding exactly who discovered it, and implying that it happened by accident, will intrigue the reader and make the content seem strange and curious.

The closing of the headline is there to answer any objections that the reader might have as soon as they read it. They might read it and think "I bet this is really hard" or "I don't want to give my birds something that could be artificial", so your last two points instantly remove their worries.

Important for headlines:

- The headline is MOST important and you must summarize the whole article or sales letter in one sentence.

- The headline must arouse the reader's curiosity.

- A headline that asks a question and promises an answer to that question is a winner.

- Get the reader to search through the article for the answer to that question.

- Spend lots of time on your headlines. Write down a few different ones and narrow them down to the best.

Chapter 3. Useful Content To Use

1. PLR articles

PLR articles are easy content for whatever you're creating. The downside is that Google will generally ignore your site if you use them because so many other people have the same content on their sites. For that reason I recommend either using it very sparingly, or not at all. Only use them to give away or to re-word.

2. Images

You should aim to have at least one image per post/page. When adding images make sure their filenames are the same as the keyword you're optimising your page for.

e.g. You've created a page on a keyword you've researched and want to rank in Google for. Let's say this keyword is "fly fishing". Your image should be named *flyfishing.jpg* and the alt text for the image should be *fly fishing*. If this is hard to understand then let me give an example of how the HTML for the image should look:

<img src="http://www.yourdomain.com/images/flyfishing.jpg" alt="fly fishing" />

3. Videos

Videos are a great way of keeping visitors on your site, while offering real SEO benefits and getting you more traffic. YouTube videos frequently appear in the first page of Google for highly competitive keywords so you know that it's worth doing.

Consumers today expect video sales pages, video testimonials and so on. The companies that do not have these can be looked upon as unprofessional and maybe even lose sales.

You don't have to create the videos yourself. If you find a video that you really like (eg. on YouTube) and want to promote it, you can email the creator asking to buy it or get permission to use it on your site. The owner of the video will usually sell it for less than $150 because he or she will be amazed that someone wants it. Most of the time the owner will simply give it to you. Then you just add your URL to it and upload it to your various video site accounts!

Keep your videos short, at a maximum of five to seven minutes. You must either mention your website or include your website in the video.

Recording your screen to create a video:

If you want to make instructional videos or record something from your computer screen, I recommend using the screen capturing software: www.camtasia.com. This is not free of charge but, in my opinion, is **simply the best.**

You can also use www.jingproject.com which lets you record five minutes maximum for a video. If you need 20 minutes of video you can record four videos of five minutes. This is free of charge.

> **TOP TIP : To avoid people stealing or copying videos from your site, you can use www.viddler.com to store your videos. People can then only see the video on the domain name that you tell them. The visitor will not be able to download the video from that domain name. Other interesting sites that you can use for storage services for your videos are: www.EZS3.com and http://aws.amazon.com/s3/**

Once you have finished a video, you can upload it to video sites in order to get traffic. ALWAYS use your keywords in the title and description when submitting a video.

The best video sites to upload your videos to are:

- AOL PR8 – www.on.aol.com
- Google Video PR9 – video.Google.com
- Viddler PR6 - www.viddler.com
- YouTube PR8 - www.youtube.com
- Brightcove PR8 – www.brightcove.com
- Buzznet – www.buzznet.com
- Daily Motion PR7 - www.dailymotion.com
- Dropshots PR6 – www.dropshots.com
- Fark PR6 – www.fark.com/video
- Flixya – www.flixya.com
- Screenjunkies PR7 – www.screenjunkies.com
- Jibjab PR6 n- www.jibjab.com
- Liveleak PR6 – www.liveleak.com
- Metacafe PR7 – www.metacafe.com
- Revver PT7 – www.revver.com
- Videovat PR6 – www.videovat.com
- Vimeo PR7 – www.vimeo.com

Tube Mogul - Sign up here to have all your videos automatically uploaded to up to 20 video hosting sites all at once - www.tubemogul.com

Myliveactor – www.myliveactor.com An actor will create your video

For video making sites:
- www.audacity.sourceforge.net free audio editing
- www.videomaker.com/youtube/

4. Flip video

This gets a separate paragraph here because I love it : On this video camera, you just press the start button to start filming and when done, simply put the built-in USB port into your computer and your video is done. No more transferring files or converting files to video-format files like you have to do with most video cameras.

Benefits:

- It fits in your pocket

- It films HD quality

- It is extremely easy to use, push-button stuff, with no manual needed

- It connects to USB port of your PC

- It is affordable

- It will record up to four hours of high quality video and audio, and more if you get the larger memory version

- Take it everywhere with you, together with a mini tripod, and you can record high definition videos wherever you are

You can get one at www.Amazon.com , search for 'flip video'.

5. Audio

Never put audio on a page if customers can't turn it off easily. This is especially important with music - if they don't share your taste it may put them off.

There are two ways of using audio content well on your site:

- Give your visitors the chance to download audio that they can listen to in their own time - every time they listen to it they'll be reminded of your site and, not only will it keep them coming back, it could be shared, bringing more users to your site.

- Have auto-playing audio that directs the visitor to the different areas of your site, gives them a clear call-to-action or testimonials from other users.

I'm sure you can think of more creative ideas. If you can fully utilise sound and video content then you'll find your content is better received.

www.sourceforge.net – a free download that lets you create audio recordings on a PC.

www.applian.com/replay-av – lets you record the music that is playing on your PC.

For royalty-free music clips:
www.publicdomain4u.com
www.royaltyfreemusic.com
www.shockwave-sound.com
www.slicktracks.com

Chapter 4. Must-have Elements on Your Website

You can download free (and payable) legal policies for your website from:

- Website Law - www.seqlegal.com

Here are the most important things your website must have to look and feel professional, and to increase your chances of ranking for search engines.

1. Disclaimer

Compulsory if you're running a site that has anything to do with health, earning money or contains information and products that could be potentially harmful.

2. Privacy policy

It's a good idea to have a privacy policy anyway, but if you're planning on installing AdSense then this is something you have to do. Add the Easy Privacy Policy plugin to your Wordpress page and this will be set up automatically for you.

3. Contact form

To install the Contact Form Plugin, visit http://wordpress.org/extend/plugins/contact-form-7.

The minimum that should be on your contact form is your name and email address. It is better to also give your address and even phone number to create more credibility.

4. Terms of use

This is a contract that the user automatically agrees to by using your site. Make sure that all legalities not covered in the Disclaimer and Privacy Policy are included here.

5. Sitemap

A sitemap is a must-have if you want Google to accurately find all the elements on your site. Install the XML-Sitemap plugin from here or visit http://wordpress.org/extend/plugins/xml-sitemap-feed and it will be done for you. If you are not using Wordpress, search for " HTML sitemap" in the help section of whatever web design software you use.

6. Copyright policy

At the bottom of every page you should have: "Copyright 2011, All Rights Reserved". This helps protect your intellectual property from people who may wish to steal your content.

7. Guarantee or refund policy

If you are selling something, make sure that you always put a money-back-guarantee on your website or a refund policy. The visitor will be more likely to buy when there is a money-back guarantee.

8. Testimonials (if applicable)

If you're selling a product or services on it is crucial to have testimonials visible. Testimonials add proof to your site and will help persuade your visitors into spending money on what you're offering.

Video testimonials are very effective.

If you put testimonials on your site, always put the full name and, if possible, the website from the person giving the testimonial. If possible, add a picture.

Audio testimonials convert better than written testimonials. Here are two websites where you can create or buy audio testimonials.

- Audio Generator - www.audiogenerator.com
- Article Video Robot - www.articlevideorobot.com

Unfortunately testimonials are not always real (you can buy testimonials from www.fiverr.com). People get paid to do them. I am sorry if I have shocked you by saying this, but it is true. If you are going to be in the IM business you need to know. I suggest that you never use made up and fake testimonials.

A lot of internet marketers know that testimonials are not always real therefore if you are selling a product related to internet marketing it is less important to put testimonials on your site.

However, you must keep in mind that your visitor or potential buyer does not know how this IM world works, who earns money from what clicks, etc…therefore it is important to put testimonials on your site if your site is outside the IM niche. Please make sure that you read the testimonials rules of the relevant websites e.g. Clickbank rules, etc...

9. 'About us' page

If possible you should put a photograph of a person on the 'about us' page. People want to know who they are buying from. If you say something about yourself and put a photograph on your page, you become a real person which helps improve your credibility. After all, you don't buy just from "anybody" on the web, so compel your visitors to buy from you. Increase your chances by increasing your trustworthiness with an 'about us' page.

Putting a signature on your site also improves your credibility. You can create a signature at www.mylivesignature.com It is free.

10. Home page

If the home page fails to tell what the site is all about, or what users can find on the site, people will leave the site more quickly.

11. Google Analytics

Google Analytics is a website statistics program that you can use for free. It is not visible to the visitor of your site. It tells you all sorts of detailed information about your site including:

- Number of daily/weekly/monthly visitors
- Your site's page views
- Bounce Rate
- From which search engines your visitors came
- What country your visitors are from
- Which browser people use
- Traffic sources
- How long people stay on your site
- How visitors found your site
- Which keywords were used to land on your site

It's crucial to have this in place so you can see exactly how well your site's doing.

You only have to sign up once and you can put Google Analytics on all your sites. The way it works: Google gives you a code and you put that code on your website. Sign up and have a look at their tutorials www.Google.com/analytics – it is completely free. There are some other good analytics tools available:

www.accesswatch.com - free

www.extremetracking.com - free

www.statcounter.com - free

www.webtrends.com - high end to pay solution

The following four pages show you an example of Google Analytics from one of my sites. This site no longer belongs to me as I have sold it. As you can see from the first graph the site did not get ANY traffic before September but it does after I improved my SEO and created a few backlinks as described in this book.

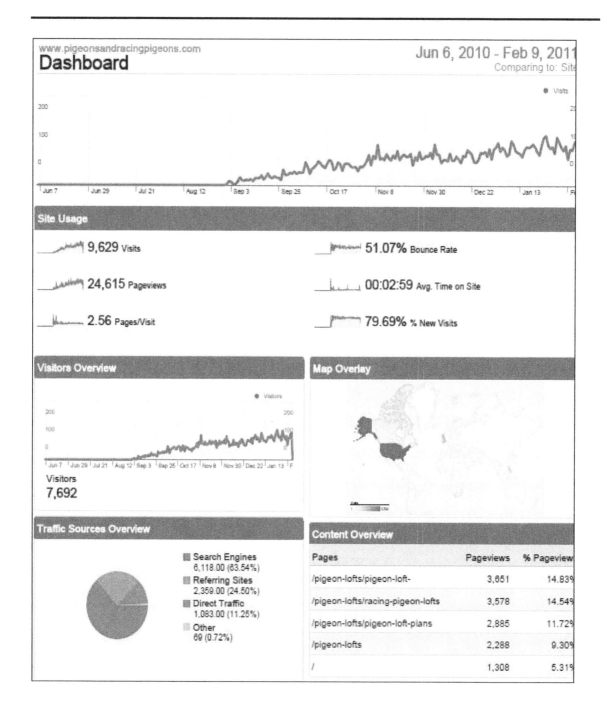

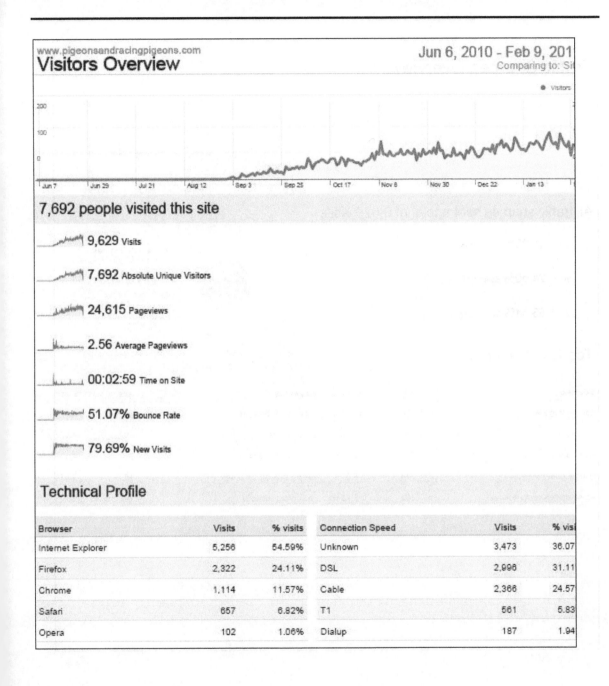

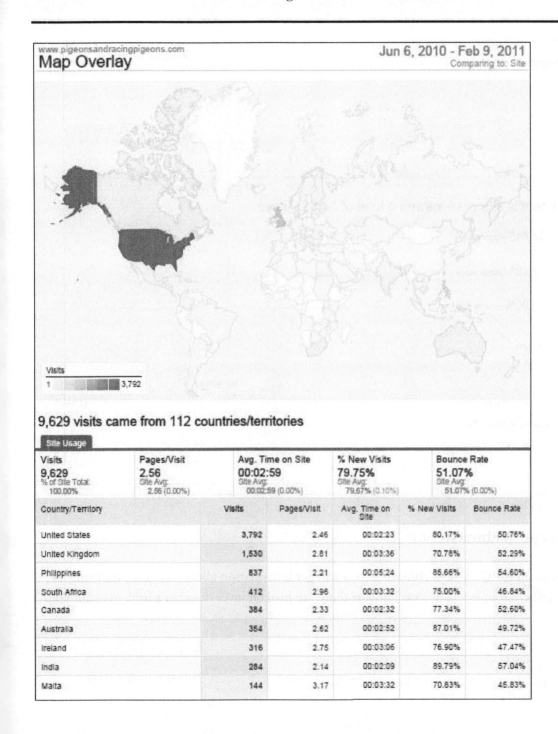

www.pigeonsandracingpigeons.com

Map Overlay

Jun 6, 2010 - Feb 9, 2011
Comparing to: Site

Visits
1 ▭ 3,792

9,629 visits came from 112 countries/territories

Site Usage

Visits	Pages/Visit	Avg. Time on Site	% New Visits	Bounce Rate
9,629 % of Site Total: 100.00%	**2.56** Site Avg: 2.56 (0.00%)	**00:02:59** Site Avg: 00:02:59 (0.00%)	**79.75%** Site Avg: 79.67% (0.10%)	**51.07%** Site Avg: 51.07% (0.00%)

Country/Territory	Visits	Pages/Visit	Avg. Time on Site	% New Visits	Bounce Rate
United States	3,792	2.46	00:02:23	80.17%	50.76%
United Kingdom	1,530	2.81	00:03:36	70.78%	52.29%
Philippines	837	2.21	00:05:24	85.66%	54.60%
South Africa	412	2.96	00:03:32	75.00%	46.64%
Canada	384	2.33	00:02:32	77.34%	52.60%
Australia	354	2.62	00:02:52	87.01%	49.72%
Ireland	316	2.75	00:03:06	76.90%	47.47%
India	284	2.14	00:02:09	89.79%	57.04%
Malta	144	3.17	00:03:32	70.83%	45.83%

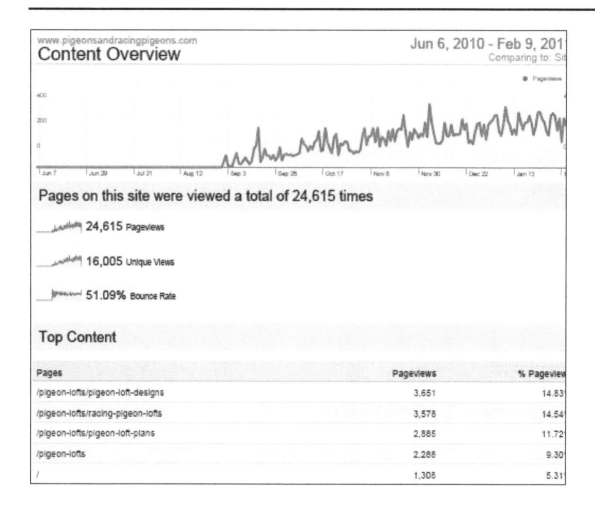

12. Google Webmasters

If you sign up for Google Webmasters you will get information about crawling, indexing and search traffic. Google will let you know if there are broken links or other problems with your site.

13. RSS feed – Really Simple Syndication

These are very popular but I have several sites that are doing well without an RSS feed. RSS stands for Really Simple Syndication and is a way for users to check on your recently updated content without having to visit your site. The most common way of subscribing to an RSS feed is by clicking on the icon that looks like this on a web page:

Users have content posted automatically to their site, or keep themselves updated on your latest posts.

If you're having trouble understanding exactly how these work then take a look at this example below. I have an RSS feed set up for the latest headlines on the BBC website. If I want to see the latest news stories I just click the button marked "Latest Headlines" and it shows me the latest news:

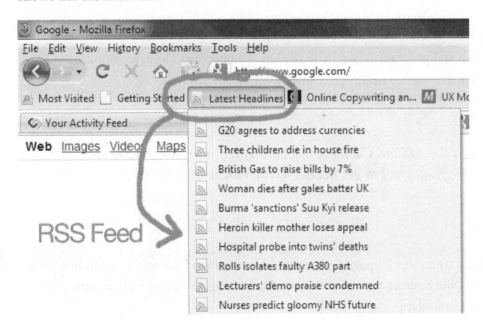

Here are some RSS resources:

www.bloglines.com

www.feedvalidator.org

www.rssfeeds.com

www.rssreader.com

The Google RSS reader is free and easy to use: www.Google.com/reader . When a new article is available for a blog that you have subscribed to, the blog will be clearly visible in your reader.

To get an RSS feed on your website (with weebly.com), follow these steps:
- search for keyword + blog or keyword + rss
- look for the orange feed button that looks like this :

- Click on the button which will take you to the RSS feed
- Copy that URL and paste it on your RSS feed in weebly.com. The URL to paste will usually be something like : www.rocketnews.com/feed
Now your website will always have fresh content.

This is explained in the AffiliateCashTactics.com video tutorials. Please visit www.VideosNewbieBook.com to get access to the video.

14. Search box

If you have a website with over 25 pages of content, I recommend putting a search box on it to make it easier for your visitors to find what they are looking for. Most web design programs have this as standard.

15.Google Map

If applicable to your site, for instance, if you have a website about physiotherapy in London, and you want to attract visitors, you MUST put a Google Map on your site to increase your ranking chances. You simply need to get the code from Google Maps and paste it onto your site. In WebPlus X4, web design program, there is a tab "insert Google map" and all you need to do is put in your postcode (zip code).

16. Online payment processor

If you are selling Clickbank products on your website, you can automatically use Clickbank as your Merchant Account. However, if you are selling your own eBook or your own products without using Clickbank, you will need an online Payment Processor or Debit and Credit Card Payment Processor to collect the money from your customers. I suggest you start with PayPal and once your sales are going, you can use others.

PayPal and Clickbank are easy to sign up with but getting your own Payment Processer (so you can take debit and credit cards over the phone or on the web) isn't easy as banks have a lot of administrative procedures. As a beginner you're better to stick with PayPal and Clickbank as these two are all you need to make money.

Some reputable payment processing companies are:
www.1shoppingcart.com RECOMMENDED
 www.2checkout.com RECOMMENDED
www.Clickbank.com RECOMMENDED
www.paydotcom.com
www.paypal.com RECOMMENDED
www.streamline.co.uk UK customers only
www.streamline.com
www.worldpay.com

17. What does Google like – my findings

So what does Google like? How can you maximise your chances to show on the first page?

What does Google like? Here's the answer from my everyday experience, not from a programmer's or internet geek's point of view. In Google type in any keyword in any niche and you will see that the following applies for quite a few of the websites shown on the first pages. This is quite a few, not all.

Here's what's officially known or mentioned in other IM courses, books and websites.

- Google likes content, meaning websites with a lot of pages with good content.
- Google likes SEO, therefore websites with good SEO work and good content have a good chance of being shown
- Google likes aged domains: buy older domain names if you can
- Google likes links: buy a domain name with links if you can
- Google likes domain name with keyword in URL
- Google likes forums
- Google likes blogs
- Google likes links authority PR4+
- Google likes Squidoo
- Google likes Ezine articles
- Google likes Yahoo answers
- Google likes Ehow.com

Google does not like :

- Squeeze pages. These are pages where you need to fill in your email address in order to get to the next page or to get a freebie of some sort. These pages aim to capture your email address so the owner of the squeeze page can send you emails, mostly with affiliate links.

- One-page wonders. These are the one-page sales letters.

- PLR articles or PLR videos.

- Websites with lots of flashing images. Don't use Flash elements - Google can't understand or read Flash, so won't know what your website is about. This will be a real problem when you start trying to get to page one of the search results.

- Splash pages. These are pages full of graphics that create a wow-factor when first visited by customers but that's where it stops: "wow" then "bye" as such sites are annoying for visitors. A splash page cannot be indexed by Google, so might never be shown.

My findings

These are my findings, according to my research over the last five years. Try it to see if it works for you. I have applied some of these rules with success.

- Google likes the following words in the Title Tags, Meta Description and Headings:
    o associations
    o benefits
    o blog
    o directory
    o easy
    o exclusive
    o exhibition
    o fast
    o forum
    o important
    o information
    o news
    o resources
    o updates
    o tips

- Google likes Adsense. Google is a commercial institution so it is only logical that it will show websites with Adsense, on its first pages. You might not find this in any Google book but in my experience, that's the way it is. Try it yourself: a lot of the websites on the first pages of Google have Adsense on them even if they have not applied good SEO-rules. Another example that Google is a commercial institution is that when you run an Adwords Campaign with Google, it will show your ads more if your CTR (Click Through Rate) is better than your competitors, even if you pay less per keyword. If more people click more on your ad, Google will earn more money from you, so will show your site closer to the top of its rankings. Want proof that Google likes Adsense? Here it is. Search for golf swing in Google and www.perfectgolfswingtips.net is the first site in Google.

golf swing

About 8,310,000 results (0.08 seconds)   Go to Go

▶ Videos for **golf swing** - Report videos

Golf Swing Steps
1 min - 7 Jul 2010
Uploaded by D34M4
youtube.com

How To Perform The Perfect
Golf Swing
9 min - 19 Jul 2006
videojug.com

Images for **golf swing** - Report images

Perfect **Golf Swing** Tips
Learn perfect **golf swing** tips and supercharge your game. Find out how to drop 10 strokes with this 1 simple secret technique...
perfectgolfswingtips.net/ - Cached - Similar

Golf Tuition - **Golf** Today
Basically it is the wrong way in which the **golf swing** has been analysed and consequently the teaching this is based on is equally wrong. ...
www.golftoday.co.uk/proshop/tuition/index.html - Cached - Similar

Now open the site and you will see that there is not a lot of content on the site at all but there is a lot of Adsense on it. Note that the domain name also has the word "tips" in it.

Important note: Google constantly changes the way it searches sites and in what is called the "Google Panda updates", sites with a lot of Adsense were hit hard and not shown in Google. Therefore if you try and find websites with a lot of Adsense on as you read this book, it might be different all together.

This of course goes against the rule about content being important for your site but that's the way it is: Google is the boss and decides which sites to show. I constantly come across these types of sites in lots of different niches. Try it yourself. You could make up a "quick and easy" site of a few pages with a good domain name and a little bit of SEO and your site might be shown. Important : these are exceptions to the rule.

-   Google likes videos. A lot of the websites on the first pages of Google have videos on them. People love videos these days. Google knows that people love videos. Google wants to please people who type in a keyword, so it puts up videos if possible. Simple logic.

-   Google likes shorter URLs as they usually perform better in the search results. This could be because shorter URLs are the older ones, and Google likes old domain names.

- Google likes Internal Page Links repeated at the top, on the left and at the bottom of the pages. Example of page links on the top and at the bottom:

Home Page	Curtain Fabrics	Curtains	Custom Curtains	Voile Curtains

Repeated page links at the bottom:

Curtains	Fabrics
All curtains	Voile fabric
Pencil pleat	Silk taffeta
Eyelet curtains	Traditional fabric
Blackout curtains	Curtain fabrics
Designer curtains	Blind fabric
Lined curtains	Sale fabric
Unlined curtains	Lining Fabric
Silk curtains	Curtain toile
Window curtains	Floral fabric
Custom curtains	Contemporary fabric
Made to measure	Plain fabric
curtains	Pvc tablecover

In most of the websites that I build I use a combination of all the factors that I think Google likes to successfully rank in Google. It really is that simple: if you know what Google likes, apply it as much as possible in order to maximise your chances of ranking.

Although I am not a big Facebook user myself, I suggest you also create a Profile on Facebook with a Fan Page and a Group in your niche. Google looks at Facebook links. When I started building my websites five years ago, this was not really important, so I have never used Facebook either to get traffic or to rank in Google.

If you are selling your own products from your site, create a video or outsource the creation for a video. Video sales letters convert better than written sales letters.

Part 8. Monetising Your Site

A video about adding monetisation with GoDaddy is included with my video tutorials. Please visit www.VideosNewbieBook.com to get access to the videos.

When you build your site you should have monetisation on your mind at all times.

By now you know how to create targeted, search-engine-optimised content for your site but how will this make you money? You need several elements on your site to make you money.

When designing and creating your site you need to be in a certain mindset: every link on your page should be there to either take the user to content that will further the chances of them being a customer (good content, sales pages) or will earn you money (AdSense, affiliate links).

The monetisation check list (or the money-making links) for your site is:

1. Opt-in box

2. Adsense

3. Clickbank products

4. Recurring affiliate products

5. Other affiliate products

6. eBook

7. Amazon products

8. CPA offers

9. Upsells (for the more advanced)

10. Exit page opportunity (for the more advanced)

11. Better CR

Important note: you do not need to put all these monetisation methods on each website. You can just put a mixture of these on. I recommend always having an opt-in form and an ebook. An opt-in form will give you the possibility to sell to your targeted customers more than once and an ebook, with a picture of the ebook on your site linked to the sales page, will create most of the sales.

1. Opt-in box

The opt-in box will earn you money with email marketing. The money is in the email list. Fact. You need to build your list and one way of doing that is by putting an opt-in box on your site for email marketing.

Why is an opt-in box so important?

The majority of your visitors will leave your site without buying anything. According to statistics, less than 5% of your visitors will buy when they first come across your site. Visitors know nothing about you, don't trust you with their money, and so are reluctant to buy. If you can convince them to give you their email address, you can email them several times to try to win their trust. Some statistics say that a customer is much more likely to buy from you after having seen your name or website seven times. Without an opt-in box, those 95% of your visitors that do not buy are gone forever and might never come back. If you capture their contact details you can get them back at a later stage.

According to a survey done in September 2008, USA online buyers visit websites differently:

62% responded to an email promotion

38% had a link from the merchant

24% entered the URL directly

20% had a bookmark

13% used search engines

62% responded to an email promotion! That's why you need an opt-in box because email marketing does work!

Source of survey : www.e-marketer.com

Also, visitors who opt-in are targeted customers. This means that they are clearly interested in your niche. Large corporations spend fortunes trying to find targeted customers by advertising, attending expensive exhibitions and so on. You can find targeted customers free by adding an opt-in box. To become an internet millionaire, you need a list of targeted interested potential customers to convert into buyers. If they buy once, they are likely to buy again. A buyer is a buyer is a buyer!

In the IM world it is generally accepted that on average, a person who has opted in to receive emails is worth about $1 a month. This may not sound like a lot, but imagine if you had 1000 email subscribers ($1000) or 10,000 subscribers ($10,000). It quickly adds up and is one of the most lucrative ways to make money online. To put it simply: 1000 opt-ins is $1000 per month, 5000 opt-ins is $5000 per month. Every time you email affiliate links to your email list, some people will buy the product, so the more people on your list, the more people will buy via your email.

Don't forget, everybody starts with a list of zero subscribers. If you work hard on building a list, you will rake the benefits over and over again. Once you have a list of 10,000 subscribers even if only 1% buys from your email at a profit of $29 per sale, you have made $2900. This will happen every time that you send a new email with an affiliate link. If you only send two emails per month, you can make $5800 per month.

Important message: get a list!

Don't have a website without a way to capture the email addresses of your visitors. Opt-in boxes for mobile phones are becoming more and more popular. Instead of sending emails to the user, you send them text messages with money-making links.

Make sure that you install your opt-in form as a matter of importance. When someone visits your site, they may never come back. If they give you their email address and you send them occasional, useful information then you increase the chances of their return hugely.

To get more email sign-ups, consider giving something away for free as an incentive. This could be a short document you've written, a relevant PLR article/eBook or free access to an email course you've prepared. People will not forget you when you give them something good and valuable for free. If the recipient of your freebie thinks "wow, this is good stuff" they will remember you. And if they remember you, they are likely to buy from you.

People will forget what you said, people will forget what you did, but people will never forget how you made them feel.

Maya Angelou

Make sure that anything you give away contains your website address. Whenever someone reads your freebie they'll find the URL of your site, resulting in more visitors.

> **TOP TIP: Put an opt-in box on each page of your website, not just on the landing page. Give yourself a second chance to get email addresses.**

What emails work?

To get an idea of what kind of emails are best at earning you money, sign up for a newsletter or get a freebie from a few websites in your niche. Remember that you can learn a lot from your competitors. Keep all the headlines that they use in a Word document and use the same type of headline that you like, but never copy it completely.

There's no need to make it complicated or follow lessons and courses on e-mail marketing.

The title of your email is what your potential customers see first. Here are some good titles:

"After you read this, your cat will never scratch a chair again"

"Things you HAVE to know when buying a micro pig"

"With these tips you WILL get the girl you want"

How to set up the best follow up messages with your auto responder

There's a fine art to properly cultivating a good email list. You don't want to send too many messages because people will stop listening, but then again you don't want to send too few because you'll be forgotten.

Follow up messages are emails that are sent automatically at regular intervals to subscribers. Some basic rules for these automatic messages are:

- Send messages frequently.
- Follow up opt-ins immediately.
- Eliminate passivity in your messages - keep your messages strong and clear.
- Keep your content balanced - give some advice, give away a great freebie and then in the next email sell something. Don't just sell, sell, sell.
- Write authoritatively.

- Clean your list to remove unresponsive subscribers.

- Keep interest high by keeping your offers hot - include limited-time-offers, say you have limited spaces available and so on.

- Do NOT overdo it! Do NOT send messages with links too often. My rule is once a month is more than enough although I am aware that a lot of gurus send links to their list, two or three times a week, which is far too often in my opinion.

On average, one of your subscribers will have to receive about seven informative or interesting emails from you before they purchase something. Take advantage of this by sending seven useful, informative emails to them before sending two emails where you are selling something.

Magic number 7:

- 7 is the number of times people need to see a name or ad in order to remember it.

- 7 is the number of seconds you have for people to either leave your site or stick around for a bit longer.

- 7 is the number of things most people can remember at once.

- $19.97 sells better than $19.99 (according to research).

What to put on your email opt-in page

Just like a sales page, your opt-in has to really sell the reasons behind your visitors signing up.

Things to look out for:

- Have a great headline.
- Strip out all extra, non-essential page elements so that the visitor has no choice but to read your sales pitch and opt-in to your mailing list.
- You have five seconds to capture the visitor's interest - if you can't get them in that time then you never will.
- Use words like "*secret*", "*easy*", "*passive*", "*income*", "*Top 10 Tips*" "FREE"

> **TOP TIP: Make sure you opt-in with one of your email addresses so you receive all your own emails and know how your customers read and view them.**

URL-shortening services or link-cloaking software

Sometimes an affiliate link is so long and looks so unattractive that you might want to shorten it before sending it to potential customers. That's what URL-shortening means. You can get this URL:

www.amazon.co.uk/Head-Ti-S6-Titanium-Tennis-Racket/dp/B001DMKZSQ/ref=sr_1_2?s=sports&ie=UTF8&qid=1294687755&sr

To this URL:

www.tennis-racket/Tintanium When people click on this they will be re-directed to the Amazon website as shown above with your affiliate link.

Here are two URL-shortening websites:
www.bitly.com
www.tinyurl.com

For more, just search for them. Make sure that you read the terms and conditions as some of these websites will automatically delete your URL if it's not used or clicked on for a certain number of days.

When to send your emails for maximum response

Mailing your list at the correct time of the day or month can have a huge impact on your sales. Email recipient behaviour is far from predictable. From all the emails that I have sent to my list I have come to the following conclusions.

Best time of the month to email your list is just after Pay Day as people haven't spent their monthly income yet. Most of the time people get paid at the end of the month, so the best time to email them is on 30th, 31st or 1st , 2nd of each month. Of course there are people who get paid weekly or every two weeks but the majority get paid monthly.

The best time of the week to email your list is Mondays and Wednesdays. Fridays, Saturdays and Sundays are the worst converting days. The best time of the day to email your list is early in the morning, between 8am and 10am. Worst time is between 4pm and 6pm.

Of course you will have to work out the different time zones and set your auto-responder to send the email in the morning of the time zone you are emailing. For instance, if you are in the UK and you want people to receive your email on a Tuesday morning, you will have to set your auto responder to send the email six hours earlier (or later) as Aweber is based in the USA.

TOP TIP: Do NOT send emails too often. People have their own lives to run and will not have the time to open five emails per day from you. Do not make the same mistake that some guru's make: sending too many emails. You have seen the screenshot of my inbox with over 11,500 emails at the beginning of this book. The majority of them will stay unopened forever.

TOP TIP: If you decide not to sign up with an auto responder but want to do email marketing, you need to be aware that some Internet Service Providers won't let you send the same email to more than 9 to 100 names. For every problem there is a solution. However you can buy cheap software with which you can send bulk emails.

You can have a look at: www.group-mail.com and www.glocksoft.com

---

Here are some interesting newsletter websites:

www.lyris.com/us-en/solutions email marketing solutions

www.emailstatcentre.com email statistics

2. AdSense

AdSense is the advertising platform run by Google. Once set up you will earn money every time someone clicks on one of the advertising links.

Creating a new AdSense unit is done as follows: Sign up here: www.Google.com/adsense/ or search for "Google Adsense Signup" if this page is no longer available.

I recommend using the same email and password as your Google Analytics account.

Once logged in select "AdSense Setup":

Click "AdSense for Content":

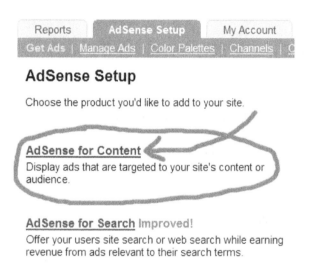

And then check the radio button next to "Ad unit" and press "Continue":

◉ **Ad unit** Text and image ads (default) ▾

Ad units contain either text ads, image ads, or both. The ads are targeted to the content of your page using contextual and placement targeting.

On the next page, select the format as a "300 x 250 Medium Rectangle" as, from my experience, this one gets the most clicks, so earns you more money.

The aim is to blend the ad into your content as well as possible. You'll find that blending will give you a much better click through rate for your ads. Change the title colour so that it matches the colour of your links, and the background colour and border to the same colour as your site's background.

Click "Continue".

Now we'll create a channel for this ad. Channels are useful because they allow you to get separate reports for the different ads that you're running. You only need to sign up with Google Adsense once and you can get all the Adsense codes for all your different sites. However, I recommend having two or three different Adsense accounts.

Let's say on some areas of your site you've got ads with colour scheme "A", and on some areas of your site you've got ads with colour scheme "B".

By separating the different ad codes into different channels, you'll be able to see which ad colour is getting the most clicks and then use this one for the entire site.

To create a new channel click the "Add new channel" link and enter a name for the channel. Normally I would simply name it after the domain name:

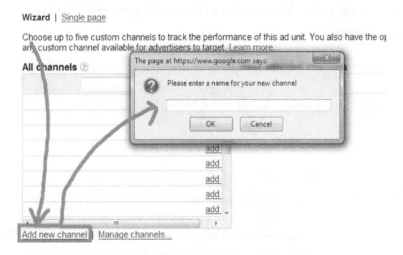

When naming your ad unit you can either leave the ad named as it is, or change it to something more useful. As we're using the AdSense Now! plugin, I'd recommend calling it something like "300x250, Adsense Now! [the date]":

AdSense for Content

Choose Ad Type > Choose Ad Format and Colors > Choose Ad Channels > **Save and Get Ad Code**

Wizard | Single page

Choose a name for this AdSense unit and then save it to get your code.

AdSense unit name:

Choose a name for this AdSense unit, so you can change its settings later. This name will appear in your code, but you can remove it if needed. ⓘ

300x250, AdSense Now! 11/11/10

e.g. Homepage, 300x250 ads, Above the fold, etc.

<< Back | **Submit and Get Code**

Press "Submit and Get Code".

You will then have your unique AdSense code. All you have to do now is copy and paste this into the box in the AdSense Now! Plugin:

This plugin will automatically place three ad units throughout any post or page you create. You can choose how these are aligned: left, centre, right or suppressed (hidden).

If you are not using Wordpress, the principle is still the same: grab your Adsense code and put it on your website.

A video about adding monetisations is included with my video tutorials. Please visit www.VideosNewbieBook.com to get access.

Increasing AdSense Earnings

Now, all your pages that are not optimised for buying keywords should be aimed to funnel visitors to these higher paying pages, which have Adsense on the page.

Here's an example:

Pages optimised for keywords may not earn you any money because they are keywords designed to gather information. All these information keyword pages should have content that drives visitors to your high AdSense payout page, by including internal page links.

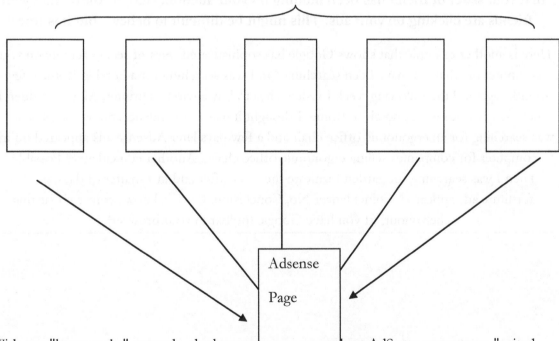

With our "horse tacks" example, the keyword with the highest AdSense payout was "gaited horse tacks". So we'd have links throughout the content on the other pages, linking to the page optimised for that keyword.

So on a page getting traffic from the keyword "white horse tacks" you would have sections in the content saying "have you seen these gaited horse tacks?", linking to the higher AdSense payout page.

This is a great trick if the high-payout keyword page is a competitive keyword, for which you'd never be able to rank highly otherwise.

Word of caution : Google is not stupid. Do not click on your own Adsense ads. Google might ban you. Do not ask friends to click on all the ads. It is illegal and certainly not ethical. The most important reason not to click on your own ads is because Google has an extremely clever system to detect fraud. Google will know that your friends are clicking on the ads because it can see who you have been chatting to, or emailed. You risk getting banned when you let your friends click on your ads. Once Google bans you from Adsense, it will be forever. It is simply not worth the risk of losing Adsense income. Even if you try to sign up again under a different name from the same computer or the same IP address, Google will know it is you! Just like eBay knows that your sister or friend has been bidding on your auction, Google knows that your friends are clicking on your ads. This might be difficult to believe, but it is true.

Here is another example that shows Google has sophisticated ways of seeing activity on your computer or what you have been searching for. I was searching for a hotel in Rome a few months ago and the following week I visited sites to buy a wireless printer. All of a sudden I saw Adsense ads about hotels in Rome. I thought it was a coincidence. Shortly after that I was searching for an ergonomic office chair and a few days later Adsense ads appeared on my computer for companies selling ergonomic office chairs. Another coincidence? Possible. Then I was searching for garden furniture the week after and in a matter of days, garden furniture ads appeared. Coincidence? No. Conclusion: Google knows your web-surfing behaviour, (if you have Google toolbar in your browser).

Although Google Adsense is my favourite and is the leader in this field, there are alternatives that you can use in case you are banned or in case you simply do not wish to do business with Google.

www.sitescout.com RECOMMENDED

www.kontera.com

www.dynamicoxygen.com

www.pocketcents.com

www.exitjunction.com

www.adbull.com

Top Tip : You can also use Clickbank ads to put on your site. These look like Adsense but Clickbank calls it HopAdBuilder instead. Whilst with Adsense, you get paid a small amount per click, with Clickbank you get paid the full commission.

When a visitor to your site clicks on a HopAd and buys the ClickBank product it promotes, you get the full affiliate commission— up to 75%, depending on the product! This can quickly add up to lots of money.

Clickbank does not pay a fee per click (unlike Adsense) and you only get paid when a purchase is made.

Visit www.Clickbank.com go to Account Settings and Hop Ad Builder, select the ad format you want and Clickbank will give you a code to put on your site.

Word of Caution: when you put Google Adsense on your site and other Pay per Click Advertising, there must be a clear distinction between the appearances of both. You must check Google's terms and conditions to avoid being banned.

3. Clickbank products

Visit www.Clickbank.com and find affiliate products on your niche. If possible, find affiliate products with recurring payments. Here's how to find Clickbank products and get the code to put on your website:

> **TOP TIP: To sign up with Clickbank, use a nickname that can be used for all your accounts, not a name with the keyword of your site in and not your own name. As you can use one Clickbank account for all your affiliate links, you do not want to be called "dog 123" when somebody buys a relaxation product from you. Your nickname will be shown on the bottom of the order form. A much better nickname would be something like "emc987" or "679kdb" which does not have a keyword in it. You can use that nickname for any products that you sell.**

Once you have set up an account with Clickbank **as an affiliate** and you have logged in, go to 'Marketplace' to find products suitable for your niche. If you are planning to sell your own products you need to sign up as a vendor, and you can then use your vendor account to find affiliate products.

> **TOP TIP: When you sign up as a vendor, the person buying from you will see your Vendor name. It is better to choose a vendor nickname that can be used for all your products, if you are not planning to set up a different Vendor account for every product you sell.**

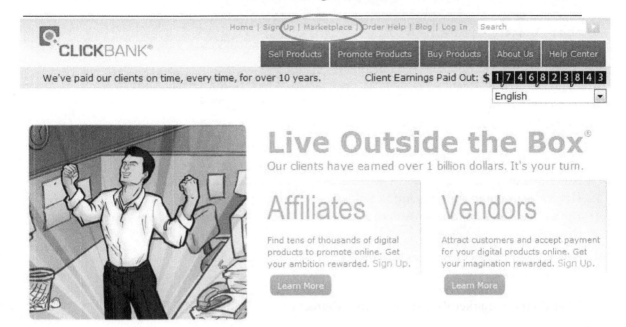

Type your keyword in the search box and click 'search':

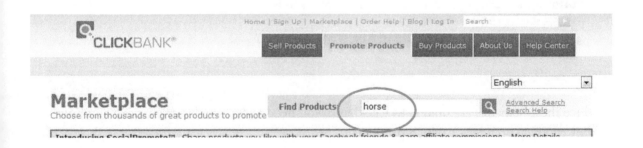

This will bring up a list of available products for you to sell. The list will give you the marketplace stats for each product.

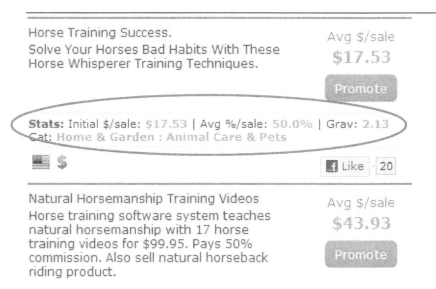

Horse Training Success.
Solve Your Horses Bad Habits With These
Horse Whisperer Training Techniques.

Avg $/sale
$17.53

Promote

Stats: Initial $/sale: $17.53 | Avg %/sale: 50.0% | Grav: 2.13
Cat: Home & Garden : Animal Care & Pets

Like 20

Natural Horsemanship Training Videos
Horse training software system teaches
natural horsemanship with 17 horse
training videos for $99.95. Pays 50%
commission. Also sell natural horseback
riding product.

Avg $/sale
$43.93

Promote

What do these marketplace stats mean? (source: www.Clickbank.com)

Once you've run your search in the Marketplace, you'll see a list of Clickbank products. At the bottom of each listing, you'll see sales statistics that look like this:

Stats: $/sale: $64.09 | Future $: $46.21 | Total $/sale: $86.37 | %/sale: 49.0% | %/refd: 89.0% | Grav: 89.70 | Cat: E-business & E-marketing : Pay Per Click Advertising

Since these statistics are unique to Clickbank, you need to know what they mean and how they can help you decide which products to promote.

Initial $/sale: This is the average amount that an affiliate earns for each sale. One-time upsell purchases (where you can buy an extra product after you have purchased the first one) are also considered initial sales. This number takes into account refunds, chargebacks and sales tax. Since vendors may offer products with different prices and commissions, the amount you earn on any given sale may not match this number exactly.

Average Rebill Total: This number is only shown if the vendor offers recurring billing products (e.g. products like memberships and subscriptions that regularly bill customers).

This number shows the average amount an affiliate makes on all of the rebilled sales. However, it doesn't include the initial sale amount.

Average $/sale: For one-time purchases, this number is the same as Initial $/sale. If the vendor offers recurring billing products, it equals the average total of the initial sale plus all rebills, divided by the number of initial sales. To put it simply, for every new purchase of this product, this is the average you'd make in total over the life of a new customer. However, this is just an average; the amount is not guaranteed.

Average %/sale: This number shows the average commission rate earned for all sales of a vendor's products, including one-time purchases, rebills and upsell purchases. Since vendors can offer different commission rates for different types of products, this number may not exactly match the commission rate you earn on any given sale.

Average %/rebill: This number is only shown if the vendor offers recurring billing products, and shows the average commission rate earned on rebills only.

Grav: Short for Gravity. This number represents a unique calculation by Clickbank that takes into account the number of different affiliates who earned a commission by promoting the product over the past 12 weeks. Since more recent transactions are given a higher value, this number can give you an idea of what products are "hot", in terms of being promoted by many affiliates and making a good number of sales. However, high gravity can also indicate that there is a lot of competition to promote this product. A gravity of 900 or higher is VERY high, which only the big gurus get.

Cat: The Marketplace category and sub-category of the site.

When I promote a Clickbank product, I am mainly concerned with:

- Gravity - This is basically a guide to how many people have bought the product. The higher the better.
- EPS/rebill - EPS is how much you will earn per sale and "rebill" is how much you'll earn every month after that (if it's a subscription service, for example)
- Commission - this is a number representing the percentage of money you earn when someone buys the product through your affiliate link

You can look at all the different websites by clicking on the title ("Natural Horsemanship Training Videos" in the screenshot below), which takes you to the sales page and order form for that product. Look at several pages, pick the one that you like or the one with a high gravity and get the affiliate link by clicking "promote". If you "ctrl+click" on each title, they will open in a different browser page, which will make it easier for you to compare the sites.

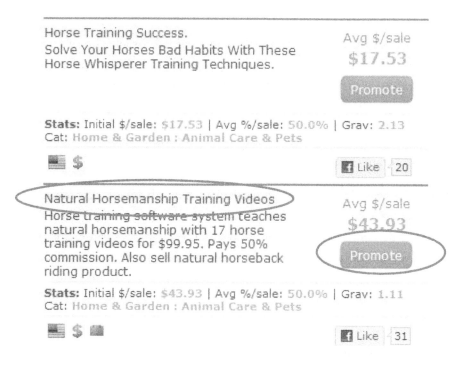

Once you click "Promote" you will see this screen:

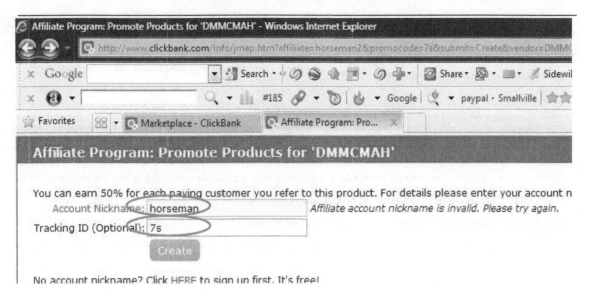

Fill in your nickname (your Clickbank username that you have set up when you opened an account with Clickbank), in this case horseman, and fill in your Tracking ID (also called TID). As explained before "horseman" is not a good nickname if you plan to sell different products from one Clickbank account. With the Tracking ID you can see in your clickbank account where the sale comes from. You do NOT need to fill in the Tracking ID. A basic hoplink does not tell you where and how you have made a sale. That is not a problem if you are only promoting a product in one way or with one traffic method. However, if you promote the same product with different traffic methods and different websites, you need to track where the sales come from by giving each traffic method a unique Tracking ID.

When you click "Create", you will see the following screen, which is the last step.

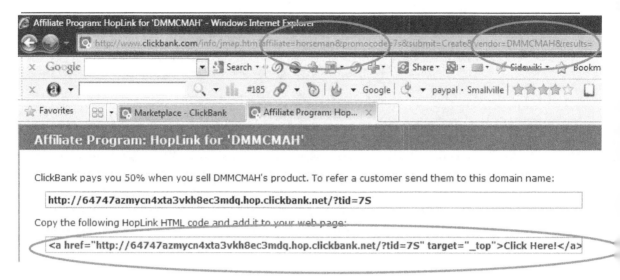

The code that appears now is the code with your hidden affiliate link, which you need to paste whenever you want to send customers to your affiliate product. This is an example of why people use url-shortening tools as discussed earlier as if you would email this code to your list, it would not look nice.

To test if it all works fine, follow these three steps:

Step 1: copy that code, starting from http://....... and paste it into the browser:

Step 2: Click "enter" and the following website will appear (Clickbank re-directs the site to the actual sales page):

Step 3: Click "Add To Cart" on the sales page to check if your affiliate code is correct:

Add To Cart

Step 4:

After you click "Add To Cart" the customer will see the order form to pay and to fill in their credit card details. If you scroll down to the bottom of the order form you will see your affiliate nickname, 'horseman'. That is how Clickbank knows that you earned commission on this sale. If it does not say horseman (or your affiliate nickname) at the bottom of the order form, you have done something wrong. IT IS VERY IMPORTANT TO CHECK THIS EACH TIME YOU CREATE A NEW AFFILIATE LINK.

iales Inc. ClickBank / 917 Lusk St / Suite 200 / Boise ID 83706.

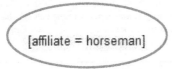

[affiliate = horseman]

Here is a screenshot from a Clickbank account with the Tracking ID showing where the sales come from. S7 is sales from www.7search.com and Miva is www.miva.com which are two PPC companies. I can see that two sales are from 7search and two sales are from Miva.

TID	Pmt	Currency	Txn Type	Item	Amount
s7	VISA	USD	Sale	1	$26.13
s7	VISA	CAD	Sale	1	$23.25
miva	VISA	USD	Sale	6	$33.90
miva	VISA	USD	Sale	6	$33.68

Every time you want a different ID, you need to click "Promote" and copy and paste the code.

I use the advanced search in Clickbank a lot but the following websites are free resources with a goldmine of information for Clickbank products. You can also create your affiliate link here.

www.CBEngine.com

www.CBTrends.com

www.cb-analytics.com

I will show you how to get your affiliate link with www.cb-analytics.com. It is very similar to how you get your link with Clickbank.

Go to *http://www.cb-analytics.com* to find Clickbank products and search for the main keywords that your site will target. This site gives detailed statistics for all Clickbank products. In this example, we want to search for things that the horse community would buy, as this is who the site is aimed at.

Searching for the keyword "horse" will bring up a list of sites, all selling Clickbank products.

3. STRADING	Bettors Bot - *Newest* Automated Betting Software	★
Gravity	12.1125 -0.98 Σ1K	Bettors' Bot will help automate **horse** racing betting! This is Hot and selling like cake...converting at a wicked 1 in 7!!! http://www.BettorsBot.com/jv.html Find websites related to BettorsBot.com
EPS / rebill	$21.95 / $29.50	
Commission / Referred %	50 / 41	
Google SEO / Adwords	0 / 0	
UVs last month / PR	0 / PR0	http://www.BettorsBot.com ▼

4. THR1VE	Train Your **Horse** & Cure Bad Habits!	★
Gravity	10.9413 +2.92 Σ2K	EBook(R) Package Revealing Powerful And Effective **Horse** Training Techniques Of Old Time Master **Horse** Trainers. Find websites related to horse<">www.trainwildhorse<
EPS / rebill	$12.24 / $0.00	
Commission / Referred %	50 / 11	
Google SEO / Adwords	26 / 0	
UVs last month / PR	7,318 / PR1	http://www.trainwildhorses.com/horsetraining1.htm ▼

Once you find one you like, click on the website link for that product, as I have highlighted.

Once you're on the site you will need to search for a link saying "affiliates" or "make money with us" or something similar. This is usually at the bottom or top of the page. In this example, it is at the bottom:

Clicking this link will take us to the affiliate page. Sometimes it will ask you to enter your name and email address to sign up, so you will need to do that.

On the next page will be a link to sign up to their affiliate scheme through ClickBank.

Follow that link and on the next page you will be asked to enter your Account Nickname and Tracking ID to create the affiliate link.

In the above image, I know that this sale came from the link with a certain Tracking ID. This helps you keep track of where the majority of your sales come from. This means you can keep tabs on which of your affiliate links are working the best, and which ones may need changing.

Back to our previous example. In the Tracking ID for this affiliate link I have put "horse site". This means that whenever we get commission from someone buying this product, it will tell us that they used the link with Tracking ID "horse site".

You can put nothing in there, or the name of the site onto which the product will be put, or anything you like. We're putting this product onto our horse site so I wrote "horse site" in the box.

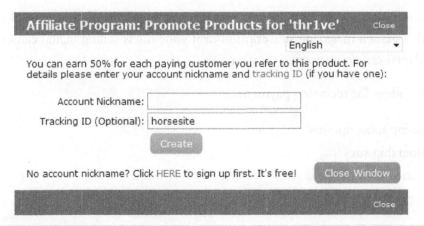

Hitting "Create" will take you to a page that looks like this:

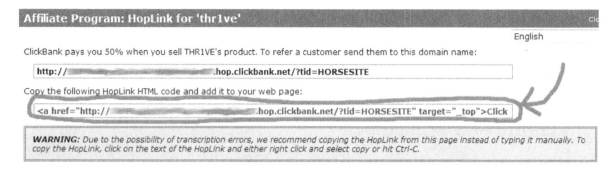

Copy the circled link as this is your affiliate link.

This link can be pasted into your site's HTML editor to produce a text link to the page with the anchor text "Click Here!".

4. Recurring affiliate products

If you will decide to purchase www.marketsamurai.com. , you can click on "Monetization" and Market Samurai will give you a list of options.

The best kind of affiliate products are those that offer a monthly subscription, meaning that from a single sale you'll be able to earn money month after month. It is always good to try to find affiliate products with RECURRING commissions. This pays you a monthly amount, on autopilot. To find recurring commissions, you could search for "membership sites" + "your keyword" to see if any of those sites have an affiliate scheme.

Here's an example: if you have a site on blooming flowers, you could put an affiliate link on your site with a garden magazine subscription or if your site is selling digital cameras, you could put a digital camera magazine on your site.

Here are a few ideas for recurring payments:

- Magazine subscriptions
- Membership sites
- Insurance
- Mortgage

- Health insurance
- Magazines
- Dating
- Newspapers
- Shopping cart
- Medication/chemist
- Vitamins
- Forex
- Diet programmes
- Book clubs
- DVD clubs
- Musical instrument lessons
- Golf memberships
- Clickbank products (some are recurring payments which are good ones to select)
- Selling hosting by promoting your host provider's affiliate links
- Monthly services/courses
- Monthly tutorials
- Sports/health clubs
- Telephone bills
- Web hosting
- Monthly payments to making-money online websites

www.lifetimecommissions.com gives you a list of affiliate products with recurring commissions. RECOMMENDED
www.magazines.com has an affiliate network. RECOMMENDED

TOP TIP : If there is a magazine available for your niche, ALWAYS put an affiliate link for that magazine on your website. It is recurring income.

LIFETIME COMMISSIONS = LIFETIME PROFITS.

Finding recurring billing products to promote on Clickbank *(source:*

www.Clickbank.com*)*

The easiest way to find recurring billing products to promote is by filtering your Marketplace search to only include these products. You can do this by selecting the Category/Sub-Category of the product you want and/or entering any search keywords, then selecting 'Recurring Billing' from the Product Type dropdown menu and clicking "Go". This will limit your search to just those products and ensure that any product you choose to promote will deliver recurring commissions.

Once you've run your search, you can get an idea of how much you can expect to make from recurring commissions by looking at the Future $ and Total $/sale amounts listed beneath each product:

d Much More! Affiliates Have Already Made $1
Future $: $93.37 | Total $/sale: $126.57
e | create HopLink

Future $ shows the average amount that affiliates make from rebills of the product. This gives you an indication of how often customers continue their subscriptions, and an idea of how much you're likely to earn in addition to the initial sale amount.

Total $/sale is the sum of the initial sale plus all rebills, divided by the number of initial sales. This number gives you an idea of how much you could expect to make over the life of a successful sale, on average. Your results may differ, but this number is the average over all sales of the product so far.

As you can see, Clickbank's recurring billing products can be a great source of regular income! If you're not already promoting recurring billing products in addition to single-sale products, give it a try to see how much they can add to your monthly earnings, without any additional effort on your part.

Make sure to read the affiliate terms for each Clickbank product with recurring commissions as sometimes the commissions paid to the affiliates stop after six months or one year.

5. Find other affiliate products

What other products could you sell as an affiliate?

- Books
- eBooks
- Training
- DVDs
- Food
- Gifts
- Videos
- Products from eBay

> **TOP TIP: All these recurring commissions are highly recommended but did you know that Web Hosting and Credit Card affiliate programs pay TOP commissions in the industry?**

Other affiliate networks to consider finding affiliate products:

www.affiliateranker.com
www.affiliatewindow.com RECOMMENDED
www.cj.com Commission Junction RECOMMENDED
www.offervault.com
www.paydotcom.com
www.shareasale.com

Or simply search for "your keyword" + "affiliate"

6. eBook

The beauty with Clickbank eBooks is that their sales pages do all the work of converting visitors into buyers, so you just have to send your visitors to the sales page, with your affiliate link.

If no eBook is available that is suitable for your site then you can have one written for you, relatively cheaply from sites like:

www.agentsofvalue.com
www.elance.com RECOMMENDED
www.freelancer.com

www.guru.com RECOMMENDED
www.ifreelance.com
www.microworkers.com RECOMMENDED
www.mturk.com
www.need-an-article.net

Help with creating an eBook:
www.easyebookcreator.com
www.ebookcompiler.com
www.ebookswriter.com
www.theebookcoach.com

Here's an example of *approximately* how much it would cost you to outsource everything to get an eBook on Clickbank:

- $600 to outsource the writing of a 120-page eBook on www.elance.com

- $600 to outsource the writing of a sales page for your eBook including the affiliate page.

- $100 to outsource a professional cover for your eBook

- $49.50 to set up a Clickbank account

Total: $1349.50. If you can do it all yourself, the only cost is $49.50 for the Clickbank listing.

BUT if there is an existing eBook already on Clickbank, it will cost you ZERO to sell it with an affiliate link and you can start earning immediately with ZERO investment. I always advise my students to build a site with an affiliate eBook link and if they start earning money with that, they can write their own eBook and let other affiliates sell it for them.

Alternatively, if you can write fairly well, you can write it yourself. I would recommend borrowing books on the topic from your local library and buying second-hand books from Amazon and eBay to base it on. Physical books tend to be plagiarised less than online articles, which makes it easier to write a more original eBook.

Submit your eBook and sales page to Clickbank (it will charge you a small fee to host it there) and then it will deal with payment processing for you. It will also put your product in its marketplace and set everything up so that affiliates can start selling your book as well!

You can set the percentage per sale that your affiliates get when they sell one of your eBooks and then sit back while other people get you sales.

You need to create your eBook in PDF-format (make sure to embed all fonts) so everybody, including Mac users, can read it. The following websites convert eBooks into PDFs:

www.acrobat.com

www.nuance.com/pdfconverter Cheaper than Adobe but does the job

www.fineprint.com You can convert some pages with a free trial

For the cover of your eBook, unless you are a design artist yourself, you can use:

www.absolutecovers.com

www.coverfactory.com

www.ebookcovercreator.com

www.ecoverexpert.com

www.killercovers.com

www.qualityebookcovers.com

7. Amazon products

A video tutorial on how to put Amazon on a Wordpress site is included in my videos. Please visit www.VideosNewbieBook.com to get access.

www.amazon.com. I love Amazon and I will explain why in a few points.

- When people click on the word Amazon, they are already in a buying frame of mind. You do not need to convince them to buy anything. Almost all of my websites contain Amazon products. Most of them have an Amazon Widget that looks like this:

Or like this:

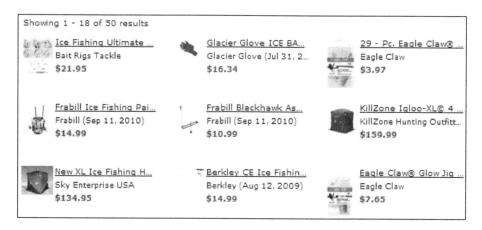

- Amazon has a vast range of products, so you can list its products for almost any niche on your website.

- Amazon pays you commission on anything that customers buy via your link. Suppose you have a website on panic attacks with a link to Amazon. Your customer orders a book from Amazon but while there they think "Oh I might as well order that video camera I was planning to buy". You get commission on the video camera as well. If the customer adds another five products to his basket, you earn commission on all seven products. Nice one!

- Amazon has a good conversion rate (the number of people visiting your link compared to the people actually buying a product via your link). Their commission starts at 3% or 4%, depending on the type of products, which is not very high BUT they have a very good conversion rate. The more you sell via your links, the more your commission (they call it referral fee or advertiser's fee) as an Amazon Associate will increase. You can earn up to 8.5% commission. This applies for most categories, but not all.

- Amazon is a trusted name so people buy without hesitation. The vast majority of your visitors have already bought something from Amazon, so there is no need to convince them to open an account.

- Amazon is a MUST for all affiliates and certainly if your income, like mine, is from multiple streams.

- If you do not have an Amazon Associates account, get one www.amazon.com

> **TOP TIP: 4% commission with a good conversion rate (as Amazon has) is better than a 15% commission with a bad conversion rate. Always put Amazon links on your site.**

8. CPA offers

CPA stands for Cost Per Action and it simply means that you, as an affiliate of a certain CPA offer, get paid for making people perform a certain action. Usually this action is filling in an email form, or giving a telephone number, or taking up a free trial. Each time a visitor to your website takes any of these actions, you get paid.

There are offers which pay out simply for a person entering their name and email address. These offers can pay out from $0.50 up to $20. Offers for free trials can pay out between $10 and $100 per lead. Most of the time the person does not have to buy anything in order for you to get paid.

If you find a high-pay-out CPA offer in your niche and place it in a good position on your website, you can earn a heck of a lot of money. I know people who ONLY focus on CPA offers who earn over $15,000 per month. So CPA is certainly worth understanding.

It is completely FREE to put CPA offers on your site, so if you drive free traffic to it as well, this is a no-brainer and a good money-making possibility.

Earlier on I spoke about finding good CPA offers in your niche. If you find one that you'd like to promote then make sure that is also on your site. Make sure you only put CPA offers in your niche on your site.

You have to fill out a sign up form for most CPA networks in order to be accepted into the network. Don't worry, this is just so that networks can see you're a serious marketer and that you know your stuff. It's easy to be accepted if you have the answers ready to the questions the networks are likely to ask you, which I will tell you later.

What is a CPA network?

A CPA network is the overall website that keeps a record of who gets paid and who earns how much. Providers can put their CPA offers on a network and affiliates can go and get a code for that offer to put on their site. Everything is done automatically. The CPA network is the company who pays your cheques. Examples of CPA offers:

CPA networks to sign up to
You can go to www.offervault.com and search for your niche. OfferVault will list the offers from a huge range of different CPA networks so, when you find an offer you like, use the following walk-through to sign up and get accepted!

There are a large number of CPA networks available on the web. Whichever you choose to work with, make sure you check them out in forums, or Google the network+review as some of them are unreliable and do not pay out.

I have worked with the following CPA networks and never had any problems:

www.neverblue.com This is one of the best CPA networks on the web. They have high paying offers and very good tracking software.

www.copeac.com This network accepts newbies without any affiliate experience, so is one to consider.

www.cxdigitalmedia.com Accepts newbies reasonably easily.

www.marketleverage.com Not easy to join but worth it, as it has lots of bonuses.

www.CPAlead.com Large selection of surveys

www.clickbooth.com

www.maxbounty.com

www.peerfly.com

Get accepted into any CPA network

Signing up to CPA networks can seem like a daunting task, especially because some of them phone you to ask you a few questions. Like anything in life, if you prepare then you'll succeed.

Most of the CPA networks give really good support and you are given an affiliate manager to help you.

The following information is the EXACT information that I have used to sign up to CPA networks and it works for me, so it should work for you!

If you're worried about stretching the truth a little bit in the phone call then look at it like this: it may not be 100% true at the moment, but it will be soon!

The sign up page

Make sure you have a marketing business style website set up and make it look professional. It doesn't matter if you're just one person; having the site will show you're serious and not just someone who will sign up and then never do anything. It doesn't have to be full of anything amazing, just make it clean, high-class and with a few pages about what you do, where you are and the kind of marketing you do.

Make sure you get an email address associated with this domain and that you're not using an address like @hotmail / @gmail / @aol. No self-respecting professional marketer would have a free email address as their business contact, so nor should you.

Say that the vast majority of your traffic comes from PPC and email marketing. This way you don't have to show them any proof, or show them any sites.

Say that you've been an internet marketer for between one and two years and you promote any offer that converts, but your main niches are health, leisure and gaming.

The phone call
Answer your phone with a "Hi, [your business name], this is [your name], how can I help?". Again, it's little touches that prove you're professional.

If you think you may miss the phone call then make sure you have a professional-style answer machine. This means no Homer Simpson voices or anything funny. It needs to be along the lines of: "You're through to [your business name], this is [your name]. Unfortunately I can't get to the phone at the moment. If you leave your name and number then I'll get back to you as soon as I can. Thanks".

These are the questions that CPA networks might ask you:

Q. How long have you been an internet marketer?

> A. "I've been marketing various offers for about two years now."

Q. How many unique visitors do you get a month?

> A. "Hard to say, exactly. I do most of my marketing through PPC networks and to my various double opt-in email lists."

Q. What kind of methods do you use to advertise?

> A. "I have an email list of about 25,000 double-opt in subscribers and spend about $5000 a month on PPC advertising. I'm looking to increase my earnings with your offers."

If they ask what PPC networks you use, say something like AdWords, as well as a number of smaller secondary networks - like 7search and Miva.

Q. Why do you want to sign up to our network?

A. "My email list is seriously responsive and I'm looking for offers that will be genuinely useful to my subscribers and earn me as much as possible. I've been told that your network is brilliant so I'd love to work with you."

Q. What kind of niches do you promote?

A. "I've got three lists in three niches: health, leisure and gaming. I'm going to be branching out into other niches over the next six months and really just want anything that converts."

TOP TIP: Don't put too many ads or CPA offers on your page. If visitors get the impression that the website is built with the only purpose of making money, visitors will immediately move away from your site. That's why you must have good content on your site. A few ads dotted here and there is much better than eight ads stacked on top of one another.

---

9. Up-sells

An up-sell is the act of making a sale after the sale. If you're selling digital cameras from your website then it's a good bet that anyone who buys one will also want accessories. Showing them a link to memory cards, carry cases, cables, or anything relating to the item they bought, makes them much more likely to buy.

Make sure you offer customers relevant items that they may genuinely need, in order to maximise your conversion rates.

10. Exit page opportunity

When a visitor leaves your website without taking any action, you can take this opportunity to try to get email addresses for email marketing. This is not really possible for beginners, as you need HTML knowledge, but for more advanced users it is perfectly possible. Give something away (a PLR-product) for FREE and put an opt-in box on your exit page. You have nothing to lose by doing this, on the contrary, you can only win and grow your list. Remember: the money is in the list. Your visitor will either subscribe, buy or leave. When he leaves, you get your second chance to earn money.

- Put another opt-in box on your site for when people leave your site or a certain page. You have nothing to lose as the visitor is leaving your site anyway. Grab your second chance to get people to leave their email address and put an exit page on your website. Visit www.exitsplash.com for more information or search for "exit page pop up".

- Put an "auto-pop-up opt-in" on your website. This is a pop-up that says something like "grab my free report NOW by filling in your email address and get instant access". Visit www.actionpopup.com for a Wordpress plugin that does exactly that or search for "auto pop ups".

11. Better CR – Conversion Rate

I have explained under "Some internet marketing terminology explained" what CR, or Conversion Rate, is. I mention CR again in this part of the book as it is a way of monetising your site as by doubling your conversion rate you double your sales.

When you log in to Webmaster Tools click "Your site on the web" and then select "Search queries"

This shows the total number of people who have seen a link to your site in the search results (Impressions) and the total number of times people have clicked on a link to your site.

Top Tips to double your conversions and double your income are:

- Don't over-use bright colours. Colour should be there to draw the eye to the object, but if everything's bright then it loses impact. The best way to do this is to have a colour scheme that's mainly whites, silvers and pale colours, with bright colour purely to emphasise what you want people to see.

- Step back, slightly un-focus your eyes and take a look at each of your pages. What are your eyes pulled towards? What do you find yourself ignoring? This is a simple, but effective way to see what the eye-magnets on the page are.

- Use the Google Analytics "In-Page Analytics" to get an idea of where people are clicking and consider ways to increase clicks on your money-making links. In-Page Analytics can be found in the side bar of Google Analytics, here:

- For small sites, make everything on your site, at most, two clicks away. Always include a "Search" box to make it easy for people to find what they are looking for.

- Get enough information "above the fold" of the site so that, even without scrolling, visitors will have a good idea of what you offer and what benefit you can offer them.

"Above the fold" describes everything you can see when you first load a website, without any scrolling down. A lot of your visitors won't bother to scroll down when they hit your site, so putting your affiliate links/email submit form at the top of the page, so they can't miss them.

- Get to grips with Google Website Optimizer and split test *everything*.

12. Split testing to create more sales

Split Testing is simply testing two different variables on your page to find out which gets the most clicks or the most sales. By variable I mean any aspect of your page. This can be the colour of your headline, the wording of your headline, the images you show on the page, the price of your product and so on. Split testing is a very powerful strategy for increasing the effectiveness of your offer. Split testing is time consuming but definitely worth the effort, if done correctly and with the right tools.

You can see a lot of split test examples on www.whichtestwon.com . *This site is definitely worth a visit.*

Say, for example, we had a box in our website sidebar with an image that, when clicked, took the visitor to a product we were promoting as an affiliate.

We would create TWO different images and set them up in Webmaster tools so that each one is shown 50% of the time, as shown below:

Image A	Image B
Shown 50% of the time	Shown 50% of the time
Links to: http://www.affiliatelink.com /?tid=ImageA	Links to: http://www.affiliatelink.com /?tid=ImageB

Each image links to the affiliate product, but with a different *Tracking ID.* These Tracking IDs will show up next to each affiliate sale you make, in your reporting section.

This means if you sell 73 products with Tracking ID "ImageA" and 150 with the tracking ID "ImageB", you know that Image B is the best at turning visitors into customers.

Date		Time	Receipt		TID		Pmt	
2010-10-07		18:35	KYJ*****				VISA	

The Tracking ID

)

Then it's just a matter of testing variations of Image B to keep pushing the conversion rate higher and selling more products.

By performing similar tests on your headlines, colour schemes and page layouts you can easily double your conversion rate or more. Testing is the main thing that separates the super affiliates from the newbies, so get testing.

These variations don't need to be amazing feats of creativity, just test anything slightly different, like the following two images side-by-side:

Image B	Image C
Shows 50% of the time	Shows 50% of the time
Links to: http://www.affiliatelink.com/?tid=ImageA	Links to: http://www.affiliatelink.com/?tid=ImageC

Remove excess navigation. This may seem like a strange one, but if you manage to get people to your sales page/sign-up page, then do NOT distract them with interesting looking links. Make sure the only thing they can do on that page is read your sales copy. If you really have to have links on that page, then have them open in a new window so you don't lose them.

Split testing is an extremely good tool for finding out which price is the best for your product. Make three different pages with three different prices and find out in your stats which price sells best.

Part 9. Things To Do Before Sending Traffic

There are four vital things you must do or must know before sending any traffic to your site.

1. You MUST TEST all the links on your website

When you've completed all the previous steps there is one final thing to be done... get people to your site! The other steps are useless if no-one can find your website - you won't make a penny.

No traffic = No visitors = No profit

Before sending traffic to your site you need to TEST, TEST, TEST everything on your site.

TEST – TEST – TEST – TEST – TEST – TEST – TEST

This is crucial, I cannot stress this enough. Have you ever come across websites with "error 404" or other errors? Or pictures that are only half shown? Or text that runs over a picture? Of course you have. Very often this is because the webmaster does not check the website regularly. You have no chance to earn money with links that do not work. You need to check your links on a regular basis – your page links as well as your affiliate links.

When you re-organise files on your computer, check your site. Depending on which company or host you use and how you have published your site, this can affect the website. When pictures have moved folders on your computer, those pictures might not show up on your website. The pictures will show as a blank frame with an 'x' - very unprofessional.

This is what you have to check regularly:

1. Check if all your internal page links are working.

2. Check ALL your affiliate links on ALL pages to see if they are working. When you click your affiliate link, you should see your affiliate ID in the browser or at the bottom of a Clickbank order form. That's how you know that your link is working.

3. Click EVERY "Add to Cart" button on ALL your pages to see if your affiliate link appears in the browser, or at the bottom of the order form if you use Clickbank products.

4. Check that all your pages display as intended.

5. Check that your AdSense looks right and does not disturb the general look of the site.

6. Check that your email auto responder is working properly. Don't forget to opt-in with your own email address for testing purposes.

7. Check that all your eBook affiliate links work.

8. Check that all hyperlinks to pages are linked to the correct page.

9. Check that customers can see in a few seconds what the site is all about.

10. Can the customer see the contact information easily?

12. Check that all your videos are playing correctly and load quickly.

13. If possible, buy your own product or ask a friend to buy it, to make sure all emails and download links work. With Clickbank, you can get a demo credit card number and buy your own product to test it. You MUST read every letter or test every step from hitting the "Add to Cart" button to receiving what's on sale. Pretend you are a customer buying your product and put yourself in your customer's shoes.

To get your test credit card, log in to your Clickbank account, go to "Account Settings" and then to "My Site".

Scroll to the bottom to get a "Test Credit Card Number".

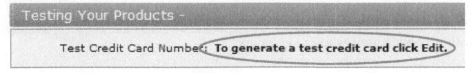

You can also give the test credit card to your friend to see what he thinks of the whole process, from ordering the product to receiving it.

14. Check if your website looks good opened with the different internet browsers: Internet Explorer, Firefox, Google Chrome, Opera, Safari (for Apple computers) and so on. Perhaps you didn't know that there are different internet browsers? Years ago I didn't either, but not everybody uses the same internet browser. Wikipedia defines internet browser as: *A web browser is a software application for retrieving, presenting, and traversing information resources on the World Wide Web. An information resource is identified by a Uniform Resource Identifier (URI) and may be a web page, image, video, or other piece of content.*

If you do not want to download the browsers, ask a friend with a different browser to look at your site but as a serious internet marketer, you should download them all yourself. You will lose potential customers if your website does not view properly with Firefox or other browsers. Not all your visitors use Internet Explorer. You can easily switch between the different browsers, so you can use the one you prefer most of the time. But when you need to test your new site, you can look at it using the five main browsers.

- http://www.browsershots.org gives a lot of information about different browsers.

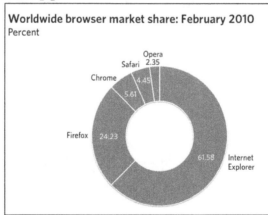

Source: Net Applications

15. If possible, create a mobile phone version of your website as there are now about 78 million people with a mobile phone who can go online.

16. Ask three friends to look at your website for their comments and criticism. Looking at a website from other people's point of view can teach you a lot. Other people will see things that you don't.

17. Have a 12 year old look at your website and read the content. Change anything that the 12 year old has problems with.

Check anything else you have on your website.

2. You must publish your website

Okay now that you have finished designing your site, it looks goods and your affiliate links work, you must publish it. It is now in finished mode sitting on your computer, but as we mentioned before: 10,000 people are not going to come to your office or lounge to look at your site, so it needs to be published for the world to see.

This is done by a protocol called *FTP: File Transfer Protocol*. It is a way of sending files securely from one computer to another. We are all involved in FTP without realising we are doing it. If you buy a song or an eBook from the web and download it to your computer, you are using FTP because you are transferring the files from the host computer to your computer.

There are three ways to publish a site:

- When using Wordpress, publishing is done automatically, so you do not need to do it. Press 'F5' and the latest version will be visible online. **Word of caution**: When developing your Wordpress site, make sure not to push F5 too often (like 20 times per hour) as Google might look at this as "invalid click activity" and consequently ban or not show your site.

- When using a web design program like Webplus, there is a "publish to" button. You need to fill in some technical information that your hosting company will be able to give you. The information that you will need will be available in "your account" with your hosting company. Most of the time all you need is your username, password and IP address.

- If using Filezilla, you drag the files from your computer to the Filezilla server.

Filezilla is FTP software and it is free. There's a huge amount of help available on the site, where you can also download it - www.filezilla-project.org.

Filezilla looks a bit scary to start with but believe me, it is easy after you have used it a few times.

Unfortunately it is impossible to explain in detail how each web design program publishes your site. Simply Google how to do it and there will be videos on YouTube to show you.

The homepage of your website must always be called index.html when using Webplus or Filezilla.

I suggest that you submit your site for publishing to these search engines:

1. Submit your site to Google here - www.Google.com/addurl/?continue=/addurl (or just Google "add url"). You must submit every web site, even if you have designed it with Wordpress. From experience I know that Google will see your site much quicker if you submit it.

2. Submit your site to DMOZ (PR8) here - www.dmoz.org/docs/en/add.html%20- DMOZ is a huge database of human-added websites. It is a human edited directory. A backlink from them to your site is a great thing to have and will greatly increase the amount of traffic you receive. If you do not get listed here at your first attempt, make some changes to your site and apply again to be listed. It will be worth the effort.

3. Submit your website to Bing : www.bing.com/toolbox/submit-site-url

4. Submit your site to Yahoo (PR8) : www.submit.search.yahoo.com

Once you have submitted your site, you can check if Google has found it by typing in Google site:www.yourwebsitehere.com and Google will show your site. If Google displays a message "Your site did not match any documents", it means that Google has not indexed your site yet.

You can also just type your URL in the search box at www.google.com. If your site appears in the results Google has indexed it. If after three weeks after submission your site is still not indexed, I suggest you submit it again. The best way to speed up getting indexed is by submitting to social bookmark sites and by getting backlinks to your site.

You can focus your submission efforts based on your target market, with this interesting information according to www.hitwise.com:

- Yahoo! searchers are younger and affluent
- Google searchers are often older, male and have a larger income
- Bing searchers are often female, within the best converting to buyers ratio

Top Search Engine - Volume

The following report shows **search engines** for the industry 'All Categories', ranked by **Volume of Searches** for the **4 weeks** ending **01/01/2011**.

Rank	Search Engine	Searches	
1.	www.google.com	69.67%	
2.	search.yahoo.com	15.17%	
3.	www.bing.com	10.60%	
4.	www.ask.com	2.49%	
5.	search.aol.com	1.45%	

(Source: www.hitwise.com)

Top Search Engines - Visits

The following report shows **websites** for the industry '**Computers and Internet - Search Engines**', ranked by **Visits** for the **week** ending **01/01/2011**.

Rank	Website	Visits Share	
1.	Google	63.40%	
2.	Yahoo! Search	12.45%	
3.	Bing	11.68%	
4.	Ask	2.17%	
5.	AOL Search	1.31%	
6.	Yahoo! Image Search	0.85%	
7.	bing Videos	0.81%	
8.	bing Images	0.59%	
9.	Yahoo! Video	0.56%	
10.	PCH Search & Win	0.40%	

(Source: www.hitwise.com

Top 20 Websites
The following report shows **websites** for the industry 'All Categories', ranked by **Visits** for the **week** ending 01/01/2011.

Rank	Website	Visits Share
1.	Facebook	11.04%
2.	Google	7.38%
3.	YouTube	3.35%
4.	Yahoo! Mail	3.04%
5.	Yahoo!	2.40%
6.	Yahoo! Search	1.45%
7.	Bing	1.36%
8.	Windows Live Mail	1.02%
9.	msn	0.93%
10.	Gmail	0.92%
11.	eBay	0.73%
12.	Aol Mail	0.68%
13.	Amazon.com	0.53%
14.	AOL	0.50%
15.	Yahoo! News	0.50%
16.	Wikipedia	0.46%
17.	MySpace	0.44%
18.	Pogo	0.40%
19.	Ask	0.25%
20.	Bank of America Online Banking	0.25%

Source: www.hitwise.com

Although 88% of all searches are through the top three search engines, below is a list of some other search engines that you can submit your site to.

www.search.yahoo.com

www.aol.com

www.ask.com

www.dogpile.com

www.entireweb.com PR6

www.exactseek.com PR7

www.excite.com

www.gigablast.com PR7

www.looksmart.com

You could also use www.addme.com for manual submission to 14 search engines.

You can find a list of the smaller search engines here: www.thesearchenginelist.com

Be prepared to receive a lot of follow-up emails from several search engines after you have submitted your site.

3. You must make sure that you can check how your website is doing

Now that your website is tested and published, you must make sure that you can see how it is doing. When you have made it to the first page of Google, you need to stay there. Once you are on the first page does not mean that you will stay there forever.

If you just want to know how many visitors have looked at your site, you can place a visitor counter on your page. Just search for "visitor counter" and you will find plenty. The visitor-counter websites will give you a code, which you put on your site.

I have already covered Google Analytics in this book (www.Google.com/analytics) but there are some other very good websites you can use:

-www.site24x7.com is a great website monitoring service and you will get instant alert when your site goes down (not free).

- www.google.com/webmasters/tools

- www.alexa.com

- www.hittail.com

- www.quantcast.com

- www.siteluck.com

- You also need to get more and more backlinks – slowly but surely.

- You must ALWAYS keep an eye on your competitors to make sure they do not overtake you.

- Visit www.delicious.com and see how many people have bookmarked your site and your competitor's site. Analyse and learn.

- Visit www.facebook.com to see who has most fans. Analyse and learn.

- Visit www.compete.com and compare both sites. Analyse and learn.

- Visit www.google.com/alerts and put your three main competitors on alert. Google will let you know when your competitors are active on the web.

4. You must avoid being banned by Google

If you follow only the guidelines in this book, you are fine and your site should not get banned. However, your site can be banned by Google for several reasons. One reason is by applying Black Hat SEO to your site.

What is Black Hat SEO?

These are techniques some people use to try to get higher search engine results in an unethical way. Some of the Black Hat SEO techniques were acceptable many years ago but not anymore. When these techniques are applied, they can result in high Google ranking very quickly. But it can also be for a short time, if Google decides to ban or never show your site.

White SEO is what we have discussed so far in this book. Google likes white SEO and it's worth pleasing Google. If it does not like your website or marketing technique it can simply ban your site.

Where does the term Black Hat SEO come from?

Remember the good old Western movies? Generally the bad cowboys wore black hats and the good ones wore white hats.

To avoid being banned, you must avoid the techniques below at all times. These techniques are generally known as Black Hat SEO techniques:

- Never use link farms.

- Never copy other people's content. Not only can you be banned from Google but you can be taken to court for violation of Copyright laws for stealing other people's content.

- Never cloak. Cloaking is when you try to fool Google by sending visitors to one site and sending Google to another site. This can be done very easily with redirects and some clever programming. Google hates it. If you type 'dogs' in your search, you do not want to open a website on crocodiles. A Google employee can manually check if you are cloaking by visiting your website. Google will not warn you before it bans you.

- Do not overstuff your page with keywords. One example of overstuffing would be to use two keywords in each sentence of your site.

- Do not use keywords not related to your content. A list of 40 keywords from a thesaurus listed at the bottom of your website is not going to do you any good.

- Do not use hidden text. Ten years ago this used to work: put a yellow banner on a site and stuff it with yellow text as your keywords. The website visitor would not see the keywords but Google would think they are all good keywords. Not any more. Google doesn't fall for that trick any longer.

- Do not distribute any viruses, Trojans or other badware.

- Do not use automated link submission programs. This is totally against Google's terms of services.

- Do not use Adwords with a landing page that is not 100% designed around Google's regulations for its landing pages. Your website can be banned from Adwords overnight without any warning. You must read Google's landing page requirements.

- Do not stuff it with SPAM. Other websites can report you, and you risk being banned.

So, don't try to cheat your way to the top. Design a white SEO site and put some decent content on it. Work to getting links to get traffic. The lazy way often means the banned way!

If you are banned, you can ask to be included again, but often it is simply better to forget the banned website and start a new one.

Part 10. Traffic – Free Traffic

Now that you know how to build a site and how to test it, you need to generate traffic, because remember:

No traffic = No visitors = No profit = No Success

I believe in the following rule: if you drive traffic in a way that is humanly possible, it is acceptable. If all of a sudden you have 1000 links to your site, and it was only submitted to Google two days ago, Google knows this is impossible for you to have done, and concludes you must have used some sort of automated software to create the links. Google does not like anything automated: automated websites, automated links, automated submissions, automated social marketing, and so on.

The aim with my method is to rank on Google's first pages and you are likely to achieve that. But you still need to send traffic to your site and to get backlinks to your site to maximise your chances of staying on the first pages of Google.

If you have a non-competitive niche you might well get and stay on the first page simply with good SEO applied to your site. If that is all you want to achieve, there is no need for you to apply any of the traffic methods in this book. However, don't forget that a lot of people do not use Google therefore you will not reach all potential customers with just Google.

The more traffic you send to your websites, the more opportunities for people to click one of your affiliate links. Sending traffic to your website is easy although very time consuming, but it is worth it. The more time you spend driving traffic to your site, the better your website and your affiliate links will do. If that is not the case, you are doing something wrong.

Without traffic, nobody will see your ad so nobody will click on your ad.

Without traffic, nobody will buy your products or your affiliate products.

Without traffic you can't build your email list.

Without traffic, you can forget it all because you will fail.

There is no such thing as "one best way" to drive traffic. You need to drive traffic to your site in different ways. Choose a few methods that you think you will enjoy.

> **TOP TIP : Never count on one way of driving traffic. You must try to build multiple streams of traffic.**

Is free traffic really free?

Some of the traffic discussed in this chapter will cost you nothing but driving it is time consuming, so ask yourself: is it still free if you spend 4 hours per day doing it? If you are employed or you have your own company, take your yearly salary, divide it by 365 days and divide it again by eight hours per day. Example: you earn $25,000 per year/365 = $68.49/8h = $8.56 per hour. So if you work two hours in driving traffic you have spent $17.12. In that way sending free traffic is not really free, if looked at from a commercial angle. However free traffic is free if you don't look at it from a business point of view, as it will only take time, not money.

I used to do all the traffic myself until I discovered outsourcing. I suggest that you work hard on your first few websites to get knowledge and experience. Once you make some profit, invest it in hiring someone from OnlineJobs – www.onlinejobs.ph Sign up and pay them monthly. As soon as you have hired a suitable person you can end your membership. I have done this several times and it works very well.

Finding a worker can't be easier: you look at their profile which gives you a list of what they are good at. You contact a suitable candidate, send a few emails and that's it. You hire one you like and if they are not as good as you thought, you find someone else. Usually you pay them per week so you can also end their services per week.

You can hire a full-time worker for $426.00 per month or £275.00 per month. Most workers have a PayPal account so you can pay them easily.

> **TOP TIP : Make some websites yourself by sheer hard work and once you are earning money and have knowledge and experience, outsource the work. While the people you hire are driving traffic, you can concentrate on building a new website.**

1. Free traffic by improving your CTR.

It's important to know the CTR (Click Through Rate) for your money-making links because, obviously, the higher it is the more clicks you'll get (and without having to increase the amount of traffic your site's getting either, which is a big bonus!).

The CTR for your links can be found in Google Analytics in the In Page Analytics section, which is found here, in your dashboard:

CTR is in this section of the book because it will increase your traffic. If you can get a better CTR then you have free traffic.

2. Free traffic with some basic SEO work

By simply improving your SEO you can increase your position in the search results. This means it is a type of free traffic because it will result in more visitors to your site.

Crafting meta description/titles that get more traffic

Let's take a look at a standard Google search result, as if we were searching for "horse tacks":

The dark blue text is the Title

Horse Tack | Horse Blankets | Bits, Breeches & Grooming ... 🛒 ☆
Horse Tack Co is a **Horse Tack** Store specializing in Horse Blankets, Horse Bits, Breyer
Horses, Riding Breeches, Horse Grooming Supplies, Horse Calendars, ...
www.horsetackco.com/ - Cached - Similar

The black text is the META description

Question: How could you get more visitors to your site without increasing your position in the search engines?

Answer: Set your Meta description with a clear call to action, which makes visitors want to visit your site.

Don't just write:

> *"Horse Tack Co is a Horse Tack Store specializing in ..."*

Write something that will make people want to click. Always include the keyword in your title, but be creative. Perhaps you could try something like:

> *"Click here to see our surprisingly good horse tacks. Our horse tacks aren't just the best on the 'net, they're the most reliable and affordable."*

Take a look at these two search results. Which do you think will get the most clicks for horse tacks?

Horse Tack | Horse Blankets | Bits, Breeches & Grooming ... 🛒 ☆
Horse Tack Co is a **Horse Tack** Store specializing in Horse Blankets, Horse Bits, Breyer
Horses, Riding Breeches, Horse Grooming Supplies, Horse Calendars, ...
www.horsetackco.com/ - Cached - Similar

Horse Tack | Horse Blankets | Bits, Breeches & Grooming ...
Click here to see our surprisingly good **horse tacks**. Our **horse tacks** aren't
just the best on the 'net, they're the most reliable and affordable.
www.horsetackco.com/ - Cached - Similar

If you use Google Webmaster Tools, you can see which of your pages are ranking for which keywords. If one of your pages shows up mainly when people search for "cheap quality horse tacks" then your meta description should be geared around this.

View meta description exactly as you view writing a headline. It should tell the viewer to click the link and give them the benefits of your page, not just what's on it.

In the screenshot below is a list of pages that are displayed when people search for pigeon lofts:

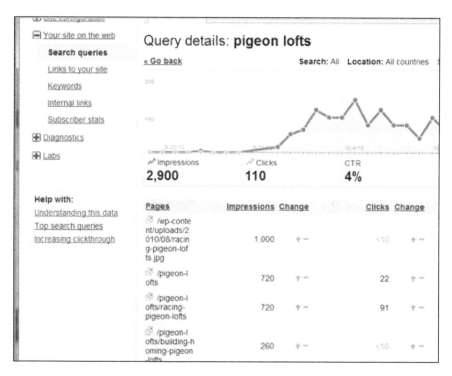

When you've got Google Webmaster Tools up and running try changing your meta descriptions to headline-style descriptions (open the page/post in Wordpress, the meta description box will be below the text editor).

I guarantee that you'll start getting more traffic without moving a single position in Google.

Go to each of those pages and add a new meta description, using the All-In-One-SEO plugin.

It may take a few days or weeks for Google to start displaying your new meta description in the results, depending on when it next visits your site, so you'll have to wait a while.

3. Free traffic from your own army of affiliates

This is an easy way to make money. If you have developed your own eBook/book or you are selling your own products you MUST find affiliates to sell for you. List your products on Clickbank and lots of other affiliate networks and let other people sell your products. You will earn less as you will give away between 20% and 70% of your earnings in commission but on the other hand *you don't have to do anything at all.* Yes that's right: *once you have an army of affiliates doing the work for you, you do not have to do anything at all.*

Very simple principle: find a potential niche, develop an eBook in that niche, put it on Clickbank and the commission will start coming in. If you have done your research right you know that people are looking for your keywords, so it is likely that a bunch of affiliates are looking for products to sell in your niche as well.

Below is a Clickbank screenshot showing that affiliates are selling for me. Do I know these guys? No. Have I ever spoken to these guys? No. All the affiliates found my site www.howtoracepigeons.com on Clickbank and have put an affiliate link on their website. Thank you realdeals5, you are doing a good job and thank you to all the other affiliates. The sales without a name under the "Affiliate" column are sales that are directly from my website, so I don't have to pay an affiliate. You can see that the affiliates are selling a lot more than I am but I am earning a lot more from them than from my own sales, even if my income is only $9.35 per sale. You can also see my low number of refunds (only 2 out of 34 sales).

Pmt	Currency	Txn Type	Item	Amount	Vendor	Affiliate	CC
PYPL	USD	Sale	2	$9.35	IMC2711	RUSSP	US
PYPL	USD	Sale	2	$9.35	IMC2711	REALDEALS5	US
PYPL	USD	Sale	2	$9.33	IMC2711	FEILAMSOL	US
VISA	USD	Sale	2	$9.35	IMC2711	ZVARNELL	ID
VISA	AUD	Sale	2	$9.35	IMC2711	REALDEALS5	AU
PYPL	USD	Sale	2	$26.72	IMC2711		US
PYPL	USD	Sale	2	$9.35	IMC2711	TOMHINTER	US
PYPL	USD	Refund	2	($9.35)	IMC2711	REALDEALS5	US
PYPL	GBP	Sale	2	$9.25	IMC2711	RMSOZZANI	GB
VISA	USD	Sale	2	$9.35	IMC2711	FEILAMSOL	US
VISA	USD	Sale	2	$9.35	IMC2711	ZVARNELL	US
VISA	AUD	Sale	2	$9.36	IMC2711	REALDEALS5	AU
PYPL	USD	Sale	2	$9.35	IMC2711	GH5649	US
VISA	ZAR	Sale	2	$9.35	IMC2711	SSSSG	ZA
VISA	USD	Sale	2	$9.35	IMC2711	MMARKM	US
PYPL	USD	Sale	2	$9.35	IMC2711	REALDEALS5	US
VISA	GBP	Sale	6				GB
VISA	USD	Sale	2	$9.35	IMC2711	SYDWTSE	US
MSTR	ZAR	Sale	2	$9.35	IMC2711	REALDEALS5	ZA
PYPL	USD	Sale	2	$9.35	IMC2711	GH5649	US
PYPL	USD	Sale	2	$9.35	IMC2711	STKRK01	US
MSTR	CAD	Sale	2	$26.72	IMC2711		US
VISA	EUR	Sale	2	$9.10	IMC2711	REALDEALS5	IE
VISA	USD	Sale	2	$9.33	IMC2711	REALDEALS5	US
PYPL	USD	Refund	2	($9.29)	IMC2711	KURLIN97	US
VISA	USD	Sale	2	$9.35	IMC2711	SMARTYMAR1	PR
PYPL	GBP	Sale	1	$16.91	MPG18	IMC2711	GB
PYPL	USD	Sale	2	$9.29	IMC2711	KURLIN97	US
PYPL	USD	Sale	2	$9.29	IMC2711	MMARKM	US
VISA	USD	Sale	2	$9.35	IMC2711	REALDEALS5	US
VISA	USD	Sale	2	$26.72	IMC2711		US
MSTR	USD	Sale	2	$9.35	IMC2711	REALDEALS5	US
PYPL	GBP	Sale	2	$9.10	IMC2711	SYDWTSE	GB
VISA	USD	Sale	2	$9.35	IMC2711	GH5649	US
MSTR	ZAR	Sale	2	$9.35	IMC2711	BIZUPFRONT	ZA
VISA	GBP	Sale	2	$9.11	IMC2711	BIZUPFRONT	GB

How to set up a new product in Clickbank?

First you need to design your Sales Page and Thank You Page (according to Clickbank rules under Clickbank Help) and publish them to the relevant domain name with your hosting company. Once that is done, setting up www.Clickbank.com is easily done in five steps:

1) Log in to your Clickbank account. Make sure you have signed up as a vendor, not as an affiliate. Go to "Account Settings", "My Site" and then click "Edit". Here you fill in your domain name and the information as it will be shown on the Clickbank Marketplace. Think about the wording carefully as this is what affiliates will see when looking for products. You also need to type in the percentage commission you want to give to your affiliates.

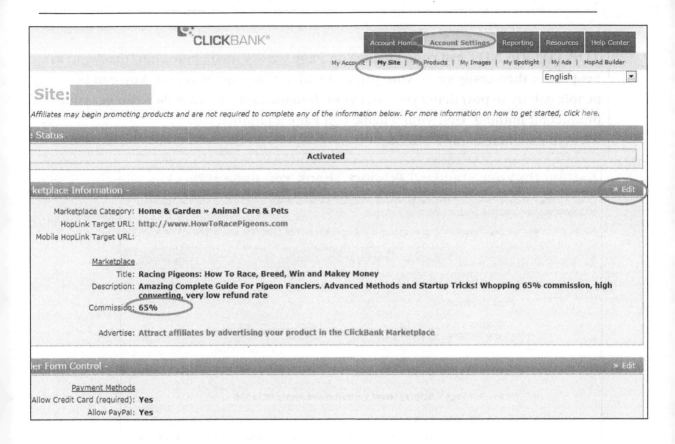

2) Go to "Account Settings" and then to "My Products" and click "Add New Product".

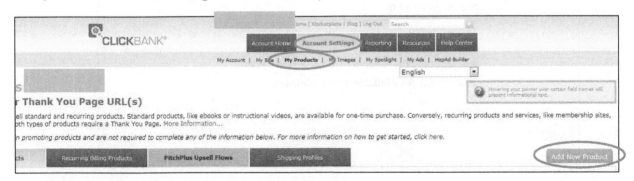

On the next screen, click "eBook" and fill in the "Item Number" (this number will be shown on your Clickbank Sales Overviews), Thank You Page URL, the Product Price and the Product Title.

TOP TIP: Do NOT call your Thank You Page www.yoursitehere.com/thankyou **as people can then easily get to your product without buying them first. You can bet people will try to put/thank you after your domain name to see if they can get your product for nothing. Give your Thank You Page a number, e.g. www.yoursitehere.com/TY12598**

Setting Up Your Standard Product Thank You Page URL(s)

Once a customer pays for your one-time purchase product, we send them directly to a "Thank You Page" or to access or download the product. More Information...

Note: Affiliates may begin promoting products and are not required to complete any of the information belo

Standard Product Editor -

Inactive:	☐
Shippable Media:	☐
*Product Type: (select one or more)	☐ Audio ☑ EBook ☐ Games ☐ Membership Site ☐ Software ☐ Video
*Item:	3
*Thank You Page:	http://www.yoursitehere.com/TY12598
*Mobile Thank You Page:	http://

Note: You must have at least one thank you page; however, you may also use both

*Product Currency:	(USD) US Dollar ▼
*Product Price:	37.00
Language:	English ▼
Product Title:	Your Product Title Goes Here.com
Product Image:	No available product images

[Save Changes] [Cancel]

Example of a Thank You Page:

Your credit card statement will show a charge from Clickbank.com

Simple Download Instructions:

Please note that you need Adobe Acrobat Reader to open the PDF file. Most computers already have Adobe Reader installed. If your computer doesn't have it, you can get a FREE version here:
http://www.adobe.com/products/acrobat/readstep2.html

Adobe Acrobat Reader has versions for both PC and Macintosh computers. The PDF documents here can be opened and read on a PC or Apple Mac with Adobe Reader.

Some items may also be placed into a compressed archive to minimize their download time. Because of this, you need an "unzip" program installed on your computer to open them if it's not installed already.

PC Users: WinZip at http://www.winzip.com - a free version is available.

Mac/Linux Users: StuffIt Xpander >http://www.aladdinsys.com.

Below you'll see your download link. To start saving it to your computer, simply click on the download link using your right mouse button. Then left click on "Save Target As" in Internet Explorer.

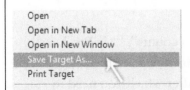

Once you select "Save Target As", a download screen asking you where on your computer you want to save the file will appear.

Simply follow the instructions and save the files to your "Desktop" or another folder you can easily find. Once you have downloaded the file, go to your desktop or the folder you saved it to and double click the eBook file to open it. This should launch Adobe Acrobat Reader and automatically display the eBook.

Right Click The Title Below and Save Target or Save File As To Download the eBook.

Click Here To Download Your Ebook.

3) Before asking Clickbank to approve your site you must test your Payment Link by requesting a Trial Credit Card Number. Go to "Account", "My Site", "Testing Your Product" and click "Edit", which will give you a credit card number to use to buy your own product. Clickbank will not approve your product unless you have done a test purchase.

4) You need to request approval for your product. Go to "Accounts", "My Products", click on the "Request Approval" button. If there is a problem with your site, Clickbank will email you to make the necessary changes after which you need to request approval again.

5) Pay a one-off $49.95 Activation Charge. The product approval team will send you instructions on how to do this.

Once it says "Approved" under Status (under "Account Settings", "My Products") your product is ready for affiliates to sell.

4. Free traffic from finding affiliates

Once your ebook is on Clickbank, affiliates will automatically find it there but how can you find more affiliates to sell your product?

- A great way to find affiliates is to buy magazines in your niche and contact the advertisers, saying that you have a product that they can sell to earn commission.

- Find blogs and forums based around our niche. Go to these blogs and forums and find the contact details of the owner and ask them if they'd like to promote your product. It really is that straight forward!

You'll find you'll start accumulating affiliates automatically because blog owners are often on the lookout for new products on Clickbank to promote.

- Visit www.Clickbank.com and find affiliates in your niche. Most products will be owners with websites in your own niche. Some of them put different ebooks on different pages on their site, their own and somebody else's.

- Go to exhibitions in your niche.

- Google "JV brokers". These are Joint Venture brokers that put affiliates and merchants together and they take a cut of the commission.

- Make sure that you have an affiliate page for your affiliates to get banners, logos, keywords and so on, to put on their sites.

5. Free traffic from article marketing

Good article marketing = more visitors to your site = increased sales

Much like the Web 2.0 properties, a well written article will rank in Google for the keyword you've optimised it for, as well as offering valuable backlinks to your domain. Most article sites will only allow you a maximum of two links per article, and these generally have to be contained within the author box at the end.

There is one other bonus to creating good articles for these sites: if your article is good then other people will post it as content on their own sites. This means each time your article is used, you get more backlinks from the links in your author box!

Article marketing rocks when done well! Article marketing is free traffic at its best.

- It works quickly as your article is mostly published in the next three days after submission.

- Google loves article directories, and this will help with your rankings for your keyword.

- It is long-term traffic, as once your article is in the directory, it will stay there. If you have chosen an untapped niche your article will constantly show up in Google. Of course if you haven't, there will be new articles and you will have to write and publish new articles as well to stay ahead.

- There are automatic submission packages available that submit your article to lots of different article directories in one click. I do not recommend using these simply because if the same article is submitted to 20 different directories, they will not be unique articles. Google does not like duplicate content of duplicate articles, so will probably only list one of your articles.

> **TOP TIP: Write 20 unique articles and manually submit them to 20 different article directories. This is a lot more work BUT you have the chance to be seen by Google on 20 article websites, not just on one. Each of your articles would be seen as unique content by Google, and so will have a better chance of showing in the search engines.**

A well optimised article can rank in Google all on its own, as well as allowing you to have two backlinks to your site.

5 Things each article MUST have:

- Keyword in the beginning of the title: Your title must have your keyword in it but it's equally significant that it's in the beginning of the title to maximise your chances of ranking. Here's an example where somebody is searching for panic attacks:

"5 Top Tips to manage your panic attacks" is a good title BUT

" Panic Attacks Gone Forever – 5 Top Tips" is better.

- Keywords and keyword phrases. Use the keywords from your niche research and write an article on several keywords.

- GOOD Article Content. Articles must read easily and provide useful information. Please do not use PLR as content, unless you re-write it, or don't copy somebody else's article. Google will look at it as duplicate content and your article will simply not show. Readers love figures, statistics, facts and tips.

- Keyword density. Spread your keywords over the article. About 3% to 4 % keyword density will give you a chance to rank in Google with your article.

- YOUR links: Don't forget to put a link to your website at the bottom of the article. Some article submission websites also allow you to put a link in the middle of the article. A brief description of your site and a resource box should always be placed at the end of your article. This link can be an affiliate link or a link to your website.

Used with my scanner method you can quickly produce a large amount of articles that can draw visitors to your websites.

Of the pages you've created in Wordpress, take the one that is optimised for the keyword that gets the most searches in Google - let's take "tack trunks".

Find another passage in one of your books that is about horse tacks and scan it. Edit it a bit and then paste it into Wordpress to let www.seopressor.com optimise it for the search engines.

Once it's got the green-light from www.seopressor.com, copy the article and upload it to several article websites.

In each article put a link, with your targeted keyword as the anchor text, to the page on your site that's optimised for that keyword, like below:

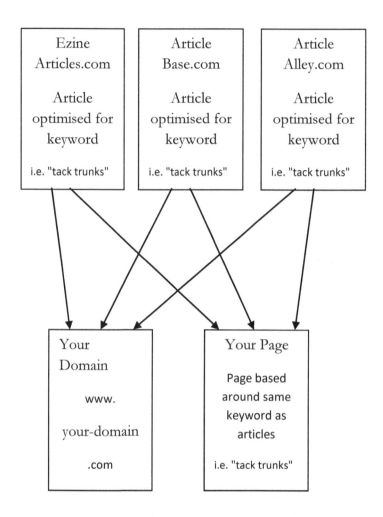

The anchor text for the links to your optimised page (http://www.yourdomain.com/yourkeyword) should be the exact keyword, like this: <u>tack trunks</u>.

Whereas the links to your root domain (http://www.yourdomain.com) should vary between three or four different anchor texts, e.g.

- horse tacks

- horse tack trunks
- horse tack
- horse saddles

It's always best to get a variety of worded backlinks to your root domain, just to keep everything looking natural and allowing you to rank for a wider variation on your keywords.

The resource box in the bottom of your article can be a straight-forward link to your website but I have found that giving away a free report works very well AND you get an extra targeted lead that you can sell to later with your auto responder. A good example to end your article would be: "For great tips on how to stop your panic attacks, download your FREE 20-page report here". The link will take customers to your website where they need to opt-in to get the free report. The only downside is you won't get anchor text backlink.

Visit a few article marketing websites and type in a keyword in your niche: look, analyse and learn. Try to answer the following questions: Which articles are shown? How are they written? How long are they? What does the title say? How many words are in the article?

Writing an article is not hard. Most people who have had some schooling can write a 400-word article. You do not have to be a professional writer to write an article. You reader will be interested in what you are saying and less in how you say it.

To get ideas on pros and cons on a certain product or subject: visit www.amazon.com and www.epinions.com read the reviews. Write down the positives and negatives that you can find to use in your article.

10 steps for successful article marketing:

1. Find a good keyword to target with your keyword research tool Market Samurai or the Google keyword tool.

2. Find a catchy title and search in Google to make sure it is unique. Eg. If your title is "10 things you did not know about preventing headaches" you must copy that text, (including inverted commas to get the exact match) and paste it into Google. As you can see from the screen shot below, no results are found for exactly the same sentence, so that means your title is unique.

"10 things you did not know about preventing headaches"   ✕   Search

Advanced search

⚠ No results found for **10 things you did not know about preventing headaches"**

Results for **10 things you did not know about preventing headaches** (without quotes):

10 Facts About Water | Scienceray
3 Aug 2009 ... **Did you** no your body is composed from around 60-70 percent water? Water can boost your metabolism up to 5%; Water can **prevent headaches**. ...
scienceray.com › Earth Sciences - Cached - Similar

Facts and Figures About **Headaches** - **Headache** Expert (UK)
Facts and Figures About **Headaches**. Headache **Headaches** Headache Causes ... Overall, migraine affects one in every **ten** adults in the world, ... prescribed to help sufferers cope with attacks and to **prevent** attacks, and for visits to GPs. ...
www.headacheexpert.co.uk › Living With Headaches - Cached - Similar

3. Join message boards and blogs and see what the hot topics around your niche are. Yahoo Answers is also a good place to see what sort of questions people are asking. You could write an article on one of these questions. Usually if people ask a question in Yahoo, they will also search elsewhere for the answer.

4. Write an article between 400 and 600 words or hire a ghost writer to write it. Make sure you check it for errors.

5. Find an affiliate product to link to at the end of your article.

6. Write an author's bio box.

7. Write your resource box, both a plain version and an HTML version. *

8. Put a keyword list together.

9. Start submitting your article and make sure you keep a record of the ones you have done.

10. Repeat with a different article and unique article.

* If possible, it is best to use anchor text in your resource box. Some article directories don't allow you to use HTML code, so you can use a direct link like this one: http://www.lifewithoutstress.com. According to studies, anchor text works better but using your website address as a link has the advantage that Google might see your website address.

The only reason why you would use anchor text rather than your URL is to get backlinks to your site.

If HTML is allowed and for maximum exposure, you can use a combination of both, something like this: "If you are looking for a life without stress (=anchor text), then check out Stress Free Tips (=anchor text) at http://www.lifewithoutstress.com (=URL)"

Don't forget to check how many links you are allowed. For most directories you are allowed at least two or three links in your resource box.

TOP TIP: In order to build up credibility and get a lot of search engine traffic, you need to regularly submit articles, not just once. I suggest for maximum results and maximum exposure you submit new articles every two to four weeks. Each article must be unique.

TOP TIP: Don't try to sell too hard in your article but focus on giving very good information. Save the sales pitch for when they get to your site. The only aim for article marketing is to get people to your site. If an article gives valuable information the reader is likely to click on your link at the end of the article.

Good article directories for publishing your article:

- Amazines – www.amazines.com
- Article Alley - www.articlealley.com
- Article City - www.articlecity.com
- Article Geek – www.articlegeek.com
- Article Snatch - www.articlesnatch.com
- ArticleDashBoard PR6 - www.articledashboard.com
- Articles Base PR6 - www.articlesbase.com
- Articletrader – www.articletrader.com
- Buzzle PR6 – www.buzzle.com
- Ehow PR7 – www.ehow.com

- EZineArticles PR6 - www.ezinearticles.com This is one of the very best article directories.
- GoArticles - www.goarticles.com
- iSnare - www.isnare.com
- Search Warp - www.searchwarp.com
- Sooper Articles - www.sooperarticles.com

Article submission services:

These are companies that automatically submit your article to several sites. Keep in mind that the same article will be submitted several times, so they will not be unique articles.

- Articlepost – www.articlepostrobot.com
- Submityourarticles - www.submityourarticle.com

These are also good websites (not purely article directories) to submit your articles to:

- Scribd – www.scribd.com
- Docstoc – www.docstoc.com
- Calameo – www.calameo.com
- Butterfly – www.butterflyreports.com
- Issuu – www.issuu.com

TOP TIP: When you list your site, make sure you put http:// in front of your website domain name or URL. For example: Instead of www.yourwebsitehere.com , you must put your links like this:
http://www.yourwebsitehere.com
Why is this important? Some website pages and email providers will automatically activate a website link but most of the time the link will be left static. In order for users to open your website link in their browser, they have to copy and paste the link. By putting the http:// in front of your domain name, the link is clickable for most email systems and web pages.

A word about article spinning

Article spinning doesn't really work any more in 2014 but I am explaining it here so you knwo what it means when you come across it. **It is ALWAYS best to write your own articles from fresh, new and unique content. I recommend you don't use spinning articles or automated article submission. The hard way is usually the best way and in this case, that means writing every article yourself and submit a unique article to each article website.**

Article marketing can be a very good way of earning money but as with everything: good things don't come easy. In order to do article marketing well you need to spend some time doing it right.

What is article spinning?

To spin an article is to create another version of it which is different to the original article. Generally 60% to 70% difference to the original counts as unique.

I usually use my scanning method as explained earlier in this book (under the public domain section) to find articles and either change them manually or use spinning software to do this for me. To do this manually takes a long time. Manual labour is best though and has given me most results. Here is an example of what a spun sentence would look like. As you can see it becomes complicated as { and | have to be put in manually in the sentence.

Here is the regular sentence:
This is what a spun sentence looks like.

Here is the same sentence in spun format:
{This is|This is an example of|Here is|Here is an example of} {just what|exactly what|what} a {pre-spun|spinnable|spun} sentence {would look|might look|looks} {like after it's spun|like once it has been spun|like}.

Source : www.bestspinnablearticles.com

Spinning articles works best when done by hand and takes a long time but the result can be multiple unique articles. You can outsource spinning articles.

The following is software that spins articles for you:

www.spinarticlepro.com

www.thebestspinner.com

6. Free traffic from directories and trade associations

A directory is a great way to source links for your site. A directory is a website that has a list of links to other sites and usually categorises in a certain order.

This is fairly simple and quick to do. Search for

- "keyword"+"directory"

- "keyword"+"directories"

- "keyword"+"trade associations"

- "keyword"+"meta-indexes" for sites with master lists of directories

Then look at all the websites that might be of interest to your niche. Sign up if need be and submit your website to the directories. Most of the time these submissions are free but even if it costs you a few dollars or pounds a year, it might be worth investing for that extra link to your site. Directories are a very good resource for generating backlinks to your site. Reciprocal directories have to be reliable. Many of these reciprocal directories want you to place a link to them before you can submit yours.

Some people say that reciprocal links don't count for Google anymore but I disagree. Their value has gone down but it is still a link that counts.

- www.dmoz.org PR8 A listing on DMOZ is worth fighting for as Google loves this directory. Make sure you choose the correct category. If your submission is rejected, try again three months later. A listing with DMOZ would give you higher rankings almost immediately.

Here are some more directories:

www.a1dir.com

www.alexa.com

www.alivedirectory.com PR6 not free

www.botw.org PR7 not free

www.directoryworld.net PR6

www.elib.org PR 7 not free

www.iozoo.com PR6

www.jayde.com PR6

www.samsdirectory.com PR4

www.superpages.com

www.thomasnet.com

www.tsection.com PR5

www.wahlinks.com PR4

www.webworldindex.com PR6

7. Free traffic from press releases

Press releases are syndicated content, which means that when you post one, a lot of other sites will automatically take it and post it onto their WebPages too.

Most internet marketers don't realise the importance of press releases and therefore under use them but they are a fantastic way to get extra visitors to your site, or to your affiliate link site.

You can use these to promote products, the launch of your site or a new section or just to raise awareness of what you're offering. Plus, optimising the press release for the keywords you're targeting will also allow it to rank in Google almost overnight!

Google loves press releases, but only if they follow a certain set of rules:

- The information you're giving must be newsworthy and specific - promoting a product, a service, a site launch, a new eBook or book and so on.
- It should not be written like a sales letter - write it as if it was going to appear in a broadsheet newspaper. It needs to be factual and well worded.

- Craft the best possible headline and then use that headline in the first sentence. You have to make your headline sound like a newsworthy topic. "Announces" or "review" or "interesting result" are good words to use. The headline should ideally not be longer than ten words.

In the first paragraph you should make it clear who you are and what you're offering. The body copy should be between 250 and 300 words.

- Explain why the reader should care - Why/how/when/where are you promoting this?
- Avoid using sensationalist adjectives like "insane", "crazy" - again, this is NOT a sales letter.
- Include ALL your contact details.
- Include city and date of the release.
- You MUST spell check and proof read.

Help to write a press release is available here:

- www.writinghelptools.com

Most press release sites are free but sometimes if you pay a one-off fee they guarantee that yours will be picked up by the major search engines. From my experience, the paid press release sites give more results. Make sure you do not forget to put your affiliate link or website link at the bottom of your press release.

Some good free press release sites:

www.businesswire.com PR8
www.eworldwire.com
www.free-press-release.com free submission to online news feeds
www.i-newswire.com free submission
www.openpr.com
www.prfree.com
www.globenewswire.com
 www.prlog.com will automatically send press releases out to a large number of other sites for you, including (potentially) Google News. Free service
www.prweb.com PR7
www.virtualpressoffice.com PR6

www.webwire.com

To find more press release sites, just Google: "free press release distribution" or "press release submission service" or "press release submission directory".

8. Free traffic from video marketing

You can submit your videos, mostly with a link to your website, to the video websites listed below. If you cannot put a link with your video, make sure your URL is shown on the video itself. You might have to become a member first before you are able to submit a video. Most of these websites are free but for some you will need a paid account.

Always use your keywords in the title and description when submitting a video. Some video sites to upload to are:

- www.youtube.com YouTube is the most popular site but lots of other sites are getting tons of traffic and are worth submitting your video to.
- http://video.Google.com Google also has a free batch uploader which enables you to upload more than one video at once. The software can be downloaded here: www.upload.video.Google.com
- www.on.aol.com
- www.buzznet.com
- www.dailymotion.com has high Alexa rank
- www.flixya.com
- www.gofish.com
- www.screenjunkies.com
- www.metacafe.com
- www.photobucket.com
- www.revver.com
- www.viddler.com
- www.vsocial.com
- www.easyanimoto.co.uk
- www.instant-traffic-geyser.com
- www.tubetoolbox.co.uk

- www.screen.yahoo.com
- www.tubemogul.com Tube Mogul - sign up here to have all your videos automatically uploaded to up to 20 video hosting sites all at once

You can search for "video hosting sites" and "video classifieds" to find more Video Hosting websites.

Informative: www.viralvideochart.com gives you a chart of the most popular viral videos. If your video is on the top 10 chart, you know you've done well! ☺

9. Free traffic from video marketing, creating your own free video

> **TOP TIP: Try this out – making a video has never been easier. You can use this method for any videos you want to make. EVERYTHING is free including all the software you will use to make the video.**

Here is a step-by-step guide on how to make your own video completely free by using free pictures, free articles and free video making software.

First step: Go to www.sxc.hu and save some royalty-free pictures regarding your niche on your hard drive. For example, if your niche is about controlling your panic attack, you can save pictures about somebody who is angry and somebody who is calm.

Second step: Go to www.gimp.org and download it free. Import the picture(s) and right-click on the picture to save it as a 700 width picture, which is a good size. Tick auto scale.

Third step: Get a PLR article regarding your niche or write a short article yourself.

Fourth step: Download Audacity: www.audacity.sourceforge.net. With Audacity you will read the PLR article and record your voice whilst you read it.

Fifth step: Open Windows Movie Maker which you should have on your PC if you are using Windows. If not, download it. In Windows Movie Maker you can import pictures, put your voice that you have recorded over the pictures and leave your website domain name at the bottom of the video. Save the video when ready.

Sixth step: Submit your video to the sites listed under "free traffic from video marketing"

ALWAYS use your keywords in the title and description when submitting a video.

10. Free traffic from video marketing and Clickbank products

Find a product on Clickbank and make a video about it in the same way as discussed above. Use a URL-shortening service to put underneath the video with your affiliate link.

11. Free traffic from backlinks

Backlinks are an imperative part of getting on Google's first page, along with content.

A video tutorial on how to get backlinks is included in my videos. Please visit www.VideosNewbieBook.com to get access.

What is Page Rank (PR)?

Let me start with an example. Suppose you have a website on hypnosis but it is not getting many visitors because it isn't on the first page of Google for any keywords. Google thinks that your site is not important because it's not getting any traffic - it's kind of Catch 22. Google gives your site a low PR, or Page Rank, and your site now has a PR0 because it has no backlinks at all. Page rank is mostly based on quality of backlinks and domain age.

However, some people may find your site and link to it from their site. When people link to your site and your Page Rank goes up, and then might be PR1. However, a link from a small insignificant blogger does not really mean a lot to Google.

All of a sudden the National Hypnosis Centre, which is a high authority website with a PR 8, finds your website and links to your page. That immediately means that your Page Rank, or Authority, will go up because Google can see that someone important ranks your site. If you can get a number of links from High Authority Sites in your niche, your PR might all of a sudden rise.

Blogging and joining forums – I will discuss these two a bit later – are a great way of improving search engine rankings. Search engines do like to see sites linking to other relevant sites. The more links Google can see, the more chances your site has to be ranked. The more inbound links that point to your site, the more people will visit it and Google will then rank you higher.

Conclusion: the higher your page rank, the more important Google thinks your site is.

What is a 'backlink' and how do they work?

To simplify: a backlink is a link from one site to another site. Backlinks are like votes. If you want to be on the first page of Google for the phrase "horse tacks" then you'll need to get backlinks to your site with the keyword "horse tacks" in them. The higher the Page Rank of the site that's linking to you, the more useful the backlink.

You can compare backlinks to an election: the person who gets the most votes wins the election. The website who gets the most votes wins in Google.

These links to your site will do the most good if they're from sites that are *relevant* to your site. This means that our horse site would do best getting backlinks from high Page Ranking horse-related web pages.

Links to your site must be keyword-links. The quality of the backlinks is more important than the quantity. In other words if you have 100 links from a hypnosis site to your dog-training-site Google will ignore these. If you have only two links to your site from a PR8 dog-training website, Google will like it.

Let's take a look at this, including a backlink from another site to our site:

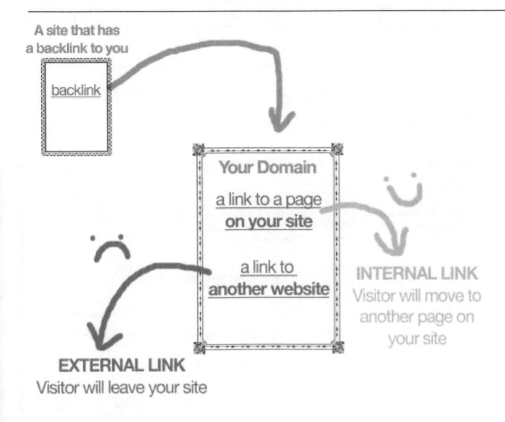

When a visitor comes to your site they will see a number of links that they'll want to click. If they click a link that takes them to someone else's website then you lose them.

> **TOP TIP: Always try to make your external links open in a new browser window. This way you won't risk your visitors moving away from your site. You can do this by adding the target=”_blank” attribute to the link.**

If the link takes them to a page on *your* site then you keep them, and so have more opportunities to sell to them.

In most web design programs, there will be a choice to open a hyperlink in a new window or the same window. Here is a screenshot of how WebPlus does this:

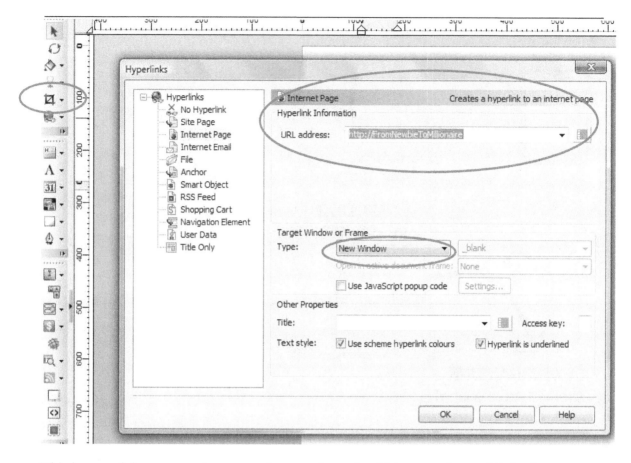

This is one of the reasons that, on each page, there should be more internal links than outbound links.

One of the ways Google calculates Page Rank is by using a concept built on "more inbound than outbound links".

To explain this it's best to think of your website as a series of buckets. Each page or post is a different bucket.

Imagine that each backlink you get to your site pours a small amount of liquid (that we'll call "link juice") into the page's bucket. Now imagine that any link on that page is a hole. An internal link is a hole that will pour your link juice into one of your other pages and keep it on your domain. An outbound link will take your link juice and lose it.

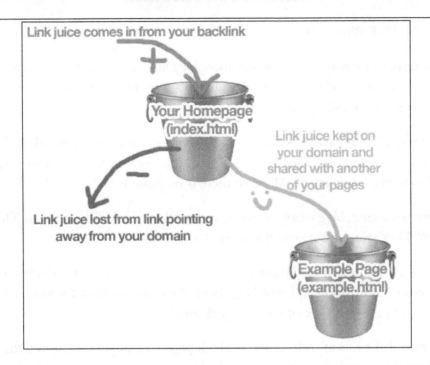

Over 50% of the links on each page should be links to other pages on your site. This helps preserve the "link juice" (aka Page Rank).

Quick backlinking methods

There is a lot of stuff on the internet that is supposed to work wonders for you and automate links. Please investigate carefully before you commit to buy. Search for reviews on the software before you decide.

A link farm is any group of websites that link to every other site in the group. Most links are created by automated programs and services and will be considered SPAM. Link farms are websites created mainly for the purpose of creating links to a page. These websites are not real and are mostly automatically created by software.

> **TOP TIP: You SHOULD NEVER use link farms that randomly link thousands of sites to your site. Another name for these link farms is FFA or Free For All sites. Your site might get banned all together and never be shown again.**

DoFollow – NoDoFollow – Do you still follow?

Word of caution: some people believe that these backlink tactics are Grey Hat SEO (not White and not really Black Hat SEO). But I know lots of people who use these methods and nobody I know has ever had a problem.

The vast majority of your backlinks need to be DoFollow (sometimes just called Follow) and not NoDoFollow (sometimes called NoFollow). A NoDoFollow link is one not searched by Google and so won't count as a backlink, so there is no point to it.

When you go to a forum, blog or any website, you need to check if the links are DoFollow or NoDoFollow. Don't waste your time if they are NoDoFollow.

Google's point of view is that government (.gov) and educational (.edu) websites have very good and relevant information and so it likes these. Backlinks on high PR sites and .gov/.edu sites can get you to the first page of Google by themselves.

There will probably be lots of websites with a high page rank in your niche and the only way of finding them is to search for them constantly. If you can find those websites that have an interactive community and where you can leave your signature or comment at the bottom of your message, then bookmark them and use them.

If you decide to purchase www.marketsamurai.com , you can click on "Promotion" for your keyword and Market Samurai will give you a list of websites to choose from.

WARNING REGARDING BACKLINKS STRATEGY

Keep the number of backlinks you get each day low at first, and then slowly build more and more per day. Google doesn't like people creating their own backlinks in large numbers because it's manipulating the search results. Steadily increasing your number of backlinks will look more natural and will avoid being penalised by Google. That is one of the reasons why sites that sell thousands of links an hour are useless and might damage your site.

IMPORTANT RULES REGARDING BACKLINKS STRATEGY

If you cannot get any backlinks from high PR sites, educational or government sites you should get as many backlinks as possible on any websites related to your niche.

> **TOP TIP: It is always good to include some .edu, . gov or .org in your outbound links. Even if they do not link back to you, according to some internet marketers, they could have some value for Google.**

There are some rather expensive but good websites that offer personal link-building services. Backlinking takes a very long time therefore if you can afford it, I recommend that you outsource it. Here is a good site www.agentsofvalue.com but you can any outsourcing sites to find people to build back links.

The best sites to get backlinks from:

- A site that has a minimum of one keyword that is the same as your site

- A site that has a minimum of one search term that is the same as your site

- A site that has text content on the page, not only links

- Links from well-known websites

- Links from sites with a high Page Rank

- Links from .edu, .gov or .org websites

Links that you do NOT need:

- Links from non-relevant pages

- Links from unethical websites full of spamming content

- Links from websites with hundreds of unrelated links on the page

- Links from adult sites

Keep in mind that most of the Automated Link Strategies Packages do not abide by the above rules.

> **TOP TIP: Only work to get backlinks from relevant websites.**

See my video tutorial "MicroPigsFirstPageProof" which shows how we got from nowhere to the first page of Google with good SEO and a few backlinks. Please visit www.VideosNewbieBook.com to get access.

12. Free traffic from commenting on blogs

If you just want to join blogs and find people in your niche, simply type in

"your keyword"+"Blog"

To maximise your efforts in creating traffic and links, you need to type in text that is a bit more complicated in order to find suitable blogs. Try to find blogs with a high Page Rank *and* DoFollow links, which is explained below. Be prepared to spend a lot of time if you are trying to get links by posting comments on blogs.

When you have found blogs, you need to contribute to the conversations, otherwise the website owner will delete your comment and you will not receive a backlink.

To find .edu blogs to comment on, search for:

site:.edu inurl:blog "leave a comment" -"comments closed" -"you must be logged in to comment" "your keyword"

You type in -"*comments closed*" because you do NOT want the sites where comments are closed. There is no point commenting on those sites. It is important that you type the – symbol before the *"comments closed"*.

You type in -"*you must be logged in to comment*" because you do NOT want sites where you have to log in first to leave a comment. It would take too long if you have to join each blog before you can leave a comment.

When the search results are displayed, if you're using Firefox and the SEO4Firefox plugin from SEOBook.com, try to get backlinks on the sites with the highest Page Rank.

So, if you are looking to build backlinks for a hypnosis website you would search for:

site:.edu inurl:blog "leave a comment" -"comments closed" -"you must be logged in to comment" "hypnosis"

If it is unlikely that you would find any .edu blogs relating exactly to your niche, search for something as similar as possible.

Look in the search results for sites that show with the highest Page Rank (this right-click will only work if you use Firefox as your browser) and open them one by one. On each one, once you have opened the site, right-click on the screen and select NoDoFollow.

All the links on the page will become highlighted on your screen:

- Blue - shows the link is DoFollow

- Red - shows the link is NoDoFollow (easy to remember as a red traffic light means NO, so a red link means NO follow).

Scroll down to the comments on each of the pages until you find one where links have been posted and they're highlighted in *blue* (meaning that they're DoFollow):

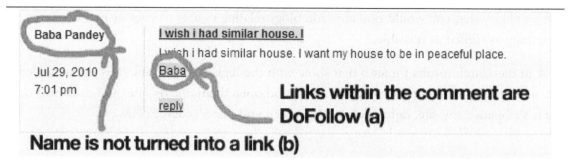

Name is not turned into a link (b)

a) As this link is within the actual comment, we can see that any link we type into the comment box will be a DoFollow link. These links can be to any website or URL.

b) Usually the name entered is automatically turned into a link pointing to the URL in the "Homepage" box in the comment form (see (1) in the next image). In these cases we would enter our keyword as our name. Here it hasn't been turned into a link, so we are free to enter whatever we want as our name.

Now that we've found a blog with DoFollow links, we need to scroll down and enter our information into the comment box:

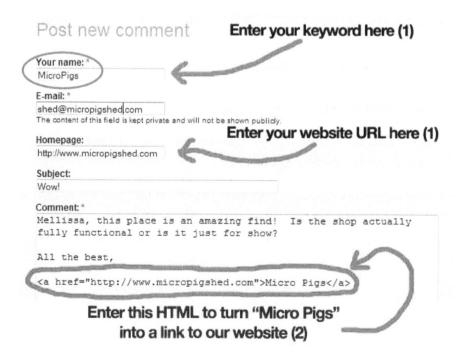

1) Enter your keyword into the "Your name" box and your domain into the "Homepage" box. In most blog comments you will only be able to enter your domain or your comment will be rejected (i.e. *http://www.micropigshed.com* not *http://www.micropigshed.com/videos/cute-piggy*).

2) Sometimes, like in this case, you will find blogs where you can enter links into your comment text. These can be linked to any page on your website, with any anchor text you like.

   To turn text into a link you need a simple bit of HTML code:

   <a href="YOUR URL">YOUR KEYWORD</a>

When you've written a comment that's relevant to the blog post (i.e. shows that you actually read the post), click the "Post Comment" button.

Normally comments will go into a *pending* status, meaning that you have to wait for the blog owner to manually approve what you posted, so write something more thoughtful than "cool post + [yourlink]".

Other ways to find blogs in your niche

Go to www.google.com/blogsearch where you can type in your keyword and Google will show a list of blogging sites. Find blogs that you think are interesting in your niche and subscribe to them with your RSS reader(www.Google.com/reader).

There are other good blog search engines/blog directories:

www.blogcatalog.com - PR7

www.bloghub.com- PR7

www.blogsearchengine.com

www.blogs.com   PR7

www.findblogs.com

www.technorati.com - PR8

13. Free traffic from forum posting

Using the Google search string to find high PR forums - as shown above - find as many high PR forums as you can. Set up accounts on each of them and put a link, with anchor text, to your site in your signature.

Some forums may require you to enter the URL in your signature in something called "BB Code". This is easy to do and is shown below (you would change the website address and anchor text to your own site and key phrase):

Alternatively, this can be done by typing your anchor text into the signature box, highlighting it, and then clicking the hyperlink button, as shown:

Just by taking part in the community and joining in with the discussions, you'll get traffic through people clicking your signature link.

Not only that, but each post you make on that forum will automatically have your signature added, which contains a backlink to your site:

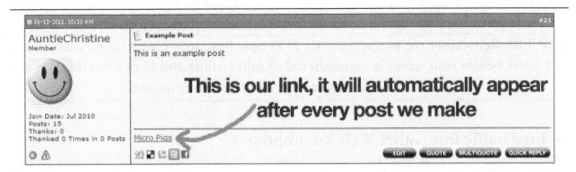

This really is my favourite way to get backlinks because, if you find some good forums, it doesn't feel like hard work. But it is time consuming.

Finding high PR forums or any other forums to comment

inurl:"forum" "your keyword"

To find a .edu forum type the following in Google:

inurl:edu+inurl:forum

To find a .gov forum type the following in Google:

inurl:gov+inurl:forum

You can also type in Google: "DoFollow" + " your niche". Here are some very good forums:

Internet marketing forums

www.affiliatesdirectory.com
www.associateprograms.com
www.forums.cafepress.com
www.clickbanksuccessforum.com
www.digitalpoint.com RECOMMENDED
www.moneymakerdiscussion.com RECOMMENDED
www.sitepoint.com RECOMMENDED
 www.warriorforum.com RECOMMENDED
www.wickedfire.com RECOMMENDED

TOP TIP: Remember the magic number 7? People have to see your name a minimum of 7 times before your name is remembered so join forums and have something to say at least 7 times before expecting decent response.

14. Free traffic from other Web 2.0 properties

*Definition from Wikipedia: The term **Web 2.0** is associated with web applications that facilitate participatory information sharing, interoperability, user-centered design,[1] and collaboration on the World Wide Web. A Web 2.0 site allows users to interact and collaborate with each other in a social media dialogue as creators (prosumers) of user-generated content in a virtual community, in contrast to websites where users (consumers) are limited to the passive viewing of content that was created for them. Examples of Web 2.0 include social networking sites, blogs, wikis, video sharing sites, hosted services, web applications, mashups and folksonomies.*

In my experience the two most loved by Google are Squidoo www.squidoo.com and Hubpages www.hubpages.com (June 2011). Below is an example of a Squidoo page shown on the first page of Google for the keywords "How to get rid of Hay Fever".

How to Get Rid of Hay Fever and Itchy Skin with all Natural Home ...
The variety and sheer number of plants with medicinal, therapeutic properties are quite astonishing. Some 70,000 plant species, from lichens to towering ...
www.squidoo.com › Topics › Healthy Living - Cached - Similar

How to Get Rid of Hay Fever | MyGetRidOfGuide.com
How to Get Rid of Hay Fever. Hay fever is medically known as allergic rhinitis. It is an alle
reaction to airborne particles that usually affects the ...
www.mygetridofguide.com/how-to-get-rid-of-hay-fever/ - Cached

Showing results for how to get rid **of** hayfever.
Search instead for the original terms: how to get rid **off** hayfever

Gooooooooogle ▶
1 2 3 4 5 6 7 8 9 10   Next

For this section we're going to talk about creating pages on a website called Squidoo.

In the words of Squidoo:

"Squidoo is the popular publishing platform and community that makes it easy for you to create "lenses" online. Lenses are pages, kind of like flyers or signposts or overview articles that gather everything you know about your topic of interest - and snap it all into focus. Like the lens of a camera, your perspective on something."

Google loves Squidoo and you'll find that pages you create there will appear in the search results much more easily than your new domain.

The first step is to create Squidoo lenses (http://www.squidoo.com) (much like you created your keyword optimised articles) to point to your page that's optimised for the same keyword. Put a bit of time into making these lenses look good because it will make a difference to the amount of visitors you get.

Make sure you are backlinking your Squidoo pages, articles and individual pages with anchor text containing the keywords.

Each Squidoo page is going to link to your similarly optimised articles AND to your optimised page, like this:

Squidoo Lens

Optimised
for keyword

i.e. "tack trunks"

Ezine
Articles.com

Article
optimised for
keyword

i.e. "tack trunks"

Article
Base.com

Article
optimised for
keyword

i.e. "tack trunks"

Article
Alley.com

Article
optimised for
keyword

i.e. "tack trunks"

Your
Domain

www.

your-domain

.com

Your Page

Page based
around same
keyword as
articles

i.e. "tack trunks"

Set up a blog on a free blog platform like Wordpress.com or Blogspot.com and post occasional updates about your niche, always linking back to your main page.

Just like the forum posts, this will help get traffic while also supplying you with a new backlink with each post.

Sign up for an account with the following Web 2.0 sites and create a page on each about your niche - always linking back to your main website:

- Squidoo - www.squidoo.com
- Wetpaint - www.wetpaint.com
- Hubpages - www.hubpages.com
- Wordpress - This type of site is hosted by the Wordpress. It will give you a site with a URL like *http://horsetacks.wordpress.com* - www.wordpress.com

Go to www.go2web20.net for a massive database of all the newest and most interesting Web 2.0 sites on the web.

Here are some other very good Web 2.0 properties:

www.blog.com
www.gather.com
www.xanga.com
www.9rules.com
www.tumblr.com

www.ning.com
www.weebly.com
www.livejournal.com
www.vox.com
www.quizilla.com
www.zimbio.com

15. Free traffic from social networks

> **TOP TIP: I wouldn't use software that automatically gets you thousands of followers/friends on Twitter, Facebook or any other social networking site. Normally the followers will be bogus in some way - either fake accounts or people who have been spammed to death. The only way you will ever get any real, potential buyers is by doing it the good old-fashioned way - yourself!**

Explaining all the different social networks would take an entire book, so I will explain them only briefly.

Social networks are places where people can interact and meet new people. Users can share things they like, upload photos, chat and do almost everything they can do in real life. Social networks aren't just for kids: everyone's using them.

The good thing about social media is that you do not need any money to be successful and start making money with it. The first thing you need to understand to be successful with social media is how huge it is. The internet world has changed forever since social media became a big thing.

Top 20 Social Networking Websites

The following report shows websites for the industry 'Computers and Internet - Social Networking and Forums', ranked by Visits for the week ending 01/01/2011.

Rank	Website	Visits Share
1.	Facebook	63.25%
2.	YouTube	19.20%
3.	MySpace	2.53%
4.	Yahoo! Answers	0.98%
5.	Twitter	0.97%
6.	Tagged	0.92%
7.	myYearbook	0.51%
8.	Mylife	0.38%
9.	Club Penguin	0.35%
10.	MocoSpace	0.28%
11.	Yelp	0.23%
12.	Linkedin	0.23%
13.	IMVU	0.22%
14.	HubPages	0.19%
15.	Classmates	0.17%
16.	myYearbook Chatter	0.16%
17.	deviantART	0.15%
18.	Tumblr	0.15%
19.	Fantage	0.14%
20.	Yahoo! Groups	0.13%

According to research Facebook now gets more page impressions than Google BUT there is a huge difference from an IM marketing point of view: Facebook users are mostly on Facebook for fun and social purposes, not to buy. If somebody searches in Google for "knee pain remedy" they are clearly looking for a specific solution and so these searches will convert a lot better.

There are 500 million Facebook users and 250 million people worldwide log on to Facebook every day. An average user has 130 friends and the community spends over 700 billion minutes per month on Facebook. You can find more facts and statistics on www.facebook.com/press

The best social networks to be a part of are:

- www.twitter.com Twitter - a micro-blogging platform with a real emphasis on communication. You can only post a maximum of 140 characters at a time so you will need to keep whatever you have to say to an absolute minimum! Check the links section at the end of this guide for some great Twitter tools.

- www.facebook.com
- www.myspace.com
- www.linkedin.com More focused on professionals. Has over 60 million users and has executives from Fortune 500 companies as members - RECOMMENDED
- www.ryze.com Not time consuming and more focused on business
- www.stumbleupon.com PR8 RECOMMENDED
- www.friendfeed.com owned by Facebook RECOMMENDED

Other social networking sites:

www.43things.com PR7
www.bebo.com PR7
www.friendster.com PR7 RECOMMENDED
www.gather.com PR6
www.hi5.com PR6 RECOMMENDED
www.livejournal.com PR8
www.meetup.com PR8
www.ning.com PR7
www.plaxo.com almost all users are over 35 years old
www.scribd.com
www.secondlife.com PR7
www.tagged.com
www.vox.com PR8
www.xanga.com PR7
www.yelp.com PR6
www.zimbio.com An interactive magazine with over 20 million readers a month
www.zorpia.com

Here are some interesting social network related sites:

- www.refollow.com - A quality way of searching for people, organising who's following you and checking social graphs of what's occurring on Twitter.

- www.autotweeting.com - The ultimate application to grow your Twitter accounts on auto pilot and schedule tweets.
- www.buzzom.com - Search for Twitterers with interest in your niche.
- www.twitter.com/search-home - Type in a keyword and it will find tweeters for you.
- www.socialoomph.com - automatically DM (direct message) your followers in one zap.
- www.tweetadder.com - Automated Twitter management software.
- www.twellow.com - Categorises Twitter users based on keywords, use the DM-system that allows to send an instant message with your links.
- www.twitterfeed.com - Automates updates by using RSS feeds from external sources.
- www.twitterfriendadder.com - Follow a number of their Twitter followers.
- www.twuffer.com - Effectively an autoresponder for tweets.
- www.wefollow.com - Find popular Twitter users in your niche.
- www.topfollowed.com
- www.opennetworker.com

16. Free traffic from social bookmarking sites

Social bookmarking is a method for people to save their favourite websites online, tagged with keywords. These social bookmarking sites allow you to post bookmarks to sites you like (which, in our case, is *your* site!) and share them with other people. People can find them by searching with a keyword. These bookmarks can then be seen and voted for by other people.

These sites show who created each bookmark and gives access to that person's other bookmarked resources. People can easily make social connections with other people in the same niche. Users can see how many people have used a keyword or tag and they can also search for all other resources that have been assigned to a keyword. All the users will develop a certain structure of keywords to find resources easily.

Social book-marking can create traffic in different ways:

- **Searching**: People searching social bookmarking sites often search on them instead of using search engines, because the results might be more interesting. So, they are more likely to click on your site than a search engine search.

- **Browsing**: People browsing the social bookmarking sites can come across your website.

- **Page Rank**: Links from social bookmarking sites with a high Page Rank can rank you higher in the search engines.

Here are my top tips for getting a big amount of traffic with social bookmarking sites:

- Use the same username and password for each account.
- Include your niche keyword in your username.
- Edit and add to your user profile so that it looks real and friendly.
- Add as many friends as you can to your account.
- Bookmark sites that you genuinely like, to build up your reputation as someone who can be trusted to know what's good.
- Send links to *your* sites to your friends.
- Bookmark your own sites.
- Vote down competing sites.
- Comment on popular bookmarks with your link in the text - don't make this obvious, try to blend it in by saying something like "this is a great bookmark, it really reminds me of some of the things I've seen on this site: [link to your site]".

Here are some social bookmarking sites. The first five are in my opinion the most important ones.

- www.reddit.com PR7 - Look for the most relevant section for your website to post your link in. Don't submit in the general section as it will just get lost in the noise. Vote your own links as much as possible, this will help them climb the ranks

- www.digg.com PR8 - This is all about friends so make your account really personal. Include your real photo and interests. To get more friends on your account add someone as a friend then, when they accept, add all *their* friends as friends

- www.technorati.com PR8 - You can post your blog in every relevant category and it combines both links, traffic and ratings. Make sure that posts on your site have been properly tagged because this will make your site appear in more places

- www.stumbleupon.com PR8 - Send pages to your friends with the Stumbleupon toolbar. Find users with similar interests to you and add them as friends. Ask them nicely to "stumble" your links (similar to giving them a good rating) and say you'll do the same in return

- www.delicious.com PR8
- www.blogcatalog.com - list blogs per directory
- www.bloglines.com PR9- publish, subscribe or search for blogs
- www.connotea.org PR7
- www.fark.com PR7
- www.jumptags.com
- www.kaboodle.com PR6
- www.kinja.com PR7
- www.meneame.net PR7
- www.newsvine.com PR7
- www.slashdot.org PR9
- www.yoono.com PR7
- www.waggit.com

Going through these social bookmarking sites is very time consuming. Go to www.socialmarker.com. It is a free service that will reduce the time and effort needed to socially bookmark a site. Set up an account and you can speed up the process of adding links to your site.

Here are some Web 2.0 marketing providers and submission programs:
www.commonplaces.com
www.onlywire.com is awesome for speedy submits. Just create an account with the sites above and you can save your logins at your Onlywire account.
www.wisitech.com

Let these providers do the work for you. Submissions to Web 2.0 sites are not always easy and time consuming. These providers know their stuff and if you have the money, I suggest you work with one of them.

17. Free traffic from Yahoo answers

Visit www.answers.yahoo.com and answer some questions with your link at the bottom. A wide range of topics is discussed. Google likes Yahoo answers (see next screenshot).

18. Free traffic from Ehow

Go to www.ehow.com and become a writer or expert.

19. Free Traffic from Wikihow

Go to www.wikihow.com/categories. Anyone can write and anyone can edit. Any person can create a new page to write about anything. Google loves Wikihow.

Want proof that eHow and Wikihow work? Here it is, with both showing on the first page of Google after my search for "how to cure a cough":

how to cure a cough

About 6,790,000 results (0.09 seconds)

How to Cure a Cough | eHow.com
How to Cure a Cough. Coughs are usually one of two types--dry or wet. Depending on which type of cough you have depends on how you cure the cough.
www.ehow.com › Drugs & Supplements - Cached - Similar

How to Cure A persistent **Cough** | eHow.com
How to Cure A persistent Cough. Dealing with a persistent cough can be ...
www.ehow.com › Healthcare - Cached - Similar
➕ Show more results from ehow.com

Home Remedies for **Cough** - Treatment & **Cure** - Natural Remedy for ...
Read about home remedies for cough and cough treatments. Also read **how to cure cough** naturally with proven home remedies.
www.natural-homeremedies.com/homeremedies_cough.htm - Cached - Similar

How to Treat a **Cough** - wikiHow
18 Feb 2011 ... This video provides information on how to treat a **cough** with over the counter medication and non-pharmacological methods. ...
www.wikihow.com/Treat-a-Cough - Cached - Similar

Home Remedies For **Cough**
Cough is a sudden expulsion of air from the lungs that clears air passages. Use garlic, olive oil, ginger and more to make your own home remedies for **cough**.
www.grannymed.com/meds/cough.aspx - Cached - Similar

Wats the best way to **cure a cough**? - Yahoo! Answers
2 Dec 2006 ... (m) goto the following website, it contains home remedies for **cough** http://www. ayurvediccure.com/homeremedie... ... if u don't want to suffer from ...
answers.yahoo.com ... › Respiratory Diseases - Cached - Similar

20. Free traffic from Wiki-Answers

Visit www.wiki-answers.com and answer some questions with your link at the bottom. A wide range of topics is discussed. Google likes Wiki answers.

21. Free traffic from All Experts

Visit www.allexperts.com which allows visitors to ask questions to experts. You can apply to become a volunteer expert and answers questions. Your response to the questions is archived on the site and can generate links for a long time.

22. Free Traffic from LinkedIn

You can answer questions on www.linkedin.com and include your website link in your answers.

23. Free Traffic from Wikipedia.

Wikipedia - www.wikipedia.org - is a lot stricter and it's more difficult to list your definition or topic. However it's 100% worth your time if you think that there is an untapped niche with insufficient information available on Wikipedia.

Simply Google "adding your own Wikipedia article" and the first site shown will probably be this one: http://en.wikipedia.org/wiki/Wikipedia:Starting_an_article. This page explains what you need to do to make your own page in Wikipedia.

Google loves Wikipedia.

> **Top Tip: Having a page approved to be published on Wikepedia.org is certainly worth the effort. I found that a good Wikipedia page combined with a good Squidoo Page (discussed later in the book) can rank you in Google in three days!**

24. Free traffic with 'share' icon on your site

You must have seen these sorts of buttons before:

To ShareThis, click on a service below:

Reddit	Digg
Facebook	MySpace
del.icio.us	StumbleUpon
Technorati	Google Bookmarks
Yahoo Bookmarks	Yahoo! My Web
Windows Live	Propeller
FriendFeed	Newsvine
N4G	Mixx
Blinklist	Furl
ma.gnolia	Mister Wong

I suggest you put a "share it with" icon on your site, even at the beginning when you will not have many Facebook fans or Twitter followers (everyone has to start somewhere). More people will talk about your website. More people will see your website on all the share-it sites. These 'share it with' buttons are free and you can download them from www.sharethis.com or www.addthis.com.

25. Free traffic from interviews

Search your keyword and contact some of the companies that show in the ranking. I suggest that you pick the websites listed on pages 9 to 20 and further because otherwise the website owner might not be prepared to speak to you as he will consider you his competition. Just because the website owner is on page 9 does not mean he does not know his trade. Speak to the boss/owner or manager and see if he is prepared to answer a few questions. Potentially he will be proud to talk to you, and happy to send the interview to his list – with a link to your website – which you agree with him prior to the interview: everybody wins. You will get extra traffic from his list.

26. Free traffic from naming images on your site

A lot of people will look under 'Images' in Google. By including a lot of images on your site and giving these images a name, you will increase traffic to your site. You must give the images a name that is relevant to the page they are on. Always make sure you include Alt and Title in your image tags.

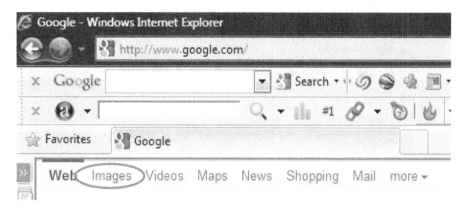

Google or any other search engines cannot recognise pictures on your website (not yet anyway) but if you give each picture a keyword Google will find it. Each page should have at least one image on it.

Google's pictures search won't find your picture of a Ferrari 458 if you are put it on the web with a reference "DCMB999002". It might show if you give your picture a name like "My Ferrari 658".

27. Free traffic from internal links

When you design your site, as mentioned before, you need to put internal links on your pages. Visitors are likely to visit more pages on your site, and search engines like internal links, so you might rank higher by doing this.

28. Free traffic from an HTML Sitemap

An HTML sitemap is a page that lists all the pages on your site. It is a page inside your site and the page links to all other pages. If you put an HTML sitemap on your site, it means that it is easier for the search engines to crawl and index your site, so it will improve your ranking.

29. Free traffic from different browsers

I mentioned under the 'Testing your site' section that you must make sure that your website can be seen on the most used browsers. You will get extra traffic this way as visitors who cannot see your site properly will immediately leave it.

30. Free traffic through offering freebies

Free giveaways travel very fast on the internet. If you have something decent to give away, you can list it on some freebie-websites. Sometimes these websites require a link back to their website from yours, but not all the time.

www.absolutefreebies.com

www.freebiedirectory.com

www.freebielist.com

www.freebiesplanet.com

www.free-n-cool.com

www.freestuffchannel.com

www.sweetfreestuff.com

www.thefreesite.com

31. Free traffic from a good hosting company

If you use a cheap or free hosting company, your pages will probably load slowly. Slow loading pages mean people will leave your site.

32. Free traffic from exchanging links

Exchanging links (reciprocal links) are links where you put a link to somebody else's site on your site, and they link back to yours. Make sure that the sites that you link to are in the same niche.

33. Free traffic from free email lists

There are a few companies as far as I am aware that send your email to their email address list free:

www.1soft.com/lists

www.groups.yahoo.com

www.lists.topica.com

This is a game of numbers: send an email to 10,000 people and a few might buy.

34. Free traffic from Froogle

Froogle is a shopping search engine from Google. If you are selling a product, you really need to be listed on Froogle. You can even list a product and use your affiliate link. For example, you can sell a specialised DVD and put a picture on Froogle with your Amazon link. When somebody clicks on the picture they will be taken to Amazon, and you earn money if the person buys.

35. Free traffic from other shopping directories

If you are selling a product that "fits in" a shopping directory, you must sign up for some directories and upload information about your products. An amazing amount of people use these shopping directories. Some shopping directories allow you to list a product with an affiliate link on.

Some good shopping directories are:

www.nextag.com

www.paiddirectory.com

www.shopping.com

www.shopping.yahoo.com

 www.shopping5.com

www.shoppingdirectory.com

www.shopzilla.com

36. Free traffic from Pinging

Pinging Services

"Pinging" means, basically, that you send a little nudge to various search engines on the internet to come and have a look at your site. This is particularly useful if you've either done a lot of updating that has yet to be indexed by Google, or your site is new and isn't yet appearing in the search results.

- Pingomatic – www.pingomatic.com Does exactly the same as Pingoat.
- Pingler - While Pingoat will only allow you to ping your domain as a whole, Pingler will let you ping individual posts and pages - www.pingler.com

37. Free traffic from a funny picture

If you publish a funny picture of a funny drawing, people might like it and pass it around to their friends. Always mention your link on the picture. Reddit has a picture section: http://www.reddit.com/r/pics/

38. Free traffic from chat rooms

Chat rooms (where you can talk to more than 1 person at a time) and message boards are still around. You can search for chat room and message boards in your niche and participate in the conversation. Now and again you will mention that you came across such a good product in your niche available at ... put your website here: www.YourWebsiteOrLinkHere.com.

Websites to visit are:

- www.chatmag.com
- www.groups.Google.com
- www.networkworld.com - Technical chats and forum

39. Free Traffic from Quizilla

Create an account with www.quizilla.com by using your product name or your website as your username. Click on "Make a creation " and add your article with anchor text (using your keyword) linking back to your landing page.

40. Free traffic with a mobile phone version of your website

Over 78 million people now use a mobile phone to go online and the number is growing. If your site does not load properly on a mobile, you will lose potential customers. Wordpress has a plugin called WPTouch that creates a mobile compatible version.

41. Free traffic from quizzes

There are a lot of people who love quizzes. You can visit www.proprofs.com to create a quiz. They have free and payable options. People who do the quiz are likely to send it to their friends.

42. Free traffic from your email address

Every time you send an email, make sure that your website link is at the bottom of your email. In Window Mails you go to Tools, Options, Signature to put your signature at the bottom of each email.

43. Free traffic from top lists

People love "Top 5" or "Top 20" or "Top 100" articles because they usually contain useful information and interesting facts. Publish these to article marketing directories or any other traffic method. You can put your own website at the bottom or an affiliate link. You could create "Top 10 best diet programmes" or "Top 10 best video software programmes". The good thing about these Top Lists is that you can put your affiliate link under each product listed in the Top List.

44. Free traffic from photo marketing

If you have a number of original photos that are based around your niche, upload them to photo sharing sites. Use relevant keywords and always include a link back to your website. These kinds of sites receive vast amounts of traffic, so are another opportunity.

Best image sharing sites:

www.flickr.com
www.i-am-bored.com
www.photobucket.com
www.picasa.google.com
You can find royalty-free pictures on www.sxc.hu

45. Free traffic from submitting links

Google "keyword" + [submit link] or"keyword + submit a link" or "keyword + add a link" and several websites will be shown where you can submit your website link.

46. Free traffic with an email newsletter

If you put an opt-in box on your site you can email the opted-in people with a monthly newsletter with links to your website.

47. Free traffic from classified ads

The following website allows your ad to be shown free in the relevant section: www.craigslist.org. Craigslist has become a very large classified ads website with billions of views each month and over 25 million users each month. They do not charge for your ad unless it is a job ad. They earn all their money from millions of new jobs that are posted each month. Your free submission ad will disappear after two weeks so you need to re-submit your ad every two weeks.

Other classified ad sites:

www.adlandpro.com

www.adpost.com

www.classifiedads.com

www.domesticsale.com

www.edirection.com

www.livedeal.com

www.postlets.com

www.usfreeads.com

www.vflyer.com

48. Free traffic from Craigslist forum

www.craigslist.org There is a discussion forum inside each city. Write posts here and include your website link when possible and appropriate.

49. Free traffic from product reviews

Go to www.epinions.com which is a product review company and write a review on a product with your affiliate link at the bottom. Your affiliate link can be your link to the Amazon shop or eBay shop.

www.consumerreports.org

www.ratings.net is another product review website.

www.resellerratings.com rating services

You can find new upcoming products, ahead of everybody else on http://uk.toluna.com/test. This is a website where brand new products are tested. You can get some great ideas here. Find a product that you believe in, make sure it is available on the market and write your review by searching for people's opinions on the product.

If you are interested in the new product market here are some websites to visit:

www.bzzagent.com

www.gizmodo.com New gadgets discussed

www.greenbook.org Guide for buyers of marketing research services

www.planetfeedback.com Complaint site

50. Free traffic from vlogs

A vlog is a personalised video journal mostly updated regularly but posted like blogs. Very often distribution is through RSS feeds.

Wikipedia defines vlogging: Video blogging, sometimes shortened to vlogging (pronounced v'LOG-ing or VEE-log-ing) or vidblogging is a form of blogging for which the medium is video, and is a form of Internet television. Entries often combine embedded video or a video link with supporting text, images, and other metadata.

Vlogs are hosted on video websites like YouTube, and they work the same as videos: you upload your vlog to the sites.

Learn more about Vlogs and Vlogging here:
www.rocketboom.com/vlog Vlog directory

51. Free traffic with your YouTube domain name

You can have your company name or domain name on www.youtube.com . Your domain can look like: www.youtube.com/ItsADogsLife.com . Create a little video showing people how to massage a dog's back (or whatever you want to show) and post it to YouTube. Write a blog article and embed the video in the article for extra traffic.

52. Free traffic from Wikidot

www.wikidot.com Create an account with Wikidot. It is a marvellous way to get your site ranked in the search engines. The educational sites are absolutely free for educational/ research purposes.

53. Free traffic from viral marketing

The term viral marketing comes from the word "viruses". Viruses can spread like wild fire and so can your website. Viral marketing can be compared with "word of mouth" but in electronic format.

With viral marketing you don't have to do anything to get visitors to your site - other people will do it for you by spreading your website link to all their friends. Those friends will forward it to their friends and so on. It is likely that you have seen video's on YouTube with 2 million views or more. They get such a high number of views through viral marketing: everybody is talking about it and showing it to their friends.

Social networking sites like Facebook and Twitter can play a large role in viral marketing.

Try creating content that is so funny that people can't help themselves but share it with everyone they know. That is what viral marketing is: people find what they see very interesting or funny and want to pass it on to people they know. It creates a buzz. There is "word of mouth" viral marketing as well as "word of mouse" viral marketing but the principle is the same: people are spreading something around by talking about it off-line or on-line.

It can be as simple as sending out an email with the subject "You may be eligible for a tax refund", which people will open quickly, thinking that they might be due some money. When they open it there is just a video of a laughing cat saying "You think you're eligible for WHAT?!" with a link to your site underneath. Sorry, I'm not a comedy writer but I think you get the idea.

54. Free traffic from radio

www.blogtalkradio.com Have your own radio show, create your own radio station. You can find some prominent people here in your niche and interview them. You can then announce your radio shows on your blog, Facebook, your email list and so on. It is an easy way to create and share radio on the web. You can sign up free and get a 30-minute show per day with 5 live callers. There are also payable options that give you a lot more possibilities. It's worth checking out.

55. Free traffic from joint ventures

You can get lots of free traffic by doing a 'joint venture'. A joint venture is basically when two people work together to maximise their profits. You can find potential people to work with by searching Google: "your niche" + Joint Venture. Most of the time the company will send whatever it is that you are selling to their email list. You can either email them or phone them explaining what you want to do. The idea here is that you split the profit into whatever margins you agree on. You can also swap your emails – in case you already have a list. If you have 3000 subscribers and your potential partner has 4000 you can probably do a deal and swap lists: you send your product to his list and he can email your list. If you have 3000 subscribers and your potential partner has 40,000 email subscribers, he probably won't be keen to swap emails. Most of the big internet guru's have lists in the "how to make money on the internet". So if you have a website on dogs, there would not be a lot of point trying to do a joint venture with one of these internet gurus. However if your site is about making money on the web, a joint venture with an internet guru is a very good place to start building *your* list (when you have your own opt-in page on your sales page).

Important: Swapping emails does NOT mean that you will actually receive the email addresses from your joint venture partner. Your joint venture partner will simply send **your** product with **his** affiliate link to **his** list and **you** will send **his** product with **your** affiliate link to **your** list.

These are good websites in the making-money online business:

www.imnewswatch.com latest news and launches

www.v3jvnotifypro.com is a great joint venture networks

56. Free traffic from your own social network

www.ning.com allows you to create your own social network in relation to your niche.

57. Free traffic from RSS feed

If you publish an RSS feed, your site visitors that subscribe to your RSS will automatically receive new content each time you put it on your site. The people that receive your new content will visit your site, creating more traffic.

58. Free traffic from slides

www.slideshare.com Slideshare allows people to share PowerPoint presentations. You can turn an article into a presentation with PowerPoint and submit your slides. Don't forget, as usual, to place your link at the top or bottom for maximum exposure.

www.myplick.com another slide sharing website

59. Free traffic from USFreeAds

www.usfreeads.com This site receives over 500,000 visitors each month and is worth checking out. You can place free ads. Pick the correct category for your ad. Then search Google for "free ads" or "free classified ads" to find more free ad websites.

60. Free traffic from safelist advertising

Safelist advertising, or free advertising through a safelist, is mailing to an opt-in subscriber list in which you can promote advertising websites, business opportunities and so on. Most of the time the members are all double-opt-in members. All members of a safelist agree to receive advertising emails from the other members. You can advertise free to a number of people via email and not have to worry about any spam complaints. Most safelist advertising sites offer you free advertising with the option to upgrade at any time to gain access to even more features.

Here are some websites:

www.gotsafelists.com

www.myfreesafelist.com

www.planetxmail.com

Google "credit based safelist" to find more websites.

http://www.supremelist.com/safelistprox/join.php

61. Free traffic from webinars

A webinar is basically a one-way audio conference or it can be a PowerPoint presentation recorded with your voice over it. In order to attend a webinar you need to register for one as you will need the link for where to watch it.

Organising a webinar is not easy and is time consuming but if carried out professionally it can be a good sales tool.

Webinars, if organised successfully, are a great way to drive traffic to your site. You can promote your webinar with any of the traffic methods in this book.

Here are some very good websites to learn about webinars. None of them are free to use.

www.gotomeeting.com

www.webex.com webinar provider

To record your screen or yourself: www.camtasia.com

62. Free traffic from teleseminars

A teleseminar is an informative seminar done over the phone. Sometimes the listeners can participate and interact in the conversation. Most of the time a teleseminar is free but sometimes the host charges admission for the call. For more information:

www.conferencecall.com

www.freeconferencecall.com

www.greatteleseminars.com

63. Free traffic from podcasting

I have not used podcasting before but I know some internet marketers that are making money with it. Basically users can download a file and listen to it on their PC or mobile phone or whenever is convenient for them.

64. Free traffic from eBay powersellers

Suppose you wrote an eBook on your niche. Type in your niche keyword in www.ebay.com and find powersellers selling products in your niche. Contact the powersellers and tell them that they can sell your eBook without having to pay a penny to you - all you want in return is the email address from the buyer who bought the eBook. This is free targeted traffic for you. All you need to do is send an email to that buyer who is likely to be interested in something that you offer that has to do with the product that he bought on eBay. I have used this traffic or lead-creation method many times with a lot of success.

You could even do this with a PLR eBook as the person selling or buying stuff on eBay might not even know what PLR is.

65. Free traffic from eBay

Wait until eBay has free listing weeks or free listing months. List your eBook or a free PLR report on eBay for $0.01 p. You can send it electronically so it costs you nothing BUT you capture the email address from a person who is interested in your niche. Send this person an e-mail and try to get him to opt-in to your list in order to send him lots of freebies, information and affiliate links.

66. Free traffic from Blog Carnival

Join www.blogcarnival.com. Bloggers write about one specific subject and the host writes a round-up post which links to all people who took part. Most of the time participants will link to each other's entries.

67. Free traffic adding a blog to your site

If you add a blog to your site, you can write new content regularly and visitors will come back more often than when you just have a static site. Search engines love blogs therefore this might increase your traffic.

68. Free Traffic adding a forum to your site

There is no point putting a forum on your site if you are getting 20 visitors per day. Once you receive over 1000 visitors per day, it might be worth adding a forum to your site. The search engines like (busy) forums. http://www.phpbb.com is free forum software.

69. Free traffic from blog contests

Several blog platforms have contests. You can participate in a contest by giving away a product or money. The blogger can then link to your site. Contest software: www.wizehive.com , www.dynaportal.com

70. Free traffic from a voting contest

Create a contest and people will vote for who the winner should be. If you have a diet website, you could ask your visitors to submit their best dieting tips. The best tips would get a prize. By doing this, people who submit tips will link to the voting and ask their friends to vote.

71. Free traffic from Google Alerts

Sign up to www.Google.com/alerts and get emailed at regular intervals whenever anyone blogs or talks about your niche. You can join the forums and blogs that are active in your niche and get free traffic to your site. You can contact the webmasters of the websites that are active in Google Alert and ask them to put your Clickbank product on their site. Use your imagination and business mind.

72. Free traffic from increasing the speed of your website

If your website does not load instantly, visitors will immediately leave. By making sure that your site loads quickly, you will generate extra traffic. Ask all your friends to see if it loads quickly on their computer. If your sites load slowly, these are the things you should check first: make sure pictures and videos are not high resolution and remove any Flash pages or complicated graphics.

73. Free traffic from your own customers' feedback

Ask your customers what they think about your site, what they would like to see different. Ask them what they are looking for and then give it to them. Let your visitors know when you have made changes to the site and they will come and visit you again.

74. Free traffic from charities

Depending on the niche you are in, you can get great free publicity from charities. Find a local charity in your niche. Donate a percentage of your sales to them. They will do the marketing for you and leave your business cards on their counter if the charity has a shop. The charity will help you make sales as they will earn money from it.

75. Free traffic from schools

Contact a local school or other educational institute and offer them a free course on your niche. The students will look at your website and some of them might buy a product.

76. Free traffic from friends and family

Tell all your friends, colleagues and family about your website. They will tell their friends and their friends will tell others, etc....and before you know hundreds of people will look at your site.

77. Free traffic from your imagination

Some of the ideas listed below will require some money to purchase the items but once bought, you will advertise your site free wherever you go.

- Put your business hat on and look, think, analyse. Think with an open business mind. Think outside the box. Make your own traffic methods.

- Watch, listen and speak. Look around you. Constantly analyse what you see on the web and around you. Could you contact somebody to get extra traffic?

- Give out business cards with your website on everywhere you go.

- Start talking about one of your niches and mention your site everywhere you go.

- Get some promotional items eg. pens, rulers, t-shirts.

- Become a public speaker at a local get-together.

- Go and visit some exhibitions and give out your business cards. Use your imagination.

There are opportunities everywhere and by using your imagination and thinking "outside the box" I am sure you will find more ways to find free traffic.

Part 11. Traffic – Paid Traffic

Paid Marketing or Paid Traffic is the fastest way to get website traffic. If you follow my way of finding a niche with the possibility of ranking highly in the search engines, you will probably make money without having to spend money on traffic. On the other hand, if you have a budget, I suggest that you try some of these Paid Traffic methods as some of them work really well. They can give you exposure and clicks on the smaller search engines or on Google if you use Google Adwords.

Below is a screenshot from the ads shown by Google for the search "telephone switchboard system". The ads are the ones in the borders. The three companies on the top of Google pay more per click than the ones shown on the side.

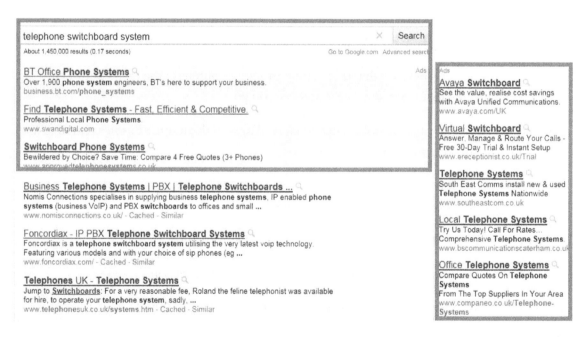

From the screenshot below you can see that the first three companies will have to pay Google approximately £4.57 or $7.49 per click. You can get this information in Keyword Tools. The average CPC will only be shown when you have logged into your account.

For the key phrase "small business telephone system" the advertiser will have to pay £9.60 or $15.73 per click. That is a lot of money (£960 or $1573) if 100 people click on the ad and the advertiser only makes one sale (based on the rule of 10)!

Keyword	Competition	Global Monthly Searches	Approximate CPC
telephone switchboard system		170	£4.57
telephone systems		74,000	£7.52
voip telephone system		3,600	£6.29
office telephone system		1,900	£6.62
small business telephone systems		22,200	£9.60
small business telephone system		22,200	£8.76
telephones systems		880	£5.55
business telephone systems		22,200	£9.05
telephone system suppliers		320	£5.69
automated telephone systems		880	£5.34
new telephone systems		1,600	£7.23
telephone switchboard		3,600	£3.90
telephone system		135,000	£7.16
business telephone system		4,400	£9.26
office telephone systems		22,200	£7.34
small telephone systems		8,100	£9.14

Paid traffic is where you pay for exposure or traffic to your site. It is the quickest way to be on page one for Google Adwords or other advertising methods on the web. The downside of course is that the minute you stop buying traffic, your exposure will stop. If you are planning to use paid traffic all the time, it does not really matter about SEO and keywords on your website as you constantly spend money for people to find your site. There are people who earn a lot of money with only paid traffic and nothing but an affiliate link. Don't forget to check Google's terms and conditions for the landing pages or you might get banned.

The pie chart below shows that although Google still has the largest slice of the pie, there are other search engines that get a lot of traffic. You can't ignore these search engines. You can see that "All Others" get 1% of the searches. 1% does not sound like a lot but 1% of 1,966,514,816 internet users worlwide * is 19,665,148 users who you can target with the smaller search engines.

* Source: www.internetworldstats.com

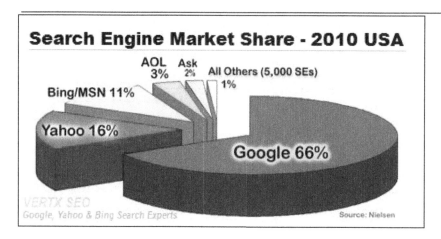

Source: www.vertxsystems.com (2010 Market Share)

If you do have money to spend on paid traffic, I recommend that you give it a try because it does work. The best way is to try several of my suggested methods, not just one. I have listed below a few of the paid traffic methods available on the web. But be aware that spending small amounts of money on advertising soon adds up.

Beware of small expenses. A small leak will sink a great ship.

---

1. Paid traffic with PPC advertising

The type of paid traffic we will discuss here is PPC (Pay Per Click) traffic. PPC advertising is my favourite form of paid traffic but ONLY with the smaller search engines.

As the name implies, this kind of traffic will cost you money for every person that clicks on your ad and visits your website. The cost of each click may cost anywhere from $0.04 (£0.03) to $80(£59) depending on the keywords you want to target.

If you can start an ad campaign for only $0.04 (£0.03) per click, there is a chance that you can make good profit from your site. $80.00 (£59) per click is for "the big boys" or only suitable if you are selling very expensive products otherwise you will probably never make any money.

Do not bid on open keywords as that will be more expensive. Find your golden keyword or long tail keyword and bid on that keyword. The days when you could earn money from PPC with a keyword like "dog" or "insurance" (open keywords) are long gone. You need to find more specific, which means cheaper, keywords to bid on.

If you decide to use Google Adwords I suggest you have a look at their Google Traffic Estimator tool (just Google it). This will tell you how much traffic you can expect, how much your keyword is going to cost per click and how much your estimated daily cost will be. On the screenshot below for the keyword "dog training" you can see that your **Average** cost per click is between £1.58 ($2.46) and the estimated clicks per day is 101 with an estimated daily cost of £164.67 ($256.49). Yes I do know it does not add up correctly but that's what it shows on Google's result.

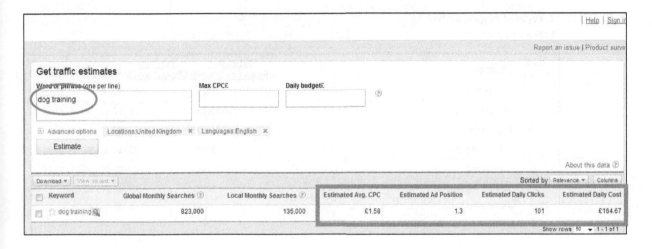

Now let me show you something pretty amazing. Remember that dog training will cost you $2.46 (£1.53) per click. Look at the screenshot below. In 7search (www.7search.com) exactly the same keyword will cost you $0.06 per click!

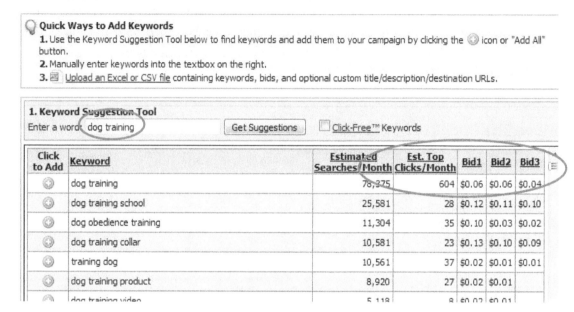

Add Keywords to 14398410 - Dog Training

Quick Ways to Add Keywords

1. Use the Keyword Suggestion Tool below to find keywords and add them to your campaign by clicking the ⊕ icon or "Add All" button.

2. Manually enter keywords into the textbox on the right.

3. ▦ Upload an Excel or CSV file containing keywords, bids, and optional custom title/description/destination URLs.

1. Keyword Suggestion Tool

Enter a word: dog training   [Get Suggestions]   ☐ Click-Free™ Keywords

Click to Add	Keyword	Estimated Searches/Month	Est. Top Clicks/Month	Bid1	Bid2	Bid3
⊕	dog training	78,375	604	$0.06	$0.06	$0.04
⊕	dog training school	25,581	28	$0.12	$0.11	$0.10
⊕	dog obedience training	11,304	35	$0.10	$0.03	$0.02
⊕	dog training collar	10,581	23	$0.13	$0.10	$0.09
⊕	training dog	10,561	37	$0.02	$0.01	$0.01
⊕	dog training product	8,920	27	$0.02	$0.01	
⊕	dog training video	5,118	8	$0.02	$0.01	

In www.miva.com ,the same keyword will cost you $0.32 (£0.32) per click for the first position (May 2011).

Okay we have clearly established that Google's advertising is more expensive compared to other search engines. Some people say that Google traffic converts better but on the other hand it will cost you a lot more money. The next thing you need to do is see if you can make money with the product that you are selling. I always use this spreadsheet to work this out in a few minutes.

	CTR Click trough rate		CR Conversion rate							
A	B	C	D	E	F	G	H	I	J	
SEARCH MONTH	% CLICKS	QTY CLICKS MONTH	% MONTH BUYING	QTY MONTH BUYING	UNIT PRICE	TOTAL SOLD £	COST PER CLICK	TOTAL SPENDING	PROFIT/LOSS MONTH	
Adwords :										
80000	1	800	1%	8	$29.75	$238.00	$2.46	$1,968.00	-$1,730.00	
80000	5	4000	1%	40	$29.75	$1,190.00	$2.46	$9,840.00	-$8,650.00	
80000	10	8000	5%	400	$29.75	$11,900.00	$2.46	$19,680.00	-$7,780.00	
7search :										
80000	1	800	1%	8	$29.75	$238.00	$0.06	$48.00	$190.00	
80000	5	4000	1%	40	$29.75	$1,190.00	$0.06	$240.00	$950.00	
80000	10	8000	5%	400	$29.75	$11,900.00	$0.06	$480.00	$11,420.00	

Conclusion: with Adwords the same keyword ("dog training" in this case) will lose you a lot of money whilst with 7search you make a bit of money even in the worst scenario with 1% CTR and 1% CR. Let me explain.

Column A = the number of searches per month. The different search engines will suggest different number of searches but in order to have an accurate spreadsheet, you need to put in the same number of searches, which I have put as 80,000.

Column B = the number of clicks your ad will receive. The first row is assuming we only get 1% of clicks. This means if our ad is shown 100 times, only 1 person will click on it. 1% is very low but you always have to find out if, even in the worst case scenario, you still make money or not. In the second row I have assumed that we get 5% clicks, which is realistic. In the third row I have assumed that we get 10% CTR, which is very high and often not achievable.

Column C = quantity of clicks our ad will receive. This is the A x B or in the first row 8000 x 1% which is 800 clicks.

Column D = Percentage of people buying your product or the Conversion Rate (CR). In other words if 800 people click your ad, which means visit your site, how many people will actually buy your product. A realistic figure here is between 1% and 5 %. If you can get a CR of over 5% you are doing very well.

Column E = number of people that will buy your product. This is C x D or in the first row 800 x 1% which is eight people will buy your product.

Column F = your profit per product that you sell, in our case $29.75.

Column G = total amount sold. This is E x F or in the first row eight people buy your product at $29.75 profit per product. 8 x $29.75 = $ 238.

Column H = your cost per click. The amount it will cost you every time somebody clicks on your ad. As we have seen before, this is $2.46 for Google Adwords and $0.06 for 7search for the keyword "dog training".

Column I = total spending for your ads. Column C (clicks per month) x Column H (cost per click). In the first row of Adwords this is 800 people x $2.46 per click, which is $1968. In the first row of 7search, this is 800 people x $0.06 per click, which is $48.

Column J = Here you can see if you are going to make money or not. This is G (total sold) – I (total spent). In the first row of Adwords, this is $238 minus $1968 which is a loss of $1730! In the first row of 7Search, this is $238 minus $48, which is a profit of $190.

Conclusion: In the worst case scenario and in the best scenario (percentage of clicks and percentage of people actually buying) you are losing money with Adwords. In the worst scenario in 7search with only 1% CTR and 1% CR, you are still making money.

Paying $0.50 per click for a product that earns you $10 per sale with a conversion rate of 2% will never make you any money as you will be paying $25 in clicks to get $20 in sales, you are losing $5.

Note: the actual cost per click once you have set up an ad campaign very often varies from the estimated cost per click.

> **TOP TIP: Never start a PPC campaign without having done your research with the spreadsheet shown above. Make sure you know your numbers and make sure that even in the worst case scenario you are still making money.**

The spreadsheet below shows that Adword advertising can work much better **IF** you are selling expensive products. I have adjusted the selling price from $29.75 to $300 per product, all the rest is the same. Result: even with a 1% CTR and 1% CR, you can make $432 (but you have to risk $1968).

	CTR Click trough rate		CR Conversion rate						
A	**B**	**C**	**D**	**E**	**F**	**G**	**H**	**I**	**J**
SEARCH MONTH	% CLICKS	QTY CLICKS MONTH	% MONTH BUYING	QTY MONTH BUYING	UNIT PRICE	TOTAL SOLD £	COST PER CLICK	TOTAL SPENDING	PROFIT/LOSS MONTH
Adwords									
80000	1	800	1%	8	$300.00	$2,400.00	$2.46	$1,968.00	$432.00
80000	5	4000	1%	40	$300.00	$12,000.00	$2.46	$9,840.00	$2,160.00
80000	10	8000	5%	400	$300.00	$120,000.00	$2.46	$19,680.00	$100,320.00
7search :									
80000	1	800	1%	8	$300.00	$2,400.00	$0.06	$48.00	$2,352.00
80000	5	4000	1%	40	$300.00	$12,000.00	$0.06	$240.00	$11,760.00
80000	10	8000	5%	400	$300.00	$120,000.00	$0.06	$480.00	$119,520.00

Here's another good example with an ENORMOUS difference in keyword bidding between 7search and Google Adwords.

Fishing in 7search: $0.04 (£0.03)

Fishing in Google Adwords: $1.079 (or £0.67)

That is A LOT OF MONEY once you start getting thousands of clicks.

7search PPC :

1. Keyword Suggestion Tool

Enter a word: fishing   [Get Suggestions]   ☐ Click-Free™ Keywords

Click to Add	Keyword	Estimated Searches/Month	Est. Top Clicks/Month	Bid1	Bid2	Bid3
⊕	fishing	45,817	1,421	$0.04	$0.03	$0.02
⊕	fishing boat	13,479	206	$0.05	$0.04	$0.03
⊕	fishing rod	4,627	188	$0.06	$0.04	$0.03
⊕	fishing charter	1,867	111	$0.07	$0.06	$0.06
⊕	fishing report	2,681	96	$0.02	$0.01	
⊕	fishing pole	109,127	90	$0.04	$0.03	$0.02
⊕	bass fishing	3,710	85	$0.05	$0.03	$0.01

Google Adwords PPC :

☐ ☆	destin **fishing** charters	🔍	▓	4,400	4,400	▂▁▆▃▅▄▅▆▅▃	£0.48
☐ ☆	discount **fishing** reels	🔍	▓	1,900	1,600	▆▄▃▅▆▆▅▆▇▃	£0.53
☐ ☆	discount **fishing** tackle	🔍	▓	4,400	2,400	▆▄▃▅▆▆▅█▅▃	£0.48
☐ ☆	discount fly **fishing** gear	🔍	▓	1,000	880	▆▇▆▇▇▆▇▇▇▃	£0.65
☐ ☆	drennan **fishing** tackle	🔍	▏	880	91	▅▂▁▄▅▄▅▁▂▃	£0.37
☐ ☆	ebay **fishing** tackle for sale	🔍	▓	170	12	▁▁ ▁ ▁▄▅▃	£0.04
☐ ☆	electric **fishing** reels	🔍	▓	3,600	1,900	▆▄▃▅▄▃▅▇▅▃	£0.38
☐ ☆	**fishing**	🔍	▓	11,100,000	6,120,000	▆▄▃▅█████▅▃	£0.67
☐ ☆	**fishing** accessories	🔍	▓	12,100	6,600	▁▁▃▄▃▅██▅▃	£0.72
☐ ☆	**fishing** australia	🔍	▏	27,100	5,400	▆▄▃██▅▄▅▆▃	£0.38
☐ ☆	**fishing** bait	🔍	▓	60,500	40,500	▁▁▃▃▅█████	£0.45
☐ ☆	**fishing** baits	🔍	▓	201,000	135,000	▁▁▁▃████▅█	£0.56

Although the majority of my sites rank in the search engines on the first two pages, I have tested some of the paid traffic methods myself. I had most success with www.miva.com and www.7search.com and by placing ads on the smaller search engines. I have had several very good campaigns where I have spent $37.14 (£23.15) and turned it into $637 (£397.00) in one month – that is 1600% profit or $599.86 (£373) in just one month from just one campaign! See screenshots a bit further. If you can find 20 good ad campaigns like that, you would be earning $11,980 per month. Of course I am still running these good campaigns. If you can find a bunch of different campaigns making that sort of money, you will soon find that the internet is not such a bad place! It took me many years and a lot of money to find profitable campaigns like this and I must admit that this one is a beauty and it keeps selling very well. It just shows how many people out there have trouble with their marriage, as this campaign sells an eBook on how to save your marriage.

I have found it difficult to earn money with *some* of my sites with Google Adwords because of their much higher prices per click. Do the test yourself: type in any keyword in a search engine and look at Adwords, the sponsored section. Type the same keyword in one or two months later and see if the same advertisers are still there. If they are, they must be making money. If they are no longer advertising you could conclude that they are not making any money - why else would they stop advertising?

However, I have sites that have been dominating Google for many years by spending an average of $1233.00 or £750.00 per month. These are only sites where I sell expensive products. I would not make any profit spending this sort of money per month if I would send traffic to a site that sells a $40.00 or £25.00 product. Ok you want proof. Here are some screenshots of one of my adword campaigns showing £756.66 spent on advertising from 17th April 2011 to 16th May 2011. Month after month my advertising expenses are paid back by the sales I make. Note the high CTR for most keywords.

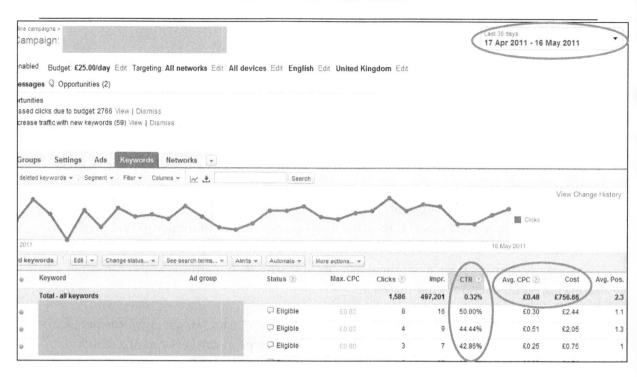

I run several PPC campaigns and I do enjoy trying out new ones to see which ones work. In a lot of my campaigns I find an interesting Clickbank product, copy and paste the headers and wording from the sales pages and I send the people straight to the Clickbank sales page (with my affiliate link obviously). These campaigns are totally separate from my websites. I do not have a website on Saving Your Marriage but I do run a very successful campaign on this subject. This is another good example of not having to sell things that you are interested in, because I have been happily married for 20 years! You can make a full time living from successful PPC campaigns.

Here is an example of a PPC campaign that I have done with www.7search.com. The screenshot from 7search shows that between 1 October 2010 and 1 November 2010 I spent

$38.14 on my campaign called "SAVMARRIAG" with an average click of $0.10.

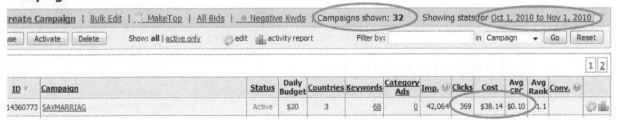

The Clickbank screenschot below shows you that I made $637 from that $38.14, in one month. That is an AMAZING return for your money. Note that I am running 32 campaigns.

What else can you see on the next screenshot?

- I have sold 27 eBooks on Save My Marriage (29 results showing but 2 are refunds).

- My TID is 7S, which stands in this case for 7search, meaning that the sales are via 7search.

- My Conversion Rate is VERY high. From the previous 7search screenshot you can see that I had 369 clicks and out of 369 visitors, 29 people have bought the eBook (two asked for a refund but refunds always happen when selling eBooks). That is almost 10% Conversion Rate which is very good indeed.

Displaying all 29 results.   Total: $637.00

Actions	Date	Time	Receipt	TID	Pmt	Currency	Txn Type	Item	Amount	Vendor
	2010-10-30			7S	MSTR	USD	Sale	1	$25.48	SAVMARRIAG 1
	2010-10-29			7S	VISA	USD	Sale	1	$25.48	SAVMARRIAG 1
	2010-10-29			7S	PYPL	USD	Sale	1	$25.48	SAVMARRIAG 1
	2010-10-28			7S	VISA	USD	Sale	1	$25.48	SAVMARRIAG 1
	2010-10-27			7S	VISA	USD	Sale	1	$25.48	SAVMARRIAG 1
	2010-10-26			7S	MSTR	USD	Sale	1	$25.48	SAVMARRIAG 1
	2010-10-25			7S	VISA	USD	Sale	1	$25.48	SAVMARRIAG 1
	2010-10-25			7S	PYPL	USD	Sale	1	$25.48	SAVMARRIAG 1
	2010-10-23			7S	PYPL	USD	Sale	1	$25.48	SAVMARRIAG 1
	2010-10-21			7S	MSTR	USD	Refund	1	($25.48)	SAVMARRIAG 1
	2010-10-20			7S	VISA	USD	Sale	1	$25.48	SAVMARRIAG 1
	2010-10-19			7S	VISA	USD	Sale	1	$25.48	SAVMARRIAG 1
	2010-10-18			7S	MSTR	USD	Sale	1	$25.48	SAVMARRIAG 1
	2010-10-18			7S	VISA	USD	Sale	1	$25.48	SAVMARRIAG 1
	2010-10-17			7S	MSTR	USD	Sale	1	$25.48	SAVMARRIAG 1
	2010-10-17			7S	VISA	USD	Sale	1	$25.48	SAVMARRIAG 1
	2010-10-15			7S	VISA	USD	Sale	1	$25.48	SAVMARRIAG 1
	2010-10-15			7S	VISA	USD	Sale	1	$25.48	SAVMARRIAG 1
	2010-10-13			7S	VISA	USD	Sale	1	$25.48	SAVMARRIAG 1
	2010-10-12			7S	VISA	USD	Sale	1	$25.48	SAVMARRIAG 1
	2010-10-07			7S	PYPL	USD	Sale	1	$25.48	SAVMARRIAG 1
	2010-10-07			7S	MSTR	USD	Sale	1	$25.48	SAVMARRIAG 1
	2010-10-04			7S	PYPL	USD	Sale	1	$25.48	SAVMARRIAG 1
	2010-10-03			7S	PYPL	USD	Refund	1	($25.48)	SAVMARRIAG 1
	2010-10-03			7S	VISA	USD	Sale	1	$25.48	SAVMARRIAG 1
	2010-10-03			7S	PYPL	USD	Sale	1	$25.48	SAVMARRIAG 1
	2010-10-02			7S	MSTR	USD	Sale	1	$25.48	SAVMARRIAG 1
	2010-10-02			7S	VISA	USD	Sale	1	$25.48	SAVMARRIAG 1
	2010-10-01			7S	PYPL	USD	Sale	1	$25.48	SAVMARRIAG 1

Word of caution on PPC Advertising: start with a small budget when you start with paid traffic and learn from your mistakes. If you are not careful you can spend a huge amount of money without ever earning your money back. Believe me, I know as I have had some money-losing campaigns myself.

You MUST set a spending budget. Without it you will just keep trying and keep losing money. You MUST be prepared to lose money with PPC as you never know if it is going to work for your niche with your ad. You will probably spend a lot of money before you start earning money with PPC. I lost a lot of money (thousands and thousands of dollars) before I started earning. But now I earn a lot of money with it and it was worth putting in the effort. I was lucky that I had some money that I was prepared to lose. Never set up an advertising campaign with PPC if you cannot afford to lose it all. You can set a maximum spend per day for your campaign but, if you are like me, you will probably put the daily budget up to see if that makes a difference. Then all of a sudden you realise you've lost $100.

Word of caution 1: Do NOT click on your competitor's Adwords ads as Google is not stupid and will eventually find out and ban your account.

Word of caution 2: As Google Adwords is like an auction you can start with a PPC of $0.20 and one year later you pay $1.75 per click. It happened to me. My competitor kept bidding higher than me to be the first one to show in Adwords. I bid higher, he big higher, and Google takes advantage and puts the price up even more.

Word of caution 3: Google can ban your account for no reason at all, without prior warning. Completely unacceptable but that's the way it is. Just because there is something that they do not like with one of your landing pages, they can ban your whole account. Make sure that you read the terms and conditions on Google's landing pages.

The list below are good PPC networks to sign up for. They will post your ad on search engines and on websites that have chosen to display ads on them. Some of these however do not allow you to put a destination URL and a display URL, which is not good if you are sending affiliate links to your visitors. The first five sites are in my opinion the best ones.

- www.7search.com – RECOMMENDED. A great, smaller network. They advertise on the smaller search engines and are the cheapest and highest converting network I've used. I've found that health products sell very well on this network.
- www.miva.com - Website no longer exists.
- www.exoclick.com – RECOMMENDED. **Extremely cheap** Pay Per Click tariffs – adult orientated only. You can make a lot of money with Clickbank products like penis enlargement, premature ejaculation and so on, on Exoclick. I mentioned at the beginning of this book that you can sell stuff in a niche that you are NOT interested in. This is yet another very good example of that. If you find something you think people will pay money for, why not try a PPC campaign for it?
- www.sitescout.com- RECOMMENDED. Used to be called Adbrite.Lots of choice for banners, text links, etc...

- www.cliksor.com RECOMMENDED

- www.chitika.com

- www.clickbooth.com

- www.clicksor.com

- https://adwords.Google.com. Google's own ad platform. This will get you a lot of traffic but the cost per click is generally much, much higher than other PPC networks. I must admit that I have not made a great deal of money with Google Adwords but I have made A LOT of money with www.7search.com and www.miva.com.

- searchmarketing.yahoo.com – for ads on www.yahoo.com. These ads are quite expensive and have comparable rates to Google Adwords. Minimum spend amount of $20 per month. You can visit www.pixelfast.com/overture to learn about the bids on keywords in Yahoo. Yahoo will also provide you with suggestive keywords. You must have a Yahoo Search Marketing account for this. If your advertising budget is under $5,000/month you will be directed to the Microsoft Advertising Adcenter to advertise with Bing and Yahoo!Search Combined:
www.advertising.microsoft.com/home
- www.adbull.com
- www.adcenter.microsoft.com PPC are much higher than low PPC networks
- www.advertise.com
- www.Bing.com: in order to advertise on Bing and Yahoo you need to sign up here:
- www.burstmedia.com ads available for niche-focused websites
- www.doubleclick.com gets high traffic. Owned by Google
- www.marchex.com has lots of distribution partners
- www.findology.com
- www.leadimpact.com RECOMMENDED
- www.mirago.com only for UK
- www.redflymarketing.com
- www.search123.com has limited distribution for your ads

Top Tip: If you use more than one PPC network you can use www.prosper202.com to manage them all and compare performances. Be prepared as it all gets a bit complicated with these types of sites but once you can master it, you can learn a lot from the statistics.

> **TOP TIP:** Bid on what I call "urgency keywords" with your **PPC** campaigns. These are keywords where people are in need of information urgently. They have a problem; they are willing to spend money to solve the problem, they are ready to buy. Experience has thought me that urgency keywords are very well converting keywords. If it is possible in your niche, bid on urgency keywords. Let me give some examples so you understand exactly what I mean. Somebody searches for "stop baby's screaming" or "remedy for ear ache" or "stop dog barking" or "cure for snoring", or "how to train my cat". These people are in need of information and clearly have a problem that they want to solve.

> **TOP TIP:** Do not sign up with www.bing.com first only to find out later that when you sign up with Yahoo.com, you have to sign up with here: www.advertising.microsoft.com/home because your advertising budget is under $5000/month. You are advertising on Bing AND Yahoo with Microsoft advertising so you do not need to sign up with Bing first. You then need to go to Bing and close your account otherwise you are paying for the same advertising twice - on Bing AND on Microsoft Advertising Centre, which is Bing and Yahoo.

2. Paid traffic with SEnuke X

www.senuke.com "It is Complete & Utter Search Engine Domination. Period. It is the Most Powerful SEO Automation Software Ever". These are their words, not mine. But it is indeed powerful stuff for getting traffic. The downside is that it costs $147 per month. There is a $67 per month version (SEnuke X Lite) that only does Niche Research and Social Network Submission, which in my opinion is not worth getting at all. If you have the money; pay for the full version and see if you like it. You have 14 days to try it free.

A big advantage of SEnuke is that you do not need a website, you can just promote an affiliate link hoping that they will be picked up by people. You can also generate your affiliate link from within SEnuke.

Here is an overview of what you can do with SEnuke X (SEnuke X is the newest version, it used to be called SEnuke):

	SEnuke X Lite	SEnuke X
Price	14 days free then $67/month	14 days free then $147/month
Wizard & Diagram Designer	No	Yes
Niche Research	Yes	Yes
Social Network	Yes	Yes
Video	No	Yes
Social Bookmark	No	Yes
RSS	No	Yes
Web 2.0 Profile	No	Yes
Forum Profile	No	Yes
Press Release	No	Yes
Indexer	Yes	Yes
Pinger	Yes	Yes

They submit videos to 30 video sites, social networking to 250 sites, social bookmarking to 32 sites, RSS feed to 23 sites but most of them are DoFollow links.

How does it work? You fill in your name, nickname and email and Senuke submits your article, video, and so on to all the sites. You do not even have to create an account with all the different sites as Senuke does this for you. It is as far as I know one of the few automated sites that does this for you. It is also the only automated software that I have used that gave me some sales (not from Google). You can also ping your sites once submission is done, which is great.

The main aim when using SEnuke is to create backlinks as they also submit to high sites with a high Page Rank.

SEnuke is great and the software does work but as usual there are a few things to know:

- Although they submit to article sites, this is not their strength as they only submit to 12 article sites. You can spin your articles to make them unique (time consuming) but if you publish the same article, it will be duplicate content.

- If you do not learn how to use SEnuke properly, you will spam the sites to death and nobody will take any notice, including Google. You will have to become a SEnuke expert and get to grips with all the functions otherwise more harm than good can be done.
- The biggest problem with SEnuke is :
    o All the accounts will be created on the same day.
    o The time of the creation of the accounts will all be approximately the same time
    o The dates of the submission will all be within a day or a few days

These three problems will immediately raise three red flags for Google and your work will have zero results.

The solution for this is to pick some accounts for submission today and pick a few other accounts tomorrow. You could also set up new accounts every week and spin the name and title but then is there any point paying $147 per month if you have to do it all the non-automated way, while you pay for automation?

In case of video submission: you can try to fool Google by giving each video that you submit a different title, so Google thinks each video is different. However, the automation aspect has no value in this case as you'll have to give a new title, submit to one video site, give a second video a different title and submit it to another video site, give the third video, you will have to do this for 30 sites. You might as well set up an account with all 30 sites and submit the video yourself.

Whatever you do with SEnuke, you have to remember that the automated publishing will never contain unique content as the same stuff will be published to all sites and you know by now that Google likes unique content. **If you are in a niche with very low competition, SEnuke can work wonders for you.**

Conclusion: SEnuke is excellent if you want to get traffic to your sites or affiliate links, hoping that people will find them all over the web. But if you want to rank in Google, it's not the best.

3. Paid traffic with banner advertising

This is also called media buying. A quick word about banner advertising: I have stopped using banner advertising all together as I have never made any money with it. On the contrary I have spent thousands of pounds trying to work out a way to earn money with it but have never earned a penny. The main reason for this is that people are truly getting fed up with them and totally ignore them. The average CTR (click through rate) is lower than 0.5%. PPC has a much higher CTR and is generally much cheaper. If you are interested in trying out banner advertising, just search for it in Google as I cannot recommend any that I have made money with. People click on text ads a lot more than they do on banner ads. Banner ads look like this:

A text ad looks like this: www.yoururlhere.com or click here for more information or it can look like an Adwords-ad.

www.doubleclick.com is one of the largest network and is now owned by Google .

4. Paid traffic with Fiverr.com

Search Fiverr.com for people who will drive traffic to your site for $5. This is a really simple tip but can get you a lot of traffic if the person you pay does it right. They will be creating backlinks for you so you will have to tell them the keywords that you are targeting.

We spoke about backlinks previously: it's these that decide your ranking in Google, so more backlinks = higher in Google = more page views = more money.

5. Paid traffic with Pay Per Post/Social Spark

This is a great service where you find people to create posts about your products on their blogs. You can set the search parameters so that you only look for blogs that get a lot of traffic, which means your site will get some serious promotion.

You can also choose the pages and the anchor text of the backlinks to your site in the post, which is another great reason to use these services.

www.payperpost.com
www.socialspark.com

6. Paid traffic with paid solo ads

What is an ezine and what is a solo ad?

An ezine is an online magazine or online newsletter that is usually emailed to the subscriber's email address. You can place your ads (for your keywords) on those ezines; these ads are called solo ads.

Solo ads are sent to opt-in email subscribers on different lists that people have built up. Basically people, like you, who have been building up their email list over a number of years, will allow you to post promotional emails to their subscribers, for a small charge.

Advertising this way takes very little effort. Just write a quick advert in an email promoting whatever you're offering, pay for X amount of email addresses you want it sent to and then you're done! You can sit back and make money from emailing people that actually *want* to buy what you're offering!

Pro: usually very cheap traffic e.g. $100 to send your email to 20,000 email addresses.

Advertising this way can be good because the publisher of the ezines usually has a good relationship with his subscribers. And the recipients of the email, with your solo ad on, will consider it trustworthy. The publisher will send an email to his list and when somebody from his list clicks on your ad they will go to your website. If you are lucky you can get lots of traffic in a very short time. Word of caution: it if sounds too good to be true, it probably is. For example, if somebody promises you 200,000 emails for $50, don't waste your money.

I have used Solo Ads successfully.

Con: those 20,000 email addresses might have received lots of other emails and might not take any notice of yours.

You can search for "solo ad" or "ezine ad" and you will find a lot of websites. Word of caution: some of them take your money but will never send your ads out. Here are some sites:

www.bestezines.com directory
www.classifiedposter.com
www.demc.com
www.directoryofezines.com a collection of niches that have ezines. Not cheap but worth it.
www.e-mailblasters.com
www.e-mailpaysu.com/advertise.html
www.ezines.nettop20.com directory
www.ezinesearch.com directory
www.ezinearticles.com directory
www.ezines-r-us.com/targeted-solo-ads
www.gotsafelists.com
www.planetxmail.com/soloads.php
www.rent-a-list.com
www.skyadboard.com/buysolo.htm
www.soloadblaster.net
www.topsurfer.com
www.traffic9.com

7. Paid traffic with renting or buying an email list

You can rent or buy an email list from:

www.businessemaillists.com

www.l-i-s-t.com

www.thrivemg.com

www.topica.com

In short this is what usually happens: you give your text email or HTML to the company that you will work with (your 'rental house') and they will send out a trial email to you and some test-emails, called 'seed names'. The rental house can send you a data card from which you choose who you want your mail to go to, based on age, gender, location, interest and so on.

At an agreed time your email will go out to whichever people you choose from the data card. The rental company will charge you, depending on how many email addresses are left over once you have made your choices from the data card.

8. Paid traffic with online classifieds

I have listed a few classified ad websites. Just Google "classified ads online" to find more.

www.citynews.com Each classified ad creates its own one-page website.

www.loot.com

www.traderonline.com

9. Paid traffic with reviews

www.reviewme.com: Advertisers can get Buzz and Traffic to their site. Bloggers get paid for doing reviews and promoting products for the advertisers.

10. Paid traffic with Sponsored Reviews

www.sponsoredreviews.com : Sponsored Reviews connects bloggers with SEO and internet marketers and advertisers looking to build links and traffic. Advertisers and bloggers can easily find each other. Bloggers write a review and post it on their blog for the world to see.

11. Paid traffic with radio show

www.blogtalkradio.com Have your own radio show, create your own radio station. You can find some prominent people here in your niche and interview them. You can then announce your radio shows on your blog, Facebook, your email list and so on. It is an easy way to create and share radio on the web. You can sign up free and get 30-minute show per day with five live concurrent callers but the payable options give you a lot more possibilities. It's worth checking out. This is also listed under 'Free traffic' as there is a free version.

12. Paid traffic with eBay

Most people know www.ebay.com mainly as an auction site but you can also advertise on eBay classified. Simply go to the eBay Classified section and post an ad. It is relatively cheap – around $10 for 30 days. You can place the ad in your chosen category.

13. Paid traffic with Amazon

Most people know www.amazon.com mainly as a shopping website but you can also advertise on Amazon to get extra traffic to your site. On most pages on Amazon, underneath the products you find the Sponsored Links. This is where your advertisement would appear. Look for the "advertise on Amazon" button and sign up.

	« Previous | **Page:** **1** 2 3 4 | Next »	
Sponsored Links (what's this?)		
1. **Document & File Scanning** ⬀	ISO 9001 Bureau Scanning Services or Complete In House Solutions	www.smsimaging.co.uk
2. **Fujitsu Scanners** ⬀	To file documents faster & more efficient with Fujitsu **Scanners**!	Fujitsu.com/**Scanner**
3. **Kodak Document Scanners** ⬀	Desktop To High-Volume Production Kodak. The Ideal Scanning Solution.	www.Kodak.com
4. **Scanning services** ⬀	Bespoke outsourced document capture solutions and services	www.capitalcapture.com

14. Paid traffic with Facebook ads

We all know www.facebook.com as a social network but you can also advertise on Facebook. Simply go to the www.facebook.com/ads and post an ad. You can place the ad in your chosen category.

15. Paid traffic with stumble upon ads

www.stumbleupon.com is a social bookmarking site that lets you advertise on their site for a very small amount per view. Your site will be shown to users. If a lot of users vote positive for your site, you might receive some extra traffic.

16. Paid traffic with Reddit ads

www.reddit.com is also a social bookmarking site that lets you advertise on their site. You will be featured on the homepage with a sponsored link. Users can vote you down or up.

17. Paid traffic with YouTube

We all know www.youtube.com as a video sharing site but you can also advertise on it by becoming a YouTubePartner. Advertising is now a major part of the site and you can place ads on your videos and paid for clicks (like Adsense). YouTube is the largest video website on the web and can be very effective, but expensive. One way to place advertising on YouTube is to sign up with Google Display Network.

When creating your ad campaign, select the "Network" tab and click "Add placements" under "Managed placements." You can then target your ads to YouTube pages by selecting "youtube.com" as a specific URL from within the Placement Tool and clicking "Get Available Sites" to see all available placements.

18. Paid traffic with mobile phone marketing and PPC

Apple iPhone, Google Android and other phones and smart phones are like mini computers and you can advertise on them like you advertise on computers. A company can send a text message to a mobile with a promotional code attached, or an ad can pop up with free vouchers to collect, or the mobile phone user can get free trials. You can pay the advertising companies per click (for a CPA offer) and when the mobile phone user gives his email address or phone number you get paid by the CPA company.

According to research, Amazon received 1 billion dollars in sales from mobiles in 2010 and eBay had 1,5 billion dollars in sales from mobiles. If you want a slice of that pie, you need to investigate paid mobile phone marketing or transfer your website to a mobile optimised site.

According to research mobile phone marketing gets a higher conversion rate compared to Facebook marketing.

How does mobile phone marketing and PPC (Pay Per Click) work – in a nutshell? Most importantly you ONLY promote mobile phone optimised CPA offers. Otherwise the ad won't display properly and you've lost your money.

a) First of all you need to sign up with some mobile advertising networks. These are companies that deal with advertising on mobile phones. You will pay these companies a price per click, every time a mobile phone user clicks on your ad. Google Adwords now also does ads for mobiles but here are some mobile phone advertising networks:

www.google.com/ads/admob

www.adsmobi.com

www.inmobi.com

www.mojiva.com

www.invoca.com

UK based:

www.valueclick.co.uk

b) You need to sign up with some CPA networks that are specialised in sending offers to mobile phones. The CPA offers for mobile phones need to be specially designed for mobile phones, otherwise you can't read them.

Here are some CPA networks that deal with mobile phone offers:

www.clickbooth.com

www.copeac.com

www.maxbounty.com

www.neverblue.com

www.peerfly.com

The negative side of mobile phone marketing is that you have to log in to your mobile phone advertising network to see how much money you have spent on advertising. Then you have to log in into your CPA network to see how much money you have made with your CPA offers. The difference between the two amounts will be your profit or loss.

If you have several offers running, tracking can become a little bit complicated. You will need some tracking software like www.prosper202.com.

You can also send your own affiliate links, like Clickbank products to mobile phone users. In that case, all you do is set up a campaign targeted to your users: boys aged between 19 and 30 or women over 60 and so on. There are many possibilities for you to investigate.

I ran (and still run) some profitable mobile phone campaigns. The ones that have been most successful for me are the ones where people have to fill in their postcode *only*.

19. Paid traffic with Click Per View (CPV) system

CPV is where you pay for advertising in the form of a pop-up screen. The ads are called pop-overs. It is also known as PPV (Pay Per View). When you visit a site and all of a sudden a pop-up advertisement displays that is not part of the site that you clicked on, that is PPV. Your pop up will mostly show on organically ranked domain names. These are the domain names that show on the left side of your screen (below the sponsored ads). You will bid on certain keywords and your ad will pop up when people click on the domain name. CPV is an aggressive form of marketing because your message will pop up in front of customers' faces to grab their attention. It is a very effective way of advertising because the customer has to look at your message or ad, if they don't click it away it stays there.

Some sites, such as some game sites, are totally free to use as long as you agree that pop-ups will show now and again. Sites like these make money from the people that click on the pop-up advertising.

Does CPV work when users have pop-ups blocked on their computer? This is a question that many people ask me during my courses. I will explain.

First of all you need to know the difference between pop-overs and pop-unders as they use different technology.

Pop-overs (CPV ads) cannot be blocked because, when triggered, the action tells the browser to open a new window. This is the reason that pop-up blockers cannot block these as they can only block programming language pop ups. Pop-overs have the benefit that they cannot be missed when they pop-up but a lot of people close them immediately.

Pop-unders can be blocked as they are loaded minimized and they are not opened in a new browser window. These ads are less intrusive. In order to see the ad, the user has to click on the taskbar.

The following sites are helpful if you are interested in CPV:

www.adonnetwork.com

www.affexpert.com

www.clicksor.com

www.leadimpact.com

20. Paid traffic with toplinked.com

www.TopLinked.com helps you build larger, more diverse and more valuable networks on the world's top social networking sites.

People who are part of TopLinked.com are people like you - they know the incredible value of being open to new opportunities and new connections - and are some of the world's most helpful and connected people.

TopLinked.com is the quick and easy way to connect with them.

Each social networking site has its own TopLinked.com "Invite Me List".

There are Invite Me Lists for LinkedIn, Facebook, Twitter, MySpace, Ecademy, Xing, Bebo, Blue Chip Expert, Fast Pitch, Friendster, hi5, Konnects, Affluence.org, Naymz, Orkut, Perfect Networker, Plaxo, Ryze, Tagged, UNYK and Viadeo.

As a TopLinked.com member you can add yourself to any (or all!) of those lists and be invited by your fellow members to connect (and/or use those lists to invite them).

21. Paid traffic with in-text ad networks

Visit www.kontera.com to find out how to advertise in text rather than with banners and ads. Kontera places your ads front-and-centre within the text of the pages. Its technology analyzes WebPages to predict user interest and intent. Your ad is then delivered to your potential customers. Here's an example how text advertising will look on a computer:

22. Paid traffic with ads in magazines

Although we live in an electronic world, there are still thousands of magazine published and sold. Find a magazine in your niche and put a very small ad in it, including your domain name.

23. Paid traffic with car stickers

Car stickers are not expensive these days and are a very effective method of advertising. Put the sticker either on the back of the car window or on the bumper. There will always be cars behind you wherever you go therefore more people will see your site. There will always be people who see your sticker when your car is in a car park. Make sure the text is large enough for people to read when they sit behind you in another car. The companies that will print your sticker can advise you on the size. Just search for "car stickers".

Ask all your friends and family to put a sticker on their car.

24. Paid traffic with television advertising

A lot of highly visited websites started with nothing and now have regular TV advertising campaigns. TV advertising is extremely expensive and is a high risk but look at www.comparethemarket.com that started out with nothing. Maybe one day this could be you.

25. Paid traffic with Yellow Pages

Advertise in the Yellow Pages. I know that this is very costly but the ad only needs to be very small, mentioning your website address. You would be surprised how many people still use the Yellow Pages to find services and products, definitely the older generation.

26. Translation traffic

Assume that you have built a website in English and it is earning money. Why not translate the whole thing into another language? If you have a site in USA on bird watching, translate it into Spanish and try to rank in www.google.es, which is in Spain. I am listing this under paid traffic as I assume most readers will not be able to translate a website into another language, and will have to outsource the work.

To give some examples:

People in Spain Google with www.google.es

People in Italy Google with www.google.it

Paid translations:

www.elance.com outsource the translation

www.atanet.org directory of translation services

www.multilingual-search.com

Free translations: If you do decide to translate yourself, please make sure that the text reads fluently. Be aware that often translations are not easy to read or understand. Free translation tools:

www.Google.com/translate

For international statistics:

www.export.gov

www.internetworldstats.com

Wordpress can use a plugin called Global Translator.

27. CD sales letter.

People generally will not read 1 hour of sales copy writing but a lot of people are willing to listen to it. You could create a CD and speak about the advantages of your products etc… You would be surprised how many people still listen to ordinary CDs rather than download the music from sites. You can post the CD to potential customers. You can also put a version to download on your site. People can listen to it in the car, on the train, etc,….

28. Paid traffic with advertising on Clickbank

Clickbank offers paid advertising opportunities for vendors who want more product visibility. You can pay for ads to be placed in any marketplace category. Find out more here: www.clickbank.com/advertise

29. Paid traffic with Clickbank

I kept the best two for last! If you have your own digital products then you must sign up with Clickbank and let other people do the work for you. This is THE BEST method of earning money on the web: get a bunch of affiliates. I have listed this under paid traffic as you will have to pay your affiliates a large chunk of your earnings, so it does in a way cost you money.

30. Paid traffic with other affiliate networks

If you have your own products, an eBook or a physical product, sign up with a few affiliate networks and let other people do the work for you. This is another VERY GOOD method of earning money on the web: get a bunch of affiliates. I have listed this under paid traffic as you will have to pay your affiliates a large chunk of your earnings, so it does in a way cost you money.

I have listed "Paid traffic with Clickbank" and "Paid traffic with other affiliate networks" separate as Clickbank does not sell physical products therefore if you sell physical products, you need to sign up with other affiliate networks, not with Clickbank.

Part 12. Ways To Make Money - No Website Needed

There are a lot of different techniques to earn money on the internet, without needing a website. In this section I'll outline some of the other ways of making money if you do not wish to follow my method or if you do not wish to build a website.

The exact methods that I use may not work as well for you. Just like anything, the best way to use this information is to build on it and change what you learn to make it on the web. The different ways of making money online listed in this chapter are not all tried and practised by myself. It is purely a list of money-making opportunities.

If you can get any of these methods to work for you, you are in for some easy money as you do not need a website, which means no fulfilment, no customer services needed, no complaints.

1. Earn money from article marketing

If you don't have the money to purchase your own domain and hosting then follow the tips to create articles, as explained earlier in this book. All you need to do is grab an affiliate link from Clickbank and use that link in your resource box at the end of your article. Be aware that some article directory websites do not like direct links to sales pages though.

This way you can sit back and earn money without doing any form of web design! I have discussed article marketing more in-depth in this book earlier on but here is a summary of the things to do:

- Write articles based on keyword research

- Put links underneath article either from an affiliate product or your own website

- Sign up with article websites

- Publish articles to article websites

- Check account to see how much you've earned

2. Earn money using Twitter and Facebook to get sales

This is a huge topic in itself, so I'm only going to give a passing overview of the basics here. Sign up to Facebook and Twitter or any other social network and search for people who list your niche in their interests.

Follow/add these people as friends and you can start promoting ClickBank products to them that you already know they'll be interested in!

3. Earn money from Blogs

Find blogs in your niche, join them, talk about your niche and now and again put your affiliate link into the conversation. Although it has been said that bloggers don't like this sort of practice, often, if you give good information some other bloggers might click on your site link.

4. Earn money from mobile phone marketing

You will need some money to spend as mobile marketing will cost money. But all you need to do is sign up with some mobile marketing companies and send your visitors to a landing page with your affiliate link. Mobile marketing is ideal for CPA marketing (Cost Per Action Marketing) where people have to leave their email address, or try some products for free, for you to get paid. Please see 'Paid Traffic' part of this book for more details about mobile phone marketing.

5. Earn money from PPC and the smaller search engines

You will need some money to spend, as you will create ads with your affiliate links as a landing page and pay search engines to show your ad. You will only pay when people click on your ad. Here's a step-by-step guide:

- Sign up with PPC networks

- Set up a campaign with your keyword

- Find affiliate products and send people to your affiliate link

I know people who have a full-time income purely with PPC and affiliate links. You will need some start up money (I suggest between $500 and $1000 to start with) as some campaigns will lose money but some will make you money. To start with the income from the ones that make money might not be enough compared to your total spending, but after a few months you can focus solely on these.

6. Earn money from Yahoo Answers

Answer some questions in Yahoo Answers and you can put your affiliate link at the bottom of the answer. People ask questions and the best answer is shown in Yahoo. www.answers.yahoo.com

7. Earn money from Wiki Answers

Answer some questions in Wiki Answers and put your affiliate link at the bottom of the answer. www.wiki.answers.com

8. Earn money from your own Blog

Visit www.blogger.com where you can start your own blog website. You can put Adsense and affiliate links on the site that can make you money. Now owned by Google so you need a Google account to sign in.

9. Earn money from Ehow.com

Write an article for www.ehow.com and put an affiliate link at the bottom. Google loves ehow.com. Try it for yourself: type in "how to make……." or "How to……." and it is very likely that articles from eHow show on the first few pages of Google.

10. Earn money from buying and selling domain names

Do some keyword research and find some untapped niches. Buy a .com domain name and simply sell it on www.flippa.com. You can earn up to $200 for a good domain. If you can buy 10 domains per week, you can earn £2,000 per week (you need to take off some of your expenses).

I have bought domains from Godaddy auctions for $39, put some decent content on them, got some more backlinks and sold them three months later for $2000.

Internet marketers like buying domains with a lot of backlinks as they know how much effort it takes to create backlinks. And because Google likes backlinks, it is a win-win situation.

11. Earn money from domain parking

Buy domain names for $8.50 and just leave them on the shelve doing nothing for years. In 5 or 10 years time you can sell them for between $100 and $5000! Google loves old domains so if you have good old ones to sell, people are prepared to pay a lot of money for them.

12. Earn money from buying and selling websites

- Buy websites on Flippa where the asking price is generally low - www.flippa.com
- Sell on eBay where the asking price is generally high - www.ebay.com
Or
- Look out for websites that have very low bids in Flippa, buy at a low price and re-list a few weeks/months later when other buyers will be online.

13. Earn money from writing

Visit www.voices.yahoo.com or www.helium.com. These sites will pay for your articles or blog posts. Some articles on specific niches can pay out about $100.

14. Earn money from photography

If you are a good photographer you can sell your photos on the web. There are thousands of people looking for specific pictures. Those people type in keywords in stock photography sites and buy the pictures that they like. All you need to do is upload your pictures (with a keyword) onto the site and each time somebody buys your picture, you get paid.

If you have decent photographs, without trademark brands or copyrights, upload them to the stock photo sites.

Here are a few good photo stock websites to seek pictures:

www.bigstockphoto.com

www.dreamstime.com

www.fotalia.com

www.istockphoto.com

www.shutterstock.com

Try to find a keyword on these sites that does not show thousands of pictures already. And if you can find the same keyword with a lot of searches in Google Keyword Tool, you might be onto a winner.

15. Earn money from becoming a paid blogger.

Visit www.payperpost.com where you can become a blogger and get paid for it.

16. Earn money from doing surveys

We all have an opinion and now you can get paid for it. If you want to make a full time living out of surveys you will have to sign up with 200 or so sites, as the payout is small, but lots of small payouts soon add up! In my opinion it is underpaid for the time it takes to do, but it might be something that you like.

Some survey companies pay in actual cash but a large amount of them pay in vouchers. Here are some survey companies that I have heard good things about:

www.acop.com

www.consumerlink.com

www.globaltestmarket.com

www.lightspeed.com

www.opinionspaid.com

www.surveyclub.com

www.surveysavvy.com

www.wowearnings.com

www.zoompanel.com

17. Earn money with Swapit

www.swapit.co.uk This is an auction site for children and teenagers. The whole thing is based on "swapits" - virtual currency. You swap online, sending the items you want to swap to the site. You can earn swapits by trading, and then use these to buy new items. This is effectively earning money, because you can now sell these new items on eBay, earning real money.

18. Earn money from lead generation

If you send a company potential customers, that company will pay you a commission. The lead generation platforms do everything automatically, and work out commissions.

19. Earn money by mystery shopping

Large companies will pay you to buy their products from several online companies to help with their market research.

20. Earn money from reading email

Some companies are prepared to pay to find out what people are saying about their website/services/products. www.htmail.com is an email marketing company with customer feedback. Most sites will pay you between one pence and 10 pence per email that you read. It will probably never earn you a lot of money. You might earn up to $100 per month which would be a lot for this type of email marketing but www.htmail.com also has a referral programme where you get paid commission for every friend that you refer to them. That's when the money can add up.

21. Earn money from product testing

www.toluna.com is always looking for new people to test products and fill in surveys. You will get paid to give your opinion on several products and niches.

22. Earn money from eBay

Become a drop shipper on eBay. For more information on drop shipping: see the drop shipping chapter.

23. Earn money from recurring commissions

Apparently there is an internet marketer who rakes in over $300,000 (£187.000) a year and all he does is sit on his computer when he feels like it and use free traffic techniques to send visitors to his recurring commissions affiliate links. His money comes in every single month without him having to get a lot of extra customers. It took him 8 years to build up his income to that level. Recurring commissions are DEFINITELY a good potential business. Earlier in this book I listed a list of potential recurring commission sites but you can also have a look at www.lifetimecommissions.com.

24. Earn money from freelance work

A lot of people make very good money as a freelancer online on outsourcing websites like the ones listed below. You sign up as "I want to work" and follow the instructions. You can then browse through all the jobs and bid to do them, hoping that you will be awarded the job and start earning.

www.99centarticles.com
www.agentsofvalue.com
www.elance.com RECOMMENDED
www.fiverr.com RECOMMENDED A huge amount of services including some funny ones!

www.freelancer.com
www.microworkers.com RECOMMENDED
www.mturk.com
www.need-an-article.net
www.odeskresources.com
www.peopleperhour.com

25. Write your own PLR articles and sell them

If you are good at writing then this is one option to consider provided that you can find an untapped niche as otherwise the competition will be vast. Webmasters are always looking for PLR articles (these are the ones who do not know that Google does not like PLR content and there are plenty like that) or they want PLR to re-write.

- Find a subject to write about

- Write the articles using relevant keywords

- Write between 10 and 20 articles and package them into one article pack

- Now the difficult part: find ways of selling your articles. Some PLR websites will buy your articles if they are in an untapped niche.

26. Sell your eBooks as hard copy books

In my product www.WorldwideSelfPublishing.com, I explain in video tutorials, EVERYTHING from A to Z how to self publish books in various formats to create multiple streams of income. The videos include how to get your hard copy book number 1 on Amazon and keep it there for years to come. You do not need a website to sell the books, unless you want to create a sales page for your eBook and let affiliates do the selling.

Once you have an eBook it is relatively easy to turn this into a hard copy book that will be sold on Amazon and other major book selling sites. It will not be possible to give you a detailed step by step guide in this book but I will give you the rough outline of what you need to do to publish your own book.

There are basically two ways of selling a hard copy book: self publishing or work with a publishing company that does all the work for you. With self publishing you have to phone around and visit book stores and basically beg them to stock your book. If you work with a publishing company they already have the main book stores as their customers and your book will automatically end up in some major bookstores and online bookstores. I always work with a publishing company. You earn less per book if you choose this way of publishing but you don't have to do any work other than bank the cheque at the end of the month.

Getting your own hard copy book on the market is not difficult. I explain everything very detailed in my Self Publishing Product www.WorldwideSelfPublishing.com,

Yes, I know, I've said this before but I realise some people don't read every page of this book therefore I am repeating myself a few times. It is important for you to have a look at this product if you want to earn money self publishing books because it is THE BEST product out there re self publishing. I created the product for the same reason as I wrote the book that you are reading now: because I could not find what I was looking for when I was searching.

Top Tip: Use a Serif font for your books and a Sans Serif font for your eBooks because Sans Serif fonts are easier to read from a computer screen and Serif Fonts are easier to read from a physical book.

Millionaire =Serif font : more rounded letters and curls, for books.

Millionaire = Sans-Serif font : simple letters, not decorative fonts e.g. Helvetica, for ebooks.

---

27. Earn money from Secondlife

www.secondlife.com Some people are making money in this virtual economy.

28. Earn money from selling leads to call centres

Getting targeted customers or targeted leads is not easy and the call centres know that. That's why they are prepared to pay for targeted leads. If they have to pay one employee $90 per day to phone around and end up with two targeted customers, they are often also willing to pay you $10 for one targeted customer lead. Contact some call centres and find out how much they pay per lead.

Part 13. Ways To Make Money - Website Needed

1. Earn money by building a list with a squeeze page

You can use all the previous methods in Free Traffic and Paid Traffic to send people to your 'squeeze page'. A squeeze page only has one purpose: to collect the email address from an interested visitor in order to build a list. Here's an example of a squeeze page. Note the arrows above the opt-in box. They work very well and convert better – according to research and split testing - than the no arrow-opt-in boxes.

"You're About To Learn Secrets That Most [NAME OF YOUR MARKET] Will Never Know About [WHATEVER IT IS YOU ARE TEACHING THEM]"

Once inside you'll learn...

- Specific, benefit-rich bullet point #1...
- Specific, benefit-rich bullet point #2...
- Specific, benefit-rich bullet point #3...
- Specific, benefit-rich bullet point #4...
- Specific, benefit-rich bullet point #5...

And that's just a *tiny* sample!

You can get all the details right now by downloading the **[TITLE OF LEAD MAGNET]** . Just fill out the short, easy form on the right to get started.

ACCESS YOUR FREE [TITLE OF LEAD MAGNET]:

Enter your email address in the form below for instant access to [TITLE OF LEAD MAGNET]...

Enter Valid Email Here

Get Instant Access ▶

**Double-check your email for accuracy to ensure you receive the report.

Privacy Assured: Your email address is never shared with anyone.

What you need:

- A domain name

- A website

- An autoresponder like www.aweber.com

- A squeeze page where you need to give your visitors a reason to opt-in to your mailing list. This can either be in the form of a free report that you give away (you can outsource this) or a PLR article that they will find useful.

Add a great headline to your squeeze page and tell people the benefits of opting in, why they need your freebie and what exciting information you're going to send them over the next few months.

Make sure you follow the rules explained earlier in this book about email marketing to prevent too much or too little contact with your opt-ins.

You can promote Amazon links, CPA offers, affiliate links and so on, to your opt-ins and earn money just from having a list of email addresses!

Google generally does not like squeeze pages (there is no content on them) so the only way for you to get people to opt-in is to send traffic to your page.

2. Creating and marketing an original eBook

You don't have to be the next JK Rowling to write an eBook.

If you know more than the average person about something, or you can learn about something and write about it in your own words, then you can produce something valuable.

Example: you have investigated a new niche and come to the conclusion that there is no eBook on "How to make a rabbit cage". This could mean two things: either there is not enough demand for such a book or yours will be the only one on Clickbank, so it will sell like hotcakes and lots of affiliates will want to sell it. If your keyword research has shown that there are a lot of searches and there is no eBook available at all on making a rabbit cage, it might be a good idea to write an eBook and put it on Clickbank for others to sell it for you. Anybody who has a website about rabbits could put your book on their site and sell it.

There are several ways to find out if there's a market for an eBook topic.

In theory you could just buy a bunch of PLR products and put them all together. Make sure that you have the right to do this when you buy the PLR products. Please refer to "Creating content for your site" to see how you can get content for your eBook.

a. Initial research

Search the ClickBank marketplace for the topic you want to create a book around. If you find two or three other books with a reasonable gravity around a similar topic then it's a good bet that the niche is profitable - start writing!

If there are too many similar books (10+) then it may be better to either narrow the focus of the book or find something different to write around. If you don't find another product about your niche, this could be because:

1. You've found an untapped niche!
2. There's not a lot of money to be made writing about your niche.

Now, neither of these are necessarily a bad thing. To judge the potential market for a product we're going to do a few simple Google searches.

-   Search for "your niche" +blog - every blogger is someone who could potentially sell your product for you. When you have the eBook written you can email them and ask them if they'd consider putting a link to it on their blog. Explain to them that they will earn commission for every sale as an affiliate, and 9 out of 10 times they will be pleased at the chance of earning some money!
-   Search for "your niche" +forum - if there are big, busy forums relating to your niche then that's another good sign. People who are passionate about things tend to congregate in groups on the internet where they can share their experiences and learn about their topic. A busy forum = active niche = potential market for you product.
-   Sign up to Google Alerts - www.Google.com/alerts - and receive email updates whenever someone on the internet talks about your niche. If you find there are a lot of blog and site updates then you've found a good niche!

When writing an eBook, the only thing that you really have to spend is time: researching, organising and writing. The internet's a huge place and you'll always find a market for your product, even if it only results in a few sales a month.

Obviously it's best to find a hungry market that is crying out for what you're going to produce, but rest assured, even if the niche you find isn't as good as you thought, you'll still earn money.

b. Topic research

You can use Public Domain Material as discussed earlier in this book.

Second hand books can be bought on eBay and Amazon for under $1 each. Get as many based around your niche as you can get your hands on. It's always worth a trip to your local library to see if they have anything you can borrow.

I recommend spending a solid week just learning about what you're going to be writing, and making lots and lots of notes.

Towards the end of the week you should be able to write the index of your book, with chapters and main headings. From there you simply have to expand.

c. How much should I write?

This is a tricky question to answer because it can vary from 10 pages to 400 pages. If there are eBooks already in your niche then buy them and see how many pages they have used. It's a good idea to buy your competitors products anyway - they can give you ideas and you'll be able to find the information they've missed out.

TOP TIP: Always buy Clickbank products via your own affiliate link, this will save you a lot of money. Simply paste your affiliate link into the browser (the link you get after you've hit Promote on Clickbank)

A general rule of thumb is to aim for between 10,000 and 20,000 words. Remember though, it's quality over quantity, so if you have information that only takes 10 pages to explain, but could save people thousands of dollars a year (for example) then those 10 pages would be enough.

It is relatively easy to write 1000 words per day, which is roughly 2 x A4 pages of text. If you write two pages per day, and you are aiming at a 40 page eBook, you will write it in 20 days.

d. How should you write?

> **The best way you write a book is the way you talk. Avoid jargon.**

- You can use contractions. Use "I've" instead of " I have" and "it's" instead of "it is". Writing like this makes you sound like a person telling a story.

- You can use common colloquialisms, it makes you sound more friendly. Instead of "enjoy" you could say "I get a kick out of it". Instead of "$10,000" you could say "ten grand".

- No gobbledygook. If people constantly have to use their dictionary or analyse your sentences, your writing is not pleasant to read. If people don't understand what you're saying, they will not buy what you are selling.

- Use everyday, easy to understand language.

- Write it so you would enjoy reading it.

- For the header of the eBook: Benefits – Benefits – Benefits. Don't tell the reader what the product will do but focus on what benefit or advantage the product will give the reader. Instead of "This tablet will stop the pain", say "The pain in your leg will be gone, and you'll be able to play football and walk in the park".

- Write clearly.

> **I believe very strongly in the following letters, which are pinned on a board in my office and I pin the same letters on a board during some of my seminars and private lessons:**
>
> **I I N I W Y S, I I I W T O P T T Y S**
>
> **It is not important what you said, it is important what the other person thinks that you said.**

It is not communication when you speak,

It is communication when it is understood.

---

e. What about the competition?

Search several eBook websites and see what the competition is doing, and what the price is for their eBook.

www.ebooks.com

www.kobobooks.com

Search for "your keyword" + " eBook"

f. Marketing your eBook

Once your eBook is written then you will have to create a site to sell it on. If you write the sales page yourself:

- You need an OMG moment in the headline (OMG = OH MY GOD for the older generation reading this book).

- Pose a problem

- Offer a solution to the problem

- Describe benefits, benefits and more benefits

- Call to action with order button

- Reassure the customer with a money back guarantee

You can hire someone to do it for you:

www.99centarticles.com
www.agentsofvalue.com
www.chilibreeze.com
www.elance.com RECOMMENDED
www.fiverr.com RECOMMENDED A huge amount of services, including some funny ones!

www.freelancer.com
www.guru.com
www.ifreelance.com
www.microworkers.com RECOMMENDED
www.mturk.com
www.need-an-article.net
www.odeskresources.com
www.peopleperhour.com

Or you can do it yourself.

If you choose to do it yourself then I recommend downloading a PLR template that you can edit with an HTML editor like the ones outlined in the links section at the end of this eBook.

The cover of your eBook will determine your sales. Covers sell books. Get it done professionally if you cannot do it yourself.

For eBook cover help:

www.20dollarbanners.com

www.absolutecovers.com

www.boxshot3d.com RECOMMENDED. In a matter of minutes you can create software boxes, eBook covers, CD and DVD boxes, binders and reports, images and business cards, brochures and cans, and so on. The only thing you need to do is create the original image yourself.

www.coverfactory.com

www.designgururyan.com

www.ebookcovercreator.com

www.ecoverexpert.com

www.groups.yahoo.com/group/ebook-community

www.killercovers.com

www.qualityebookcovers.com

www.websiteheaders.net

www.xheader.com

The best places to pick up easy sales page creating software:

www.wordpressppc.com - RECOMMENDED

g. How much should you sell your eBook for?

- Deciding on the price is difficult because too cheap and people think it can't be any good whilst too expensive and people will not buy it. I charge $37 (£27) for the majority of my eBooks in a variety of niches. Don't forget that your affiliates have to earn money and you have to earn money. From the sale of a $19.97 (£12) eBook, you will only receive $7.99 (£4.98) if you give your affiliates 60% commission. Sell your eBook at $37 (£27) and you will receive $14.80 (£9.28).

- EBooks are subject to VAT if sold in the UK from a UK-based company but paper books are not. EBooks that are sold to countries outside the UK are not subject to VAT in the UK. Keep this in mind when setting your selling price.

- Make sure you check out the legalities and VAT requirements in your country before you start selling eBooks and determine the price.

- If there is a competitive eBook, see how much they charge and charge a little bit less.

- Go by how much you would be prepared to pay for your eBook.

- Most eBook s are sold between $9 (£6) and $29.99 (19). EBooks on IM topics are usually between $19.99 (£12.50) and $47 (£29)

- People are prepared to pay for useful and hard-to-get information.

- I suggest that you start with a very low price and if the eBook starts selling, slowly put the price up. Remember:

The product is too expensive when the value is too small.

TOP TIP: Buy your own eBook from your affiliate page on Clickbank. Get an affiliate link (click "promote" on your own product) and paste that link into the browser. Get a second PayPal account and ask a friend to buy it for you. The very small investment of buying your own eBook - with your own affiliate link – will definitely be worth it as without doing it, potential affiliates will not promote your product because most of them will not know what N/A* means. Visit Clickbank and you will see that in any category there are eBooks with N/A* next to them.

This is how your product will look on Clickbank when nobody has bought the product yet (N/A next to the product):

It is not very appealing to affiliates as they cannot even see how much they will earn. It looks like no money will be paid and/or no book has ever been sold. It does not look professional and affiliates are unlikely to promote the eBook for you.

This is how it will look once you have bought your own eBook, much more professional:

3. Set up a Wordpress blog that updates itself (also called "Autoblogging")

With a program like Wordpress Robot you can set up a blog in a matter of minutes and then never touch it again!

You give the easy to use bit of software a few keywords that describe your niche, and then it goes and finds content all over the internet to post on you site - it really is as easy as that.

You can tell it:

- How often you want it to post
- Where you want it to get content from - article sites, ClickBank, YouTube, Yahoo! Answers and so on
- What kind of ads you want to display - AdSense, eBay, Amazon and so on
- How to lay out the content

You can literally set up your blog and forget it, while it grows and grows and earns you money!

The downside of this is some people consider this as blackhat, although it is done by many website masters in different niches in the first pages of Google.

Word of caution: the content will not be unique content if other internet marketers in the same niche as yours also have autoblogging on their website.

4. Get a free website and drive traffic to it

Visit www.homewebsitecenter.com This is a great website. Here you can have your own website with an eBook to sell in three easy steps. Simply fill in your PayPal address and your website is ready. There's a choice of several niches. There are several upgrades possible but even with the completely free version, your website is created in less than five minutes. Simply drive traffic to your site and start earning money. It's highly recommended for newbies who want to test driving traffic to a site. The paid version gives you a bunch of website statistics as well. You can also visit www.weebly.com for free websites.

5. Misspellings opportunities

There are still some opportunities in the misspelling/typo market. People who type in a misspelled word land on your website and you sell them your stuff or some affiliate links from the misspelled word niche. Although Google autocorrects misspellings nowadays, some people ignore this and click on the sites with misspelled words. Your website could be: www.artritispainrelief.com instead of www.arthritispainrelief.com. Don't worry about it not being professional as only the people typing in the misspelled word will get to see your misspelled domain name and they probably don't even know they've misspelled it. Needless to say, you would spell all the words correctly on all your pages once people have clicked on your domain name.

6. Sell resell rights products

> **TOP TIP: Create an opt-in box on your sales letter or website so you can constantly buy different Resell Rights Products in the same niche and send them to your list. The income from the sales of only one product will give you the money to buy a second product in the same niche.**

Some good websites to visit if you want to earn money this way:
www.master-resale-rights.com
www.theplrstore.com

Or search for "your keyword + resell rights".

7. Top 10 reviews websites

Buy a domain name "Top 10 best music recording software" or "Top 10 – your keyword-here" and put some decent content on your website with your affiliate link to buy the products dotted all over the pages. Five years ago I used to believe Top 10 websites. Now I realise that very often the first one in the Top 10 listed products is the product the website developer makes most money with.

8. Join new product launches websites

Join www.jvnotifypro.com and www.imnewswatch.com . When a new product is being launched you build a website e.g. "keywordhere-review.com" or "keywordhere-scam.com" and describe the pros and cons of the product, with your affiliate link dotted all over the pages.

9. Start a membership site

Search for "keyword"+"membership" to see if there are any membership sites available in your niche. If there aren't and your research tells you that there is a lot of demand for your niche, a membership site is certainly something you could consider. It will be hard work as you have to make sure that you have something to tell your members each month, but the spreadsheet below shows what your income could be.

Membership at $19.99 per month.

MONTH	MEMBERS	TOTAL MONTH	TOTAL YEAR
$19.99	10	$199.90	$2,398.80
$19.99	20	$399.80	$4,797.60
$19.99	30	$599.70	$7,196.40
$19.99	40	$799.60	$9,595.20
$19.99	50	$999.50	$11,994.00
$19.99	60	$1,199.40	$14,392.80
$19.99	70	$1,399.30	$16,791.60
$19.99	80	$1,599.20	$19,190.40
$19.99	90	$1,799.10	$21,589.20
$19.99	100	$1,999.00	$23,988.00
$19.99	200	$3,998.00	$47,976.00
$19.99	300	$5,997.00	$71,964.00
$19.99	400	$7,996.00	$95,952.00
$19.99	500	$9,995.00	$119,940.00
$19.99	600	$11,994.00	$143,928.00
$19.99	700	$13,993.00	$167,916.00
$19.99	800	$15,992.00	$191,904.00
$19.99	900	$17,991.00	$215,892.00
$19.99	1000	$19,990.00	$239,880.00

Membership at $7.99 per month.

MONTH	MEMBERS	TOTAL MONTH	TOTAL YEAR
$7.99	10	$79.90	$958.80
$7.99	20	$159.80	$1,917.60
$7.99	30	$239.70	$2,876.40
$7.99	40	$319.60	$3,835.20
$7.99	50	$399.50	$4,794.00
$7.99	60	$479.40	$5,752.80
$7.99	70	$559.30	$6,711.60
$7.99	80	$639.20	$7,670.40
$7.99	90	$719.10	$8,629.20
$7.99	100	$799.00	$9,588.00
$7.99	200	$1,598.00	$19,176.00
$7.99	300	$2,397.00	$28,764.00
$7.99	400	$3,196.00	$38,352.00
$7.99	500	$3,995.00	$47,940.00
$7.99	600	$4,794.00	$57,528.00
$7.99	700	$5,593.00	$67,116.00
$7.99	800	$6,392.00	$76,704.00
$7.99	900	$7,191.00	$86,292.00
$7.99	1000	$7,990.00	$95,880.00

Whichever membership you choose, remember:

- Make the sign up process simple, quick and easy. If there are too many pages to fill in, people will leave in the middle of the sign up process.

- Make sure you choose one with a drip-feed possibility: this means that every week you can allow new members access to some new content on your site. If they can see all content at once immediately, they've no incentive to return and will get their money back after a week or so. If they know there is fresh stuff to come every week, they are more likely to stick around.

- Make it interesting to sign up for a $1 trial. I have found that a $1 trial is better than a free trial. After 7 days of the $1 trial, their card is automatically charged the first monthly fee, unless they've asked for a refund.

- Content is essential if you want to keep your members.

- You must give the members their money's worth each month.

- The more you give the more you get: if you give a lot of good stuff, your members will stay longer.

- Most members love video content so give it to them. PLR videos are available in a lot of different niches, simply Google "your keyword" + " PLR video".

- If your membership sites is a success and you start to get 5000 or more members, you must be prepared to give customer service. Set up the site accordingly with telephone numbers and support email addresses. You can get Helpdesks to sort this out for you (just Google help desks).

You must spend a lot of time evaluating each membership site before you purchase because they all give different possibilities. Here are some sites you can evaluate:
www.amember.com
www.easymemberpro.com
www.memberfire.com
www.membergate.com can't use PayPal to check out and doesn't do drip feed
www.memberspeed.com
www.yourmembership.com

Information about memberships:
www.5minutemembershipsites.com

www.membershipacademy.com
www.membershipsiteowner.com

Visit www.clickbank.com and look at the websites with the highest gravity, these are the sites that are selling well. Analyse the sales pages and see what you can learn from them.

11. Transfer public domain into an eBook

Find a Public Domain book and change it into an eBook, put the eBook on Clickbank and let affiliates sell the eBook for you.

You can duplicate the content from a Public Domain book and keep all the profit when you sell it as an eBook. Is there an easier way to write a book?

And it gets better: you can change the content, add stuff to it and then sell it as your own book. If you change it enough you can obtain a Copyright to the work – to **your** work.

12. Buy and sell sites on Flippa

- Buy a website on www.flippa.com .

- Drive traffic to it and get backlinks for the site

- Sell the same site on Flippa again

- You can make anything between $200 and $5000 in a matter of weeks or months.

13. Buy an old domain name and sell it on Flippa

- Buy an old domain name e.g. 10 years or older

- Sell it on Flippa or any other domain auction site, without doing anything to the domain name. People are prepared to pay money for old domain names. It takes a long time to find a good old domain name on GoDaddy but is worth looking out for one.

14. Buy an old domain name, put content on it and sell it.

- Buy an old domain name e.g. 10 years or older

- If possible buy one that has a minimum of 500 backlinks

- Put content and monetisation on the site

- Sell it on www.flippa.com or any other domain auction site

- You can make between $1000 and $10,000 in a matter of weeks or months

15. Fulltime website flipper

- Find keywords and a website with potential with the methods in this book

- Build a website with the methods explained in this book

- Sell your website

That's what a website flipper does: develops sites and sells them.

16. Earn money with CPA

You can use the smaller search engines to place ads and send them directly to a landing page with a CPA-offer on it. This method will cost you money to advertise but once you have found a niche that works for you, you can make money.

17. Earn money with selling advertising space

Once you have mastered how to get traffic to your site, you can make some extra easy money. You can contact website owners in your niche or even businesses who do not have a website and ask if they are interested in placing a banner ad on your website. If you cannot design a banner yourself, you can outsource it: www.elance.com. You can also go to www.20dollarabanners.com and have some made. All you need is a picture and when somebody clicks on the picture, the visitor goes to the advertiser's website. Don't forget to make sure that the advertiser's website opens in a new browser window so your website stays open.

To make a simple banner all you need is the free graphic editor software paint.net. A standard size horizontal banner is 468 x 60. A block ad format can be 250 x 250. Whatever you use to make the banner look nice, do not use flashing banners and do not use clashing colours. Your banner can be just text with or without a border around but must be eye-catching.

You could sell banner space to 10 different companies. For one banner you can ask approximately $200 per month x 10 banners per site = $20000 per month for doing nothing. If you have 10 different websites with 10 banners on each website= $20,000 per month.

Selling banners' space is a little bit of work to start with but can work really well. The money it brings in even with one banner can pay for a full time freelancer who can do a lot of other IM work for you.

18. Earn money with Adsense only

I bet you have come across websites that basically have a little bit of content on their pages and the rest is ONLY Adsense. Well it is indeed an easy way of earning money but is also considered greyhat policy. An Adsense click pays on average between $1 and $1.50 per 1000 views. To earn $200 a month you would need about 200,000 page views!

As an alternative to Adsense, you also need to check out other platforms, for instance www.sitescout.com.

19. Earn money with White Label Strategy

White Label Strategy is when you can turn a product or service into your own, and brand the product as your own. It is the same principle as in the food/car/computer industry: a computer called XYZ might use exactly the same components as the computer brand ABC, they're just branded differently. But because it is "White Labelling" nobody knows that XYZ and ABC are actually the same computer. There are plenty of white label products. All the design work is done for you. All you need to do is get traffic to your site.

www.whitelabeldating.com is a dating site where you are able to set up your own dating site free of charge. All you need is a domain name. They take a percentage of your takings.

20. Make money with iPhone apps

Creating an app (application) for an iPhone is not that complicated these days. One site where you can make free apps is www.seattleclouds.com

21. Earn money with drop shipping/eCommerce

I have listed drop shipping/eCommerce in this chapter because it is another great way of making lots of money. It is a very large part of my income so I've devoted a complete chapter to it.

Whether you are designing a Wordpress site or any other website, the same applies for drop shipping and e-commerce sites: SEO is extremely important, your images need to have a keyword description, driving traffic to your ecommerce sites can be done with the same traffic methods as mentioned in this book, etc… In other words, most of what is discussed in this book can be applied to e-commerce or drop shipping sites with the only difference that you are selling physical products.

www.liquorice-licorice.co.uk is one of my (small) eCommerce sites. So if you like liquorice, you know where to get it!

I have shown you earlier for which keywords the site ranks well for.

Note: searches vary therefore every day different websites are shown by Google.

Part 14. Drop Shipping and eCommerce

You can buy my book "Drop Shipping and eCommerce. What You Need and Where To Get It" on Amazon or as an ebook here: www.dropshippingandecommerce.com

Drop shipping can be a VERY profitable business. It may take some time to fully grasp it all but once you have got your website set up with products from reliable suppliers, and you've decided on your card processing company, all you need is traffic to your sites. Drop shipping is a category in the eCommerce or "shopping cart software" side of internet marketing that should be explored. eCommerce has been booming for the last few years and is growing year after year.

Drop shipping and eCommerce are well worth a look. I have some very successful drop shipping/eCommerce sites and I started with zero knowledge. The Streamline Income Screenshots shown in this book are from eCommerce sites. On some days, I sell over $10,615 (£6800) products per **day** with the combined sales from a few sites!

March 2013 update: **Since I've created a lot of income from self publishing books I've sold several of my drop shipping sites as it is very time consuming. The income from self publishing books becomes autopilot income once the work has been put in. That does not apply to drop shipping. As I have to try and reduce the time I work on the computer, for my neck condition, I decided to publish more and more books and reduce my drop shipping sites. You already know where to check out my product re self publishing:** http://www.worldwideselfpublishing.com/

1. What is eCommerce?

You may have heard of the phrase before but it's important to define it. eCommerce (or Electronic-commerce) is a broad term used to describe the selling of products or services online or on the internet. Established businesses that have "brick and mortar" stores or online-only stores - operated by large businesses or a single individual - can all participate in eCommerce. Basically, anyone with a computer, a website, and a product, can participate and benefit from eCommerce. Yes, this means you! This ability to create a website and sell products online can generate you loads of cash and profit, right from the comfort of your own home! The number of people who buy online is increasing every day.

eCommerce occurs when someone makes a sale or an online purchase. It is certainly going to expand and grow as more and more people get access to internet, have their own computer, and are generally more accustomed to buying products or services online. Even today, people don't necessarily have to own a computer to participate in eCommerce! They can make purchases over the phone!

The possibilities of eCommerce are endless. Generating value for other people can help you generate a lot of money online. However, there are a couple of things that you should know in order to effectively participate in eCommerce. Keep in mind, that if you don't read anything else in this book, the remaining pages in this chapter can generate a lot of cash for you - relatively quickly.

The first thing you need to have is an actual website, so that people will be able to log on to the internet, go to your internet address, and review what you have to offer – and buy! The next thing you need to create is a way for people to pay you, collect funds, and to notify you when they purchase an item - otherwise known as a payment platform. Of course, you will need a product to sell. And lastly, you need to generate a way to ship or deliver your product to each of your customers when they order from you.

This is where "drop shipping" comes in. Drop shipping is where stores have displays of products (online retailers will simply display images on their website). The products are then ordered by your customers and are shipped from a warehouse or manufacturer directly to your customer.

2. What is drop shipping?

Wikipedia: "Drop shipping is a supply chain management technique in which the retailer does not keep goods in stock, but instead transfers customer orders and shipment details to either the manufacturer or a wholesaler, who then ships the goods directly to the customer. As in all retail businesses, the retailers make their profit on the difference between the wholesale and retail price."

Here's another definition: It's a method of selling an item whereby an individual retailer will advertise, sell, and collect the money, then contact a larger merchant or warehouse where the item is actually stored and have them ship the item to the consumer for a percentage of the profit. The consumer usually does not know that the larger merchant or warehouse is involved in the process at all. This is a great way to start a home-based internet business!

Think of it as the same as affiliate marketing, except instead of getting a set percentage of the sale you mark the product up in price and pocket the profit.

A drop shipping site looks like any other "shop" on the internet and the visitor will not know that it is a drop shipping site. As with all websites, the problem will be to get traffic to your drop shipping site (SEO is also very important, e.g. naming your product with a keyword) but once your customers find the site and start ordering, you can make a lot of money with drop shipping.

Here is one examples of a drop shipping site:

www.laptopstands.co.uk

Drop shipping is a big part of the process in delivering your product to your customer. Since we are talking about an online business here, we need to be able to have a few things set up. The first is storage space if you decide to store the products yourself. Where are you going to store your product(s)? The process of drop shipping allows you to have the manufacturer send your orders directly to your customers. You get the customer to buy from you but you can also ship the products yourself. Most shopping cart services, including www.Ultracart.com provide immediate notification to your drop shipper (which may or may not be the manufacturer). An email to your drop shippers system will tell them where to send the product, how many products are ordered, and what type of postage to use (first class, overnight). Some manufactures that supply products do not provide "drop shipping" services. So, you will need to have a "fulfilment house" which is a business that picks up or receives your wholesale order, safely stores your inventory, and ships out your products when your shopping cart notifies them via email.

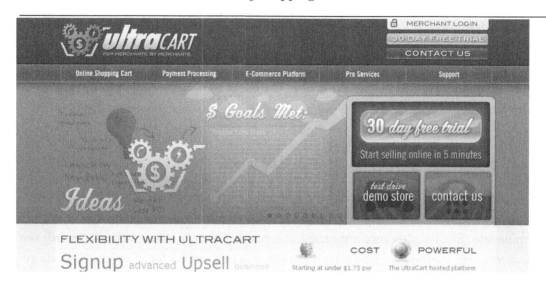

Using a drop shipper allows you to focus on product development, marketing, and customer support – and ultimately spending time growing your business! Remember, if you wanted to work in a stock room, you wouldn't have started your own online business!

So how do you find your own drop shipper? Well, very often the manufacturer of the product will be able to provide this service or recommend one of their partners. Trust me, if the manufacture doesn't provide this service, they will want to recommend someone who does. After all, they want to see their products move out and into the hands of consumers just as much as you do!

Nevertheless, they may recommend a "fulfilment house" or business which helps to "fulfil" the ordering process for you. A fulfilment house acts as a drop shipper and sends your product to your customers. They store your products on a shelf and mail them out in the manner specified. In addition, most fulfilment houses also can put various things into your package, such as coupons, instructions, fliers, or free give away products that many customers love!

Each fulfilment house works a little differently and charges for different things too. So, do your homework. Again, don't worry about the time involvement here. One afternoon of researching and picking a fulfilment house will be worth it – and you won't have to think about it again!

Remember, the most important thing that drop shipping offers is a way to "automate" your business, which is what you want!

A slightly negative side of drop shipping is that in most cases you need to collect the money from your customers. So you will need to sign up with a Debit/Credit Card Processing Company. This is not easy when you are starting up. You can start with www.Paypal.com and www.2checkout.com which are payment processing companies that will approve your application reasonably easy.

The difference between drop shipping & eCommerce

eCommerce is a great way to generate money through your own website, with your hand in each part of the sales process: selecting the product, purchasing products wholesale, collecting the money, and creating the system by which money is taken and the product is delivered to the customer. Affiliate drop shipping programmes are similar, but you are essentially dealing with creating a website, developing web traffic and web conversions. As an affiliate, your job is more of a "front end" venture where you get people to purchase items and you let the manufacturer or drop shipper take care of the rest.

For example, let's say you are a personal trainer and you write a blog or website about health fitness and exercise. Your credibility and large client following makes you a great candidate for developing a "Drop Shipping" affiliate relationship with one or more manufacturers. Perhaps you want to partner up with a protein shake company. As an affiliate, all you would need to do is focus on increasing your traffic and developing conversions from your website. The actual drop shipper will take care of the rest!

There are manufacturers who have their own drop shipping website templates and all you need to do is put that template on your website. People who find your fitness website through Google will end up on your **own** shop but you never have to do any work once you have received a sale. eCommerce on the other hand would take a bit more effort to reap your rewards. It would require you generate a product and develop a payment platform on your website where customers can take orders from you directly. You would be primarily responsible for delivering those orders back to your client. So, with eCommerce you have to do all the work yourself from A to Z and deal with your customers for any questions they might have. With drop-shipping all you have to do is get traffic to your drop shipping site, charge the customer for the purchase and the rest is done by your drop shipping company.

3. Why drop shipping and eCommerce?

Today, it is fairly difficult to find anyone who regularly uses a personal computer that hasn't already purchased a product or service online. The fact is that every day, more and more people use the internet to buy the things they need and want, easily, safely and conveniently from their own home. Since the internet is accessible to anyone in any part of the world, an online business has unlimited potential to reach customers in any region of the globe.

This new computer usage is great news for budding entrepreneurs because it can give them the potential to offer their very own product - or variety of products - to their customers from the comfort of their own home! Imagine, making great money by providing any number of great products, right from your kitchen table? Yes, it's possible!

4. How does drop shipping work?

Typically, a customer makes a purchase, and you take the money or handle the transaction via credit card processing. Once you receive payment, you then forward the order to your supplier for fulfilment. The supplier ships the goods to your customers with your labels on the package. You pay your supplier via credit card transaction – and everyone is happy!

The big advantage is you pay your suppliers the buying price for a certain product but YOU can decide the selling price. With this regard, you are in total control of your profit margins. Keep in mind that you need to carefully study the competition and not overprice the products or potential customers will look elsewhere. You also need to calculate your monthly expenses and fees (see further) in your selling price.

- You do not need to ship or post any products.

- You are not responsible for customer services.

- You never have to speak to anybody about the orders or sort out any problems.

All this is done by your drop shipping company. **The stages of drop shipping:**

The people involved:

1. The Seller - You!
2. The Buyer - Someone who's looking for what you're selling.

3. The Supplier - The person who stocks and sells the item you're selling.

The steps involved:

a) The Buyer is looking for an item and finds it on The Seller's website. The Buyer then places an order with The Seller and sends payment.
b) The Seller sends order to The Supplier.
c) The Supplier sends the product to The Buyer.

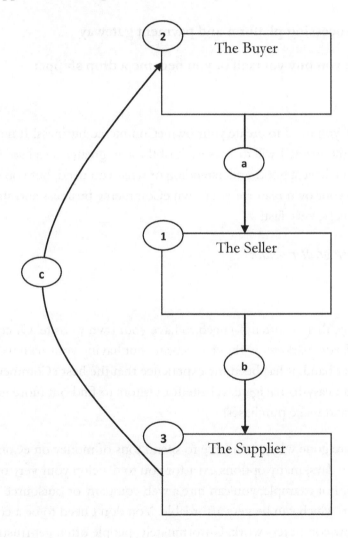

5. What do you need to start up?

To sum up, here are basic items you need to participate in eCommerce:

a) **A website**

b) **A payment processing platform and payment gateway**

c) **Products that you buy yourself or you become a drop shipper**

d) **Customers!**

And that's it! That's all you need to create your own eCommerce business! It may sound overwhelming, but don't worry, I will discuss each of these in greater detail so that by the end of this, you will not only have a good understanding of what you need, but you will be ready to move forward with your own plan for your own eCommerce business and start making yourself some money very, very fast!

So let us discuss these in greater detail:

a) **Your website:**

With affiliate marketing, there is often no need to have your own website. Of course, you can still be an effective affiliate marketer without a website, but having your own website is beneficial. On the other hand, it has been my experience that the best eCommerce solution is to have and maintain an easy-to-navigate website for visitors to find out more information about your product – and make purchases!

Fortunately, the days are gone where you have to spend tons of money on eCommerce website creation. These days, many options exist for you to develop your very own website affordably and quickly. For example, you can hire a web company or outsource your website creation to a freelancer, which can be very affordable. You don't need to be a computer whiz or even understand how computers work. Unfortunately, people often get frustrated or fearful of computers, and get bogged down thinking about all the "technical" stuff behind the scenes. Don't do this! Don't get sidetracked by the technical stuff! Sure, it's helpful to know some technical terms, but it's really not necessary to know everything. For example, let's take "electricity" as a subject. Most people do not understand how electricity works, and how to generate it or even how to transport it. The details of how electricity is carried into our bedrooms remains a mystery to most people. Yet, do we worry about electricity? Nope. Not at all! Same is true with websites. All you need to know is how to flip the switch and when to pay the monthly electricity bill.

You can outsource the creation of your website and I have listed some outsource companies before in this book. You can also use one of the many "Do-It-Yourself" web development programs offered by a number of sites – like www.godaddy.com or www.1and1.com which are a great alternative for the beginner. www.ekmpowershop.com and www.actinic.com are great sites to do it yourself with very good tutorials. You can set up a simple shop with these sites in just a weekend.

Even sites like WordPress, which offers blogging templates, can set you up with a great looking site that you can manage on your own – and relatively inexpensively.

Your website should be easy to navigate, easy to read and free of spelling errors. In addition, you should have a homepage, a contact page, about us page, a Frequently Asked Questions (FAQ) page and of course a product information page. You don't need to get too flashy with your website but you must add an image of your product.

b) A payment processing platform

A "payment platform" is just a fancy term that describes the method of how you will actually get paid. If you sell something, you have to provide a way for the customer to pay you. Collecting payment is an important aspect of eCommerce and your business! And since we are dealing with credit cards and the financial details of our customers, it's important to get this part right. Fortunately, there are great ways to do this that are easier than ever! In the old days, you were really on your own when it came to figuring out how to collect, store, and process financial information and then be able to transfer it to your bank account. And now to do it safely with a high emphasis on consumer protection against fraud - what a difference a few years makes!

Today, collecting information, storing it, and getting paid is easier than ever! Many companies have recognized that they could make a healthy profit helping people to process their transactions.

PayPal is a very popular payment platform which provides a way to send and receive money easily. PayPal also allows you the convenient ability to generate "order now" buttons which you can easily place on your site. So, for example, if you sell necklaces, you can place graphics (or photos) of the necklaces and create an order button for each product. When the customer clicks on the order button, PayPal will direct the customer to enter their credit card and shipping information. PayPal will take the order, collect the payment from the customer and route the money directly into your PayPal account. They will charge you a minimal fee per transaction. Yet, the good thing is that you never have to worry about collecting, storing, and maintaining any financial information. This process also allows people to feel safe and confident that they aren't going to get ripped off, and provides a level of confidence that you will deliver your product.

PayPal is not the only company that provides this type of service. www.E-junkie.com , for example, can also provide these services and generate another easy platform which can take the customers' information and send you the money for a small fee per month. You can also use a third party e-commerce cart solution, which is a "shopping cart" platform. This type of service can provide you with an "order now" button or with a specific product link, which you will need to set up and generate within their system. For example, I have used the shopping cart company www.UltraCart.com . UltraCart allows you to set up an account, establish your product links, and allows you to set up a connection between your bank account, so that you get paid! In addition, **and this is very important**, UltraCart notifies your fulfilment house to "drop ship" your product to your customer by email.

There is also a missing piece we haven't talked about and that is often missed when setting up your account. For a traditional shopping cart system, you need to be able to connect the "cart" to your bank. To do this you need a payment gateway. This payment gateway works as a guarantee that the credit card transaction occurs without any hiccups. Credit card companies like Visa or MasterCard won't process money without a "payment gateway" to guard against fraud or misuse of credit card information. The payment gateway basically protects you and the customer against getting conned – which doesn't always work but it definitely helps. The gateway confirms that there is enough money in the account or in the available balance and charges the account. If you have seen a credit card declined for insufficient funds or the card is unauthorized for use, you can be sure that the "payment gateway" is working. This path or "gateway" is the route where the collected money gets transported back and forth, from one account to another. It serves as a way to connect your merchant account to your payment platform.

As mentioned earlier, your shopping cart account generally requires a "merchant account" which collects the money from the shopping cart system through the "gateway." This establishment of a gateway serves as a way to protect the transaction from credit cards. Getting a merchant account through your bank requires you have decent credit. If your credit is a little rusty, then you can use "higher risk" merchant accounts, which charge a bit more a month – though the charge is still minimal.

You might wonder why you need a payment gateway or processor of your transaction. Your shopping cart network serves only as a "face" to your company's ability to take orders. It specializes in setting up your products to order. The credit card company doesn't deal with any products whatsoever. The only thing the processor does is process the payment, makes sure that it is a real credit card number, preventing fraud and approving the payment. Once the approval and credit card information is processed, then the money lands in your merchant account. If you are unable to get a merchant account, you can rely on services from PayPal.

When you become a drop shipper or if you have an eCommerce site, you will need to collect money from your customers. Therefore, you will need an online payment processor or a Debit and Credit Card Payment Processor. This is very difficult to get if you are just starting up. You could start just by using PayPal, but lot of people do not have a PayPal account and may be required to sign up to pay you. This creates a barrier of inconvenience for the customer, and often results in no sale.

A question that many people have is: why not just tie or connect the payment into your personal checking? The reason is that the payment gateway or the payment processor requires that a merchant account exist. This type of account prevents fraudulent activity. As mentioned, your shopping cart service will notify your drop shipper usually through your fulfilment house.

In summary, your payment platform setup may look complicated at first, but it really isn't as difficult as it seems. Think of it as a series of "connections" so that you are able to collect money. Your payment platform comprises several parts. The "face" of the platform can be your website's shopping cart system.

So:

- Website

- Click to Shopping Cart

- Shopping Cart is seen – it is where the actual order is placed

Your shopping cart sends the credit card information punched in by the customer through a "payment gateway," which then determines if the credit card numbers are legitimate, if there's enough money in the account, and if everything checks out, it then processes the payment. The payment is then placed into your merchant account.

So again, here are the pieces of the small puzzle:

- **A website** – you can create this yourself or pay someone to develop this for you.

- **Payment platform:** This could be PayPal or a **shopping cart** service, such as www.UltraCart.com. It requires two additional items: a **gateway processor** and **merchant account**, which you can set up through your bank. The most popular gateway service company is www.Authorize.net. As mentioned, you also need a **shopping cart service:** This allows you to create "links" for your product, connects to your payment gateway, and notifies your drop shipper (often your fulfilment house) that they need to send the product to your customer.

If it sounds a little complicated, it is only because you are not familiar with the process. However, most people find that everyone in this process is familiar with each other, and will generally help you out. It is important to remember that everyone wants you to be successful and to get you on your feet as quickly as possible. After all, once you start making money, they start making money too – and everyone is happy!

Because this might be confusing, I will provide a quick flow chart that will help you to understand the backend of the process. Don't worry, after it's all set up you won't have to think of it much. In fact, if you don't think about it, then everyone is doing their job. Keep in mind that everyone along this payment chain will collect some funds or make money. Your shopping chart, for example, might charge a monthly fee and maybe a small transaction fee. (www.UltraCart.com at this time does not charge per transaction.). However, the processing gateway, such as www.Authorize.net charges a monthly fee, and then a small transaction fee. And your merchant account also charges a minimal monthly fee. Yes, these charges add up, but they are nothing in comparison to the costs of actually opening up your own physical store, hiring employees, paying for the electricity, rent, insurance and business district fees!

The question I often get is, why deal with this entire process? If you want to accept a variety of different payment options, such as using Visa, MasterCard, or other credit and debit cards, you need to ensure your transaction process runs smoothly for everyone.

c) Products

This is truly the fun part! Your product is what you are selling. It could be anything from t-shirts to blueberry jam. If you want to sell hats, shoes, dresses, or even your own art work, you can! Your product is anything that you plan on offering on your website. Are you unsure what to sell? There are plenty of products that are available to you to "resell" to customers.

Consider looking at several wholesale providers of products and discover the hundreds of thousands of products you would be able to buy and sell. Often, a wholesaler will sell you a bundle of products at a steep discount. The price you sell on your site would be the retail price. Often, people charge anywhere from 40% to 300% of the price they buy the product for. So for example, if you buy a product that costs $10 per item from a wholesale distributor, you might consider turning it around and selling it for $29 or $39.

Remember, you still need to pay for the website and all the transaction fees, including shipping (you may also charge a shipping fee through your shopping cart) and of course, you want to make a profit!

Here is a diagram that illustrates this further:

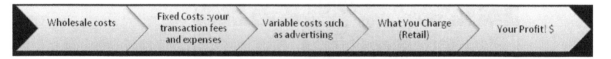

Drop shipping for affiliates

Often, you won't even have to purchase any products in advance. Many manufacturers or international distributors simply have well supported programmes that allow affiliate marketers to sign up to sell their items directly from their websites, email marketing campaigns, or blogs. This is a great way to make money, because you don't have to buy any inventory, you don't have to ship any items or deal with returns, and you don't have to deal with any customers. All you have to do is generate traffic and conversions directly from your website!

If you are searching for an already developed site, you can buy ready-made-drop shipping sites on www.flippa.com (put "drop shipping" in the search box), but be warned as transferring the site becomes a bit technical. You'll have to tell the seller of the site that complete transfer has to be included in the price before you release the funds. You will have to give the seller your log-in details of your hosting account.

d) Customers

Once your site is up and running, the same applies as to any other website: you need web traffic and you need to do some seriously good SEO management. You can use most of the traffic methods described in this book. And the most important thing to do for SEO is to make sure that you name your various categories of products with the keywords that people would type in a search engine to find your shop (website).

6. How much does it cost to set up?

To run an eCommerce website or drop shipping site is surprisingly affordable. Setting up your site if you use www.ekmpowershop.com is free if you do it yourself – and it is easy. Your main monthly expenses are:

- $32 (£19.99) per month for your shopping cart software e.g. www.ekmpowershop.com

- $32 (£19.99) per month for your payment processing company e.g. www.streamline.com

- $16 (£9.99) per month your hosting (including your domain name) e.g. www.godaddy.com

$80 (£49.97) per month in total. That might look like a lot but once your site starts selling you will be happy to pay the unavoidable expenses.

The above are fixed monthly fees. On top of that you will have to pay the following:

- A percentage of the selling price of the product for your payment processing company. This can be anything between 2% and 15% depending on your negotiating skills and how many you sell per year.

- A percentage of the selling price for your payment gateway which is the same as the above.

- A fee for your fulfilment house if you use one. This can be a fixed monthly fee that depends on the volume of sales or again it can be a percentage.

Here is a breakdown of what you need to do:

Create a website – either hire someone, use a service or use www.ekmpowershop.com where you just import your images, give them a title, description and price, and that's it.

Choose a product – your product will determine the look and feel of your site. Find a wholesaler that you can work with or buy a readymade drop shipping site from www.flippa.com

Find a shopping cart service e.g. www.ekmpowershop.com

Open a merchant account (not always necessary, but helpful) with a payment processing company e.g. www.streamline.com

Contact Authorize.net to help you secure your ability to process payments. Ekmpowershop has a payment gateway build in.

Find a drop shipper or a fulfilment house if applicable

Start generating traffic and making sales!

With www.ekmpowershop.com **and** www.actinic.com **(and others) all you need to do is follow the screens and fill in the necessary fields and everything is done in the background for you. However you will need the information from your payment processing company before you can complete the process.** www.ekmpowershop.com **has its own payment gateway, so you do not need to worry about that.**

Some good websites to design your shop:

www.ultracart.com RECOMMENDED. Ideal for drop shipping as it has all you need built in.
www.ekmpowershop.co.uk RECOMMENDED, very good SEO which is extremely important
www.ekmpowershop.com
www.actinic.com
www.cubecart.com

I believe all of these have a free trial period, so sign up and try to create a few products to see which one you like best.

My site www.liquorice-licorice.co.uk is designed with www.ekmpowershop.co.uk shopping cart software.

If you want more examples, simply search "shopping cart software" and look at all the different companies. Review the one you are going to use.

Some reputable payment processing companies are:

www.1shoppingcart.com RECOMMENDED
www.2checkout.com RECOMMENDED
www.E-junkie.com
www.paypal.com RECOMMENDED
www.streamline.co.uk RECOMMENDED UK customers only
www.streamline.com

www.worldpay.com Does not like to deal with transactions for delivery of online digital products

Trust me, it is not as difficult as you think. After a few days of your time, you could generate a whopping amount of cash with your shop!

I love www.ekmpowershop.co.uk and use this platform for many of my shops. It is all optimised for SEO: each page can have a header with a keyword and so can each product. You simply create a product under a specific category, give it a description, upload a picture, set a price and hey, it's done.

It's pretty easy to get started. Here are a few screenshots to show how the platform looks once you are inside:

Screenshot 1: You can see that you can give each category a description with keywords. Each product can be altered simply by clicking edit, or delete or you can change the order of appearance on the site.

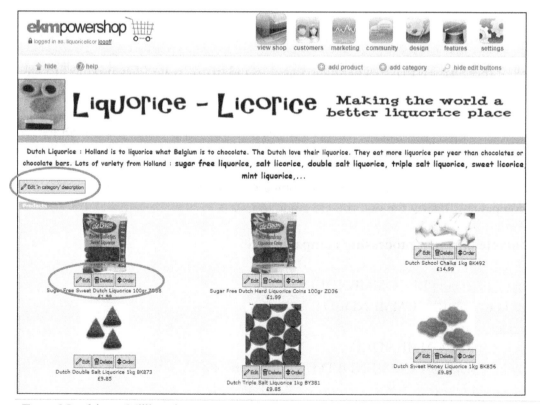

Screenshot 2: You can give your product a title (with keywords) and a product description with keywords.

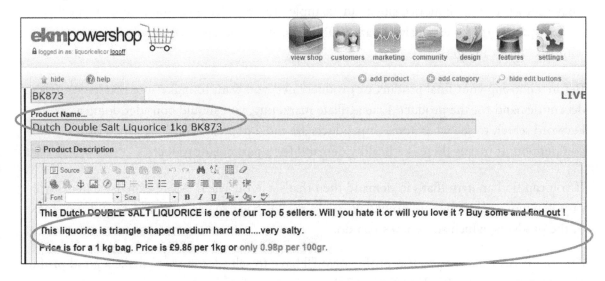

Screenshot 3: For each product, you can create a Meta Title, Meta Description and fill in Meta Keywords. That is brilliant for SEO !! I really love www.ekmpowershop.co.uk and their service is brilliant too.

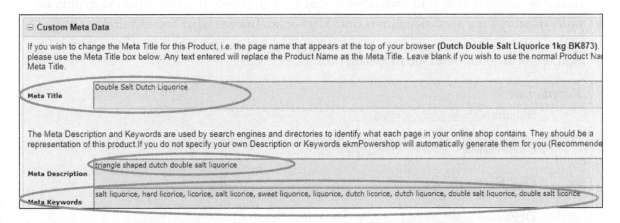

Top Tip: **Never** give your product a title with a reference number **only**. You **must** always give your product a name with the **keyword** in. Nobody will search for BK873 (my reference number for the product) but people will search for "Double Salt Liquorice". So my product name or title in www.ekmpowershop.co.uk is "Dutch Double Salt Liquorice BK873". Many people ignore this aspect with eCommerce which is vital for SEO.

7. What items are good to sell?

I have shown you my liquorice site as an example but I also have ecommerce sites in other niches: spare parts for expensive boats, binoculars, spectacles, gardening, etc.... all niches with BIG profit margins.

Before choosing your final product or product lines, you want to make sure you have a fairly decent demand for the product. Like affiliate marketing, you should consider doing a keyword search to see what items or products are most popular. Don't be afraid of competition. It means there is a healthy demand for a particular product.

If you can find an item that's in demand then that's a good seller! More expensive items will earn you more profit, but are potentially more risky if you can't sell them and you have stock of the products, which sometimes you do.

Cheaper items will earn you less profit so you'll have to sell a lot more to make a good profit. However, if you get refunds or can't sell them, then you lose less money.

If you want to stock the products yourself, you'll have to find products first. There will be plenty of wholesalers in your own country that want to supply you and often the minimum order quantity for a good discount is only $700 or so. Just see what you can find.

Sign up for accounts with the following sites:

Supplier sites

> Alibaba - www.alibaba.com

> Chinavasion - www.chinavasion.com

> Deal Extreme - www.dx.com

> DHGate - www.dhgate.com

Some of the suppliers on these sites require you to buy containers at a time but if you keep looking, there will be somewhere the minimum order value is only $1000.

Auction sites

> eBay - www.ebay.com   Amazon - www.amazon.com

For more help, you can search for "your keyword" + "drop shipping" to find directories and products that you want to sell.

Amazon has its own fulfilment service and works really well for thousands of sellers.

8. Step-by-step guide for drop shipping on eBay

1. Sign up to a supplier site. You may need to supply your credit card details in order to get a verified sellers' account. Don't worry, this is just a security check.
2. Search for an item that you want to research and, possibly, sell. As soon as you start searching you'll see the huge range of products available; you'll just have to try to choose!
3. Research, research, research. Login to eBay and search for the item you're researching.
4. Check "Completed listings"

This allows you to see items that have sold, in green, and auctions that ended unsold, in red:

* *Note the items that received bids, but did not sell. This indicates items that had interest, but where the reserve price was set at more than people were willing to spend. If you find lots of instances of your chosen item going unsold, but getting bids, you could dominate the market by underselling the reserve prices other people are setting (assuming you can do this and still make a profit).*

5. Search the list of results. If you find that the vast majority of the item you want to sell is finishing as "Sold" then this may be a great product to sell. If you find that your item is a hot seller then that's even better. Check how many items are selling every day and every week. Your best bet is to find lots of items that are selling at the "Buy It Now" price because this makes it easier to calculate how much profit you'll make.

6. Login to DHGate and Alibaba and find someone that stocks the item you want to sell. Keep an eye on the minimum orders that these suppliers ask for. Some will require a minimum order of 10 - 1000 which won't be possible if you're just starting out. You want to find someone who allows you to order single items or, if you think the item will sell well, 10 at most.

TIP: If your supplier says it will take two days for the product to be sent to the customer then, on your sales page, state "four days for delivery". This way, if your supplier requires a minimum order, you have two days in which to sell the minimum order amount. If you feel it will take you more than two days then add more days for delivery. Be careful not to make it too long though because this'll definitely put some people off buying.

7. Contact the seller. Sometimes the price per unit won't be listed so

8. you'll have to get in touch to find out their pricings; you'll also need to make sure that they have the item in stock. A good supplier will be one that speaks good English (because this will make your life a LOT easier if anything goes wrong) and is open and clear about what they sell.

9. Now to create the listing:
   Search back through the listings that ended with the item being sold and copy and paste it into your new listing. Add any information from your supplier that's missing in the listing, your Terms and Conditions and refund policy, and you're good to go!

> **TOP TIP**: Do not "oversell" your product. If you're completely honest about what you're selling then you'll get fewer refund requests. This doesn't mean you should undersell yourself, just don't say anything that isn't 100% true.

10. Now that your listing is live, you'll have to answer any questions that you're sent, and sit back and watch as the bidders go crazy for what you're offering!

11. When the item sells you need to remember that PayPal will hold your funds for around 15 days, or until you get positive feedback.

12. Order the item(s) from the supplier(s) and request that they're sent to the addresses you've received from the buyers. Make sure you tell the supplier not to put the price anywhere on the packaging!

13. Rinse and repeat! If you find that your initial few items sell really well then attack it hard and put up a lot of the same item. He who dares wins!

Keep tabs on what sells and how much profit you make overall for each item. Eventually all items will stop selling as well. I'd recommend setting up a spreadsheet with the time and date that each of your items sold, along with a running total of the profit you've made. This will allow you to keep track of the rate at which these are selling, and to notice when sales are starting to slow down.

Aside from the initial investment in the first batch of stock you should not put any more of your own money into selling these. If you keep that mentality then you'll never lose money from drop shipping.

9. Important legalities for a drop shipping business.

- You must be a legitimately registered business in the UK and in the US you will need a State Tax ID number.

- In the UK (in May 2011), you do not need to register for VAT unless your income exceeds £70.000 (or $113.000). You can voluntarily register if you wish to claim VAT back.

- It is impossible for me to list all the legal requirements in all the countries that this book will be available in. Therefore check your official government sites or give a local accountant a call. A local accountant will probably answer some questions free of charge hoping that he will win your business once you are successful.

10. The key to success.

The first key to success and to sell lots of products is to find products that are not widely available and that have reasonably low competition. Examples: hard to find records, old tapes, XXXL sizes in clothing or shoes, parts for remote control helicopters, etc…

The second key to success is to apply good SEO as explained in this book. Remember the comparison with the high street shops? You must make sure that customers can see your shop if you are in the high street and your shop must be located in the busiest part of the high street. The same applies for your online shop. If customers cannot find your shop when typing in a keyword, you will not sell a lot and you won't survive just like a high street shop won't survive on the edge of the high street where nobody ever goes.

You can buy my book "Drop Shipping and eCommerce. What You Need and Where To Get It" on Amazon or as an ebook here: www.dropshippingandecommerce.com

Part 15. My Success Formula Explained

1. My success formula is simple.

To recap this book or my success formula in 13 steps:

1) Get your niche. You must spend a lot of time doing your research and investigating your competition and potential.
2) Get a domain name (keyword must be in the domain name) and hosting.
3) Find your long tail keywords to target and make one separate page on your site for each keyword. I suggest you make a minimum 10 pages.
4) Get decent content and lots of it.
5) Apply good SEO to your site and apply what Google likes.
6) Monetize your website so wherever people click, makes you money. Put a Clickbank ebook on your site and if the ebook sells, develop your own ebook.
7) Test all your links.
8) Publish your site.
9) Apply the free traffic methods.
10) Apply the paid traffic methods, if you can afford it.
11) Create your own eBook and put it on www.Clickbank.com with a one-page-sales wonder and let affiliates do the work for you. You can create your own ebook when you have sold a lot as an affiliate or if you find a gap in the market for an ebook, create the ebook immediately yourself.
12) Create your own hard copy book from your ebook and publish it.

Multiply – keep the template and find a different niche.

13) Create an e-commerce or drop shipping site and apply good SEO to the site and drive traffic to it.

OR: Only do steps 11) and 12): find a niche with potential, use relevant keywords and create an ebook for Clickbank and a hard copy book for Amazon. The affiliates will do the work for you to sell your ebook and Amazon will do the work for you to sell your hard copy book. Talking about auto pilot! ☺ Don't forget you will still have to do your niche and keyword research, which will be vitally important to succeed!!

2. My internet success formula rules

1) Start a niche *with potential.*

2) Don't put all your eggs in one basket. Have lots and lots of sites all in different niches or sub niches. I have sites in all of these niches: ice fishing, tarantulas, micro pigs, hypnosis, racing pigeons, recording studio, food processors, organic gardening, panic attacks, stand up comedy, cyclists, golf trolleys, bladeless fans, horses, iguana, discuss fish, wedding planning, cat training, green house, body building, magnetic therapy, hoarding, golfer's elbow, sports injuries, liquorice, nougat, gout, chickens, arthritis, lizards, cats, goats, osteophytes, peafowls, diabetes, music and more.

3) You must have multiple streams of income on your sites. I build all my websites so that visitors are likely to click on something that makes me money. Lots of little amounts add up very quickly. Some people will click on Adsense, some people will order a book from Amazon via your affiliate link, some people will buy your eBook and some people will fill in a CPA-offer from your site.

4) You must have different types of websites. On some of your sites you can concentrate on selling your own eBooks, on other sites you will put your Adsense very visibly because it is a high Pay Per Click pay out. I recommend that you also have some drop shipping/eCommerce sites as they make up a large part of my income.

5) Create your own products and let an army of affiliates sell for you. On some of my websites I focus on selling my own eBook. The home page for selling my eBook is never my sales page. I put a picture from my book on the page and once people click on the picture, they will see the sales page. If I put the sales page my home page, Google would not like my site and as you know by now, you need good content and decent SEO on your site to rank.

6) You must put your own eBook on Clickbank and other affiliate networks and let affiliates do the work for you. In this case you can make the sales page a One-Page-Wonder Sales Page.

7) You must have an opt-in box on each site. You can always find some PLR stuff to give away. Remember: a buyer is a buyer is a buyer AND the money is indeed in the list. For some of my websites, I don't have an opt-in box in case I can't find many products to sell as an affiliate.

> **Don't forget: A winner is a loser who kept trying.**

3. My step-by-step guide for sites and ebooks/books.

You can make it your step-by-step action plan. I have spoken about all the different steps in this book but not on great detail for some of them. I suggest that you search the internet for tutorials on the steps that you do not completely understand or you can watch the video tutorials listed later.

My steps for you to copy:

1. Find a niche with my method described in this book

2. Buy a domain name with the niche-keyword in it

3. Put content on your site with one of the methods described in this book

4. Put an opt-in box on each page of the site

5. Monetise the site with CPA offers, Adsense, Amazon, a Clickbank eBook and any other good affiliate products that you can find. I will not write my own book to start with, as I want to see first if the book is selling after my site ranks in Google.

6. Put all the necessary items like contact details, privacy policy and so on, on your site

7. Publish the site to the search engines

8. Design a Squidoo lens

9. Spend a lot of time in article marketing

10. Drive free traffic to your site with several of the methods described in this book

11. Try some paid traffic

12. Create follow up emails for the next six months in www.aweber.com with affiliate links to email to your opt-ins

Once the Clickbank eBook that I have put on my site sells an average of ten per month, I will either write my own eBook or outsource the writing of the book, provided the competition is not too big on Clickbank and on Amazon. The steps below are what I apply when I outsource the writing of the book.

13. Write a job description and put it on Elance www.elance.com

14. Study the providers on Elance who quote for the job and select a provider

15. Put the funds in Escrow on Elance

16. When the eBook is finished you can either use the cover that the Elance provider has made or outsource the cover. Most Elance writers are not designers therefore sometimes they supply a very simple cover. A cover sells a book (as a hard copy book) therefore the cover needs to look professional and attractive

17. Replace the Clickbank eBook on your site with your own eBook as that will earn you more money

Now that I have my own eBook I will design a sales page for it and put it on Clickbank and other comparable sites and let affiliates sell for me. Here are the steps I follow to do this:

18. Buy a domain name with the keyword in it for my sales pitch page for my eBook

19. Write the text for a sales page or outsource it on Elance

20. Make an affiliate page on the Clickbank sales page site

21. Put the product on Clickbank as a vendor

22. Other affiliates will drive traffic to your sales page and all you need to do is check your Clickbank account to see how much you've earned

Now that I have my own eBook I also sell it as a hard copy book and lots of different book formats. To find out more, visit www.worldwideselfpublishing.com.

Duplicate all the above again and again in different niches and in 1 year you could have a reasonable income on autopilot.

Important notes that apply to all the spreadsheet screenshots below:

- The total of all the figures can vary. I just want to give you some rough idea on costings and potential income per site. It would be an endless list of spreadsheets if I were to show every variable.

- The income figures per site are estimated rather low but are realistic. I am sure that people will be able to create more income per site than the figures shown. The income depends on how many visitors you drive to your site using the free (or paid) traffic techniques discussed in this book. If nobody ever gets to see your site, the income will be zero.

- All income figures shown are including VAT and all expenses are shown excluding VAT. It is of course your responsibility to reclaim the VAT or to pay taxes on all your income and to take care of the VAT, if you are VAT registered, in whatever way it applies in your country.

- Clickbank commissions need to be taken off the Clickbank sales totals. These are only small amounts. The spreadsheets are complicated enough so I have decided not to show these separately.

4. How much money does it all cost?

The spreadsheet below shows how much all the different steps above (1 to 22) will cost you. The numbers that are *not* listed in the spreadsheet below and that are listed in the step-by-step action plan are steps that will not cost you any money. I have skipped the paid traffic step as obviously it is up to you how much money you want to spend on paid traffic. The number in the picture below refers to the number in the step-by-step guide.

Number	Description	Price $	Price £
1	Find a Niche with Market Samurai	$97.00	£59.17
2	Buy domain name.com & hosting go daddy $19/year	$1.58	£0.96
12	Autoresponder www.aweber.com = monthly fee	$19.00	£11.59
13	Elance job to write an ebook (100 pages)	$600.00	£366.00
18	Buy domain name.com for sales page ebook	$1.58	£0.96
19	Elance job to write sales page for ebook	$600.00	£366.00
21	Put the sales page domain on Clickbank as a Vendor	$49.95	£30.47
	Get an ISBN number New Publisher Fee	$42.00	£25.62
	Get an ISBN number for hard copy book	$9.00	£5.49
	Set up book with publisher	$42.00	£25.62
	Get an ISBN number for eBook	$9.00	£5.49
	Set up ebook with publisher	$21.00	£12.81
Total		1492.11	£910.19

The items listed above underneath the Number 21 row are explained in more detail in my Self Publishing Video Tutorials.

The total cost is $1492.11 (£910.19). If you would do all the work yourself, the total would be $292 ($1492.11 minus $1200) or £162.00 (£910.19 minus £748) as I have calculated $1200 (£748) outsourcing fees in the total price.

Remarks on the spreadsheet shown above:

- .co.uk domain names are cheaper than .com ones

- Market Samurai is a one-off fee

5. When will you get your money back?

Okay now you have some idea of the costings involved, you will probably want to know how quickly you will get your money back. I have assumed that it will take you three months to build your very first website (if you can do it full time) from your initial research to your site being live. Realistically it will take you three months as you will have to do a lot of reading, a lot of research and as everything you do will be new to you, it will take you a long time. Your second website will probably be done in one month but I am not the type that promises an easy ride, I am very realistic.

Here are some spreadsheets showing estimated income figures:

				Monthly sales	
Month	Description	$	Qty.	Total $	Total £
3	Clickbank Ebook sales per month=60%	$17.98	7	$125.86	£76.77
3	Amazon Commission from website 3%	$150.00	3%	$4.50	£2.75
3	Adsense Commission from website	$0.35	50	$17.50	£10.68
3	CPA commission from website	$5.50	10	$55.00	£33.55
3	Other afilate commission from website	$200.00	7%	$14.00	£8.54
	Total month 3 when site is finished			**$216.86**	**£148.08**
5	Affiliate sales from Clickbank sales page=30%	$8.98	30	$269.40	£164.33
6	Hard Copy Book sales lightingsource	$8.90	20	$178.00	£108.58
6	Ebook sales lightingsource	$8.50	10	$85.00	£51.85

During month 4, 5 and 6, while you are working on your Clickbank sales page for your ebook and whilst you are working to get your hard copy book published, your sales from your website will continue to come in so I am adding these to the total :

Month	Description	$	Qty.	Total $	Total £
4	Month 4 same income as month 3			$216.86	£148.08
5	Month 5 same income as month 4			$216.86	£148.08
6	Month 6 same income as month 5			$216.86	£132.28

During month 5 and 6 you will also start to create sales from your email marketing to your opt-ins. Month 6 shows more income then month 5 as your opt-in list should grow every month.

Month	Description	$	Qty.	Total $	Total £
5	Email marketing sales from opt-ins	$8.98	10	$89.80	£54.78
6	Email marketing sales from opt-ins	$8.98	20	$179.60	£109.56

Income after 6 months :				$1,669.24	£1,018.24

Conclusion:

If you write the eBook and the sales page for your eBook yourself, or if you decide not to make an eBook and hard copy book, you will have your money back after approximately one month. The total cost for setting it all up was $292 (£162) and the total income is $216.86 (£132.28).

To outsource the eBook and sales page the total cost was $1492.11 (£910.19) and the total income after six months is $1669.24 (£1018.24). This means that after six months you will have earned your money back. All sales created after 6 months will be pure profit as all expenses made have been paid back. The only expenses you will have are monthly fees like www.aweber.com and any other subscriptions you might have.

How many businesses do you know that get their original investment back after six months and where all income after that is pure profit? None is probably your answer. That is one of the reasons why IM is such a great business.

Remarks on the income spreadsheet shown above:

- **Clickbank eBook sales per month = 60%** : I have assumed that the price of the Clickbank eBook that you are selling on your site is $29.95 and that you are earning 60% commission, making your commission $17.98. I have assumed that you only sell seven eBooks per month but realistically you can sell a lot more.

- **Amazon commission from website 3 %** : I have assumed that the total Amazon sales created via your website is $150 and that your Amazon commission as an associate is 3%. You would usually earn more commission, even up to 8.5% but I have put the sales very low and the commission very low.

- **Adsense commission from website:** Earnings are, again, estimated rather low because most Adsense keywords will pay out more than $0.35 and it is very likely that you will receive more Adsense clicks via your site.

- **CPA commission from website**: I have assumed that you will earn $5.50 per CPA (Cost Per Action) and that 10 people have earned you money. As you can guess, $5.50 for a CPA offer is not very high and only 10 people taking action per month is estimated very low.

- **Other affiliate commission from website:** This income refers to whatever other money making links you have put on your site from affiliate networks. For a website on relaxation, you could put affiliate links to shops that sell relaxing candles.

- **Affiliate sales from Clickbank sales page:** 30% : This income starts on month five as it takes several weeks once you have your own website ready, to have an eBook written and a sales page written resulting in your own Clickbank-ready product. The commission is now set as 30% because you are now the vendor of the product and I have assumed that you will give 70% commission to your affiliates. I have assumed that the selling price for the eBook on Clickbank is $29.95 which is a realistic price for a 100-page eBook. You can see although you are earning a lot less per sale, this figure is the highest income. ***The affiliates will be doing the work for you.*** I have assumed that you will get five affiliates each selling six eBooks per month. The total of sales created from your Clickbank sales page will probably be much higher.

- **Hard copy book sales Lighting Source** : The earnings per book totally depend on how much margin you give to the retailers (book shops) that will be selling your book. This is not an easy decision. The more margin you give them, the less you earn but on the other hand the less margin you give them the less they earn, so they might not "push" the sale of the book. You will need to give between 35% and 60% profit margin to the retailer. You must make calculated business decisions to do this. There is not rule therefore I cannot give you one. I have assumed that your selling price for your book is $16.99 and your net profit per book is $8.90 after having paid Lighting Source its commission. The estimated sale quantity of 20 is *extremely* low.

- **Ebook sales Lighting Source**: Low estimate once again as you will probably sell a lot more eBooks per month. Profit margins for eBook retailers and for Lighting Source are higher than for hard copy books. I have set the selling price for the eBook (on eBook selling sites) as $16.99.

- **More earnings with your own eBook.** After month five when your own eBook is finished, you would replace the Clickbank eBook that you have on your site with your own eBook. You would earn the full 100% of the sale of your own eBook (less Clickbank commissions) instead of 60% as an affiliate therefore the total income for the first row "Clickbank Ebook sales per month" should be higher in month 5 and 6. But in order to show that, I would have to make the spreadsheets even more complicated!

How many visitors do you need to your site to get this level of income?

Now that is a really difficult question to answer because there are several factors that will influence if people will buy from your site or not. If your site looks a mess or does not have any decent content on it or does not load properly, people are unlikely to buy from you.

Well:

- Assuming that you have done your niche and keyword research right

- Assuming that you have followed all the rules that I have discussed in this book and consequently you have a pleasing looking and informative site

- Assuming that all your money-making links are working

- Assuming that the majority of your visitors are *targeted* customers

- Assuming that you spend a lot of time in sending traffic to your site and building backlinks

- Assuming that you are not selling ice fishing tents to people living in the Sahara ☺

With the above assumptions in mind, you should be able to get between 1500 and 4000 unique visitors per month (between 66 and 133 visitors per day) and chances are that your income will be over $500 per month.

Getting between 2000 and 4000 visitors per month to your site in today's competitive IM environment is not easy and would be an excellent achievement for a newbie. Here is a screenshot from one of my sites showing 9629 visitors between September 3 and January 13 which is 5 months = 1925 visitors per month. My site was finished end of August which was when I started getting backlinks and traffic to my site. This shows that you can get 1925 (in my case) visitors per month to your site after only five months of hard work. If all goes well and you keep on working on the site, the visitors will soon double.

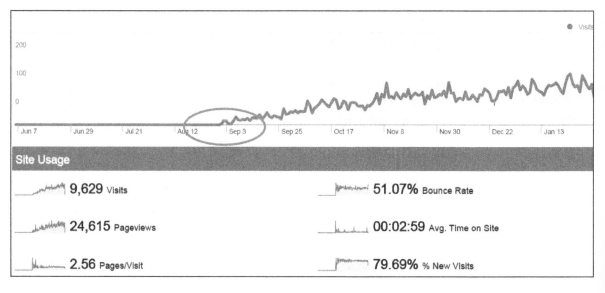

Never believe companies or websites that promise you 50,000 visitors per month. To get between 5000 and 10,000 *targeted* visitors to your site is *extremely* difficult and you can only achieve that if you focus on one site for at least 6 to 8 months. Yes sure, you might get 100,000 visitors to your site an automated system but these visitors will not be targeted, so won't buy anything.

I aim to get between 1500 and 4000 visitors per month *every* month to each of my sites. Don't forget that I recommend untapped niches with long tail keywords for a beginner, so the worldwide searches per month for my keyword might only be 35,000. Sure you could get over 100,000 visitors per month to one site if you are extremely clever in building sites and sending traffic and if your niche is in the ones that I do *not* recommend e.g. insurance, mortgages and so on.

I do not think you have a chance against the "big boys". A lot of people/companies who show you screenshots of traffic, like 600,000 per month and more, have spent thousands and thousands of pounds in non-targeted automated traffic just to show you a screenshot with those figures. Why do you think that most of the time they will not show you their Traffic Sources overview (like the one I show below from my site)? Could it be because none of their traffic comes from the search engines? I wonder. Massive companies might get massive amounts of traffic but the average "small" site won't.

You can see on my Google Analytics screenshot below that the vast majority of visitors come from search engines (63.54%). The referring sites traffic is mostly from article marketing and Squidoo.

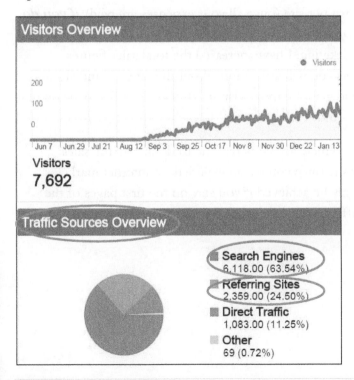

This screenshot from My Google Analytics shows that the average time on my site is almost three minutes, which is good.

6. How much money can you realistically earn per site per month?

Here is an overview of what you can earn per site (once all your expenses are paid) *if you do not have your own eBook or hard copy book*. The income is purely created from your money-making links and from email marketing. I have increased the total sales figures compared to the previous spreadsheet as you will learn more about the internet and about driving traffic to your site, so you should get a lot more visitors after six months than you did during the third month. More visitors = more sales.

Don't forget that these estimates are extremely low. It is realistic to double all the sales figures, earning over $1000 (£623) per site once you are an experienced internet marketer. However, these levels of income can only be achieved if you stay on the first pages of the search engines, unless you use paid traffic which consequently will result in less profit.

Description	$	Qty.	Total $	Total £
Clickbank Ebook sales per month=60%	$17.98	10	$179.80	£109.68
Amazon Commission from website 3%	$250.00	3%	$7.50	£4.58
Adsense Commission from website	$0.35	50	$17.50	£10.68
CPA commission from website	$5.50	20	$110.00	£67.10
Other affilate commission from website	$200.00	7%	$14.00	£8.54
Email marketing sales from opt-ins	$8.98	20	$179.60	£109.56
Total income per month for 1 site no ebook or book			**$508.40**	**£310.12**

Here is an overview of what you can earn per site if you have your own eBook and *if you have your own hard copy book to sell.* Note that the first row of figures is now 100% as you now have your own eBook on your own site, which means you do not have to pay any affiliate commission and all the profit is yours. These sales exclude any sales from drop shipping.

Description	$	Qty.	Total $	Total £
Clickbank Ebook sales per month=100%	$29.95	7	$209.65	£127.89
Amazon Commission from website 3%	$250.00	3%	$7.50	£4.58
Adsense Commission from website	$0.35	50	$17.50	£10.68
CPA commission from website	$5.50	20	$110.00	£67.10
Other affilate commission from website	$200.00	7%	$14.00	£8.54
Affiliate sales from Clickbank sales page=30%	$8.98	30	$269.40	£164.33
Hard Copy Book sales lightingsource	$8.90	20	$178.00	£108.58
Ebook sales lightingsource	$8.50	10	$85.00	£51.85
Email marketing sales from opt-ins	$8.98	20	$179.60	£109.56
Total income per month for 1 site + own ebook + own book			**$1,070.65**	**£653.10**

I strongly recommend that you get your own sales page with an eBook and put it on Clickbank as a vendor as that represents most sales per month in the Monthly Sales spreadsheet above. All those sales were created by other affiliates who are doing the hard work getting traffic to your site. Other people making websites will be looking for Clickbank products to put on their site. People who are doing article marketing will be looking for Clickbank affiliate links to put in their article.

> **You have to remember: become a vendor on Clickbank as soon as you can by having your own sales page with your own eBook. That's where the real "lazy" money is. Yeah, that's right. I can say towards the end of this book that you can be lazy and earn money on autopilot once you know how to make money on the internet. But first, there's a lot of work to be done.**

Want proof that the sort of income on the above screenshots can be achieved? Below are some income screenshots.

Don't forget this sort of income will only be possible after having worked really hard for several years. I just want to show you what sort of income you could have after years of hard work. Lots of little amounts add up to one large amount, which is exactly how I earn money.

One Adsense account showing earnings of $2709.81 or £1654.71 for December. Remember that you only need to sign up once with Adsense and you can use the same Adsense account for all your sites. The screenshot below does not represent earnings from one website.

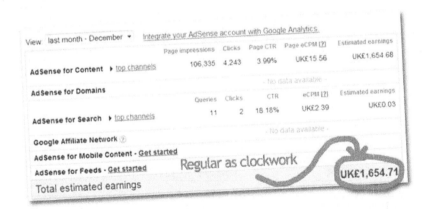

One Amazon account showing total earnings of $2105.68 or £1292.26 for November 2010: You can also use the same Amazon associate account for different sites.

Once Clickbank account showing a total income of $3593.38 or £2205.62 from two weeks sales: 3 December to 17 December. This is $7186.56 or £4411.24 per month. **One** Clickbank account can be used for different websites. So the sales from 20 different ebook can all be together in one Clickbank account. As a vendor I usually open a different Clickbank account for each product as I prefer it that way.

I do however use the same Clickbank account for all my sales as an affiliate. I can see where the sales are coming from with my TID (Tracking ID).

Daily Sales Snaps		
Fri	Dec 17	$290.64
Thu	Dec 16	$320.15
Wed	Dec 15	$210.20
Tue	Dec 14	$99.60
Mon	Dec 13	$358.60
Sun	Dec 12	$189.63
Sat	Dec 11	$320.50
Fri	Dec 10	**$125.88**
Thu	Dec 09	$420.99
Wed	Dec 08	$75.80
Tue	Dec 07	$89.66
Mon	Dec 06	$358.74
Sun	Dec 05	$89.60
Sat	Dec 04	$189.50
Fri	Dec 03	**$453.79**

Another Clickbank account showing $2654.73 or £1629.47 in sales during October 2010.

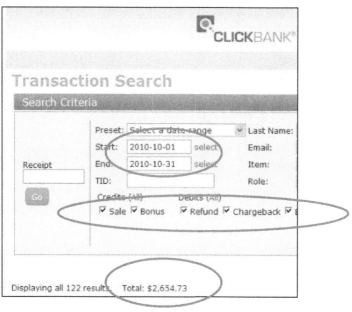

One PayPal account showing $628.99 or £385.93 income during 12 days, which would be $1572.47 or £964.82 per month:

Date	Type	Name/Email	Payment status	Details	Order status/Actions	Gross	Fee	Net amount
22 Mar 2011	Payment From		Completed	Details	Print postage label ▼	£13.84	-£0.67	£13.17 GBP
22 Mar 2011	Payment From		Completed	Details	Print postage label ▼	£27.68	-£1.28	£26.40 GBP
19 Mar 2011	Payment From		Completed	Details	Print postage label ▼	£17.02	-£0.78	£16.24 GBP
17 Mar 2011	Payment From		Completed	Details	Print postage label ▼	£35.34	-£1.40	£33.94 GBP
17 Mar 2011	Payment From		Completed	Details	Print postage label ▼	£10.99	-£0.57	£10.42 GBP
17 Mar 2011	Payment From		Completed	Details	Print postage label ▼	£23.98	-£1.02	£22.96 GBP
16 Mar 2011	Payment From		Completed	Details	Print postage label ▼	£24.28	-£1.03	£23.25 GBP
16 Mar 2011	Payment From		Completed	Details	Print postage label ▼	£22.84	-£0.98	£21.86 GBP
16 Mar 2011	Payment From		Completed	Details	Print postage label ▼	£16.99	-£0.78	£16.21 GBP
16 Mar 2011	Payment From		Completed	Details	Print postage label ▼	£21.49	-£0.93	£20.56 GBP
14 Mar 2011	Payment From		Completed	Details	Print postage label ▼	£11.49	-£0.59	£10.90 GBP
12 Mar 2011	Payment From		Completed	Details	Print postage label ▼	£39.62	-£1.55	£38.07 GBP
11 Mar 2011	Payment From		Completed	Details	Print postage label ▼	£23.64	-£1.00	£22.64 GBP
10 Mar 2011	Payment From		Completed	Details	Print postage label ▼	£39.17	-£1.53	£37.64 GBP
10 Mar 2011	Payment From		Completed	Details	Print postage label ▼	£39.20	-£1.53	£37.67 GBP
9 Mar 2011	Payment From		Completed	Details	Print postage label ▼	£35.40	-£1.40	£34.00 GBP

One of my Publishing accounts showing $1080 or £665.28 from one month's sales (MTD means Month To Date).

		Lightning Source United Kingdom Operating Unit - GBP Transations Publisher POD Compensation Report for Internet Marketing Business For Period of CUSTOM			Run Date: 02/12/2010 Period: 02/10/2010 To 31/12/2010 Page: Summary			
		This report includes an open period, the amounts are not final.						
	(All transactions are liable to VAT at 0%)							
Summary Totals	Quantity	Net Sales	Print Charge	Setup Recovery	Other	Net Pub Comp	Rec Rem
Total Sales							
MTD	112	922.88	-257.60	0.00	0.00	665.28	

The total of all the above income screenshots is $12,388.60 or £7578.66 per month based on the average Clickbank sales total.

Clickbank account showing high monthly income of $7,186.56 or £4,411.24, as shown on first Clickbank screenshot.

Income Source	$ Per Month	£ Per Month
Adsense	$2,709.81	£1,654.71
Amazon	$2,105.68	£1,292.26
Clickbank	$7,186.56	£4,411.24
Paypal	$1,572.47	£964.82
Lightingsource	$1,080.00	£665.28
Total	$14,654.52	£8,988.31

Clickbank account showing "low" monthly income of $2654.73 or £1629.47 : as shown on second Clickbank screenshot.

Income Source	$ Per Month	£ Per Month
Adsense	$2,709.81	£1,654.71
Amazon	$2,105.68	£1,292.26
Clickbank	$2,654.73	£1,629.47
Paypal	$1,572.47	£964.82
Lightingsource	$1,080.00	£665.28
Total	$10,122.69	£6,206.54

Clickbank account showing average monthly income of $4920.64 or £3001.59 : based on the two Clickbank screenshots.

Income Source	$ Per Month	£ Per Month
Adsense	$2,709.81	£1,654.71
Amazon	$2,105.68	£1,292.26
Clickbank	$4,920.64	£3,001.59
Paypal	$1,572.47	£964.82
Lightingsource	$1,080.00	£665.28
Total	$12,388.60	£7,578.66

I am going to include some of my Commerce and/or drop shipping accounts just to show you what the potential earnings are (after many years of hard work). These screenshots are from my debit/credit card processing account www.streamline.com.

The reason I am not including these eCommerce sales screenshots in the total above is because I have not included e-commerce sales in my step-by-step guide.

A good day of ecommerce sales:

24 Nov 2010	Pur	Accepted	707.66 GBP	58590969658262000384	VP
24 Nov 2010	Pur	Accepted	1,610.98 GBP	58590969658262000383	VP
24 Nov 2010	Pur	Accepted	358.02 GBP	58590969658262000376	VP
24 Nov 2010	Pur	Accepted	185.44 GBP	58590969658262000379	DE
24 Nov 2010	Pur	Accepted	50.09 GBP	58590969658262000387	DE
24 Nov 2010	Pur	Accepted	579.91 GBP	58590969658262000377	DE
24 Nov 2010	Pur	Accepted	778.25 GBP	58590969658262000382	DE
25 Nov 2010	Pur	Accepted	633.41 GBP	58590969658262000402	DE
25 Nov 2010	Pur	Accepted	126.93 GBP		
25 Nov 2010	Pur	Accepted	207.68 GBP		
25 Nov 2010	Pur	Accepted	88.30 GBP		
25 Nov 2010	Pur	Accepted	197.98 GBP		
25 Nov 2010	Pur	Accepted	88.39 GBP		
25 Nov 2010	Pur	Accepted	39.64 GBP		

On 24th November, daily total sales:

$10,615!

(£6,804)

A "bad" day of ecommerce sales:

17 Nov 2010	Pur	Accepted	28.20 GBP	585909696582620002	
17 Nov 2010	Pur	Accepted	11.94 GBP	585909696582620002	
17 Nov 2010	Pur	Accepted	296.04 GBP	585909696582620002	
17 Nov 2010	Pur	Accepted	93.95 GBP	585909696582620002	
17 Nov 2010	Pur	Accepted	186.02 GBP	585909696582620002	
17 Nov 2010	Pur	Accepted	11.74 GBP	585909696582620002	
17 Nov 2010	Pur	Accepted	185.98 GBP	585909696582620002	
17 Nov 2010	Pur	Accepted	246.48 GBP		2
17 Nov 2010	Pur	Accepted	32.44 GBP		2
17 Nov 2010	Pur	Accepted	28.19 GBP		2
18 Nov 2010	Pur	Accepted	79.67 GBP		3
18 Nov 2010	Pur	Accepted	116.10 GBP		2
18 Nov 2010	Pur	Accepted	191.47 GBP		3
18 Nov 2010	Pur	Accepted	465.11 GBP	585909696582620003	

On 17th November, daily total sales:

$2,343

(£1,502)
(This was a bad day)

The average of the above two Streamline screenshots is $6479.00 (£4039) per day. The payments from Streamline are only processed on weekdays by my staff as they do not work during the weekends. The amount of $129,580(£79.043) in the next spreadsheet is calculated as follows:

$ 6479 per day average (£4039)

x 240 days per year (365 days – 104 days for weekends – 21 days as holidays leaves 240 working days per year)

Equals $1,554,960 (£975.000) per year

This is $129,580.00 (£79043) per month.

Income Source	$ Per Month	£ Per Month
Adsense	$2,709.81	£1,654.71
Amazon	$2,105.68	£1,292.26
Clickbank	$4,920.64	£3,001.59
Paypal	$1,572.47	£964.82
Lightingsource	$1,080.00	£665.28
Total excl. ecommerce	$12,388.60	£7,578.66
e-commerce sales	$129,580.00	£79,043.80
Total incl. ecommerce	$141,968.60	£86,622.46

Total per year	$1,703,623.20	£1,039,469.52

That is over $1,700.000 per year created from multiple streams of income.

Important: Total income does not mean total profit. There is a big difference! VAT needs to be deducted where applicable and all expenses need to be deducted from the earnings in order to calculate the taxable profit. On top of that taxes need to be paid, after which your net profits can be calculated.

---

7. Multiply. It's a game of numbers

With these Internet Success Formula rules, it is very realistic to earn $508.00 per site (without your own eBook or hard copy book and without eCommerce sales), per month. This is, *as an average,* as explained in this screenshot, shown earlier:

Description	$	Qty.	Total $	Total £
Clickbank Ebook sales per month=60%	$17.98	10	$179.80	£109.68
Amazon Commission from website 3%	$250.00	3%	$7.50	£4.58
Adsense Commission from website	$0.35	50	$17.50	£10.68
CPA commission from website	$5.50	20	$110.00	£67.10
Other affilate commission from website	$200.00	7%	$14.00	£8.54
Email marketing sales from opt-ins	$8.98	20	$179.60	£109.56
Total income per month for 1 site no ebook or book			**$508.40**	**£310.12**

Multiply your system in different niches and build several websites. This is what I have been doing very successfully. From the screenshot below you can see that lots of little earnings can make you a large amount of money. These shots are based on my step by step guide only excluding any eCommerce/drop shipping sales.

Income per month for 100 sites, from monetized website only, without your own ebook and without your own hard copy book.

Income Per Month 1 Site	Income Per Year 1 Site	Nr. Of Sites	Total Income Year $	Total Income Year £
$508.40	$6,100.80	5	$30,504.00	£18,607.44
$508.40	$6,100.80	10	$61,008.00	£37,214.88
$508.40	$6,100.80	20	$122,016.00	£74,429.76
$508.40	$6,100.80	50	$305,040.00	£186,074.40
$508.40	$6,100.80	100	$610,080.00	£372,148.80

With your own eBook and your own book and without any eCommerce sales, it is realistic to earn $1,070.65 per site, as explained in this screenshot, shown earlier:

Description	$	Qty.	Total $	Total £
Clickbank Ebook sales per month=100%	$29.95	7	$209.65	£127.89
Amazon Commission from website 3%	$250.00	3%	$7.50	£4.58
Adsense Commission from website	$0.35	50	$17.50	£10.68
CPA commission from website	$5.50	20	$110.00	£67.10
Other affilate commission from website	$200.00	7%	$14.00	£8.54
Affiliate sales from Clickbank sales page=30%	$8.98	30	$269.40	£164.33
Hard Copy Book sales lightingsource	$8.90	20	$178.00	£108.58
Ebook sales lightingsource	$8.50	10	$85.00	£51.85
Email marketing sales from opt-ins	$8.98	20	$179.60	£109.56

Total income per month for 1 site + own ebook + own book	**$1,070.65**	**£653.10**

Income per month for 100 sites from monetized website AND from your own ebook and your own hard copy book.

Income Per Month 1 Site	Income Per Year 1 Site	Nr. Of Sites	Total Income Year $	Total Income Year £
$1,070.65	$12,847.80	5	$64,239.00	£39,185.79
$1,070.65	$12,847.80	10	$128,478.00	£78,371.58
$1,070.65	$12,847.80	20	$256,956.00	£156,743.16
$1,070.65	$12,847.80	50	$642,390.00	£391,857.90
$1,070.65	$12,847.80	100	$1,284,780.00	£783,715.80

Note: takings per site are based on average. Some sites might create $1200 per month and others might only create $25 per month.

With "only" ten sites, you can create an income of $128,478 per year if you choose to create your own eBook and your own hard copy book, and $61,008 per year without eBook or book.

So what are you waiting for? Find yourself some profitable niches and start working.

If you have a job and can only work on your site in the evenings or a few hours per week, you can still build one site per month, once you are experienced.

Once you have 15 to 20 sites you are going to need help and I suggest you find a good VA (Virtual Assistant outsourcer) or take on an employee to expand your internet business.

If you follow all the steps correctly there is a very good chance that you will earn money BUT I never said it was going to be easy. You will have to work at it but it will be worth it.

You need to be confident that you can do it; you need to have a positive attitude towards it. You do not need to be experienced; you just need to be confident.

The one with confidence, not experience, is the one followed in the battle.

Never believe that making money on the internet is easy because it isn't. Once you know how to make money with one site, you will soon want to develop more sites.

Rome was not built in a day and your internet empire won't be ready in a short period of time. If you expect to be rich in a few months time, you will fail. You need to plan how you are going to tackle this, you need to plan when to build your first site and when to build your second site. You need to set yourself a realistic goal.

So from now on, if you are serious about starting to earn on the internet, don't arrive in front of your computer without a "to do" list.

Fail to plan and plan to fail.

A goal without a deadline is nothing more than a wish.

8. How I decide if there is potential for an eBook or book?

March 2013 : I have just launched my new product www.WorldwideSelfPublishing.com which explains in video tutorials from A to Z how to self publish and earn money from niche books.

Here are all the things that I analyse in order to decide if I think an eBook/hard copy book will sell well or not. I sometimes outsource the writing of an eBook/book and outsource the design of the sales page for Clickbank without ever building a website around the niche. The Clickbank Affiliates, Amazon and other book shops will do the work for me and sell the product.

A friend told me recently that she wanted to get rid of mice in her house and did not know how. Being an internet marketer, the first thing that goes through my mind is: "Maybe there is potential for an eBook about getting rid of mice". These are the steps that I research before deciding if there is a market for an eBook on mice/getting rid of mice.

1) Investigate total monthly searches. I type in the keywords "mice" and "get rid of mice" in GoogleKeyword Planner : https://www.adwords.google.co.uk . Then I make sure "locations all" and "Languages English" is ticked as our book will be written in English, so it must be suitable for the online English market. Make sure that "exact" is ticked in Keyword Tool.

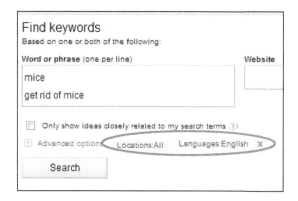

I have selected the keywords that relate to "how to get rid of mice" and the spreadsheet below shows that the total searches is 42,290 per month. That is a good amount of searches. I always look for searches between 35,000 and 100,000 in order to take my investigation to step two. Therefore if the keyword total was 10,000 I would not investigate the next step but would look for a different keyword.

Keyword how to get rid of mice	Global Monthly Searches
[how to get rid of mice]	9900
[mice in house]	4400
[getting rid of mice]	3600
[how to get rid of mice in your house]	2900
[get rid of mice]	2400
[mice infestation]	1600
[best way to get rid of mice]	1300
[mice repellent]	1300
[mice droppings]	880
[mice in walls]	880
[how to catch mice]	720
[catching mice]	720
[mice cages]	720
[how to keep mice out of your house]	590
[mice in attic]	590
[getting rid of mice in house]	590
[mice in the house]	480
[how to get rid of mice naturally]	480
[how to get rid of mice in the house]	390
[mice deterrent]	390
[how to breed mice]	390
[how to get rid of mice in the walls]	390
[get rid of mice in home]	320
[natural mice repellent]	320
[how do i get rid of mice]	320
[mice in the attic]	320
[mice infestation in house]	320
[how do mice get in houses]	260
[get rid of mice in house]	260
[how do you get rid of mice]	260
[exterminating mice]	260
[how to repel mice]	260
[exterminator mice]	260
[how many mice are in my house]	260
[trapping mice]	260
[get rid mice]	260
[how to get rid of house mice]	210
[best way to catch mice]	210
[how to get rid of mice in apartment]	210

[what attracts mice]	210
[best way to get rid of mice in the house]	210
[getting rid of mice in the home]	210
[gestation period for mice]	210
[mice and mouse]	210
[mice in the walls]	210
[how to catch mice in your house]	170
[catching mice in the house]	170
[how to get rid of mice in house]	170
[mice repeller]	170
[how to trap mice]	170
Total exact searches per month	**42290**

I do **not** analyse the keyword in Market Samurai as I do not want to design a website on getting rid of mice, I only want to make a Clickbank ready product and a hard copy book on mice. The person who will design the website should study the potential of ranking in Google and they will come and find your eBook on www.Clickbank.com.

2) Investigate Clickbank potential. I go to www.Clickbank.com and type in the keyword "mice" and "how to get rid of mice". Result are in the screenshots: no products on mice available, as nothing is shown. Another successful step. If there is a vendor on Clickbank with our keyword, he has not done a good job!

3) Investigate Amazon potential I go to www.amazon.com . You can also have a look at www.amazon.co.uk (or whatever country you are in) but if amazon.com looks good I do not investigate any further because the American market is large.

I type in the keyword "get rid of mice" under books and surprisingly only 6 books are shown – I expected this to be a lot more - and out of those six most are not directly related to my keyword. The one that is, is dated 2008. People prefer to buy books from more recent years.

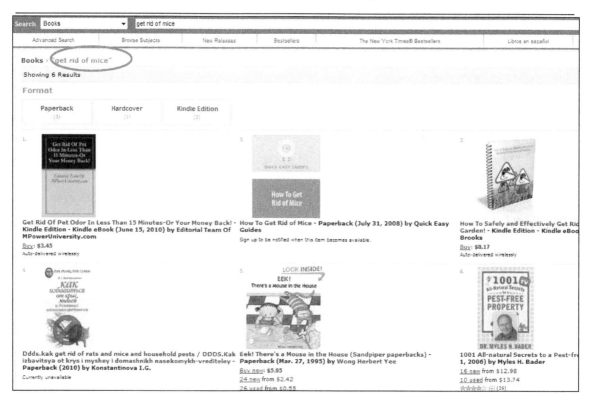

I type in "mice" in Amazon and the first book is dated 2001. Most of the books on the 10 first pages are children's books. Some people say that this is not good because there are not a lot of books about mice on Amazon, so there is no market. I look at it differently: if there is no book on Amazon and there are a lot of monthly searches, I call it potential. I might be proven wrong when my book is published and it does not sell but hey, positive thinking. No try, no win. I realise that you can only say that if you have $1000 / £1000 or more disposable income. So I recommend that you double and triple check everything that you have learned and take a decision, go with your gut feeling.

Part 15. My Success Formula Explained

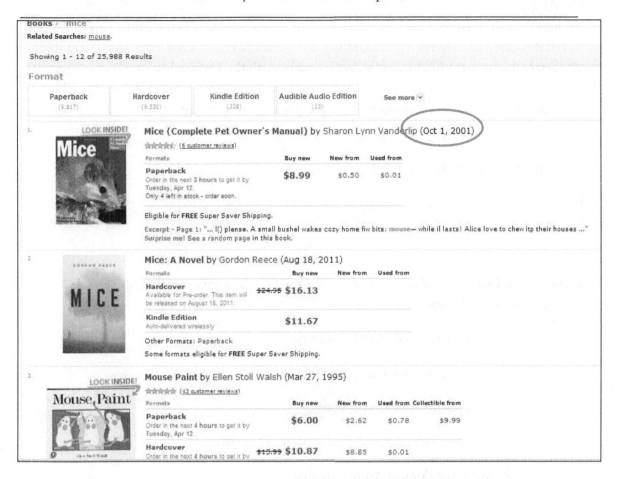

4) Google both keywords and open every site on the first ten pages. I analyse if my eBook would fit on the websites that I open. Elsewhere in this book I say that people do not look past the first three pages in Google. But websites that are on page 10 today could be on page one tomorrow, so they are all potential customers for my book. I decide that there is potential. You can send these websites an email when your eBook/book is finished to suggest they sell your book as an affiliate. This step in my investigation is the least decisive factor, as lots of affiliates will sell the book without having their own website (e.g. article marketing, social marketing) or will get traffic with paid methods.

5) Research domain name potential for your sales letter on Clickbank.

Remember you must try to get keywords in your domain name if you want to rank in Google but in this case, we only need a domain name for our Clickbank sales letter so it is not that important. However, I have found a domain name with the keywords: www.waystogetridofmice.com for an eBook on how to get rid of mice. I did not buy the domain name as I am not looking for new products at the moment.

Order or Transfer a Domain

✓ Congratulations! The domain name is currently available.

Domain name : waystogetridofmice.com

Conclusion: I have scored five out of five for my five steps investigation, so a new eBook/book could be born.

1) Investigate total monthly searches

2) Investigate Clickbank potential

3) Investigate Amazon potential

4) Google both keywords and analyse other sites

5) Research domain name potential

The extra advantage for the "get rid of mice" keyword is that it is a "need" or "solution" keyword. People who type in the keyword clearly have a problem and very often people are willing to pay money for a solution to their problem. A good sales letter will sell the solution and make people buy the product.

Some people say that you can find all the information you need on the internet, so nobody would buy a book on "how to get rid of mice". My argument against that is: Clickbank sells one eBook every three seconds, Amazon is one of the biggest websites around and sells hundreds and thousands of books each month. *Source : www.rampant-books.com.* How can you argue against those facts?

If people have a choice between browsing for hours on the web to find answers, or finding all the answers in one eBook, many will choose for the latter. If you provide a product to make their life easier, to save them time, they will buy it. A lot of searchers are busy business people who want answers immediately, in a few clicks.

I think I might have killed "two books with one stone" as not only is there potential for "how to get rid of mice" but there is also potential for keeping a mouse as a pet. It's up to you to research the potential.

Once my new eBook/book is ready, I apply steps 13 to 28 as described under " My step-by-step guide that I apply to each site or each eBook/hard copy book".

Warning: My 5 step investigation is a very quick investigation that I do for a potential new niche. If you outsource everything, it will cost you approximately $1200 (£751) before your eBook and sales page is ready, as I have explained before. If you do not sell a single book, you will lose all your money. Make sure you are aware of this.

If you do not want to risk $1200 (£751), I suggest that you investigate a niche's potential by other ways discussed in this book, or you write the book and the sales page yourself instead of outsourcing.

Visit www.WorldwideSelfPublishing.com for very detailed video tutorials about self publishing books.

9. How I decide if there is potential for a website to put the eBook on

Once I have decided the potential of a new eBook, I will investigate the potential to build a website around the same niche. The factors that influence my decision are:

1) I do the keyword research with www.marketsamurai.com. as explained in 'Part 4 Keyword Research' and as explained on my videos. I am looking for searches over 35,000. I do not base my decision solely on the Market Samurai Result.

2) I type my keyword in Firefox and look at the Page Ranks of the sites shown on the first 2 pages. If most websites are PR0, PR1, PR2 or PR3, I would consider that a good thing as I could, with hard work, possibly overtake these sites. If most of the websites are PR6 and higher I would not investigate further as getting above them would be hard. I would therefore decide not to build a website and only publish an eBook and a book, then let others do the selling for me.

3) Assuming that the previous step is positive, I investigate if a lot of the domains on the first pages of Google have the keyword in the URL. If not, that is good. Remember that I told you a lot of domains are already taken but where are they all? If they are taken and are not shown in Google, it means the webmaster has not succeeded to rank in Google but maybe you can.

4) I Google my keyword and open all websites on the first three pages of Google and analyse the View Source (right click). With which keywords, meta description have those sites managed to get there? I also analyse the content on all these sites. Do they have forums on with thousands of members? If most sites do not have a lot of content on them, maybe I could overtake them with extremely good and unique content.

5) I open all the websites on pages 4, 5, 6, 7, 8, 9, 10 in Google and analyse "View Source" on all these sites. Why did these sites **not** rank in Google and can I better them? I also look at the Page Ranks on these sites and see if I can beat them.

6) I investigate all the potential monetization elements as explained under 'Part 8 Monetising Your Site'.

Make sure you investigate steps 2 to 5 several times, not just once, as Google keeps changing the sites that it shows. If you Google the same keyword at 9AM or at 3PM, completely different sites could be shown. Google is in charge and we are all players trying to win the game.

10. How I investigate the potential of a new niche in 20 steps.

Here is a quick overview of the 20 things that I investigate when I am considering starting a website in a new niche with the aim of ranking in Google for that site.

Important: If you are planning to build a website and drive traffic to your site with paid traffic or viral traffic, don't worry about any of these (except for numbers 19 and 20).

The one thing that would put me off on the overview most is number 14. If all sites on the first pages of Google are PR6 or higher, I will not develop a new site and I will investigate a new keyword.
If you are investigating a very popular niche, you could start with number 14 and make a quick decision.
I always start with number 1 as I usually know (from years of experience and searching the web) that I am going for a "niche with potential".
Not all 20 need to have a positive outcome in order for me to decide to "go for it". I cannot really say exactly what score you need as it can vary per niche but aim for a minimum score of

12 out of 20. I have to leave this up to your business instinct, common sense and professional judgment.

Keyword Research : Tick when done

1	Check if keyword total searches is over 35.000 per month for long tail keyword	
2	Do keyword research Market Samurai for title competition	

Products available to monetise

3	Check if there are Amazon products available to sell	
4	Check if there are Clickbank products available to sell	
5	Check if Adsense pays well for your keywords	
6	Check if there are CPA offers available at good pay-outs	
7	Check if there are other physical products available on other affiliate networks.	
8	Check if there is a magazine available with recurring commission	
9	Google "keyword" + "affilates" to see if other products are available	

Google the keywords you want to target and analyse all websites that appear on the first 2 pages of Google. Check all these :

10	Competition's keywords in URL for all websites.	
11	Do View Source for al the sites, analyse and learn. Can you better the SEO ?	
12	Check if there is lots of content on all the sites. Can you better it ?	
13	Is there Adsense on the websites? If not, you can put it on yours.	
14	Check Firefox Page Ranks for all the sites. If all are PR6 and more, forget it.	

If you are considering writing an ebook/book :

15	Check competition on Clickbank - if already 20 ebooks, forget it.	
16	Check competition on Amazon. If already 50 recent books, forget it.	
17	Google "keyword" + "ebook". Are there already a lot of ebooks available ?	
18	Are their a lot of sites on the first pages where your ebook would "fit in"?	

In case you want to investigate potential of Adwords :

19	Check competition in Keyword Tools	
20	Do Traffic Estimator with Keyword Tools	

11. Another way of finding potential earners.

Go to www.clickbank.com and find products with a high gravity in any niche.

Follow steps 1 to 6 as above and decide if you could design a website around that nic

Part 16. Conclusion

You have taken the positive steps to earn money online. I hope that you use your acquired knowledge from this book and put it into practice. Even if you use only a few of the ideas discussed in this book, you might create some extra income even if you don't quite make it to the top. Maybe you will find your own success formula.

I started with nothing at all. I started with one website that I built all on my own, at home. I created a second one and a third one. When my first few sites were up and earning money I realised I had found my own system that was working well. I decided to take on a full time employee and invest the money that I made so he could build more sites. At the moment I have 96 sites. Not all make money but the majority do.

1. Mistakes not to make.

A lot of internet marketers make one or more of the mistakes listed below, including myself. Here's a list of mistakes that I suggest you avoid:

1. Not setting goals

2. Inadequate planning

3. Underestimating the time it would take

4. Building a site that was not search engine friendly

5. Saying what I want to say instead of saying what my visitor wants to hear

6. Leave a site to die without ever updating it

7. Waiting for somebody to knock on my door with a message "I have traffic for you"

8. Not using statistics and learning from them

9. Not being able to admit that I was doing it all wrong when it wasn't working

10. Not putting an opt-in form on my site

11. Wanting to do it all myself when I had over 10 websites. You can't. Full stop.

12. Not investigating keywords and niches enough

13. Building the site and then doing SEO instead of the other way around

14. Cramming too much info on one page

15. Using PLR stuff without editing it, because it is easy

16. Putting too many links squashed together in one small space

17. Building difficult site navigation. If a 12 year old cannot work with your site, other people can't either and they will leave your site instantly.

18. Joining too many affiliate networks

19. Betting on one horse or putting all my eggs in one basket

20. Submitting websites to FFA directories – Free For All directories

21. Pricing products too high – your must study your competition

22. Failing to check links on a regular basis

23. Having too much competition

24. Posting ads on forums

25. Shouting or using capitals in forums or blogs. People hate it.

26. Using free hosting and email accounts – looks unprofessional

27. Placing affiliate links right in your visitor's face. Let people browse a bit first.

28. Playing around too much instead of investing a bit of money in some professional tools

29. Selling the wrong product to the wrong market

30. Sending the wrong traffic

31. Spending too much money on the wrong paid traffic

2. So what's next?

Congratulations, you have made it to the end of the book (almost the end anyway). You are now ready to start creating your own Internet Success System.

You need to believe in yourself. If you think you can do it: you will!

You need to get organised.

You need to set yourself a realistic goal.

You need to set up a system, a step by step process of what you are going to do.

You need to get yourself a notepad to make a list of:

- all the usernames you will set up and the passwords

- all the affiliate and CPA networks you will be signing up with and the passwords

- all the forums and blogs you will be signing up with and the passwords

- all the online accounts you will sign up for and the passwords

- all the things you still have to do

- all the money you have earned

You too can enjoy financial freedom with the money making possibilities of the web and with the Power Of The Internet.

Good things never come easy. You can bet on it that you will have to work hard to start with, but it will pay off if you do it right, if you persist and if you believe you can do it.

Internet marketing works if you work at it.

---

3. Do you need to set up a business?

A lot of people ask me how it works with setting up a company and how to set up an internet marketing company. Basically setting up an internet marketing company is the same as setting up any other company: you will need to get a business name, register your business, pay taxes, etc…

I suggest that you do not worry about this at all at the beginning of your internet marketing venture. Set up a website (or two or three,…), see if you are actually making money and if you do, start worrying about setting up a business, income taxes, VAT, etc…. You might not enjoy being an internet marketer, therefore it would be silly to set up a registered business right from the start.

- Once you are successful and you are making money, you need to find out how to set up a business in your own country. This is very easy, affordable and straightforward these days (well, it is in the UK) and all aspects of it can be done online.

- It is impossible for me to list all the legal requirements in all the countries that this book will be available in. Therefore check your official government sites or give a local accountant a call. A local accountant will probably answer some questions free of charge hoping that he will win your business once you are successful.

- Once you have found out how to set up your own business or how to run a business from home as a sole trader, start working towards even more success.

- In the UK (in May 2011), you do not need to register for VAT unless your income exceeds £70.000 (or $113.000). You can voluntarily register if you wish to claim VAT back on your purchases.

- You must comply with all legal requirements regarding sales taxes and so on. Just because you are selling online does not mean you do not have to pay taxes on your income.

This "State of mind Poem" says it all. If you think you will fail, you most probably will.

4. State of your mind

<u>State of Mind Poem</u>

Anonymous

If you think you are beaten, you are;
If you think you dare not, you won't;
If you like to win, but don't think you can,
It's almost sure you won't.

If you think you'll lose, you're lost;
For out in the world you'll find
Success begins with a fellow's will
It's all in a state of mind.

For many a game is lost
Even a play is run,
And many a coward fails
Even his work is begun.

Think big and your deeds will grow,
Think small and you'll fall behind;
Think that you can and you will;
It's all in a state of mind.

If you think you are out classed, you are;
You've got to think high to rise;
You've got to be sure of yourself before
You can ever win a prize.
Life's battles don't always go
To the stronger or faster man,
**But sooner or later, the man who wins
Is the fellow who thinks he can.**

> # The only difference between try and triumph is a little umph.

5. Be human on your way to the top

Once you are making good money, don't forget to enjoy it with your family and friends. Help your friends and family when you can. Make somebody happy with your money. Be rich but be human. Never become a money-robot and forget the most important things in life: health, love and happiness.

> **No extraordinary activity is more important than the family having dinner together.**
>
> **The Best Things In Life Are Not Things.**
>
> **Measure your wealth by things you have that no one could buy at any price.**

6. Remember your friends

Don't let the money go to your head, and look down on your friends or family. The friends you had before you made money should still be your friends. Make sure you tell your friends that you are still the same person, just with more money.

7. Look after your health

- Sit on your computer in an ergonomic chair and in the correct posture. If you can afford it, go to www.breakremindersoftware.com and buy it, which will help prevent office-related injuries (Not available for Apple computers) www.workpace.com is similar, more sophisticated software and I believe available for Apple computer.

- Read www.PainInTheThumb.com book about Repetitive Strain Injury. You will be shocked by the real life horror stories. The book is also available on Amazon.

8. Don't ever forget the art of giving back

I give to charities every month. I strongly suggest that you donate a percentage of your income to a charity. It will make you feel good, it will keep you going and keep you focused and there's no reason to be the richest person in the cemetery. You can't do any business from there ☺.

9. Back up your data

It is vital to back up all your data at least once a week and if possible once a day. Back up everything relating to your sites. You will spend a lot of time building your site and you certainly do not want to lose it all if your computer crashes.

10. Keep up to date

There will always be new stuff going on in the IM World. Keep up to date. Here are some sites that I enjoy and learn a lot from.

www.clickz.com online news

www.imnewswatch.com

www.searchengineland.com

www.seobook.com

www.whichtestwon.com

www.wired.com technology news

The day you stop learning is the day you stop earning.

---

11. You have to do the rest

My mother tongue is Dutch and I am not a qualified writer but I have tried to explain how to earn money on the web in plain, easy-to-understand language. I have not outsourced this book but written it myself. If you have come across some matters that were not explained clearly enough, I apologise. **I have done my best, now you have to do the rest.**

It would be impossible to explain every single aspect of internet marketing in detail in one book. A lot of the things you will have to figure out yourself with trial and error, no matter how detailed things are explained to you.

I end this book with two of my favourite one-liners:

EXCUSES ARE YOUR LIMITATIONS.

NO BEES NO HONEY

NO WORK NO MONEY

Good luck. I really hope that you make it as an internet marketer.

Now go and make some money!

Christine Clayfield

Author, Entrepreneur, Infopreneur, Internet Marketer, Personal Tutor, Book Publisher

... and don't forget Churchill's famous seven words:

Don't give up, don't ever give up.

Part 17. Make Money With My Products

You can make money by selling my products as an Affiliate.

1) This book, From Newbie To Millionaire:

1) Sign up with Amazon as an Associate and search for "From Newbie to Millionaire" in the book section, get your affiliate code and put it on your website or email the affiliate code to your friends, family and colleagues.

2) This book is on Clickbank. Sign up as an affiliate: www.FromNewbieToMillionaire.com/affiliates.html

2) My book explaining how I find new niches: "Finding Niches Made Easy"

Buy the eBook here: www.FindingNichesMadeEasy.com

Buy the hard copy book: search for it on Amazon.

Earn money as an affiliate: www.FindingNichesMadeEasy.com/affiliates

3) My Drop Shipping and Ecommerce book:

To buy the eBook is: www.DropshippingAndEcommerce.com..

You can get your Clickbank affiliate link here:
www.DropshippingAndEcommerce.com/affiliates.html

Simply get your affiliate code and put it on your website or send it to your friends, family and colleagues.

4)My Self Publishing Success System explained step by step in video tutorials.

Product: Worldwide Self Publishing Business Training. The very best Self Publishing Training available. I know because I bought all the other ones!

I publish a new book, on average, every 6 weeks. These books are all in different niches and I outsource all aspects of the book, including writing and cover design, except for the publishing, which I do myself. You can found out how I find new niches and how I self publish my books here: www.WorldwideSelfPublishing.com.

I have books in all of the following niches: ice fishing, tarantulas, micro pigs, hypnosis, racing pigeons, recording studio, food processors, organic gardening, panic attacks, standup comedy, cyclists, golf trolleys, bladeless fans, horses, iguana, discuss fish, wedding planning, cat training, green house, body building, magnetic therapy, sports injuries, peafowl, African pygmy hedgehogs, puffer fish, dementia, bone spurs, flying squirrels, hoarding, and a lot more!

Buy the video tutorials to watch online: www.WorldwideSelfpublishing.com

Read what people say about the videos: www.WorldWideSelfPublishingTestimonials.com

Earn money as an affiliate: www.WorldwideSelfpublishing.com/affiliates.html

5) My Break Reminder Software

I have to try and reduce the time I spend on my computer due to my neck-injury. I used to use www.workpace.com, which is software that forces you to take breaks whilst on your computer. I had my own simplified version developed, which you can buy here: www.BreakReminderSoftware.com. Sorry, not available (yet) for Apple computers.

Earn money as an affiliate: www.BreakReminderSoftware.com/affiliates.html

6) My Print Screen Software

When I was looking for a very simple screen software application, without all the bells and the whistles, I couldn't find it, therefore I had my own developed.

You can buy it here: www.PrintingYourScreen.com

Earn money as an affiliate: www.PrintingYourScreen.com/affiliates.html

Printing Your Screen, Screen Capture

⭐⭐⭐⭐⭐ The Software that Makes Printing Screen Shots And ⭐⭐⭐⭐⭐

Saving Screen shots *instant*.

Final Words

I hope that you have enjoyed reading this book and that you have learned a lot. If you did, please leave a 5star review on Amazon. I would appreciate that. Even if you have bought the eBook version of this book, you can still leave a review on Amazon.

Don't forget to tell your friends, family and colleagues about it. Support a hard working woman:-).

For any suggestions or comments (good or bad) about this book, email me: Christine@FromNewbieToMillionaire.com

If you would like to be notified when my next product is launched or when I will be speaking on stage, please visit www.FromNewbieToMillionaire.com and opt-in. I will NOT send you a bunch of crappy affiliate links. Just not my style!

By the way, did I mention that my husband is the band manager of a fantastic 60's and 70's band called www.thevintagecorporation.co.uk ? Now you know why this is not a good domain name for a band from an internet marketer's point of view. He'll be well happy now that I've mentioned his band twice☺. I know I said at the beginning of the book that I wouldn't mention the band again but hey, he's worth it!

List of Video Tutorials

It is my aim that together with these video tutorials and my book, you are ready to start making money online.

Please visit www.VideosNewbieBook.com to get access to the video tutorials. Below is a list of the video tutorials that you will receive when you buy them. You have a 60 days No Quibble Money Back Guarantee. If you think you are not receiving value for money, simply request a refund. As you WILL receive BIG value for money because you get access to over 9 hours of video tutorials for a small price, I am convinced you won't be asking for a refund☺.

The videos will give you a great "head-start" to make money online.

1). Keyword Research with Market Samurai, Monetization in Wordpress and Proof that my system works as the site www.micropigshed.com shows up in Google on the first page (9 Videos - Total Time 38:36s).

Important note: Some of these video tutorials refer to a website www.micropigshed.com. This website was set up especially to make the videos. I have not driven any traffic to that site and the website is not a finished site with money-making affiliate links. These videos are recorded by Will, my webmaster.

If you are not familiar with Wordpress, please watch 3) Wordpress Videos first in order to understand the videos 5 and 6 better.

1. Keyword Research in Market Samurai, 9:51s
2. Buy Domain Name MicroPigShed, 3:48s
3. GoDaddy Setting up Hosting, 1:30s
4. Install Wordpress,2:22s
5. Install Theme and Plugins Wordpress, Install Google Analytics, 10:10s
6. Adding Monetisation Elements : Adsense, Amazon, Clickbank, etc..., 7:52s
7. Getting Backlinks To YourSite 5:40s
8. First Page Google Proof, 2:33s
9. Scan With Abbey Fine Reader, 1:59s

2). Affiliate Cash Tactics Videos: A complete system from A to Z that can be followed step by step to make money on the internet. No money needed at all. (30 videos – Total Time 293 minutes or almost 5 hours).

Video 1	Getting Started	8 minutes
Video 2	How to pick a niche on Clickbank	10 minutes
Video 3	Opening your affiliate account	2 minutes
Video 4a	Article Marketing-Create an article	4 minutes
Video 4b	Article Marketing-Keywords	27 minutes
Video 4c	Tiny URL	3 minutes
Video 5a	Weebly.com	21 minutes
Video 5b	Publish to .weebly.com	10 minutes
Video 6	Traffic Generation dig, delicious, propeller	12 minutes
Video 7	Traffic Generation mix, reddit, socialmarker	5 minutes
Video 8	Setting up blog + RSS + pingoat	9 minutes
Video 9	Article Marketing, articledashboard.com	13 minutes
Video 10	Articlealley.com, ezinearticles.com and more	19 minutes
Video 11	Squidoo	17 minutes
Video 12	Hubpages.com	5 minutes
Video 13	Press releases Header, body, etc..	7 minutes
Video 14	Press releases Write press release	6 minutes
Video 15	Press releases : submit	19 minutes
Video 16a	Video Hosting Websites and free pictures	8 minutes
Video 16b	Pictures : gimp.org	6 minutes
Video 16c	Audacity to record your voice	7 minutes
Video 16d	Windows moviemaker	10 minutes
Video 17a	Video Marketing Part 1	12 minutes

Video 17b	Video Marketing Part 2	4 minutes
Video 18	Get More Traffic : Google blog search	5 minutes
Video 19	System Recap	5 minutes
Video 20a	Find Niches : Amazon	7 minutes
Video 20b	Find products Keyword tool + Clickbank	9 minutes
Video 20c	More keyword tools	15 minutes
Video 20d	Magazines.com	8 minutes

3). A Complete Set of Wordpress Video Tutorials

(36 Videos, Total Time 2 hours, 7min, 18s)

If for some reason you cannot access/watch the videos, please email me:
Christine@FromNewbieToMillionaire.com

Lightning Source UK Ltd.
Milton Keynes UK
UKOW06f1903170215

246459UK00010B/478/P